CRITICAL ISSUES IN
GLOBAL SPORT MANAGEMENT

The social, cultural and economic significance of sport has never been more evident than it is today. Adopting a critical management perspective, this book examines the most important themes and challenges in global sport management. From match-fixing, doping, bribery and corruption to corporate social responsibility, governance and new media, it helps students, researchers and practitioners to understand the changing face of the global sport industry.

Written by leading international sport management experts, *Critical Issues in Global Sport Management* includes twenty chapters and real-life case studies from around the world. It examines contemporary governance and management issues as well as the ethical challenges faced by the global sport industry, including questions of integrity and accountability in recent drug scandals that have been widely reported and debated. This book deals with such questions and many more, highlighting the fact that the global sport system is in urgent need of new and innovative solutions to these ongoing problems.

Based on cutting-edge research from the US, UK, Australia, Europe and beyond, this book will add depth and currency to any course in sport management, sport business, sport development or sport events.

Nico Schulenkorf is Senior Lecturer for Sport Management at the UTS Business School, Sydney, Australia. His research focuses on the social, cultural and health-related outcomes of sport-for-development and event management projects. Nico has worked with local and international NGOs, Government Agencies, Sport Associations and Ministries in developing capacities to implement development projects in countries such as Sri Lanka, Israel/Palestine and the Pacific Islands. Nico is co-editor of *Global Sport-for-Development: Critical Perspectives* (Palgrave, 2014) and *Managing Sport Development: An International Approach* (Routledge, 2016). He is also co-founder and editor of the *Journal of Sport for Development*.

Stephen Frawley is the Director of the Australian Centre for Olympic Studies at the UTS Business School, Sydney, Australia. His research is focused on the organisation and management of the Olympic Games and associated sport mega-events. He has published widely on the Olympic Games and the Football World Cup and is the editor of *Managing the Olympics*, *Managing the Football World Cup* and *Managing Sport Mega-Events*. Stephen's academic work is informed by his experience working on sport mega-events. From 1998 to 2001 he worked for the Sydney 2000 Organising Committee for the Olympic and Paralympic Games and he was an advisor to the Melbourne 2006 Commonwealth Games Organising Committee.

CRITICAL ISSUES IN GLOBAL SPORT MANAGEMENT

Edited by Nico Schulenkorf and Stephen Frawley

Routledge
Taylor & Francis Group

LONDON AND NEW YORK

First published 2017
by Routledge
2 Park Square, Milton Park, Abingdon, Oxon OX14 4RN

and by Routledge
711 Third Avenue, New York, NY 10017

Routledge is an imprint of the Taylor & Francis Group, an informa business

British Library Cataloguing-in-Publication Data
A catalogue record for this book is available from the British Library

Library of Congress Cataloging in Publication Data
Names: Schulenkorf, Nico, editor. | Frawley, Stephen, 1969- editor.
Title: Critical issues in global sport management / edited by Nico Schulenkorf
and Stephen Frawley.Description: Milton Park, Abingdon, Oxon ; New York, NY :
Routledge, 2016. | Includes bibliographical references and index.Identifiers:
LCCN 2016020603| ISBN 9781138911222 (hardback) | ISBN 9781138911239
(pbk.) | ISBN 9781315692883 (ebook)Subjects: LCSH: Sports administration.
| Sports and globalization.Classification: LCC GV713 .C77 2016
| DDC 796.06/9--dc23LC record available at https://lccn.loc.gov/2016020603

ISBN: 978-1-138-91122-2 (hbk)
ISBN: 978-1-138-91123-9 (pbk)
ISBN: 978-1-315-69288-3 (ebk)

Typeset in Bembo
by Fish Books Ltd.

Nico – to Anja and Henry
Stephen – to Tanya, Tara and Alanna

CONTENTS

FIGURES

TABLES

CONTRIBUTORS

Johanna A. Adriaanse is Senior Lecturer in the Business School at the University of Technology, Sydney, and a member of the University's Centre for Corporate Governance. Her area of interest and expertise focuses on investigating the relationship between gender and sport. Currently, she is conducting research on gender dynamics in the governance of sport organisations globally. She has published her work in prestigious academic journals including the *Journal of Sport Management*, *Sport Management Review*, and the *Journal of Business Ethics*. In addition, Johanna is a strong public advocate for women, sport, and gender equality. She has completed projects with UN Women in New York, served as the co-chair for the International Working Group on Women and Sport (IWG) from 2006 to 2014, and given presentations at conferences all over the world. She obtained her Ph.D. and master of education at the University of Sydney after completing her bachelor of education (Physical Education) and bachelor of psychology in Amsterdam.

Pamela H. Baker is an Associate Professor of Special Education and Director of the Division of Special Education and Disability Research at George Mason University. She earned her doctorate in leadership studies from Bowling Green State University, and her M.Ed. and B.S. from the College of William and Mary. In addition to numerous presentations and publications, Dr. Baker has served as an investigator on a variety of state and federal grants to support teacher preparation and sport diplomacy projects with funding in excess of US $8.7 million dollars. She is currently involved in an ongoing cooperative agreement with the U.S. Department of State's SportsUnited Sports Visitors and Envoys programme.

Robert E. Baker is a Professor and Director of the Center for Sport Management and Division of Sport Recreation and Tourism at George Mason University. He earned his doctorate from the College of William and Mary, and his M.S. and B.S.

from Pennsylvania State University. He has served as President of the North American Society for Sport Management, as a founding commissioner of the Commission on Sport Management Accreditation, and a founding board member of the World Association of Sport Management. Dr. Baker received NASSM's 2010 Distinguished Sport Management Educator Award and NASPE's 2011 Outstanding Achievement in Sport Management Award. In addition to publishing numerous books and articles, Dr. Baker has served as the principal investigator on several grants to support sport diplomacy projects totalling U.S. $6 million. He is currently involved in a cooperative agreement with the U.S. Department of State's Sports United Sports Visitors and Envoys programme.

Christoph Breuer is a full Professor at the German Sport University, Cologne, specialising in research on sport demand, sport organisations and sport sponsoring. His research mostly relates to forecasting sport demand, identifying key drivers of viability of sport organisations, and measuring the economic value of sport sponsoring. His work has been published extensively.

Markus Breuer is the Dean of the M.A. Sport Management program at the SRH University Heidelberg, Germany. After graduation in business administration and economics in Braunschweig and Chemnitz, Professor Breuer received a Ph.D. in Sport Economics from the University of Jena. From 2011 to 2014, he joined the KPMG transfer-pricing office in Hamburg. He obtained his master's degree in international taxation from the University of Hamburg in 2014. Professor Breuer lectures regularly at various local and foreign universities and presents his latest research findings at international conferences.

Katherine Bruffy is a Lecturer of Sport Management and Programme Leader in the Department of Sport at Unitec Institute of Technology, Auckland, New Zealand. Katie's passion for sport began as a youth swimmer and continued through her time as a collegiate synchronised swimmer. She began teaching in higher education in 2006 at Ohio State University, where she also earned her Ph.D. researching sport nostalgia. Particular research areas of interest include: sport marketing, consumer behaviour, governance and sport development. Katie has worked within these research areas as a consultant for the Skycity Breakers Basketball Team, Auckland Mystics Netball Team, and Auckland Cricket.

Sarah Cobourn (originally from Toronto) is the Senior Officer of Corporate Social Responsibility (CSR) at Hitachi. Sarah completed a Ph.D. focused on Creating Shared Value in professional sport at the University of Technology Sydney (UTS). Sarah continues her research through the Australian Centre for Olympic Studies at UTS Business School. Previously, she has worked as a consultant, working with organisations across Australia, North America and the United Kingdom to develop innovative policies and programmes that create shared economic and societal value. Sarah also holds a bachelor's degree in science from Western University (Canada) and a master's in sport management from Bond University (Australia).

Harry Collins is Distinguished Research Professor and Directs the Centre for the Study of Knowledge, Expertise and Science at Cardiff University. He is an elected Fellow of the British Academy and a winner of the Bernal prize for social studies of science. He has served as President of the Society for Social Studies of Science. His 18 published books cover the sociology of scientific knowledge, artificial intelligence, the nature of expertise, and tacit knowledge. He is continuing his research on the sociology of gravitational wave detection, expertise, fringe science, science and democracy, technology in sport, and a new technique—'the Imitation Game'— for exploring expertise and comparing the extent to which minority groups are integrated into societies. He is currently writing books on science and democracy, on artificial intelligence, on technology in sport, and on the Imitation Game.

Geoff Dickson has an honours degree in leisure management and a doctorate from Griffith University. In between degrees, Geoff was General Manager of the Coorparoo Australian Football Club in Brisbane. He began his academic career in 1996 at Central Queensland University. In 2004, Geoff moved from Australia to New Zealand to work at Auckland University of Technology as a director of Gymsports New Zealand and Tennis North Harbour. He is currently Chair of AFL New Zealand and President of the Sport Management Association of Australia and New Zealand. Geoff's research interests focus on interorganisational relationships – federated networks, collaborations, partnerships, co-opetition, clusters and cliques. These relationships include sponsorship and ambush marketing. Geoff has presented his research in every continent, except Africa and the Antarctic.

Robert Evans is a Professor of Sociology in the Cardiff School of Social Sciences. He specialises in Science and Technology Studies (STS) and has published extensively on the nature of expertise. Together with Harry Collins he is the author of the influential 'Third Wave of Science Studies' paper (Social Studies of Science, 2002) and *Rethinking Expertise* (University of Chicago Press, 2007). His current work has two main elements. The first continues to refine and extend the theory of expertise that underpins the Third Wave programme in STS. The second focuses on the development of the Imitation Game as a new method for social research. This methodological work, which is funded by the European Research Council (#269463, IMGAME), operationalises the idea of interactional expertise and provides a means by which its distribution can be measured and its content explored across a wide range of domains and topics.

Stephen Frawley is the Director of the Australian Centre for Olympic Studies, which is located at the UTS Business School, University of Technology, Sydney, Australia. Stephen is the editor of *Managing Sport Mega-Events* (Routledge) and co-editor (along with Daryl Adair) of *Managing the Olympics* (Palgrave Macmillan) and

Managing the Football World Cup (Palgrave Macmillan). Stephen has significant experience working in sport having worked in the Sport Division for the Sydney 2000 Olympic and Paralympic Games from 1998 to 2001.

Bill Gerrard is an economics graduate of the University of Aberdeen and Trinity College, Cambridge, and received his doctorate from the University of York. He is currently Professor of Business and Sports Analytics at Leeds University Business School. Bill has published academic papers in sport management on the football transfer market, measuring team quality, coaching efficiency, stadium naming rights, and the sporting and financial performance of pro sports teams. He is a former editor of the *European Sport Management Quarterly*. Bill holds the UEFA B football coaching licence. In recent years, his work has mainly focused on the development of coach-led analytics. He was the technical analyst for Saracens (rugby union) from 2010 to 2015. Bill has also provided statistical analysis to support the Sky Sports coverage of Super League (rugby league). Bill has worked with several U.K. and Dutch football clubs, an Australian rugby league team, a South African Super 15 rugby union team, the Oakland As and various Olympic sports.

Lisa Gowthorp is a full-time Assistant Professor at Bond University and has previously worked in high-performance sport for over 12 years, with organisations such as the NSW Institute of Sport, the Australian Institute of Sport (AIS), and Australian Canoeing. Lisa has managed teams at the World Championships and was the gymnastics section manager on the Australian Olympic Team in Beijing in 2008.

Lisa's research interests include the governance and management of the Australian high-performance sport system, especially government involvement in elite sport, sport governance and regulation, high-performance sport management issues, and contemporary issues surrounding the Olympic Games. She regularly consults with industry on governance issues and sport policy. Lisa is also the Secretary-General of the Sliding Sports Australia (SSA), working towards the development and implementation of good governance practices and procedures for this new Olympic NSO.

Annette Greenhow is an Assistant Professor in the Faculty of Law at Bond University, having joined the faculty in 1996 as an adjunct during her private legal practice career. She is now a full-time member of the faculty and teaches Global Sports Law and Governance, Sports Law, Business Associations and Land Law. Annette's research interests focus on the intersection between sport, law, regulation, and governance and her research evaluates the regulatory responses of the Australian football codes to concussion management at the elite levels. Annette has authored and co-authored publications on sports-related concussion and has delivered presentations on this topic at national and international conferences since 2011. She has a keen interest in understanding the interdisciplinary perspectives on sports-related concussion and contributing to the design and delivery of sustainable concussion management solutions for a broad range of stakeholders.

Larena Hoeber earned her Ph.D. in sport management from the University of British Columbia. She is an Associate Professor in the Faculty of Kinesiology and Health Studies at the University of Regina. Her research interests include gender issues in sport, use of innovative research methods, organisational culture, and amateur sport organisations. She teaches in the areas of sport management and marketing, sociology of sport, volunteer management, and qualitative research methods. She has published her research in the *Journal of Sport Management*; *Sport Management Review*; *European Sport Management Quarterly*; *Gender, Work and Organisation*; *Qualitative Research in Sport, Exercise and Health*; *International Journal of Sport Management and Marketing*; and *Sex Roles*.

Orland Hoeber received his Ph.D. in computer science from the University of Regina (Canada) in 2007. After five years at Memorial University (Canada), he returned to the University of Regina as an Associate Professor in 2012. His primary research interests are in the domains of information visualisation, visual analytics, mobile computing, social media analytics, the process of innovation, and the use of software to support the collection and use of data in business and academic research contexts. His research has been funded by both the Natural Sciences and Engineering Research Council of Canada and the Social Sciences and Humanities Research Council of Canada.

John Horne is Professor of Sport and Sociology at the University of Central Lancashire, Preston, U.K. He is a Fellow of the Academy of Social Sciences (FAcSS), Vice-Chair of the British Sociological Association, and Vice-President of the International Sociology of Sport Association. His research interests include sport, leisure, and globalisation; the socio-cultural, political, and economic impacts of sports mega-events; sport and social theory; and consumer culture. He is the author, co-author, editor, and co-editor of over 150 books, edited collections, journal articles and book chapters including: *Understanding the Olympics* (2nd ed., 2016), Routledge; *Mega-Events and Globalization: Capital and Spectacle in a Changing World Order* (2016), Routledge; *Sport and Social Movements* (2014), Bloomsbury Academic; *Understanding Sport* (2nd ed., 2013), Routledge; *Sport in Consumer Culture* (2006), Palgrave; *Sports Mega-Events* (2006), Blackwell; *Football Goes East: Business Culture and the People's Game in China, Japan and South Korea* (2004), Routledge; and *Japan, Korea and the 2002 World Cup* (2002), Routledge.

Brett Hutchins is an Australian Research Council Future Fellow and Associate Professor in the School of Media, Film and Journalism at Monash University in Melbourne, Australia. His Fellowship project, 'The Mobile Media Sport Moment: Markets, Technologies, Power' (http://artsonline.monash.edu.au/mobilemediasport/), investigates how smartphones, tablet computers, and mobile communications are transforming the production and circulation of sport content around the globe. Brett's latest journal articles appear in *Convergence*, *International Communication Gazette*, *Telematics and Informatics* and *Journal of Sport and Social Issues*.

His books include *Digital Media Sport: Technology, Power and Culture in the Network Society* (co-edited with David Rowe, 2013), Routledge; and *Sport Beyond Television: The Internet, Digital Media and the Rise of Networked Media Sport* (co-authored with David Rowe, 2012), Routledge. He is also the co-editor of a recent special issue of the journal, *Media International Australia*, on 'Media Sport: Practice, Culture and Innovation' (No. 155, May 2015).

Sebastian Kaiser holds a Chair of Business Administration, particularly sport management, at Heilbronn University, Germany. Sebastian graduated at German Sport University Cologne and received a Ph.D. in sport economics (2005). He is Section Editor (Social Sciences) of the *German Journal of Sports Science* and author/ co-author of a range of books, book chapters, and journal articles on sport management. Sebastian lectures regularly at various international universities and is an international professor at the Russian International Olympic University in Sochi.

Wolfram Manzenreiter is Professor of Japanese Studies and Vice Head of Department at the Department of East Asian Studies at the University of Vienna. His research is concerned with the social and anthropological aspects of sports, emotions, work and migration in a globalising world. He is author of several books and numerous articles and book chapters mainly on sport, leisure, popular culture, and social issues in contemporary Japan. As a scholar of globalisation, his research also extends into the larger East Asian region and the transnational networks of the Japanese diaspora. Book publications of note include *Sport and Body Politics in Japan* (2014), Routledge; and the co-edited volumes on *Migration and Development; New Perspectives* (2014, in German), ProMedia; *Governance, Citizenship and the New European Championships, The European Spectacle* (2011), Routledge; *Sports Mega-Events* (2006), Blackwell; *Football Goes East: Business Culture and the People's Game in China, Japan and South Korea* (2004), Routledge; and *Japan, Korea and the 2002 World Cup* (2002), Routledge.

Michael Naylor is currently a Senior Lecturer in Sport Management at Auckland University of Technology in New Zealand. Born in Toronto, Canada, Michael also spent time in the United States as both a practitioner and scholar in the sport industry. His research interests include sport marketing, consumer psychology, and social media. The projects he undertakes are based in a variety of participant and supporter contexts around the world.

Hayden Opie is the Director of Studies, Sports Law Programme, Melbourne Law School, the University of Melbourne. Hayden pursues research and teaching interests in all areas of sports law and is recognised internationally for his work in the field, especially in regard to sports integrity. He has been researching and writing on legal aspects of anti-doping since 1987 and has served on various committees and advisory boards in the anti-doping field. He is the founding

President of the Australian and New Zealand Sports Law Association and served as a legal member of the Australian government's Anti-Doping Rule Violation Panel from 2010 to 2015. He is a member of the Court of Arbitration for Sport. Hayden teaches the master's-level subject, 'Sports Integrity and Investigations', with Catherine Ordway on the Melbourne Sports Law Programme.

Catherine Ordway is currently Professor of Practice (Sports Management), La Trobe University and Senior Fellow, Melbourne Law School, the University of Melbourne. Catherine holds a bachelor of arts in jurisprudence and law degree from the University of Adelaide, a Graduate Diploma of Legal Practice from the University of South Australia, and a Graduate Diploma in Investigations Management from Charles Sturt University. She is internationally recognised for her work in the field of regulatory review in international sport integrity. Catherine is also a member of the Australian and New Zealand Sports Law Association (ANZSLA) and acted for the Australian Olympic Committee in the lead up to the Sydney 2000 Olympic Games. Catherine lectures at the master's level in sports law and sports management subjects at La Trobe University (risk management), at the University of Melbourne (sports integrity and investigations) with Hayden Opie, the University of New South Wales (anti-doping), and the University of Canberra (performance integrity). Catherine has also taught undergraduate sports management units as Senior Lecturer at the University of Canberra. She is currently completing her Ph.D. in governance, leadership, and sports integrity.

Geoff Pearson is Senior Lecturer in criminal law at the University of Manchester in the United Kingdom. He has utilised ethnographic research to research football fan behaviour and the impact of legal and policing responses on football crowds since 1995, approaching the subject from a socio-legal and human rights perspective. He has been engaged in research, consultancy and police training on football crowd management throughout Europe and has published extensively on the issue, most notably *Football Hooliganism: Policing and the War on the English Disease* (2007), Pennant; *An Ethnography of English Football Fans: Cans, Cops and Carnivals* (2012), MUP; and *Legal Responses to Football Hooliganism in Europe* (in press), TMC Asser. Geoff is co-founder of the Annual Ethnography Symposium and between 2003 and 2014 he was Director of the unique MBA (Football Industries) programme. He is a Manchester United season-ticket holder.

Joel Rookwood is a Senior Lecturer in the Faculty of Business, Sport and Enterprise at Southampton Solent University, United Kingdom, and a Visiting Fellow in Sport Management at the University of Vic, Spain. He studied football science at the undergraduate level and earned master's degrees in performance analysis and sport management, before being awarded a Ph.D. for his thesis entitled 'Fan perspectives of football hooliganism' at the University of Liverpool's Management School in 2008. He has conducted research and written for various media publications, covering football matches in 110 British grounds, and in stadia across 70 countries spanning six continents. He reported on and conducted research at the 2002, 2006, 2010, and 2014 World Cups; the 2004, 2008, and 2012 European Championships; and at confederation equivalents in Asia, Africa, North America, and South America. He has worked in and published widely on sport-for-development, football fandom, violence, peacebuilding, sports mega-events, and sport and social identity.

David Rowe is Professor of Cultural Research, Institute for Culture and Society, University of Western Sydney and Honorary Professor, Faculty of Humanities and Social Sciences, University of Bath. His books include *Popular Cultures: Rock Music, Sport and the Politics of Pleasure* (1995); *Globalization and Sport: Playing the World* (co-authored with Toby Miller, Geoffrey Lawrence and Jim McKay, 2001); *Sport, Culture and the Media: The Unruly Trinity* (2nd ed., 2004); *Global Media Sport: Flows, Forms and Futures* (2011); and *Sport, Public Broadcasting, and Cultural Citizenship: Signal Lost?* (co-edited with Jay Scherer, 2014). His work has been translated into several languages, including Chinese, French, Turkish, Spanish, Italian and Arabic. In the specific field of sport management, Professor Rowe has published in *International Journal of Sport Management and Marketing, Australasian Leisure Management*, and *European Sport Management Quarterly*; and delivered a Keynote Address to the 2005 Sport Management Association of Australia and New Zealand Conference.

Katie Rowe is a Lecturer in the sport management programme at Deakin University and currently teaches units in Sport Development, Sport Performance, and Sport Practicum. She completed her Ph.D. studies in 2013 with focus on women's cycling participation in Australia. Katie's research interests include sport and recreation participation, women's engagement in sport, and the ways in which sport can be used as a tool to improve community health and wellbeing (sport-for-development). Her research to date has focused on participation issues in sports such as cycling, table tennis, and netball and she is interested in exploring opportunities for development through sport initiatives in local government contexts. Katie has presented at sport management and physical activity conferences both nationally and internationally.

Christopher Rumpf researches and teaches in the field of sport management and sport marketing at the German Sport University, Cologne. His current studies explore the impact of colour and animation on sponsorship outcomes and the affective and behavioural response to sport marketing activities. His articles have appeared in the *Journal of Sport Management, Psychology and Marketing*, and *Marketing Review St. Gallen*, among others.

João M.C. Malaia Santos has a bachelor's degree in history and a doctorate in economic history from University of São Paulo (USP), Brazil. He began his academic career in 2010 at University of Rio de Janeiro (UFRJ), where he developed his postdoctoral research on international sports competitions hosted in Brazil (1919–2016). João is currently director of São José Rugby Club and works on the master's programme in sports management at the University Nove de Julho (São Paulo, Brazil). João's research interests focus on organisational theory, critical management, international relations, history of sport, sociology of sport, and sports economics. In 2015, he was a commentator for ESPN Brazil's coverage of the Rugby World Cup.

Nico Schulenkorf is Senior Lecturer for Sport Management at the University of Technology, Sydney (UTS). His research focuses on the social, cultural, and health-related outcomes of sport-for-development and event-management projects. He is particularly interested in the role of sport as a vehicle for sustainable development and peacebuilding within and between disadvantaged communities. For his long-term contribution to the advancement of social justice on an international level, Nico was awarded the 2008 UTS Vice Chancellor's Human Rights Award. Nico is co-founder and editor of the *Journal of Sport for Development* and serves on the editorial board of the *European Journal for Sport and Society* and *Sport and Entertainment Review*.

Emma Sherry is an Associate Professor within the La Trobe University Centre for Sport and Social Impact, specialising in the area of sport development. Emma has completed a bachelor of arts at the University of Melbourne and a masters of business (Sport Management) and a Ph.D. at Deakin University. Emma's Ph.D. studies investigated conflict of interest in the Australian Football League. Her current research interests include community development through sport activities, undertaking a broad range of research projects with national and regional sport organisations in Australia and Oceania, including Netball Australia, National Rugby League, Australian Football League, and Tennis Australia. Additional research areas include access and equity in sport participation, and sport and recreation for at-risk and marginalised communities. Emma is currently supervising a number of Ph.D. students in the areas of sport-for-development in India and with refugee communities, para-sport athlete wellbeing, and elite athlete career transition.

Olan Scott is an Assistant Professor in Sport Management at University of Canberra. His research into sport media particularly focuses on the mainstream media and fan engagement in social media. Dr. Scott is heavily involved in industry-focused research including social media marketing, fan development, strategic planning, and brand-awareness market research in the Canberra community. His investigations examine how events are framed by the media for audience interpretation. In addition, he also researches the use of social media, leading projects involved in social media marketing for professional sports teams. He has also been a board member of the Canberra Cavalry since March 2015. Dr. Scott's research provides a greater understanding of the way sports governing bodies, teams, and players interact with the paying public to build their loyalty base. Understanding and improving the way the industry approaches and engages fans offers sports an opportunity to improve its positive societal role.

Clifford Stott is Professor of Social Psychology at Keele University in Staffordshire, United Kingdom. His work revolves around crowd psychology, collective conflict, and public order policing. He has published over 50 articles in leading interdisciplinary journals and co-authored and edited three books, one of which was on the 2011 English 'riots'. He works regularly with police forces, governments, and football authorities across the world and is widely recognised as a global expert in his field. In 2014, he was awarded the Economic and Social Research Council's (ESRC) national award for the impact of his work on public policy. In 2015, his work was acknowledged by the ESRC as one of its 'Top 50' achievements in its 50-year history. His research underpins recent human-rights-based reforms of public order policing in the United Kingdom, Sweden, Denmark and Queensland, Australia.

Jules R. Woolf is an Assistant Professor at Adelphi University in the Department of Exercise Science, Health Studies, Physical Education and Sport Management. He completed his Ph.D. in Sport Management at the University of Texas at Austin where he also earned a master's degree in exercise physiology. His multidisciplinary background informs his practice as he attempts to combine his research training in physiology, management, and communications. His research interests involve the ways in which institutional and organisational forces impact the nexus between sport and health. In essence, he is interested in the ways that sport is managed to promote positive and avoid negative health outcomes. A main focus of his research examines doping in sport. His research has been published in the *Journal of Sport Management*, *International Journal of Sport Policy and Politics* and the *British Journal of Sports Medicine*, among others.

ACKNOWLEDGEMENTS

This book was conceived with the assistance of several people. From within the global community of sport management scholars, we received widespread encouragement and support for the book, with several colleagues engaged as contributors. The international expertise and thoughtful reflections of these authors has provided profound insights into critical aspects of sport management. Thank you for sharing your knowledge and for taking time to write, edit, and amend the chapters.

As editors, we were conscious of the need to make the material research driven yet accessible and relevant for a wide audience of students, academics, and practitioners of sport management. Each of the contributing authors has honoured our intent; we thank them for their collegiality and enthusiasm in achieving that research goal. We also wanted to ensure the overall quality of the book and subjected all chapters to rigorous editorial feedback. We believe that this approach has been important to secure coherence and continuity in the development of different concepts and issues presented in the book. We especially thank Dr Natasha Black for her outstanding editorial advice.

We also wish to acknowledge the encouragement and professionalism of the Taylor and Francis editorial team: Simon Whitmore (Senior Commissioning Editor), William Bailey (Editorial Assistant), and Cecily Davey (Editorial Assistant). Finally, and perhaps most importantly, we like to express our love and gratitude to Anja, Henry, Tanya, Tara and Alanna who cheered from the sidelines as this book evolved.

1

CRITICAL ISSUES IN GLOBAL SPORT

Nico Schulenkorf and Stephen Frawley

Background and context

Sport holds significant social, cultural and economic importance to people all over the world. Every year, billions of dollars are spent on sporting goods and services, including sport equipment, broadcasting licenses, naming rights and live entertainment. From a business perspective, the sport sector employs millions of people and presents a crucial component of many national economies. For example, sport's contribution to the English economy has reached over £20 billion, about 2 per cent of the total economy (Sport England, 2013). This places sport up in the top 15 industry sectors above motor vehicles, telecommunication services, legal services, accounting, publishing, advertising and the utilities. However, sport is more than simply a business. Sport also provides important opportunities for social engagement and active participation contributes to a healthy lifestyle. Overall, the significance of sport is felt on the sporting fields around the world where professional sport managers, development officers, programme coordinators, coaches and volunteers are focusing on growing the potential of athletes, clubs, businesses and (sport) communities.

With the sport industry experiencing exponential growth, sport managers, sport management academics and graduates of sport management programmes are increasingly required to be experts across a number of disciplines in a fast-changing business environment. Therefore, universities around the world are providing numerous sport-specific subjects, including sport management, sport development, sport globalisation, sport marketing, sport and the media to equip students with the required knowledge to master imminent social, cultural, technological and economic challenges. While in the past sport management was often seen as a by-product of business education, today more and more sport management degrees are offered at reputable universities at both the undergraduate and postgraduate levels.

At the same time, research in sport management has developed into a well-respected and rigorous field of study. Dozens of high-quality academic journals and book publishers provide important outlets for sport management academics to publish their latest research findings.

Critical Issues in Global Sport Management was conceived with the clear intent to engage a wide range of sport management scholars including academics, students and the wider sport community in current, critical and applied sport management issues. To achieve this goal – and against the background of an increasingly global sport audience – this book provides 20 intriguing chapters and topical case studies from around the world. This collection of chapters is written by leading international sport management experts and examines contemporary issues and the latest challenges faced by the global sport industry. For example, in recent years the issues of integrity and ethical behaviour in professional sport and sport management have been widely reported and debated. Such topics are receiving significant media attention and they provide a continual challenge for sporting administrators who have to address issues such as match-fixing, doping, bribery and corrupt governance structures. *Critical Issues in Global Sport Management* deals with such concerns and many others from a critical management perspective, highlighting the fact that not all is well with the global sport system and that cultural change may be required.

Purpose of the book

In the past, sport programmes, projects and events have been examined from a number of academic perspectives including history, sociology, politics, marketing, management, strategy, urban planning and economics. What was lacking, however, was a book that identified and evaluated the current issues and complexities faced by those charged with the responsibility of managing sport in compound business contexts as well as intricate social environments. With *Critical Issues in Global Sport Management* we want to address this issue and provide a book that discusses the latest trends and issues faced by sport managers around the world. Moreover, we want to provide an attractive text for students, one that brings sport management education to life. In short, we want to assist in making reading, learning and classroom discussions relevant, meaningful and enjoyable!

In contrast to "plain' sport management textbooks that describe concepts and standard aspects of management in a pre-defined and often restricted manner, this compilation of research-based chapters goes beyond standard management knowledge to explore and discuss a wide range of current issues and global developments in the management of sport. In other words, we put *Critical Issues in Global Sport Management* above standard introductory sport management books; it should be used for advanced undergraduate or postgraduate coursework programmes, or as a supplementary volume that complements standard texts (e.g., Beech and Chadwick, 2013; Hoye, Smith, Nicholson and Stewart, 2012; Rosner and Shropshire, 2010) with more critical and in-depth analyses of contemporary sport management topics.

To achieve the goal of providing an attractive yet rigorous sport management book, we have secured an impressive array of acclaimed authors who have contributed chapters and expert knowledge in their favourite areas of research and practice. With contributions from the United States, United Kingdom, Australia, New Zealand, Germany, Austria and Brazil, the group of authors also contributed to the global flavour and cross-cultural perspectives reflected in this book. We have asked all authors to link critical theory with current practice to bring their chapters to life through real-life cases and practical examples. In this way, *Critical Issues in Global Sport Management* combines research-based investigations into current global issues in sport management with dedicated critiques of contemporary cases in their own right. For us, these aspects set our book apart from other textbooks and we are convinced that *Critical Issues in Global Sport Management* will allow for timely debates, rigorous discussions and critical reflections in the classroom and beyond – something we consider crucially important in an increasingly global (sport) world.

About this book

In this introductory chapter we have briefly provided the background, purpose and context for *Critical Issues in Global Sport Management*. In the remaining 19 chapters of this book we invite readers to explore, learn, discuss and reflect on the latest concepts, issues and trends in managing sport. In particular, readers will enjoy timely chapters that are broadly categorised into three overarching sections: Governance, integrity, and welfare (Chapters 2–7); Globalisation (Chapters 8–14); and Technology and social media (Chapters 15–19). Finally, in the last chapter of the book we as editors provide a brief reflection on the issues discussed and we look forward to future challenges in sport management.

The section on governance, integrity and welfare in sport begins with Chapter 2, provided by Johanna Adriaanse, Sarah Cobourn, and Stephen Frawley. Their chapter engages with the critical topics of governance, CSR and diversity management. The authors examined how the three constructs have developed in sport, and how they are related to one another. Implications for sport managers are suggested and recommendations for future research in this growing field are provided. Continuing with the theme of governance and diversity management, in Chapter 3, Johanna Adriaanse goes into more detail discussing the topic of gender diversity in the governance of international sport federations. Her chapter showcases that while women's participation in many sports has been increasing over time, female representation in leadership positions remains a serious challenge. Adriaanse provides empirical evidence for her findings through a recently conducted audit of gender distribution in the composition of the executive boards of international sport federations. The negative and potentially damaging consequences of the omission of women in executive roles are clearly outlined.

In Chapter 4, Catherine Ordway and Hayden Opie define and discuss the concepts of integrity, corruption, doping, match-fixing and betting in sport. The authors suggest a number of approaches and strategies towards managing corruption issues and protecting the integrity of sport. Next, in Chapter 5, Markus Breuer and Sebastian Kaiser continue with the theme of corruption and discuss the timely topic of match-fixing and manipulation in sport. Their focus is on the consequences of betting and manipulation of individuals, clubs and leagues, as well as the potentially damaging influence that powerful multi-club investors/owners may have on 'their' clubs. In Chapter 6, Jules Woolf explores the challenge of how to manage drug use in sport. He explains the complexity of dealing with doping from a sport management perspective and provides an analysis of the World Anti-Doping Agency's current strategies and tactics. Finally, in Chapter 7, Annette Greenhow and Lisa Gowthorp deliberate sport-related head injuries and concussion issues from a medical, legal and managerial perspective. Illustrated through two international case studies, the chapter specifically discusses the regulation and governance of sports-related concussions and the implications for sport managers and their organisations.

The section on globalisation is introduced by Geoff Dickson and João Malaia who in Chapter 8 discuss a number of key domains in which globalisation can be evidenced in today's sporting world. The consequences of topics such as global recruitment of players and their merchandising options, the global broadcasting of media content and scheduling of games in foreign markets, as well as overseas investment in sporting clubs and teams are critically discussed and implications for sport managers are provided. In Chapter 9, Wolfram Manzenreiter and John Horne critically investigate the (un)intended socioeconomic impacts of global sport mega-events. They illustrate their arguments through a case study of the 2012 London Olympics, which provides numerous implications and lessons learnt for sport event organisers. Next, in Chapter 10, Olan Scott, Michael Naylor and Katherine Bruffy discuss the timely topic of social media with a focus on international fan engagement. The authors provide a number of contemporary social media examples to illustrate opportunities and challenges in this space; they also outline the lessons learnt for an effective use of social media aimed at maximising marketing potential and engaging fans from all over the world. Next, Joel Rookwood in Chapter 11 reflects on his long-term experiences in researching the complex topic of hooliganism in sport. He focuses on English football when outlining the issues caused by hooligans for other sport stakeholders, and he provides managerial implications for preventing and controlling hooligans in and around the stadium. In a related topic, Geoff Pearson and Clifford Stott discuss current developments in the science of football crowd management. In Chapter 12, they call for a more holistic, engaged and evidence-based approach towards understanding and managing football crowds.

Chapter 13 introduces the concept of sport-for-development (SFD) and provides an overarching review of theoretical and empirical work done in this field of study. SFD uses sporting projects as a vehicle for achieving social, cultural, psychological, educational economic or health-related outcomes for disadvantaged communities. Nico Schulenkorf, Emma Sherry and Katie Rowe highlight current strengths and weaknesses in SFD research and practice, and they provide recommendations for future work in this emerging field. Chapter 14 connects with the previous one as it discusses the topic of sport and international diplomacy. Authors Robert Baker and Pamela Baker critically analyse diplomacy efforts on various levels and showcase an intriguing international sport-for-diplomacy initiative they have been engaged with for a number of years.

The final section on technology and social media in sport begins with Bill Gerrard's Chapter 15 on analytics and technology in high performance sport. It explores how in recent years, technological developments have revolutionised the collection of performance data with profound consequences for performance analysis. In particular, the impacts, opportunities and challenges of tracking data are discussed and managerial implications are provided. In Chapter 16, Harry Collins and Robert Evans critically examine the role of technologies in supporting match officials and argue that getting the 'right' outcome should be seen as a problem of increasing 'justice' rather than increasing 'accuracy'. The authors suggest that technology must be used by officials wherever possible – a standpoint that should provide for some interesting debates between sport traditionalists (or romanticists?) and supporters of video referees.

In Chapter 17, Brett Hutchins and David Rowe engage in a critical discussion on global mobile media, digital communication and traditional television – a challenging management context they describe as 'the tyranny of perpetual inno-vation'. The authors explain why professional sport managers and sport business owners tend to struggle in their attempts to lead – rather than react to – develop-ments in mobile and digital media. In a closely related contribution, Larena Hoeber and Orland Hoeber discuss the opportunities and challenges of social media analytics in Chapter 18. In an applied manner, the authors provide examples of different social media analytics software which they believe should be an essential element of any sport organisation's social media strategy. Finally, in Chapter 19, Christopher Rumpf and Christoph Breuer discuss how the adoption of digital technology can impact on sport management research and practice, and how it may enhance the efficiency and effectiveness of sport sponsorship. The authors provide an overview of technology-based measurements that may be used to better manage, assess and improve sponsorship activities.

In Chapter 20, we as editors reflect on what the eclectic combination of chapters in this book has revealed about contemporary and critical issues in global sport management. This is done against a background where each of the chapters has provided relevant theory, practical examples and managerial implications. Therefore, the final chapter allows us to use comparisons and draw links to provide the bigger picture regarding current trends and future challenges in global sport management.

References

Beech, J. and Chadwick, S. (2013). *The business of sport management*. Harlow, UK: Pearson Education.

Hoye, R., Smith, A., Nicholson, M. and Stewart, B. (2012). *Sport management: Principles and applications* (3rd ed.). Abingdon, UK: Routledge.

Rosner, S. and Shropshire, K. (2010). *The business of sports* (2nd ed.). Sudbury, UK: Jones and Bartlett Learning.

Sport England. (2013, July). *Economic value of sport in England*. Retrieved from www.sport england.org/media/177230/economic-value-of-sport.pdf

PART 1

Governance, integrity and welfare

2

GOVERNANCE, CSR AND DIVERSITY

A critical field of study in global sport management

Johanna A. Adriaanse, Sarah Cobourn and Stephen Frawley

Governance has only emerged in the last couple of decades as an explicit field of study, primarily in response to management failures of corporate entities around the globe since the 1980s. Failures of large corporations, such as Enron in the United States and OneTel in Australia, have emphasised the need for adequate corporate governance to protect the rights and interests of the stakeholders. According to one of the pioneering researchers in the field, Bob Tricker (1993), the impetus for research into governance was the poor performance of corporate leadership. The role and structure of boards were therefore investigated with the aim of improving performance and thus enhancing the sustainability of the corporate entity.

As with the field of governance, the study of corporate social responsibility (CSR) is a relatively new phenomenon. According to Harjoto and Jo (2011), 'One of the most significant and contentious corporate trends of the last decade is the growth of corporate social responsibility' (p. 45). While CSR as a concept has received a great deal of scrutiny over recent years, the fundamental purpose for an organisation's CSR involvement remains very much uncertain. Friedman (1970) suggested that CSR is a tool employed by organisations to generate shareholder returns while also benefiting broader society. A more detailed discussion of how CSR is defined is outlined later in this chapter, but in general terms, CSR describes 'how firms manage the business processes to produce an overall positive impact on society and refers to serving people, communities, and the environment in ways that go above and beyond what is legally and financially required of a firm' (Harjoto and Jo, 2011, p. 45).

Before the recent increase in CSR as a corporate strategy, the discussion within management circles (both academic and industry) was very much centred on understanding the fundamentals of good corporate governance. This theme has dramatically accelerated since the emergence of the global financial crisis in 2008.

As a consequence of this event, the role and importance of both CSR and corporate governance have been highlighted and reinforced (Harjoto and Jo, 2011). Hopkins (2001), for instance, outlined more than 15 years ago that the concept of corporate governance needed to extend to incorporate CSR.

The purpose of this chapter therefore is to first examine, within the context outlined above, how governance and CSR have developed in sport. Secondly, the chapter will explore the relationship between governance and CSR and, further, their relationship with diversity practices. Areas for future research will be discussed.

Governance: 'pilot versus watchdog'

Governance involves the exercise of power relations in organisations and the frameworks that prevail within the duties of directing, monitoring and regulating that comprise their core business. Governance, however, needs to be distinguished from management. Tricker (1984) explained that the role of management is to ensure that the business operations run efficiently and effectively. This involves the coordination of the processes of product planning, design, marketing, production and distribution. By contrast, governance is not concerned with the day-to-day operations of an organisation; its focus is of a higher order.

There is an emerging literature describing the nature of corporate governance and different approaches. Of particular importance is describing the 'function' or 'purpose' of governance. For example, Thomas Clarke (2004), in his introduction to *Theories of Corporate Governance: The Philosophical Foundations of Corporate Governance* wrote that the Organisation for Economic Cooperation and Development (OECD) provides a useful definition for the function/role of governance. Clarke (2004) cited the following extract from an OECD report on governance and management:

> Corporate governance is the system by which business corporations are directed and controlled. The corporate governance structure specifies the distribution of rights and responsibilities among different participants in the corporation, such as the board, managers, shareholders and other stakeholders, and spells out the rules and procedures for making decisions on corporate affairs. By doing this, it also provides the structure through which the company objectives are set, and the means of attaining those objectives and monitoring performance.
>
> *(p. 1)*

Others have a different view of the function of governance; for instance, Cadbury defined it as follows:

> Corporate governance is concerned with holding the balance between economic and social goals and between individual and communal goals. The

governance framework is there to encourage the efficient use of resources and equally to require accountability for the stewardship of those resources. The aim is to align as nearly as possible the interest of individuals, corporations and society.

(as cited in Clarke, 2004, p. 2)

This means that boards are not only accountable for the financial resources of the company, but also have a responsibility to consider the needs of stakeholders. Yet another approach emphasises the dynamics of corporate governance, described as 'a continuing process through which conflicting or diverse interests may be accommodated and co-operative action may be taken' (Commission on Global Governance; as cited in Clarke, 2004, p. 2).

Despite variations in approaches to corporate governance, it is evident that board members or directors play a critical role. The board of directors is active at all stages throughout the life of a company. As Clarke (2007a) commented, the board of directors is 'the fulcrum of corporate governance, the critical nexus in which the fortunes of the company are decided' (p. 33). In the early stages of a company, it represents the DNA or blueprint for the company's lifespan. As the company grows, the board of directors represents the source of values and objectives that will further develop and sustain the company.

According to a number of leading researchers in the field of corporate governance, in fulfilling their duties, all boards have to balance the strategy and accountability elements of their contribution in ways that encourage performance while maintaining effective control (Daily, Dalton and Cannella, 2003; Johnson, Daily and Ellestrand, 1996; Zahra and Pearce, 1989). Based on this literature, the key roles of boards may be considered as follows:

- *Control*: Monitoring management and ensuring accountability.
- *Strategy*: Approving the strategic direction of the organisation.
- *Counsel*: Providing advice and counsel to management.
- *Institutional*: Building institutional relationships with investors, stakeholders and the community.

 The metaphor 'pilot versus watchdog' captures the tension in the function of governance between directing – such as setting strategic goals and objectives – and monitoring – such as protecting the interests of stakeholders (Carter and Lorsch, 2004; Clarke, 2004; Hoye and Cuskelly, 2007).

Situating sport governance within governance

Governance is relevant for any group of people who organise themselves for a common purpose. However, governance of corporate entities needs to be distinguished from governance of non-profit organisations. There has been a recent orthodoxy in corporate governance, with a focus on protecting and enhancing shareholder value (though this is contested by approaches based on a wider concern for stakeholder interests; Clarke, 2007a). The focus in non-profit governance is more clearly on providing a community service or facilitating the engagement of members in a social activity. After examining several perspectives on the differences in governance characteristics of corporate versus non-profit organisations, Hoye (2002) concluded that there are five main differences. Compared to profit-oriented organisations, non-profit organisations have

- multiple measures of organisational performance,
- shared leadership between an executive and board chair,
- more diversity in board membership,
- a diversity of constituents to serve,
- pressures to maintain volunteer decision-making structures and processes.

(Hoye, 2002, pp. 21–22)

Although there are many types of sport organisations, the majority of those providing participation opportunities in sport and physical activity can be classified as non-profit, as their main purpose is to provide a service to members rather than making profits and increasing shareholder value.

Sport governance is a relatively new concept and relates to the governance of sport organisations. As a field of study, it emerged approximately a decade after the commencement of research into corporate governance. In *Sport Governance*, Hoye and Cuskelly (2007) documented the scholarly literature since the inception of the field in the late 1980s. They defined *sport governance* as 'the structures and processes used by an organisation to develop its strategic goals and direction, monitor its performance against these goals and ensure that the board acts in the best interest of its members' (Hoye and Cuskelly, 2007, p. 9). It is apparent that the pilot versus watchdog metaphor, as previously described, is also applicable in the realm of sport. Further, Hoye and Cuskelly identified the main research themes related to sport governance as generated by the following questions:

- What are the core roles and responsibilities of the board?
- What board structures and processes are most effective for sport organisations?
- What relationships exist between the board and management? Who exerts authority and power?
- What are the key influences on governing boards and its members?

The main research themes that emerge from these questions include board members' roles, board structures and processes, board-staff relations and key influences in sport governance.

A somewhat different perspective was suggested by Ferkins, Shilbury and McDonald (2005). Although they recognised research themes that were similar to those proposed by Hoye and Cuskelly (2007), they presented an integrated model of sport governance research consisting of three components: (a) environmental dynamics, (b) sport governance factors and (c) governance capabilities. An adaptation of their model is presented in Figure 2.1. The purpose of the model is to provide an overview of research themes in the current literature on sport governance and their interrelationships. The first component, *environmental dynamics*, includes both influences – those that are external to the organisation and those that are internal and specific to a sport. For example, compliance with legal requirements is an external influence, while funding sources and membership numbers are internal influences (i.e., specific to a particular sport organisation). The second component, *sport board dynamics*, includes board composition, board roles and responsibilities and directors' interactions – which are comparable to some of the research themes suggested by Hoye and Cuskelly (2007). The third component of the integrated research model, *sport governance dynamics*, considers the development of a strategic direction, monitoring management and building relationships with key stakeholders. This component appropriately reflects the nature of governance, which has previously been characterised as being a pilot versus a watchdog.

Ferkins *et al.* (2005) argued that the strategic role of the board is a major factor in the governance of sport organisations due to the transition of many national sport bodies from predominantly volunteer-based to professional management structures. The introduction of paid professionals in sport organisations has led to the change from a council of representatives to a modern board of directors to govern the sport. Since the day-to-day operations are now managed by paid professionals, the role of the board has changed to providing strategic direction and counsel to management. A critical part of an organisation's strategic plan nowadays is the inclusion of a CSR strategy. Therefore, the development of a CSR strategy as part of an organisation's overall strategic direction has emerged as a major research theme.

Despite the variations in perspectives in the research literature on sport governance, one of the main themes has been board structure and composition. In reviewing the sport governance literature to date, Ferkins *et al.* (2005) found that this theme has been scarcely addressed by sport management scholars. They recommended more research into this critical area of knowledge development. Hoye and Cuskelly (2007) also referred to the dearth of studies exploring board composition in sport organisations. Yet, they argued that composition is an essential issue: 'The questions of who should comprise the board and how they get elected, appointed, selected or invited to a position as a board member are central to the governance of non-profit sport organisations' (Hoye and Cuskelly, 2007, p. 74). They suggested that one of the key aspects of board composition is the diversity of its members, which should reflect the organisation's membership and the stakeholders whom they are representing. The types of diversity that may be usefully represented in the boardroom include age, gender, ethnicity, culture, religion, profession and life experience. Although all these aspects of diversity are important, the main focus in the academic literature has been on gender diversity.

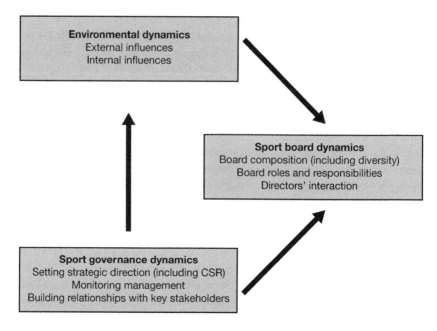

Figure 2.1 Integrated research model of sport governance

CSR: what is it, really?

CSR is a broad field that has been attracting a great deal of academic attention in recent years. CSR as a concept encompasses terms such as sustainability, community engagement, corporate citizenship and shared value. The fundamental principle of CSR is that businesses are responsible for their actions and therefore should embrace societal concerns within their operations and in interactions with key stakeholder (Porter and Kramer, 2006). Despite its growing history and increasing prominence in business discourse, there is significant confusion regarding how CSR should be defined. This has led to an expansion of terms and definitions to describe similar concepts such as corporate citizenship, corporate accountability, sustainability and sustainable capitalism. These terms are synonymous and therefore interchangeable. Clarke (2007b) specifically noted the confusion in the definition of sustainability. For instance, in some definitions, CSR is subsumed under the sustainability banner, while in others, sustainability is considered a component of CSR. However, despite other competing, complementary and overlapping terms, CSR is the most widely used and will therefore be the central term debated in this chapter.

Given the proliferation of terms, finding a widely accepted definition for CSR has been a common challenge across multiple disciplines and sectors. Nonetheless, five key dimensions have emerged as commonalities among the various definitions (Carroll, 1999; Dahlsrud, 2008):

- *Environment*: protecting the natural environment.
- *Social*: managing the relationship between business and society.
- *Economic*: managing socio-economic or financial impacts.
- *Stakeholders*: interaction with stakeholders, such as suppliers, customers and so on.
- *Voluntary*: actions not prescribed by law, based on ethical values, beyond legal obligations.

Given the points outlined above, one of the most commonly cited definitions refers to CSR as follows: 'The manner in which businesses manage their economic, social and environmental impacts as well as their stakeholder relationships in their key areas of influence: the workplace, the marketplace, the supply chain, the community and public policy realm' (John F. Kennedy School of Government, 2008, p. 1). Until recently, CSR was mostly viewed as a business cost to be traded off with profitability. However, over the past decade, companies have realised that CSR activities can benefit both society and business at the same time (Cobourn, 2014).

CSR and sport

Sport is a prominent international social and economic institution (Jenkins, 2012). The global sport industry has grown rapidly over the past four decades and is now worth an estimated US$1.2 trillion (Plunkett Research, 2014). The economic value of sport and the ripple effects of revenue creation reflect the substantial power of the industry. In today's business environment, many sporting organisations operate as business franchises and are, therefore, expected to act within legal and ethical boundaries and societal expectations. Many stakeholders in global sport management have been active in community initiatives for decades, from athletes visiting children in hospitals, to teams promoting healthy lifestyles and participation in physical activity. However, over the past decade, there has been a dramatic increase in the level of support within the sports industry for CSR. This is best evidenced by the large number of social and environmental initiatives and programmes that have been put in place.

As sport has become increasingly globalised, this has resulted in key sport stakeholders becoming much more influential members of the global community. As a result of enormous team revenues, player salaries and increasing ticket prices, pressure has been placed on professional sporting organisations to implement more meaningful community-based programmes (Babiak, 2010). Some sport organisations have met this demand with efforts to give back to local communities using a variety of strategies and tactics (Cobourn, 2014). For instance, a number of sport organisations run community outreach activities to 'address important social issues, build good-will in their communities and, at the same time, enhance their public image' (Babiak, 2010, p. 562). Sport, therefore, has become a lens through which larger social perspectives of identification, community and sociability are examined (Hunt, Bristol and Bashaw, 1999; Melnick, 1993; Sutton, McDonald, Milne and Cimperman, 1997). CSR across all industries covers an increasingly wide range of issues, including employees, operations, customers, suppliers, environmental sustainability, community, ethics and human rights. The specificity of each of these responsibilities does vary according to the type of industry or business.

Governance, CSR and diversity

Increasingly, a key feature of CSR strategy for sport and non-sport organisations has been the focus on social inclusion and encouraging diversity. *Diversity* 'is defined as real or perceived differences among people that affect their interactions and relationships' (Bell, 2007, p. 4). Similarly, diversity refers to 'differences between individuals on any attribute that may lead to the perceptions that another person is different from self' (van Knippenberg, De Drue and Homann, 2004, p. 1068). There are various types of diversity, including – but not limited to – age, gender, race and ethnicity, education, religion, physical appearance or ability, sexual orientation and culture.

In the application of CSR, the growing concern for diversity in governance has often been termed *diversity management*. Managing diversity is about 'creating a climate in which the potential advantages of diversity for organisational or group performance are maximised while the potential disadvantages are minimised' (Cox and Beale, 1997, p. 2). In a business context, diversity management is the 'proactive management technique designed to utilise employee differences in order for an organisation to glean a competitive advantage in the marketplace' (Fink and Pastore, 1999, p. 313).

The embracing of diversity has grown in importance across many industries and contexts in alignment with the growing CSR movement. The focus on diversity can be attributed to a number of factors:

- Changing demographics in many communities has resulted in an increase in the median age, the proportion of racial minorities and women in the workplace.
- Social pressures have shifted in a manner that leads organisations to fulfil an ethical obligation to have diverse workplaces.
- Legislation has been enacted requiring equal employment or access to opportunities irrespective of an individual's demographic characteristics or background.
- The *value-in-diversity hypothesis* suggests that diversity can positively influence desired individual group and organisational outcomes.

(Cunningham, 2011, p. 10)

Therefore, organisations are increasingly realising that effective management of their social and environmental risks (and obligations) can improve business performance (Margolis and Walsh, 2003). Until recently, the terms *diversity and inclusion* and *social responsibility* were used together as organisations attempted to legitimise equity as part of the triple bottom line. Sustainable organisations use a triple-bottom-line approach to track ecological and social performance in addition to traditional financial performance (Savitz and Weber, 2006). However, sustainability refers to more than simply the environment, and many organisations are now further pursuing social responsibility by launching diversity and inclusion initiatives as part of their business strategies (Savitz and Weber, 2006). The incorporation of social responsibility and diversity and inclusion has progressed to a growing understanding of how diversity and inclusion are vital to the core business strategy of a sustainable organisation (Applegate and Puentes, 2009).

Governance, CSR and diversity in sport

Effectively managing diversity is now critical in light of the social and economic pressures that sport organisations are facing in the twenty-first century (Spracklen, Hylton and Long, 2006). According to Doherty and Chelladurai (1999), sport organisations need new and diverse perspectives, ideas and approaches for success. Given that sport organisations are not immune to the influence of environmental changes, increasing diversity is expected in these organisations, among athletes, coaches, officials, staff and administrators. Furthermore, the dependence of many sport organisations on volunteers can increase the importance of managing diversity. Examples of current and increasing diversity-related CSR issues for organisations include, for example, women and racial minorities in coaching and management; the international and interracial composition of professional sporting teams; the inclusion and employment of people with disabilities; the interaction of younger and older volunteers; and issues with athlete migration and racism, especially in football, with the trade of players from Africa to Europe (Bailey, 2005; Cornelissen and Solberg, 2007; Doherty and Chelladurai, 1999).

Given that diversity is now a critical issue for people working in sport, it is vital that the sport workforce understand the dynamics and impacts of diversity in order to maximise the benefits of having a diverse workforce. Sporting managers must strategically address the opportunities and challenges of managing an increasingly diverse workforce. According to Mai-Dalton (1993), *social responsibility* – the moral obligation to treat people fairly – should be the first and only reason for supporting diversity in organisations. However, Wright, Ferris, Hiller, and Kroll (1995) also noted, importantly, that if competitive advantage is based on human and organisational resources, then increasing diversity not only requires embracing reality, but also changing policies and procedures to align with the needs of the changing marketplace. For example, when NASCAR sought to increase the diversity of its spectators, it sought the help of NBA star, Ervin 'Magic' Johnson. NASCAR's chief operating officer at the time, George Pyne, noted the following: 'Magic will help NASCAR achieve its goals to better educate new audiences and facilitate greater participation among the industry and communications of colour' ('Magic Johnson to help NASCAR', 2004, p. 1). Overall, diversity influences important benefits to organisations such as cost savings, access to talented human resources and competitive advantage (Robinson and Dechant, 1997). Diversity can also facilitate business growth in areas such as increasing creativity and innovation, improving problem-solving and enhancing leadership capabilities (Cunningham, 2011).

These outcomes far outweigh any potential negative effects (Cunningham, 2011).

Gaps in practice and research

In an introductory survey of interest on the interplay between ideologies of race and identity within sport cultures, Carrington (2004) claimed that significant progress has been made since the 'intellectual lacuna' (p. 1) of the 1990s. In particular, the works of Back, Crabbe and Solomos (2001); Carrington and McDonald (2001); Garland and Rowe (2001); Williams (2001); and Ismond (2003) have established strong epistemological literature on race, ethnicity and diversity in social studies of sport. However, despite greater attention to racial equality in sport in recent years, the research and practice of sporting organisations towards creating equality of outcomes has been limited. Little work has been done at the intersection of strategic CSR implementation and diversity policies. Whilst the theoretical proposition that diversity has subsequent economic benefits for organisations is strong, as identified above, the empirical research to investigate this is limited. Further research is needed in this area to assist sporting organisations in understanding, articulating and enhancing these benefits.

In a comprehensive review of gender diversity in corporate boards including 400 publications, Terjesen, Sealy, and Singh (2009) found that, among other results, women directors were more committed to CSR than men, who were more concerned about economic performance. In particular, findings from the review indicated that boards with three or more women directors were more inclined to consider non-financial performance measures such as CSR involvement and stakeholder satisfaction. Similarly, in the context of sport organisations, future research should investigate the influence of gender diversity in board composition on the organisation's non-financial performance measures including CSR.

In addition, diverse sport boards by definition draw their directors from a wider range of the population. This often results in a better representation of the key stakeholders of the organisations as well as enhanced sensitivity to a wider range of perspectives (Terjesen et al., 2009). This raises the following questions: To what extent do these diverse boards contribute to building positive and ethical relationships with their key stakeholders, which is a salient aspect of CSR? Key stakeholders of sport organisations include the players, fans, employees, sponsors and media. If boards indeed have a positive impact on relationship building, in what manner are relationships with these partners developed? There is a clear gap in the literature that has not addressed this issue to date, with important implications for sport management practice.

In order to fully realise the extent to which an organisation is successfully implementing CSR, it must measure its progress on both social objectives and the degree to which these objectives improve the economic value for business. Measurement of CSR initiatives is an area that requires much more attention from both sport management and management researchers in the future. Despite the relatively widespread interest in CSR, the measurement tools to evaluate impact are still in their infancy. Organisations require a systematic model to assess the impact of CSR initiatives on stakeholders and society, not just the business itself (Lemon, Roberts, Raghubir and Winer, 2011). This area remains a significant gap in the current CSR literature.

Whilst organisations are increasingly realising that strong CSR and governance in diversity and inclusion may improve financial performance, there is a large gap in the sport literature regarding the actual link between CSR initiatives and financial performance. Future research could use financial data to examine the direct link between CSR policies and initiatives, and the subsequent financial return on investment. By highlighting the direct connection between addressing societal and governance issues and achieving economic value creation, organisations will be better able to articulate, understand and improve their CSR initiatives.

Conclusion

As the above discussion illustrates, the intersection of CSR, governance and diversity has become a central topic across most industries. The world has become more heterogeneous in many ways, from demographics and attitudes to beliefs and preferences. Further work is now needed to continue exploring the theoretical and practical aspects of the intersections of CSR, governance and diversity within the sporting context.

References

Applegate, B. and Puentes, S. (2009, August). *Diversity and inclusion: The next step in social responsibility*. Retrieved from the Center for Association Leadership website: www.asaecenter.org/Resources/ANowDetail.cfm?ItemNumber=43374

Babiak, K. (2010). The role and relevance of corporate social responsibility in sport: A view from the top. *Journal of Management and Organization, 16*, 528–549. doi:10.1017/S183336 7200001917

Back, L., Crabbe, T. and Solomos, J. (2001, December 17). The changing face of football: Racism, identity and multiculture in the English game. *The Guardian*. Retrieved from www.theguardian.com/us

Bailey, R. (2005). Evaluating the relationship between physical education, sport and social inclusion. *Educational Review, 57*, 71–90. doi: 10.1080/0013191042000274196

Bell, M. P. (2007). *Diversity in organizations*. Mason, OH: South-Western.

Carrington, B. (2004). Introduction: Race/nation/sport. *Leisure Studies, 23*, 1–3. doi:10. 1080/0261436042000182272

Carrington, B. and McDonald, I. (eds). (2001). *'Race', sport and British society*. London: Routledge.

Carroll, A. B. (1999). Corporate social responsibility: Evolution of a definitional construct. *Business and Society, 38*, 268–295. doi:10.1177/000765039903800303

Carter, C. B. and Lorsch, J. W. (2004). *Back to the drawing board: Designing corporate boards for a complex world.* Boston, MA: Harvard Business School Press.

Clarke, T. (ed.). (2004). *Theories of corporate governance: The philosophical foundations of corporate governance.* London: Routledge.

Clarke, T. (2007a). *International corporate governance: A comparative approach.* London: Routledge.

Clarke, T. (2007b). The materiality of sustainability: Corporate social and environmental responsibility as instruments of strategic change? In S. Benn and D. Dunphy (eds) *Corporate sustainability: Challenges for theory and practice* (pp. 219–251). London: Routledge.

Cobourn, S. D. (2014). Battle for the community: Key features of community engagement in professional sport. *International Journal for Sport and Society, 4,* 25–32. Retrieved from http://ijr.cgpublisher.com/product/pub.191/prod.2

Cornelissen, S. and Solberg, E. (2007). Sport mobility and circuits of power: The dynamics of football migration in Africa and the 2010 World Cup. *Politikon: South African Journal of Political Studies, 34,* 295–314. doi:10.1080/02589340801962619

Cox, T. and Beale, R. L. (1997). *Developing competency to manage diversity: Readings, cases and activities.* San Francisco, CA: Berrett-Koehler.

Cunningham, G. (2011). *Diversity in sport organizations.* Scottsdale, AZ: Holcomb Hathaway Publishers.

Dahlsrud, A. (2008). How corporate social responsibility is defined: An analysis of 37 definitions. *Corporate Social Responsibility and Environmental Management, 15,* 1–13. doi:10.1002/csr.132

Daily, C. M., Dalton, D. R. and Cannella, A. C. (2003). Corporate governance: Decades of dialogue and data. *Academy of Management Review, 28,* 371–382. doi:10.5465/AMR.2003.10196703

Doherty, A. and Chelladurai, P. (1999). Managing cultural diversity in sport organisations: A theoretical perspective. *Journal of Sport Management, 13,* 280–297. Retrieved from http://journals.humankinetics.com/jsm

Ferkins, L., Shilbury, D. and McDonald, G. (2005). The role of the board in building strategic capability: Towards an integrated model of sport governance. *Sport Management Review, 8,* 195–225. doi:10.1016/S1441-3523(05)70039-5

Fink, J. S. and Pastore, D. L. (1999). Diversity in sport? Utilizing the business literature to devise a comprehensive framework of diversity initiatives. *Quest, 51,* 310–327. doi:10.1080/00336297.1999.10491688

Friedman, M. (1970, September). The social responsibility of business is to increase its profits. *New York Times Magazine, 13,* 32–33.

Garland, J. and Rowe, M. (2001). *Racism and anti-racism in football.* Basingstoke, UK: Palgrave.

Harjoto, M. A. and Jo, H. (2011). Corporate governance and CSR nexus. *Journal of Business Ethics, 100,* 45–67. doi:10.1007/s10551-011-0772-6

Hopkins, M. (2001, January). What, if any, is the relation between corporate governance and corporate social responsibility? *World Bank Monthly Report.* Retrieved from www.worldbank.org/

Hoye, R. (2002). *Board performance of Australian voluntary sport organisations* (Doctoral thesis). Retrieved from www120.secure.griffith.edu.au/rch/file/69bfc7da-436d-45ac-3456-b11a76fbbeeb/1/02Whole.pdf

Hoye, R. and Cuskelly, G. (2007). *Sport governance.* Amsterdam: Elsevier.

Hunt, K. A., Bristol, T. and Bashaw, R. E. (1999). A conceptual approach to classifying sports fans. *Journal of Services Marketing, 13,* 439–452. doi:10.1108/08876049910298720

Ismond, P. (2003). *Black and Asian athletes in British sport and society: A sporting chance?* Basingstoke, UK: Palgrave.

Jenkins, H. (2012). *CSR in sport: Investigating environmental sustainability in UK Premier League football clubs* (Working Paper No. 68). Cardiff, UK: Cardiff University, the Centre for Business Relationships, Accountability, Sustainability and Society.

John F. Kennedy School of Government. (2008). *Defining corporate social responsibility.* Retrieved from www.hks.harvard.edu/m-rcbg/CSRI/init_define.html

Johnson, J., Daily, C. and Ellestrand, A. E. (1996). Board of directors: A review and research agenda. *Journal of Management, 22,* 409–439. doi:10.1177/014920639602200303

Lemon, K. N., Roberts, J. H., Raghubir, P. and Winer, R. S. (2011). Sustainability performance assessment. In M. Tonello (ed.) *Sustainability matters: Why and how corporate boards should be involved* (pp. 61–70; Research Report No. R-1481-11-RR). Retrieved from The Conference Board Website: www.conference-board.org/retrievefile.cfm?file name=TCB_R-1481-11-RR1.pdf&type=subsite

Magic Johnson to help NASCAR diversity efforts. (2004, May 20). *Sports Illustrated.* Retrieved from www.si.com/

Mai-Dalton, R. (1993). Managing cultural diversity on the individual, group, and organizational levels. In M. M. Chemers and R. Ayman (eds) *Leadership theory and research* (pp. 189–215). San Diego, CA: Academic Press.

Margolis, J. D. and Walsh, J. P. (2003). Misery loves companies: Rethinking social initiatives by business. *Administrative Science Quarterly, 48,* 268–305. doi:10.2307/3556659

Melnick, M. J. (1993). Searching for sociability in the stands: A theory of sport spectating. *Journal of Sport Management, 7,* 44–60. Retrieved from http://journals.human kinetics.com/jsm

Plunkett Research. (2014, November 11). *Industry statistics sports and recreation business statistics analysis.* Retrieved from www.plunkettresearch.com/sports-recreation-leisure-market-research/industry-statistics

Porter, M. E. and Kramer, M. R. (2006). Strategy and society: The link between competitive advantage and corporate social repsonsibility. *Harvard Business Review, 84*(12), 78–92. Retrieved from https://hbr.org/

Robinson, G. and Dechant, K. (1997). Building a business case for diversity. *Academy of Management Executive, 11,* 21–31. Retrieved from http://cursos.itam.mx/

Savitz, A. W. and Weber, K. (2006). *The triple bottom line: How today's best-run companies are achieving economic, social and environmental successes – and how you can too.* San Francisco, CA: Jossey-Bass.

Spracklen, K., Hylton, K. and Long, J. (2006). Managing and monitoring equality and diversity in UK sport: An evaluation of the Sporting Equals Racial Equality Standard and its impact on organizational change. *Journal of Sport and Social Issues, 30,* 289–305. doi:10.1177/0193723506290083

Sutton, W. A., McDonald, M. A., Milne, G. R. and Cimperman, J. (1997). Creating and fostering fan identification in professional sports. *Sport Marketing Quarterly, 6,* 15–22. Retrieved from www.fitinfotech.com/smqEletricVersion/smqWVU.tpl

Terjesen, S., Sealy, R. and Singh, V. (2009). Women directors on corporate boards: A review and research agenda. *Corporate Governance: An International Review, 17,* 320–337. doi:10.1111/j.1467-8683.2009.00742.x

Tricker, R. I. (1984). *Corporate governance: Principles, policies, and practices.* London: Gower.

Tricker, R. I. (1993). Corporate governance – the new focus of interest. *Corporate Governance: An International Review, 1,* 1–3. doi:10.1111/j.1467-8683.1993.tb00001.x

van Knippenberg, D., De Drue, C. K. W. and Homann, A. C. (2004). Work group diversity and group performance: An integrative model and research agenda. *Journal of Applied Psychology, 89,* 1008–1022. doi:10.1037/0021-9010.89.6.1008

Williams, J. (2001). *Cricket and race.* London: Berg.

Wright, P., Ferris, S. P., Hiller, J. S. and Kroll, M. (1995). Competitiveness through management of diversity: Effects on stock price valuation. *Academy of Management Journal, 38,* 272–287. doi:10.2307/256736

Zahra, S. A. and Pearce, J. A. (1989). Board of directors and corporate financial performance: A review and integrative model. *Journal of Management, 15,* 291–344. doi:10.1177/014920638901500208

3

GENDER DIVERSITY IN THE GOVERNANCE OF INTERNATIONAL SPORT FEDERATIONS

Johanna A. Adriaanse

A significant milestone for women's presence in sport governance was reached in 2013 when football's international governing body, FIFA, welcomed Lydia Nsekera, President of Burundi Football Association, to its Executive Committee. For the first time in its 100-year-old history, a woman was elected to take a seat at the FIFA executive table alongside 24 male members (FIFA, 2013). Since women and girls gained access to football clubs several decades ago, football has emerged as one the fastest growing participation sports for females. The first Women's World Cup in football took place in 1991 in China, demonstrating evidence of its popularity at a global level. While participation rates for women playing football have grown exponentially, women's participation in the governance of the sport remains a serious challenge. The election of the first woman on the FIFA executive was an important step; however, with only one woman out of 25 directors (4 per cent), women remain markedly under-represented. On a wider scale, it appears that gender diversity in sport governance is a critical issue not only for FIFA, but also for many international sport federations (IFs).

Yet, the business case for women's participation in the governance of organisations has been solidly established. When a coach picks the best team for the field, she or he considers the entire pool of players, all the talent available. In contrast, when the best team is selected for the board room, half of the population is currently ignored. Clearly, the pool of talent and skillsets will significantly increase when women are included in the selection process. Against this background, Terjesen, Sealy and Singh (2009) conducted a review of research on women directors on corporate boards based on more than 400 publications in the past 30 years. They found that gender diversity mainly had a positive impact on the organisation's performance. Women's participation on the board led to more sensitivity to other perspectives, which contributed to better problem solving and decision making. Women also demonstrated a critical approach by frequently asking questions which enhanced the board's independence. Further, the researchers found that boards with three or more women were more active in going beyond financial performance measures such as stakeholder satisfaction, innovation and corporate social responsibility.

A growing number of studies have investigated the relationship between gender and sport leadership, in particular the issue of women's under-representation in sport governance. Researchers have examined this issue in a range of countries, including Australia (Adriaanse and Schofield, 2013; McKay, 1992, 1997; Sibson, 2010), Canada (Hall, Cullen, and Slack, 1989; Inglis, 1997; Shaw and Slack, 2002), Germany (Doll-Tepper, Pfister, and Radtke, 2006; Pfister and Radtke, 2009), the Netherlands (Claringbould and Knoppers, 2007, 2008), New Zealand (Cameron, 1996; Shaw, 2006), Norway (Fasting, 2000; Hovden, 2000, 2006; Skirstad, 2002, 2009), the United Kingdom (Shaw and Hoeber, 2003; Shaw and Penney, 2003; White and Brackenridge, 1985) and the United States (Burton, Grappendorf, and Henderson, 2011; Schull, Shaw, and Kihl, 2013). These studies have all focused on the governance of national sport organisations. At an international level, Henry and his colleagues (Henry *et al.*, 2004; Henry and Robinson, 2010) investigated women's representation in the governance of IFs. These studies are of great significance; however, they have included only those federations that are part of the Olympic Movement. Considering that less than half of the IFs are actually part of the Olympic Movement, there is a lack of research into gender representation in the governance of the broader group of IFs. The present study seeks to fill this gap and extend the prevailing knowledge and understanding by examining gender diversity in the governance of both Olympic and non-Olympic IFs.

The research questions that framed the study were: (a) What is the gender ratio on boards of IFs with reference to board directors, chair and chief executive? (b) To what extent has gender balance and/or a critical mass of women been achieved on IF boards? (c) In light of the findings, what are the implications for sport management practice? The study is based on the Sydney Scoreboard (www.sydney scoreboard.com/) – a global index for women in sport leadership – which gathers and displays data on women's representation in sport governance globally.

The chapter begins with a review of the literature on gender diversity in sport governance and explains the theoretical framework. This is followed by a description of the methodology, which comprised an audit and comparison of IF boards ($N = 76$) in 2012 and 2014. Next, the results of the audit, including the percentages of women board directors, board chairs and chief executives, are presented and discussed. The chapter concludes with a discussion of the implications of the study's findings for sport management practice.

Women's under-representation in sport governance

In a comprehensive review of research, based on nearly 100 publications over the past 40 years, Burton (2015) provided a multi-level examination of scholarship that contributes to understanding the scarcity of women in sport leadership positions.

She distinguished research at three levels: macro, meso, and micro. From a macro-perspective, where the focus is at the societal and/or sport sector level, the under-representation of women suggests that sport is a gendered institution with hegemonic masculinity as the norm. The sport sector shows institutionalised masculinity as an operating principle, which is evident in the findings of a range of studies on the gendered structure of sport organisations (Hall *et al.*, 1989; Hovden, 2010; Shaw and Slack, 2002; White and Brackenridge, 1985).

At a meso-level, where the focus is on analysis within sport organisations, Burton (2015) contended that the scarcity of women is explained through stereo-typing of leaders, issues of discrimination, and gendered organisational cultures. Some of the more notable findings involved men's privileged position in sport leadership roles (Adriaanse and Schofield, 2014; Fasting, 2000; Inglis, 1997; McKay, 1992; Pfister and Radtke, 2009; Sibson, 2010) and the discrimination in recruitment processes (Claringbould and Knoppers, 2007; Hovden, 2000).

Analysis at the micro-level focuses on the individual men and women within the sport context and how they make sense of their experiences of power, policies, and procedures. Scholars have often used discourse analysis to help understand how constructions of gender are embedded in organisational discourses that inhibit women from advancement to sport leadership positions. Key findings demonstrate that governance and senior management roles are dominated by discourses of masculinity and that subordinate positions are associated with those of femininity (Claringbould and Knoppers, 2012; Shaw and Hoeber, 2003).

A common thread throughout the research on gender and sport leadership at all three levels is the focus on the concept of power and related notions of gender hierarchy, hegemonic masculinity, male privilege and exclusionary power. According to Connell (2009), an internationally acclaimed scholar on gender, power is a key dimension of gender relations. It is about the way in which control, authority, influence and force are exercised along gender lines. Power relates to the concept of patriarchy, a gender order in which men dominate women. According to Connell (2009), 'The power of husbands over wives and fathers over daughters is still an accepted idea in much of the world, even in modified forms such as the idea of the father as "head of the household"' (p. 76). The concept of gendered power relations in the context of managing organisations including sport organisations is further explored in the next section.

Gendered power relations in organisational management

The control of men over women not only occurs at an individual level, but is also impersonally realised through institutions or the state. The work of Kanter (1977), Burton (1987), and Wajcman (1999) provide important examples of institutionalised power. Kanter's pioneering study on gender dynamics in U.S. corporations in the 1970s disclosed that the prevailing gender hierarchy in organisations was not the result of individual differences between men and women, but that of the structure of the organisation. Gender inequality arose because women were located in dead-end jobs at the bottom of the organisation or appeared as tokens at the top. This ultimately led to the notion of a gendered institution in which hegemonic masculinity prevails. Kanter further found that relative numbers or ratios are significant for affecting behaviour in organisations. One or two women tend to have limited influence, but when a minority group obtains a presence of one-third or more, it is thought to become a critical mass and therefore able to influence the culture of the organisation. Such groups can form alliances with other minority members and contribute to the organisation's governance in ways that can bring about change. Kanter identified *balanced groups* as those in which the gender ratio ranges between 40 and 60 per cent. In such groups, gender-based differences become less important. In other words, women are more likely to be seen as individuals with their own skills and perspectives, and not as representatives for women.

Kanter's (1977) notion of gender balance in groups parallels that in the context of public policy in governance. In this context, gender balance refers to gender parity in the number of directors on the board. As a measure of gender parity, a minimum of 40 per cent representation of each gender on the board is generally adopted. This approach is often described as the 40:40:20 target, which means including 40 per cent women, 40 per cent men, and 20 per cent of either gender in the composition of the board. This target has been recommended by the Australian Human Rights Commission (2010) in their *2010 Gender Equality Blueprint* report and internationally, for example, by the European Parliament as a non-binding resolution to be achieved by 2020 (Australian Human Rights Commission, 2010; Whelan and Wood, 2012). The present study examines board composition in sport governance by investigating the gender ratios on IF boards. In particular, it aims to analyse to what extent boards have obtained gender balance and/or a critical mass of women in their composition.

Method

An audit was conducted of the gender distribution in the composition of IF boards. Both Olympic and non-Olympic IFs that were members of SportAccord were selected for inclusion. SportAccord is an umbrella organisation (not-for-profit) based in Lausanne that coordinates and supports IFs through knowledge sharing (SportAccord, n.d.). It provides expertise and resources on critical issues commonly faced by the international sport bodies, such as good governance, anti-doping, integrity, social responsibility and digital media.

Data were collected through the Sydney Scoreboard, an interactive website, which collects and displays data on the gender composition of boards of national sport organisations, national Olympic committees and IFs. In relation to the latter – which represents the focus of this study – data include the name of the IF, the number of male and female directors on each board, gender of the board chair and gender of the chief executive. The *board* is defined as the group of officials (directors) empowered through the constitution to govern and oversee the running of an organisation. *Director* is understood as a person who is on the board of directors of an organisation either through election or appointment. Finally, a *chair* is the person responsible for leading the board; in some organisations the board chair is named president. The *chief executive* is the senior executive (usually paid) who is responsible for the organisation's overall operations and performance and who operates in accordance with the delegations and directions given by the board. He or she may also be referred to as general manager, managing director, or secretary-general.

Data were collected during two periods of time. The first period was between September 2010 and December 2012, while a repeat audit was conducted between January and September 2014. An open invitation to submit data was sent to all 6,000 members of the International Working Group on Women and Sport (IWG) network via the organisation's e-newsletter. The IWG is an independent coordinating body comprising representatives of key government and non-government organisations from different regions of the world to empower women and advance sport. Every four years, it hosts a world conference and the Sydney Scoreboard is the official legacy of the fifth IWG World Conference on Women and Sport which took place in Sydney in 2010.

In addition to providing data on the gender distribution of boards of the international sport bodies, participants were also asked to identify the source of information (e.g., annual report or official website of the sport organisation) and the date of data collection. Further, information for those IFs whose data was not provided by the IWG network was gathered from the official website of the IF. Subsequently, the data for each IF were entered on the Sydney Scoreboard database. Using these data, tables were created showing percentages of women board directors, women chairs, and women chief executives on boards of 76 IFs for the two time periods ending 2012 and 2014.

Results

Table 3.1 shows the percentage of women directors on 76 IF boards in 2014 and 2012.

As can be seen, in 2014 women's representation ranged from 0 to 100 per cent, with a global mean of 13.3 per cent. Three of the 76 IFs have between 40 and 60 per cent women's presence, which means that they have obtained the recommended gender balance in the composition of their board. They are the International Skating Union, the International Hockey Federation and the International Triathlon Union. A critical mass, defined by a minimum of 30 per cent women's representation, has been obtained in four federations: the International Equestrian Federation, the International Federation of Sleddog Sports, the International Surfing Association and the International Gymnastics Federation. The majority of federations, 44 of 76 IFs, show women's representation between 4 and 28.6 per cent. At the bottom of the table are 24 federations without any women on their board, including several

TABLE 3.1 Percentage of women directors on boards of international sport federations (N = 76)

International Federation	Female Board Directors 2014 (%)	Female Board Directors 2012 (%)	Difference + / −
INF: International Netball Federation	100	80	+20
ISU: International Skating Union	45.45	29.41	+16.04
FIH: International Hockey Federation	40	37.5	+2.5
ITU: International Triathlon Union	40	42.86	−2.86
FEI: International Equestrian Federation	33.33	14.29	+19.04
IFSS: International Federation of Sleddog Sports	33.33	35.71	−2.38
ISA: International Surfing Association	33.33	25	+8.33
FIG: International Gymnastics Federation	30.43	28.57	+1.86
ISA: International Rowing Federation	28.57	25	+3.57
IFF: International Floorball Federation	27.27	8.33	+18.94
IOF: International Orienteering Federation	27.27	9.09	+18.18
FIRS: International Roller Sports Federation	25	27.27	−2.27
ICU: International Cycling Union	25	0	+25
ISAF: International Sailing Federation	25	18.18	+6.82
WCF: World Curling Federation	25	25	0
WDF: World Darts Federation	25	28.57	−3.57
IAAF: International Association of Athletics Federations	22.22	15	+7.22
FIBA: Federation Internationale De Basketball	21.74	21.74	0
IFMA: International Federation of Muay Thai Amateur	20.59	0	+20.59
TWIF: Tug of War International Federation	20	20	0
UIAA: International Mountaineering and Climbing Federation	20	0	+20
WSF: World Squash Federation	20	25	−5
United World Wrestling	19.05	9.09	+9.96
WDSF: World DanceSport Federation	18.75	18.18	+0.57
IRF: International Racquetball Federation	16.67	27.27	−10.6
WFDF: World Flying Disc Federation	16.67	18.18	−1.51
BWF: Badminton World Federation	14.29	7.69	+6.6
CMAS: World Underwater Federation	14.29	9.52	+4.77
IIHF: International Ice Hockey Federation	14.29	13.33	+0.96
ILS: International Life Saving Federation	14.29	5.26	+9.03
FIL: International Luge Federation	13.33	12.5	+0.83
IFBB: International Federation of Body Building and Fitness	13.33	7.14	+6.19
FIVB: International Volleyball Federation	12.5	13.33	−0.83
IWWF: International Waterski and Wakeboard Federation	12.5	22.73	−10.23
IBU: International Biathlon Union	11.11	20	−8.89
FIDE: International Chess Federation	10	8.33	+1.67
ICF: International Canoe Federation	10	13.33	−3.33
IFAF: International Federation of American Football	10	0	+10

TABLE 3.1 Continued

International Federation	Female Board Directors 2014 (%)	Female Board Directors 2012 (%)	Difference + / −
IFSC: International Federation of Sport Climbing	10	30	−20
UIPM: International Modern Pentathlon Union	9.52	10.53	−1.01
CMSB: Federation Mondale Des Sports de Boules	9.09	13.33	−4.24
IPF: International Powerlifting Federation	9.09	0	+9.09
WBF: World Bridge Federation	9.09	13.04	−3.95
FIM: International Motorcycling Federation	7.69	7.14	+0.55
WKF: World Karate Federation	7.69	7.69	0
FMJD: Worlds Draughts Federation	7.14	7.14	0
IGF: International Golf Federation	7.14	25	−17.86
WTF: World Taekwondo Federation	7.14	8.82	−1.68
WAKO: World Association of Kickboxing Organisations	5.88	5.88	0
IWF: International Weightlifting Federation	4.76	0	+4.76
FINA: Federation Internationale De Natation (Swimming)	4.17	4.55	−0.38
FIFA: Federation Internationale de Football Association	4	0	4
AIBA: International Boxing Association	0	7.14	−7.14
CIPS: Confederation Internationale De La Peche Sportive (Sport Fishing)	0	0	0
FAI: The International Air Sports Federation	0	4.65	−4.65
FIAS: International Amateur Sambo Federation	0	0	0
FIBT: International Bobsleigh and Skeleton Federation	0	0	0
FIK: International Kendo Federation	0	11.76	−11.76
FIP: Federation of International Polo	0	0	0
FIPV: Federacion International De Pelota Vasca	0	0	0
FIQ: Federation Internationale des Quilleurs (Bowling)	0	12.5	−12.5
IAF: International Aikido Federation	0	0	0
IBAF: International Baseball Federation	0	0	0
ICC: International Cricket Council	0	0	0
CSF: International Casting Sport Federation	0	0	0
IFA: International Fistball Association	0	0	0
IGF: International Go Federation	0	0	0
IHF: International Handball Federation	0	0	0
IJF: International Judo Federation	0	4.76	−4.76
IRB: International Rugby Board	0	0	0
ISSF: International Shooting Sport Federation	0	0	0
ITF: International Tennis Federation	0	6.67	−6.67
JJIF: Ju-Jitsu International Federation	0	0	0
PI: Pentathlon International	0	9.09	−9.09
WCBS: World Confederation of Billiard Sports	0	0	0
WMF: World MiniGolf Sport Federation	0	0	0
Global Average	13.32	12.00	1.32

that govern popular global sports: the International Tennis Federation, the International Cricket Council, the International Rugby Board, the International Handball Federation and the International Baseball Federation. At the other end of the spectrum is the International Netball Federation that is governed by women directors only (100 per cent). This portrays a 'reverse' case of gender inequality where men are under-represented; in fact, men are not represented at all.

Regarding women's representation as chair (or president) of the federation, six of the 76 IFs (8 per cent) in 2014 had a woman in this leading position. They include the World Underwater Federation, the International Equestrian Federation, the International Federation of Sleddog Sports, the International Netball Federation, the International Triathlon Union and the World Curling Federation (see Table 3.2).

In addition, this table provides an overview of the federations with a female chief executive, also known as secretary-general in IFs. In 2014, women occupied the chief executive position in 15 out of 71 IFs (21 per cent). They include the governing bodies of popular global sports such as handball, netball, and triathlon. It is noted that five of the 76 IFs operated without a chief executive at the time of the study.

When comparing the 2014 results with those of 2012, a trend over time emerges (see Table 3.3). First, the percentage of women board directors of all IFs that participated in this study slightly increased from 12 per cent in 2012 to 13.3 per cent in 2014. This represents a change of 1.3 per cent for the two periods. An

TABLE 3.2 International sport federations with women chairs and women chief executives in 2014

Leadership Position	IFs
IFs with women chair/ president (6)	CMAS: World Underwater Federation, FEI: International Equestrian Federation IFSS: International Federation of Sleddog Sports, INF: International Netball Federation, ITU: International Triathlon Union, WCF: World Curling Federation.
IFs with women chief executive/secretary-general (15)	FIBT: International Bobsleigh and Skeleton Federation, FIQ: Federation Internationale des Quilleurs (Bowling), IBU: International Biathlon Union, IFSC: International Federation of Sport Climbing, IGF: International Go Federation, IHF: International Handball Federation, IJF: International Judo Federation, INF: International Netball Federation (IFNA), IOF: International Orienteering Federation, ITU: International Triathlon Union, IWWF: International Waterski and Wakeboard Federation, JJIF: Ju-Jitsu International Federation, UIAA: International Mountaineering and Climbing Federation, UIPM: International Modern Pentathlon Union, WDSF: World Dance Sport Federation.

TABLE 3.3 Percentage of women as directors, chair and chief executive of IFs in 2014 and 2012

Leadership Position	2014	2012	Change
Women directors	13.3	12	+1.3
Women chairs	8	7	+1
Women chief executives	21	9	+12

upward trend has also occurred with reference to women in the leadership positions of chair and chief executive. Women's representation as chair of an IF has increased from 7 per cent in 2012 to 8 per cent in 2014. Finally, a more significant change can be seen in women's presence as chief executive: from 9 per cent in 2012 to 21 per cent in 2014, a remarkable increase of 12 per cent.

Discussion

Gender balance and critical mass on IF boards

The findings of the study indicate that although women's presence as directors on IFs' boards has increased between 2012 and 2014, women remain markedly under-represented in the governance of global sport. Overall, the gender dynamics on IF boards are characterised by a prevailing gender hierarchy in which men continue to dominate women. Only three federations have obtained what is described as gender balance (at least 40 per cent of women on the board) and another four federations have a critical mass of women (over 30 per cent) on their board. The likely consequence for the 69 of the 76 international federations that failed to achieve either gender balance or a critical mass is loss of potential. As discussed previously, the business case for gender diversity in governance is strong. In other words, whilst gender diversity on boards is an ethical and democratic issue in terms of adequate representation of all stakeholders, it also impacts on the organisation's performance. Terjesen et al. (2009) found that gender diversity on boards contributed to more effective corporate governance. Several other studies have concluded that in order to reap the benefits of gender diversity, a minimum of 30 per cent women's representation is required (Joecks et al., 2013; Konrad, Kramer and Erkut, 2008; Torchia, Calabro and Huse, 2011). After empirically testing Kanter's critical mass theory with German organisations, Joecks et al. (2013) found a link between gender diversity on the board and firm performance. They found the critical mass to be approximately 30 per cent women's representation because when it reaches this threshold it can influence the culture of the organisation. If women's presence is less than the critical mass of 30 per cent, gender diversity is likely to result in having no influence or even a negative influence on the performance of the organisation. This means that those international sport federations that lack a critical mass of women – which are the vast majority of IFs – may well be under-performing. In short, they lack a diversity of perspectives on the board which may result in diminished capability to be innovative, solve problems, and make sound decisions. This also applies to the International Netball Federation, the reverse case, which lacks a critical mass of male directors.

Similarly, although women's representation in the positions of board chair and chief executive of IFs has increased between 2012 and 2014, neither indicator has achieved either gender balance or a critical mass globally yet. The most powerful and influential positions, namely the board chair and chief executive, remain largely occupied by men. Again, the lack of gender diversity suggests that the governance of sport from a global perspective is being compromised and not reaching its full potential. The 12 per cent increase of women's presence in the chief executive role to 21 per cent in 2014, however, is promising. Chief executives can be regarded as the pipeline for board directors and therefore bode well for an increase of female directors in the future. Nevertheless, based on the current status, the question arises as to how we can accelerate gender diversity in the governance of international federations. The next section considers implications of the study's findings for sport management practice.

Strategies to accelerate gender diversity on IF boards

A common intervention to accelerate gender diversity in governance has been the introduction of gender quotas and targets. Both refer to the requirement of a minimum number or percentage of women or either gender, but a key difference is that quotas are mandatory while targets are voluntary (Whelan and Wood, 2012). One of the strongest examples of using quotas which brought about profound change is the case of Norway. In 2005, Norway became the first country in the world to pass a quota law requiring a minimum of 40 per cent of either gender on the board of directors of public limited liability companies by 2008 (Torchia et al., 2011). Sanctions for non-compliance included the dissolution of the company. As a consequence, women's representation on these Norwegian boards increased from 7 per cent in 2003 to 40.3 per cent in 2010.

In the context of sport governance, Adriaanse and Schofield (2014) have examined the impact of gender quotas on gender diversity on boards of national sport organisations in Australia. They found that a quota of a minimum of three women was an effective way to increase women's presence in governance, but it was only a first step towards achieving gender diversity. It needed to operate in conjunction with several other conditions, including women assuming influential board positions and, most importantly, directors adopting gender diversity as an organisational value.

In contrast to quotas, gender targets operate as a voluntary, aspirational goal for the level of gender representation in an organisation. In 1996, the International Olympic Committee chose to adopt targets over quotas for women's membership in national Olympic committees and international sport federations associated with the Olympic Movement. Although many organisations responded positively to the proposed target of 20 per cent female representation by 2005, by 2010, aspirations had not yet been achieved, with the percentage of women on national Olympic committees reaching 17.6 per cent and on IFs, 18.3 per cent (Henry *et al.*, 2004; Henry and Robinson, 2010). It is evident from this example that voluntary targets have limited impact. Accordingly, using quotas may be a more effective intervention for achieving gender diversity on sport boards. Nevertheless, the introduction of quotas is often opposed on the grounds that they represent additional regulation and therefore limit the efficiency of business. Critics also argue that quotas undermine the principle of merit, with many women believing they will be viewed as tokens when hired on the basis of fulfilling a quota (Whelan and Wood, 2012).

Another strategy to accelerate gender diversity is to adjust the recruitment and selection process. As previously mentioned, discrimination in the recruitment of directors has been identified as inhibiting the presence of women on sport boards (Burton, 2015; Claringbould and Knoppers, 2007; Hovden, 2000). Men can control boards by framing the selection process in a manner that maintains the male-dominated culture of the sport board. This happens when male board members select those with similar characteristics in an attempt to 're-create themselves'. Moreover, the common strategy of searching in networks of friends and colleagues for potential board members re-confirms the existing gender structure. Based on their research into women's participation in the governance of the Olympic Movement, Henry and Robinson (2010) therefore recommended that IFs develop a list of potential candidates for 'posts of responsibility within the … IF. This list would be gender-balanced with a minimum target of 40 per cent representation from either gender' (p. 15). When board vacancies occur, suitable candidates – both men and women – can be nominated from this pool of potential candidates.

A final strategy to advance gender diversity is to adopt gender reporting. This involves federations monitoring the gender distribution in the composition of their board and reporting the results on a regular basis (e.g., bi-annually). The advantage of this strategy is that it raises the awareness of this critical issue in sport governance – in other words, it puts gender equality firmly and officially on the map. Further, regular gender reporting tracks the progress of gender diversity in the governance of global sport in a statistical way with 'hard' data that allows for the identification of good practices and effective interventions. Gender reporting can be adopted on a voluntary basis by the individual IF. Alternatively, international bodies such as the International Olympic Committee or SportAccord could make it a requirement for membership of their organisation.

Conclusion

Despite compelling research evidence that shows the benefits of gender diversity in governance, the findings of this study indicate that women's participation in the governance of IFs remains a serious challenge. The study was based on an analysis of data from the Sydney Scoreboard: a global index for women in sport leadership.

In 2014, the global average for women's representation as board directors was 13.3 per cent, while board chair/president was 8 per cent and chief executive/secretary-general was 21 per cent. These findings suggest that women continue to be largely under-represented in the key leadership roles in global sport. A trend over time discloses that women's representation on all three key indicators has improved; however, few federations (seven of 76 IFs) have achieved either gender balance or a critical mass of women on its boards in 2014. The most promising result was in reference to the position of chief executive, which demonstrated a 12 per cent increase in women's presence between 2012 and 2014.

The governance of global sport reflects a prevailing gender order in which men and masculinity continue to occupy a privileged position. Given the paucity of international federations that achieve gender balance and/or a critical mass of women in the composition of its boards, it is evident that the vast majority of IFs fail to adhere to ethical business practices. This is because important stakeholders are under-represented or not represented at all. Further, it is evident that these federations fall short of maximising the organisation's performance potential. In particular, a lack of different perspectives can impair the board's decision-making and problem-solving capability.

Considering the implications of the study's findings for sport management practice, three key strategies to advance gender diversity are suggested. First, although the introduction of gender quotas and targets are usually met with some resistance, they have proven to be effective in the acceleration of gender diversity in governance. Second, to counteract bias in recruitment processes, the establishment of nominating committees is recommended with the task of identifying suitable male and female candidates for board positions. Finally, it is suggested to adopt gender reporting to monitor progress towards gender diversity in the governance of sport globally.

References

Adriaanse, J. A. and Schofield, T. (2013). Analysing gender dynamics in sport governance: A new regimes-based approach. *Sport Management Review, 16*, 498–513. doi:10.1016/j.smr.2013.01.006

Adriaanse, J. A. and Schofield, T. (2014). The impact of gender quotas on gender equality in sport governance. *Journal of Sport Management, 28*, 485–497. doi:10.1123/jsm.2013-0108

Australian Human Rights Commission. (2010, June). *2010 Gender equality blueprint*. Retrieved from www.humanrights.gov.au/sites/default/files/document/publication/Gender_Equality_Blueprint.pdf

Burton, C. (1987). Merit and gender: Organisations and the mobilisation of masculine bias. *Australian Journal of Social Issues, 22*, 424–435. Retrieved from www.aspa.org.au/publications/ajsi.html

Burton, L. J. (2015). Underrepresentation of women in sport leadership: A review of research. *Sport Management Review, 18*, 155–165. doi:10.1016/j.smr.2014.02.004

Burton, L. J., Grappendorf, H. and Henderson, A. (2011). Perceptions of gender in athletic administration: Utilising the congruity to examine (potential) prejudice against women. *Journal of Sport Management, 25*, 36–45. Retrieved from http://journals.humankinetics.com/jsm

Cameron, J. (1996). *Trailblazers: Women who manage New Zealand sport.* Christchurch, NZ: Sports Inclined.

Claringbould, I. and Knoppers, A. (2007). Finding a 'normal' woman: Selection processes for board membership. *Sex Roles, 56,* 495–507. doi:10.1007/s11199-007-9188-2

Claringbould, I. and Knoppers, A. (2008). Doing and undoing gender in sport governance. *Sex Roles, 58,* 81–92. doi:10.1007/s11199-007-9351-9

Claringbould, I. and Knoppers, A. (2012). Paradoxical practices of gender in sport-related organisations. *Journal of Sport Management, 26,* 404–416. Retrieved from http://journals.humankinetics.com/jsm

Connell, R. (2009). *Gender.* Cambridge: Polity.

Doll-Tepper, G., Pfister, G. and Radtke, S. (eds). (2006). *Progress towards leadership: Biographies and career paths of male and female leaders in German sport organisations.* Cologne: Sportverlag Strauss.

Fasting, K. (2000). Women's role in national and international sport governing bodies. In B. L. Drinkwater (ed.) *Women in sport: Volume VIII of the encyclopaedia of sports medicine, an IOC Medical Committee publication* (pp. 441–451). Oxford: Blackwell.

FIFA. (2013, May 31). *Overwhelming support for FIFA reforms and resolution on the fight against racism and discrimination; First woman elected to Executive Committee* [Press release]. Retrieved from www.fifa.com/aboutfifa/organisation/bodies/congress/news/news id=2089615/index.html

Hall, M. A., Cullen, D. and Slack, T. (1989). Organisational elites recreating themselves: The gender structure of National Sports Organisations. *Quest, 41*(4), 28–45. doi:10.1080/00336297.1989.10483906

Henry, I., Radzi, W., Rich, E., Shelton, C., Theodoraki, E. and White, A. (2004). *Women, leadership and the Olympic movement.* Loughborough: Institute of Sport and Leisure Policy, Loughborough University and the International Olympic Committee.

Henry, I. and Robinson, L. (2010). *Gender equity and leadership in Olympic bodies.* Loughborough: Centre for Olympic Studies and Research, Loughborough University and International Olympic Committee.

Hovden, J. (2000). 'Heavyweight' men and younger women? The gendering of selection processes in Norwegian sports organistions. *NORA – Nordic Journal of Feminist and Gender Research, 8,* 17–32. doi:10.1080/080387400408035

Hovden, J. (2006). The gender order as a policy issue in sport: A study of Norwegian sport organisations. *NORA – Nordic Journal of Feminist and Gender Research, 14,* 41–53. doi:10.1080/08038740600727127

Hovden, J. (2010). Female top leaders – prisoners of gender? The gendering of leadership discourses in Norwegian sports organizations. *International Journal of Sport Policy and Politics, 2,* 189–203. doi:10.1080/19406940.2010.488065

Inglis, S. (1997). Roles of the board in amateur sport organisations. *Journal of Sport Management, 11,* 160–176. Retrieved from http://journals.humankinetics.com/jsm

Joecks, J., Pull, K. and Vetter, K. (2013). Gender diversity in the boardroom and firm performance: What exactly constitutes a 'critical mass?' *Journal of Business Ethics, 118,* 61–72. doi:10.1007/s10551-012-1553-6

Kanter, R. M. (1977). *Men and women of the corporation.* New York: Basic Books.

Konrad, A. M., Kramer, V. and Erkut, S. (2008). Critical mass: The impact of three or more women on corporate boards. *Organizational Dynamics, 37,* 145–164. doi:10.1016/j.orgdyn.2008.02.005

McKay, J. (1992). *Why so few? Women executives in Australian Sport.* Canberra: National Sports Research Centre.

McKay, J. (1997). *Managing gender: Affirmative action and organisational power in Australian, Canadian, and New Zealand sport.* Albany, NY: State University of New York Press.

Pfister, G. and Radtke, S. (2009). Sport, women and leadership: Results of a project on executives in German sports organisations. *European Journal of Sport Science, 9*, 229–243. doi:10.1080/17461390902818286

Schull, V., Shaw, S. and Kihl, I. A. (2013). 'If a woman came in … she would have been eaten up alive': Analyzing gendered political processes in the search for an athletic director. *Gender and Society, 27*, 56–81. doi:10.1177/0891243212466289

Shaw, S. (2006). Gender suppression in New Zealand regional sports trusts. *Women in Management Review, 21*, 554–566. doi:10.1108/09649420610692507

Shaw, S. and Hoeber, L. (2003). 'A strong man is direct and a direct woman is a bitch': Gendered discourses and their influence on employment roles in sport organisations. *Journal of Sport Management, 17*, 347–375. Retrieved from http://journals.humankinetics.com/jsm

Shaw, S. and Penney, D. (2003). Gender equity policies in national governing bodies: An oxymoron or a vehicle for change? *European Sport Management Quarterly, 3*, 78–102. doi:10.1080/16184740308721942

Shaw, S. and Slack, T. (2002). 'It's been like that for donkey's years': The construction of gender relations and the cultures of sports organisations. *Culture, Sport, Society, 5*, 86–106. doi:10.1080/713999851

Sibson, R. (2010). 'I was banging my head against a brick wall': Exclusionary power and the gendering of sport organisations. *Journal of Sport Management, 24*, 379–399. Retrieved from http://journals.humankinetics.com/jsm

Skirstad, B. (2002). *Shortage of females in local, national and international sport structures.* Paper presented at the Belgium Olympic and Interfederal Committees Colloquium 'La Femme et les Structures Sportives,' Brussels, Belgium.

Skirstad, B. (2009). Gender policy and organisational change: A contextual approach. *Sport Management Review, 12*, 202–216. doi:10.1016/j.smr.2009.03.003

SportAccord. (n.d.). Mission. Retrieved from www.sportaccord.com/about/mission/

Terjesen, S., Sealy, R. and Singh, V. (2009). Women directors on corporate boards: A review and research agenda. *Corporate Governance: An International Review, 17*, 320–337. doi:10.1111/j.1467-8683.2009.00742.x

Torchia, M., Calabro, A. and Huse, M. (2011). Women directors on corporate boards: From tokenism to critical mass. *Journal of Business Ethics, 102*, 299–317. doi:10.1007/s10551-011-0815-z

Wajcman, J. (1999). *Managing like a man.* Sydney: Allen and Unwin.

Whelan, J. and Wood, R. (2012). *Targets and quotas for women in leadership: A global review of policy, practice and psychological research.* Melbourne: Melbourne Business School, Centre for Ethical Leadership.

White, A. and Brackenridge, C. (1985). Who rules sport? Gender divisions in the power structure of British sports organisations from 1960. *International Review for the Sociology of Sport, 20*, 95–106. doi:10.1177/101269028502000109

Further reading

Adriaanse, J. A. and Schofield, T. (2014). The impact of gender quotas on gender equality in sport governance. *Journal of Sport Management, 28*, 485–497. doi:10.1123/jsm.2013-0108

Burton, L. J. (2015). Underrepresentation of women in sport leadership: A review of research. *Sport Management Review, 18*, 155–165. doi:10.1016/j.smr.2014.02.004

Henry, I. and Robinson, L. (2010). *Gender equity and leadership in Olympic bodies*. Loughborough, United Kingdom: Centre for Olympic Studies and Research, Loughborough University and International Olympic Committee.

Joecks, J., Pull, K. and Vetter, K. (2013). Gender diversity in the boardroom and firm performance: What exactly constitutes a 'critical mass?' *Journal of Business Ethics, 118*, 61–72. doi:10.1007/s10551-012-1553-6

Pfister, G. and Radtke, S. (2009). Sport, women and leadership: Results of a project on executives in German sports organisations. *European Journal of Sport Science, 9*, 229–243. doi:10.1080/17461390902818286

4

INTEGRITY AND CORRUPTION IN SPORT

Catherine Ordway and Hayden Opie

Sport looms large in the lives of many people around the world. With the practice of sport comes the many pleasures and rewards of physical exercise, feats of athletic skill, competition and contest, self-esteem, social connection and entertaining spectacle. Important human values are found, taught, and reinforced through sport; for example, the pursuit of excellence, honesty, fair play, respect for rules and laws, non-discrimination and respect for others, the educational value of good example, ethical behaviour and peaceful existence (see, for example, International Olympic Committee (IOC), 2015; World Anti-Doping Agency (WADA), 2015). Specific examples of those values grouped under the label of sportsmanship include teamwork and team spirit, playing earnestly and never giving up, accepting the umpires' decisions, humility in victory and graciousness in defeat. All of those attributes demonstrate the value of sport to individuals and society as well as contribute to a collective love of sport for both participants and spectators (for a summary of research on participant motivation and behaviour, see *Sport Participation in Australia*; Richards and Murphy, 2015). In significant measure, they underpin the ongoing support that governments and commercial enterprises of many kinds show for the development of sport.

However, over the past few decades, dark clouds have begun to dim this shining vision of sport. From doping by famous athletes to the misappropriation of funds at the highest levels of international sports organisations, such clouds are considered threats to the integrity of sport. In 2011, the then IOC president, Jacques Rogge, in his address to celebrate the hundredth year of the Japanese Olympic Committee said, 'We have made doping a top priority, and now there is a new danger coming up that almost all countries have been affected by and that is corruption, match-fixing and illegal gambling' ('Jacques Rogge: Corruption', 2011, para. 2).

The doping scandal surrounding the American cyclist and seven-time winner of the Tour de France, Lance Armstrong, attracted worldwide attention. As a supreme athlete, cancer survivor, and philanthropist, Armstrong was an inspiration to many. He encapsulated so well the values associated with sport. When Armstrong was revealed as a serial doping cheat and liar who pursued aggressively and remorselessly those who claimed he doped (U.S. Anti-Doping Agency, 2012), not only was Armstrong's reputation severely damaged, but so was that of his sport. Other international superstar athletes who have been caught doping have included Ben Johnson (Dubin, 1990) and Marion Jones (Shipley, 2007). Doping has not only been at the initiative of individual athletes. Through the 1970s and 1980s, the East German government maintained an extensive and hugely successful doping programme across many sports in an effort to prove to the world the superiority of its political and social system (Franke and Berendonk, 1997; Ungerleider, 2001). In Australia, an unresolved doping scandal, now in its third year, has raged around the Essendon Football Club of the Australian Football League over an ill-fated 'supplements program' (Le Grand, 2015).

Doping damages the integrity of the sporting competition as well as the values of sport (e.g., Lumpkin, 1983). Not only are athletes disgraced as 'cheats', but suspicion of doping falls on other winning performances via the unproven suggestion that a victory could not have been achieved, or a record broken, without doping. Athletes disinclined to dope come under pressure to do so because they come to believe that they can never succeed when everyone, or nearly everyone, at the highest levels is breaking the rules. On the other hand, the increasingly stringent rules against doping can sweep up athletes who have unwittingly consumed a prohibited substance and it becomes very difficult for at least some of them to avoid an undeserved 'disgraced drug cheat' epitaph to their sporting careers.

There have been some notorious instances of fixing the outcome of a sporting competition or some event within it in return for payment. Fixing is commonly associated with betting. Arguably the most famous fixing case of all time is the 'Black Sox Scandal' in the United States. This is a play on the name of the famous Major League Baseball (MLB) team the Chicago White Sox, whose players were alleged to be involved. It gave rise to the infamous expression, 'Say it ain't so, Joe', and launched the sporting administration career of MLB's first Commissioner, the larger-than-life figure Judge Kenesaw Mountain Landis. The heavily favoured Chicago White Sox lost the 1919 World Series to the Cincinnati Reds. Although the eight accused players were acquitted of criminal charges by a jury (the confessions of three of them had vanished mysteriously), Commissioner Landis placed all of them on the permanently ineligible list which amounted to a life ban (Sigmund, 2004). More recently, major incidents have included scandals in German association football (Harding, 2005), English cricket,[1] rugby league in New South Wales (Massoud, 2014),[2] and association football in Victoria,[3] resulting in criminal convictions and substantial or life bans for some of those involved.

The integrity of the governance of the world's largest sports federation, the Fédération Internationale de Football Association (FIFA), has been called into question with ongoing controversy over whether the decisions to award the hosting rights for the 2018 and 2022 World Cups to Russia and Qatar, respectively, were tainted by bribery and improper voting deals and should be cancelled (Davis, 2015). Also, various FIFA officials and others in the 'football family' from the Americas have been detained in Switzerland with a view to their extradition to the United States to face serious criminal charges relating to commercial dealings in football ('FIFA Scandal', 2015).

While the integrity of sport has in recent years become a widely used term,[4] and protecting it a cause worthy of significant effort, it is essential to understand exactly what the term means and what safeguards and responses protection involves. That is the purpose of this chapter, which will commence with an analysis of the meaning of the terms *integrity of sport, corruption, doping, match-fixing* and *sports betting*. In the second part of the chapter, strategies originating from beyond sport will be drawn upon to identify and explain possible risk countermeasures and mitigation solutions. These range from good governance practices through intelligence-gathering and enhancement of athlete welfare to disciplinary and penal measures. It is intended that practitioners and students of sports administration will be able employ an understanding of these terms and strategies to promote integrity in sport.

Terminology

Integrity of sport and associated terms such as corruption in sport and match-fixing are widely used with the assumption that there is a common international understanding of their meanings. It is also often believed that the behaviour they reflect is of recent origin. Neither is accurate. However, the scale of occurrence, public attention, and regulatory responses linked to that behaviour are now unprecedented.

Commensurate with the human values found, taught, and reinforced through sport, it is suggested that attaining and maintaining a state of integrity should be the aspiration of athletes, sports administrators, and sports organisations alike. What then is meant by the term integrity of sport and what is the scope of its operation?

Integrity of sport

The *Macquarie Dictionary* provides the following definition of integrity: '*Integrity* (noun) 1. soundness of moral principle and character; uprightness; honesty 2. the state of being whole, entire, or undiminished 3. sound, unimpaired or perfect condition' ('Integrity', 2001, p. 984).

These meanings can be applied to sport in the sense that the audience is entitled to rely on the outcome of a match or competition on the basis that it has been played in accordance with the sport rules. This suggests that the outcome, or elements of the competition leading to the outcome, have not been affected by either cheating to win (e.g., by doping) or cheating to lose (e.g., match-fixing). In that sense, not only does the competition have integrity, but so do the athletes who participate in it. This provides a normative, formal, or rule-based definition of the integrity of a sporting competition.

Reliance on that rule-based approach can present difficulty in some commonly encountered circumstances. Should a batter in cricket who has lightly glanced the ball into the hands of the wicketkeeper 'walk' or await the call of the umpire who may not have observed the snick? Is it acceptable to not try as hard to win as one might in order not to risk injury or to preserve energy for a later stage of a competition? Furthermore, is it acceptable to deliberately lose so as not to meet a strong opponent in the next phase of a tournament or to gain a favourable selection in an end-of-season draft for uncontracted players in a professional league? In the sport of Sumo, it has been known for leading wrestlers to intentionally lose to young, inexperienced opponents so they may have a share of winnings and help build their fledgling careers. In each of these circumstances, the formal rules may not be broken, but is there a lack of integrity? If so, in which ones and why?

The Australian Sports Commission (ASC, n.d.) expands on this rule-based approach by defining integrity as 'the integration of outward actions and inner values' (ASC, n.d., para. 1), and a sport as having integrity where it remains 'true to its values, principles and rules' (ASC, n.d., para. 6). By introducing principles and values, more reference points become available to determine the integrity of particular behaviour. The standards thereby reached may not result in sanctions under the rules of the sport, but may take form as unwritten rules or customs (e.g., in association football, returning the ball to the opposition after a stoppage to treat an injured player) or simply attract the disapproval of fellow participants and spectators. These customary standards may evolve into formal rules of the sport.

For sports administrators and sports organisations, the attainment of integrity applies to behaviour principally off the field of play. Compliance with established constitutions and rules governing the sport's organisation as well as respecting the laws of the land are to be expected. As with the conduct of the sporting competition, the notion of integrity extends beyond the formal rules. For an organisation to project an image of integrity, it has been suggested that its individuals should be 'considerate, compassionate, transparent, honest, and ethical' (Duggar, 2009, p. 2). Sport participants and others dealing with a sports organisation should be able to place their trust in the organisation with justifiable confidence. A dilemma may arise for an organisation whose mission is to protect the integrity of sport. Is it consistent with integrity to engage in 'sharp practice' or employ arguably unethical (but not illegal) measures so as to disrupt or successfully prosecute behaviour which breaches the anti-doping or anti-match-fixing rules of a sport? In other words, does the end justify the means?

A number of elements of the behaviour of sports administrators and sports organisations off the field of play which lack integrity are often considered under the rubric of 'corruption'. This term will now be examined.

Corruption

3

The *Macquarie Dictionary* provides the following definition of corrupt: '*Corrupt* (adjective): 1. dishonest; without integrity; guilty of dishonesty, especially involving bribery; *a corrupt judge* 2. debased in character; depraved; perverted; wicked; evil' ('Corrupt', 2001). Transparency International (n.d.), a respected watchdog of government and business behaviour worldwide, defines corruption as 'the abuse of entrusted power for private gain' ('How Do You Define Corruption?' section). The United Nations Convention against Corruption describes corruption in these terms:

> Corruption is an insidious plague that has a wide range of corrosive effects on societies. It undermines democracy and the rule of law, leads to violations of human rights, distorts markets, erodes the quality of life and allows organized crime, terrorism and other threats to human security to flourish.
> *(U.N. Office on Drugs and Crime, 2004, p. iii)*

Corruption cannot occur without the involvement of people who lack integrity. The higher up the leadership ladder corruption occurs, the more evil it becomes. The more endemic corruption is in a society, the more difficult it is as a practical matter to impress on athletes and sports administrators that corruption in sport is wrong and that a path of integrity should be followed.

In sport, corruption has been identified as relating to money, power, status and privilege (Unger, 2015). It is usually found in sports organisations in connection with commercial activities such as broadcasting and sponsorship deals and the allocation of hosting rights to major events. In the field of organisational governance, corruption typically raises its head in the rigging of elections, making grants for facilities and development programmes and in patronage and kickbacks to friends and allies of those in power.

Doping

The *World Anti-Doping Code* creates ten categories of anti-doping offence which are known as 'violations'. These include the use of prohibited substances or doping methods, the possession or trafficking in prohibited substances and refusing to undergo testing (WADA 2015).[5]

Match-fixing

A number of terms have been used to describe the phenomenon of improperly influencing the outcome of a sporting contest or the happening of some element within it. These include match-fixing and *spot fixing, manipulation* (Council of Europe, 2014) and *sporting fraud* (Legal India, 2013). Match-fixing and spot fixing will be used here.

Match-fixing involves a lack of sporting integrity. Not only might it be contrary to the rules of sport, it may also amount to a crime. There is, however, no agreed-upon definition of match-fixing. This is in part attributable to the circumstance that some instances of 'match-fixing' may not be regarded as wrongful if done for some strategic or tactical sporting reasons.[6] Other forms of match-fixing may contravene the rules of sport, but not the criminal law. The criminal law is more likely to become involved when the fixing is associated with gambling.

Heron and Jiang (2010) suggested that match-fixing involves 'improperly influencing the outcome or any dimension of a sports event for financial or personal benefit' (p. 99). Carpenter (2013) described match-fixing as 'a dishonest activity by participants, team officials, match officials or other interested parties to ensure a specific outcome in a particular sporting match or event for competitive advantage and/or financial gain which negatively impacts on the integrity of sport' (p. 215).

Match-fixing can involve deciding not only who wins and loses, but the winning margin too. Spot fixing entails the improper influencing of an event or contingency *within* a sporting competition. That might include the time and rate of scoring, the score at certain times, the occurrence of particular events such as who scores first, the number of penalties awarded and so on.

In its most common form, match-fixing involves an intentional underperformance by players. Also of significance are instances where referees unfairly favour a particular player or team. The instigator of the fix may offer the corrupted individual or team a bribe in the form of payment of money or some favour, such as career advancement or access to prostitutes. Particularly in the case of individuals, the corrupting request may follow a period of 'grooming'. The term *grooming* here is used in the same way as criminologists describe sexual predators incrementally gaining the trust of their potential victims in child abuse cases (Salter, 2003). In the sports setting, organised criminals, or former athletes, attempt to create friendship bonds with vulnerable players. They seek to attend the same social venues, and provide gifts such as alcohol, prostitutes, and gambling accounts before requesting information about playing conditions and coaching strategies which can be used as a form of gambling insider trading.[7] Additionally or separately, the corrupted individual may be blackmailed by threats of violence or the prospect of exposure of some indiscretion, such as using banned doping agents or illicit drugs which might have been supplied by the instigator in the first place.[8] The prospects for links to organised crime are obvious.

J. Anderson (2012) suggested that it is important to draw a distinction between 'gambling-led corruption' and non-betting related match-fixing, such as instances where a participant might bribe an opponent so that the instigator may progress in the competition. It is the explosion in Internet-based sports betting (to which national borders offer only modest impediment) that poses the most significant threat to the integrity of sport: 'The danger is that from illegal betting comes match-fixing, and you see more … attempts to manipulate matches. It is as dangerous as doping for the credibility of sport. It's only the beginning of a huge battle' (Lane, 2011, p. 9).

Sports betting

There is no international legal system for the regulation of betting on sports. Individual nations adopt different approaches. Some prohibit betting in all its forms, while others allow some betting and in yet others many types of betting are available. Both Australia and the United Kingdom have relatively unrestricted sports betting opportunities, while in China, India and the United States, sports betting is either illegal or heavily constrained (P. M. Anderson, Blackshaw, Siekmann and Soek, 2012). Whether sports betting should be lawful and, if lawful, how much betting and under which circumstances it should be permitted remain contested social issues globally. However, it is suggested that lawful sports betting should not in isolation be regarded as a sports integrity issue.

In countries where sports betting is lawful, it may be either extensively or lightly regulated. *Grey markets* is a term that refers to lightly regulated betting markets because it becomes difficult to trace bets and establish the bona fide of either or both gamblers and betting service providers, despite a level of regulation. Black (illegal) and grey sports betting markets are believed to offer greater prospects for betting participants to be linked to match-fixing, money laundering, and organised criminal activities. The Internet is progressively breaking down national regulatory approaches to sports betting with those willing to use Internet-based grey and black market operators finding it relatively easy to do so.

Three solutions: anti-corruption strategies and their application to sport

In his 2010 article 'A Critical Mass of Corruption: Why Some Football Leagues Have More Match-Fixing than Others', leading academic and investigative journalist in the field of match-fixing in sport, Declan Hill (2010), argued that

> the data indicates that when similar conditions exist in a football league in a different country with a different cultural background – England in the 1950s [or China in the 2000s], players also engaged in match-fixing. I argue that it is the introduction of new market alternatives, combined with situations of relative deprivation and expectations of corruption, that lead to high levels of corruption and the eventual collapse of the leagues.
>
> *(p. 222)*

For sports administrators, sports boards, and those funding sports (whether government agencies or sponsors/partners), it is worth examining what can be done to the micro-conditions inside individual clubs or sports to make them more resistant to corrupt practices.

Leadership: ethical decision-making

The basic premise in looking to leadership to reduce the risk of corruption is that although the most robust structures can be set in place (and some of them will be referred to below), if the people entrusted with the stewardship of the organisation are open to – or actively engaged in – corrupt practices, then corruption within the organisation will thrive.

The influence of leaders in setting the culture of an organisation, both positively and negatively, has been researched extensively (Duggar, 2009). In its report, *Safe Hands: Building Integrity and Transparency at FIFA*, Transparency International (2011) observed that if sports, such as football, are perceived to be led by a culture of corruption, then they will, in turn, have a higher probability of threats to their integrity.[9] Corrupt leaders will set the tone for the organisation, and demonstrate that cheating and other corrupt practices are not only condoned, but might be actively encouraged.[10] On the other hand, it is thought that negative, self-motivated or other corrupt practices are extremely unlikely to be instigated or permitted by leaders with integrity. This effect increases when the leader is positioned higher on the ladder of authority. One of the leading anti-corruption think tanks, the Australian Commission for Law Enforcement Integrity (ACLEI, n.d.-b), recognises that 'individuals vary in their motivation and decision-making processes' and that therefore organisations must vary their integrity strategies based on a values alignment ('Values Alignment' section, para. 1). It is therefore important for sports organisations to assess both the *hard skills* (knowledge and experience) and *soft skills* (values, inter-personal and emotional intelligence) in their decision-makers (Edwards and Clough, 2005).

Attracting and developing people with integrity is an obvious risk management strategy for a sports organisation. It is therefore important for sports organisations to possess an understanding of how skills and values associated with integrity might be developed. There are a number of models that describe adult cognitive development. A model such as 'vertical leadership: 7 leadership action-logics' developed by Rooke and Torbert (2005; Torbert, 2004) from the transformational leadership work made popular in the 1980s, is one model that describes a staged developmental approach to *vertical development*. Vertical development fosters higher or later stages of vertical leadership. This concept is based in adult development theory which has stages describing levels of cognitive, emotional, and relational capabilities. Cook-Greuter (2004) described vertical development as the capacity to

> learn to see the world through new eyes, how we change our interpretations of experience and how we transform our views of reality. It describes increases in what we are aware of, or what we pay attention to, and therefore what we can influence and integrate.
>
> *(p. 276)*

Each stage of thinking becomes increasingly more complex, incorporating the previous level(s) and expanding awareness and capability as it increases the way a person makes sense of reality.[11]

While a minority of people could be described as 'born leaders', Rooke and Torbert's (2005) research supports the idea that sophisticated leadership skills can be taught. Therefore, the identification and development of positive vertical leadership traits in sport decision-makers is crucial. Using models like action-logics, and implementing its profiling and vertical development tools, could assist sport decision-makers in moving from a culture of people operating at the lower 'opportunistic' levels of leadership, to those who have the ability to lead effectively and inspire others. Termed 'Transforming (Strategist)', 'Alchemists', or 'Ironic/Ionist' leaders in the action-logics model, these leaders are able to generate personal and organisational transformations, exercise powers of mutual inquiry, vigilance and vulnerability and are conscious of paradox (Brown, 2013).

Nelson Mandela's striking example of exemplary sport leadership is described by Mohamed Muhsin (2013), himself said to be a visionary and highly functioning leader, as follows:

> Mandela, in one of the most audacious political gambles of his career, appeared before the mostly white crowd of 62,000 wearing a Springbok jersey to shake the players' hands before kick-off. The-then All Blacks coach Laurie Mains said the entire stadium was electrified at the sight of South Africa's first black president sporting a garment that was indelibly associated with the apartheid regime.
>
> *(para. 4)*

That outward display of unity and reconciliation set the tone for wider developments. It might therefore be suggested that if sports organisations have leaders who are focused prominently on promoting an ethical vision for the organisation, ahead of self-interest and greed, then the risk of on-field integrity issues would be significantly diminished.

Partnerships: information-sharing and inter-agency collaboration

It has been recognised for some time by the sports industry that, in order to protect sport from various integrity threats, it must work closely with governments and agencies with access to relevant information, knowledge, and resources. In the anti-doping environment, then WADA President, John Fahey, introduced the *Guidelines for Coordinating Investigations and Sharing Anti-Doping Information and Evidence* (WADA, 2011a), stating the following: 'For some time now we have been saying that testing alone is not enough to lead the fight against doping in sport, and that ADOs need to develop stronger relationships with law enforcement agencies' (WADA, 2011b, 'Guidelines' section, para. 3). One major limitation of testing as a detection method is that it only applies to athletes, and therefore, coaches, doctors, and others involved in doping are not exposed through this approach. The other major limitation is that current testing methods cannot detect all prohibited substances (or the detection windows are very short) – for example, peptide hormones (Barroso, Mazzoni and Rabin, 2008). Those involved in administering or trafficking in prohibited substances, including athlete support personnel, therefore need to be identified through means other than testing. One way is through developing partnerships with law enforcement agencies.

In May 2005, WADA and the Anti-Doping Norway Anti-Doping Symposium identified cooperation with police and customs as two of 18 factors for selecting athletes for detection purposes. This thinking was reflected in new powers given to the Australian Sports Anti-Doping Authority in 2006 (Ings, 2007). The Australian Sports Anti-Doping Authority was the first national anti-doping organisation to have legislated powers of information disclosure to allow it to exchange information with other sports and law enforcement bodies, such as Australian customs, the state and federal police, the Therapeutic Goods Administration, national anti-doping organisations, and the International Sports Federations (IFs). Sharing information between government agencies is consistent with the commonwealth 'whole of government' approach, particularly for bodies with investigative powers (Carson, 2003).

In 2007, WADA (2007) described 'a new era in anti-doping', recognising that the illegal manufacture and distribution of performance-enhancing drugs (such as that seen in the U.S. Bay Area Laboratory Co-Operative scandal) required coordination with law enforcement. In 2006, the International Criminal Police Organisation (INTERPOL) and WADA committed to work together to identify areas for cooperation (WADA, n.d.-b). The 2008 Memorandum of Understanding set out a framework for cooperation in tracking doping, in particular in the area of evidence-gathering and information-sharing. This arrangement included the provision by the French government of a seconded officer based at INTERPOL's headquarters in Lyon to liaise between WADA, the governments, and the sport movement (WADA, 2008; 'WADA Advances Cooperation', 2008). The cooperation agreement between INTERPOL and WADA (2009) was formally signed in 2009.

Similarly, in relation to match-fixing, it has been recognised that 'no organisation can tackle the problem of match-fixing alone' (INTERPOL, 2015, para. 4). In May 2011, INTERPOL and FIFA entered into a joint initiative with FIFA (2011) pledging to contribute €20 million over ten years to INTERPOL's Integrity in Sport programme. INTERPOL and FIFA stated that a cross-sector approach is necessary at national, regional, and international levels in order to successfully reduce match-fixing. Further, 'strategies should incorporate partnerships between national football associations and betting organizations as well as public authorities including law enforcement and regulators' (INTERPOL, n.d., 'A Multi-Faceted Approach Section', para. 2). The first phase of the programme (2011–2014) focused on raising awareness, with the second phase from 2014 onwards, addressing capacity building with targeted training courses delivered to participants in all regions of the world (INTERPOL, n.d.). This has included the opening of a multimillion dollar INTERPOL Global Complex for Innovation building in April 2015 in Singapore (INTERPOL, 2013; 'Interpol Opens New Singapore Headquarters', 2015).

The enthusiasm for public–private partnerships of this nature may have cooled somewhat after INTERPOL announced its decision to suspend the agreement in June 2015, following the FBI investigations into corruption against football's governing body, which included a freeze on the use of the remaining financial contributions from FIFA. That raises concerns over INTERPOL accepting money from organisations it could potentially be investigating, as its independence would be called into question (Simons, 2015).

Good governance: transparency and accountability

Many of the IFs and major games organisers, such as the IOC, are based in Switzerland. This location was arguably chosen because of the favourable tax status enjoyed, but also, as private organisations are not subject to the level of corporate accountability that might be expected in many other jurisdictions (Fridman, 1999). Over the last 15 years, Swiss taxation and corporations laws have been reviewed with the aim of tightening up governance requirements relating to private corporations (Geeraert, 2014; Jones, 2013; Zulauf and Weder, n.d.). In the absence of any sweeping changes coming through in the near future, the Action for Good Governance in International Sports Organisations, has developed the Sports Governance Observer (SGO) tool ('Sports Governance Observer', 2015). The SGO is an example of a mechanism to shine a light on the IFs in a consistent way to demonstrate the extent to which these organisations implement best practices in good governance. The headings used by the SGO include

1   Transparency and public communications,
2   Democratic process,
3   Checks and balances, and
4   Solidarity (Chappelet and Mrkonjic, 2013).

Under the heading of 'Democratic Process', the SGO assesses whether the organisation 'has gender equity guidelines for its leading officials' (Alm, 2013, p. 219). There is mounting evidence in the corporate world (Ruigrok, Peck and Tacheva, 2007; van der Walt and Ingley, 2003) and in anti-corruption research (Transparency International, 2014a) that leadership diversity – and gender equity in particular – is a risk management tool that could also positively impact integrity outcomes in sport. Requiring organisations in the sports movement to report on the gender split of their executive, senior managers as well as their coaching, high performance, and officiating staff would also promote transparency (Alm, 2013; Sydney Scoreboard, n.d.).

Another method for creating greater transparency is the publishing of independent governance reports. This can occur at the instigation of the sports body, governments, or private watchdogs. At the international level, a number have appeared in recent years, including the following:

- FIFA (football): *Safe Hands* report (Transparency International, 2011);
- International Cricket Council (cricket): Lord Woolf and PricewaterhouseCoopers 2012 report and *Fair Play: Strengthening Integrity and Transparency in Cricket* (Transparency International, 2013); and
- Union Cycliste Internationale (cycling): Cycling Independent Reform Commission 2015 report.

Surprisingly, it has taken the recent crisis involving the prosecutions of current and former senior members of the FIFA Executive ('FIFA Scandal', 2015) for the IOC to announce the introduction of independent auditing of the governance and funds provided to the IFs (Play the Game, 2015).[12]

Awareness and education

No behavioural change strategy is complete without both awareness and education programmes. Outward communication channels with the aim of creating general awareness of the challenges and possible solutions are made available for the general public, media outlets, school children and stakeholders with an indirect association with the sports industry. Those directly impacted by integrity risks need to have more detailed and targeted education programmes.

Education and advocacy have been the primary strategies used by the national anti-doping organisations since anti-doping first became a serious issue on the agenda for sports ministers around the globe (e.g., *Australian Sports Drug Agency Act*, 1990). To combat match-fixing, education and awareness have also been prioritised. For example, prior to the recent suspension of the relationship, INTERPOL and FIFA adopted the following strategies to lower the risk of match-fixing:

- **Prevention:** Prevention measures include awareness raising, training, and education.
- **Information:** All partners – including stakeholders, key actors, and targets – need general details about match-fixing to ensure there is a shared understanding of the problem. Each group also needs specific advice that can directly assist them in their individual roles in protecting the integrity of sport (INTERPOL, n.d., p. 2).

A similar approach has been adopted through a partnership between the German Transparency International chapter and the German Professional Football League. Since 2014, the German Transparency International chapter has been advising the

German Professional Football League on the project, 'Transparency and Integrity in Football', which focuses on how to prevent match-fixing. Germany was the first pilot country involved in Transparency International's (2014b) education sessions, workshops, and media events on how to stop match-fixing.

Sport industry regulatory frameworks

Sports have gradually improved the documentation of their policies and procedures so that it is clear to athletes and their entourage what level of behaviour is expected of them. Leaving aside considerations of the appropriateness of imposing 'role model' status on elite athletes, it is now very common for athletes to be contractually bound to codes of conduct or ethics codes, team and sponsorship agreements, and nutritional, medical, and anti-doping policies. These agreements prohibit behaviour 'bringing the sport into disrepute' or against the 'spirit of sport'. For example, the Australian Olympic Committee (2015) *Team Membership Agreement* for the 2016 Rio Olympic Games sets out the athlete's obligations as follows:

> As a member of the Team, I shall:
>
> ...
>
> 2) respect the spirit of fair play and non-violence and behave accordingly;
>
> ...
>
> 4) not at any time engage in conduct (whether publicly known or not and whether before or after the date of my selection), which has brought, brings or would have the tendency to bring me or my sport into disrepute or censure.
>
> *(Clause 4.1)*

The anti-doping policies have developed in sophistication from the simple 1928 ban by the then International Amateur Athletic Federation on the 'use of stimulating substances' (International Association of Athletics Federations, 1928) to the current four-part, 152-page *World Anti-Doping Code* (WADA, 2015) which serves as a model for adoption by sports organisations worldwide under the leadership of WADA. The *Code* sets out that 'doping is fundamentally contrary to the spirit of sport' (WADA, 2015, p. 14). This harmonised approach received the support of national governments via the UNESCO (2005) International Convention against Doping in Sport (see also Marriott-Lloyd, 2010).

Included in INTERPOL and FIFA's match-fixing prevention strategies are deterrent regulations involving sanctions for unprofessional behaviour (INTER-POL, n.d.). INTERPOL and FIFA reflect WADA's standardised and harmonised approach by reiterating the importance for 'all stakeholders [to] operate in a coordinated manner, especially at national level, to ensure a comprehensive and unified approach to both the prevention of match-fixing and responses to allegations of match-fixing' (INTERPOL, n.d., para. 2).

Early warning systems

For law enforcement agencies investigating corruption, money laundering and fraud offences, it is crucial to be able to follow the money trail. Investigations are often triggered by financial thresholds or other irregular accounting practices (Australian Transactions Reports and Analysis Centre, 2011). Similarly, to identify possible match-fixing, sports organisations are using quantitative analyses of betting market statistics (e.g., SportRadar; www.sportradar.com/). By analysing regulated and some grey betting markets (though not usually the unregulated or black markets), recommendations can be made on whether to allow the match to go ahead, or which matches warrant further investigation. Initial piloting work is currently being done to analyse performance measurements based on patterns, trends, decisions and behaviour in play (motivation, decision-making, intensity and vulnerability) to identify those players who attract suspicion and warrant further investigation (e.g., SportsWizard; http://sportswizard.com/).

In anti-doping, qualitative analytics on athletes' motivations to dope, such as return from injury, career progression (breaking in or prolonging) and reference events, have been taken into account in assigning target testing for many years (Hanstad and Loland, 2005). This work has more recently been supplemented by quantitative data collected from 'biological passports' (WADA, n.d.-a). The *World Anti-Doping Code* allows for anti-doping rule violations to be proven via 'any reliable means' (WADA, 2015, Article 3.2). Over the last 15 years approximately, anti-doping organisations have used markers and biological indicators to be able to assess an individual's 'normal' thresholds (Ashenden, 2002; Schumacher and Pottgiesser, 2009).

Whistleblowing and reporting systems

It is important that people with knowledge about corrupt practices have the opportunity to safely report their concerns and information to the investigative bodies. Integrity organisations have a strong interest in protecting whistle blowers, particularly when the information may relate to the activities of organised, and possibly highly dangerous, criminals. Therefore, some sports organisations have encouraged people to provide information anonymously or via encrypted services. Conversely, investigators need to be able to verify the source of the information provided in order to be able to determine its reliability. Using law enforcement tools, sport and anti-doping agencies receiving information via well-publicised 'Stamp Out Doping' (or similarly named) integrity hotlines[13] assess the information to exclude the possibility that information may be erroneous or mistaken, or provided with the intention to adversely impact competitors.

Integrity units, officials and networks

While there is no standardised understanding of what an 'integrity officer' duty statement might contain, a number of sport organisations have established integrity units to develop and enforce their own codes of conduct and ethics policies. Many sport organisations have focused on recruiting and/or developing intelligence and investigative skills, such as in horse racing,[14] cricket,[15] and tennis.[16] Government agencies, such as the Australian National Integrity of Sport Unit (NISU), have tended to have a purely policy-based role. NISU is focused on education, facilitating an integrity network of state government, sport and law enforcement personnel and providing template documents to support the work of other integrity units (Australian Government Department of Health, 2013).

Legislation and the role of penal measures

At the international governmental level, participants at the fifth World Conference of Sports Ministers in May 2013 adopted a range of recommendations calling on UNESCO Member States to enact legislation to protect the integrity of sport from the threat posed by transnational organised crime, doping, the manipulation of sports competitions and corruption (UNESCO, 2013; see also Bang, 2013). The Intergovernmental Committee for Physical Education and Sport has also included 'better integrity in sport' for the first time in the latest draft version of the *International Charter of Physical Education, Physical Activity and Sport* (Andersen and Alvad, 2015; UNESCO, 2014).

In relation to match-fixing, Australia is one of the leading nations in adopting a national policy and prescribing a maximum ten-year jail term (Australian Government Department of Health, 2014). By way of comparison, while Australia also has a national anti-doping framework[17] and a national anti-doping organisation established through its own Act of Parliament, Australia (along with WADA) does not consider it appropriate to criminalise doping in sport.[18]

Asset protection: athlete welfare

In the context of integrity in organisational models generally, ACLEI (n.d.) cites *asset protection* as one of its corruption prevention key concepts. ACLEI's (n.d.) asset protection model 'recognises that investment and proper management of integrity and professional standards builds the capability of an agency, in the same way that investing in people or information does' ('Asset Protection Model' section, para. 2). This concept can be applied specifically to the sports context. Integrity in the organisation can be seen as an asset in the same way as both athletes and staff need to be developed and empowered by their sports within an integrity framework. In his book *The Insider's Guide to Match-Fixing in Football*, Declan Hill (2013) went further by arguing that the first priority is to address baseline survival issues. Hill called on sports organisations to reduce integrity risks through providing for the athletes' welfare, paying them appropriately and on time and supporting vulnerable athletes (e.g., those with gambling and prescription drug addictions). WADA has also funded a number of important social science studies into doping athletes' motivations and rationale in order to assist in shaping the education and welfare programmes (Moston, Engelberg and Skinner, 2015). It is clear from both WADA's and Hill's research that financial rewards are motivators both in cheating-to-win (doping) and cheating-to-lose (match-fixing) scenarios which leads to the conclusion that measures aimed at minimising the financial vulnerability of players will, at least in some cases, head off such cheating activity.

Anecdotal evidence suggests that differences in the approach of sports organisations to player welfare impacts on integrity issues. For example, the Australian Football League has taken a strong 'health' approach to tackling illicit drug use among its players, which arguably has paid dividends in both assisting the players and in protecting the sport's brand (Harcourt, Unglik and Cook, 2012). By way of comparison, there have been questions raised in connection with the match-fixing case involving Ryan Tandy (Massoud, 2014) about the role the sport (rugby league) and the club should have played in disrupting/detecting suspicious behaviour.[19] Although an independent investigation appointed by the National Rugby League (NRL) Integrity Unit cleared Canterbury Bulldogs' General Manager of Football Operations, Alan Thompson, and the NRL's Head of Football, Todd Greenberg, of knowing about Tandy's gambling debts, and failing to act ahead of the fix, more importantly, questions remain about the extent to which the club/NRL should have supported Tandy to help overcome his gambling and drug addictions ('Greenberg Cleared', 2014; 'NRL Reportedly Investigating Todd Greenberg', 2014; Welch, 2014).

Research and the facilitation of new ideas and approaches

A number of organisations have committed funding and/or supported new ideas and research through paper prizes and other grants and competitions to encourage people interested in integrity in sport issues to share and develop their solutions. In the anti-doping field, since 2001, WADA has committed US $60 million to research (WADA, n.d.-c). The IOC (2014), National Olympic Committees and sports on the Olympic Program have a number of different PhD and other research grants available to those interested in promoting integrity aims.

General anti-corruption competitions have also awarded prizes for sport integrity initiatives (International Anti-Corruption Conference, n.d.). Transparency International has continued its commitment to integrity in sport by promoting, what it terms as a

> space for new analysis, commentary and recommendations by leading voices in the field of sports governance to strengthen transparency, accountability and participation [to] showcase the work of TI national chapters and the wider anti-corruption movement in tackling corruption in sport.
>
> *(Sweeney, 2015, para. 5)*

In the spirit of people-powered approaches to anti-corruption (Beyerle, 2014), there have been recent social media campaigns to try to return control of sports organisations to the fans and the players. For example, the New FIFA Now campaign (www.newfifanow.org/), led by European Parliament members Ivo Belet and Emma McClarkin, held a coalition meeting in Brussels on 21 January 2015. The summit sought to establish a FIFA Reform Commission and published a Charter for Change (New FIFA Now, 2015) and Guiding Principles for Democracy, Transparency and Accountability (New FIFA Now, n.d.-a). It remains to be seen whether initiatives of this kind can exert sufficient pressure to create lasting change in the otherwise largely unaccountable sports organisations.

Conclusion

> Here muscles win, and speedy feet, not lots of money spent to cheat
> ('Cheating in the Ancient Olympics,' para. 1)[20]

Whether the motivation is to uphold the intrinsic positive values of sport, or otherwise to protect a sport's brand from a purely commercial perspective, it is clear that it will only become more important that sports administrators have a good understanding of what the possible threats to the integrity of sport are and how those threats might be dealt with.

Cheating has long been present in every human endeavour causing some psychologists to spend their entire careers examining why we cheat (Fang and Casadevall, 2013). Sport presents unique challenges that go beyond the traditional temptations of corruption: fraud, nepotism, and other self-serving abuses of trust. Cheating to win (doping) and cheating-to-lose (match-fixing) incentives have only been further exacerbated by the vast financial gains made by athletes through sponsorships, prize money, and season contracts, or via the punters eager to participate in the various regulated or poor-to-unregulated gambling markets.

As has been outlined in this chapter, and in the chapters to follow in this book, there is no 'silver bullet' or single solution to solve all the integrity challenges facing sport today. Whether by tackling cultural and leadership issues through awareness and education campaigns, enforcing sport rules and legislative processes, improving relationships with like-minded entities or creating greater transparency around pre- and post-reporting mechanisms, it is clear that sport must look to other industries for guidance and solutions. Sports organisations will have to adopt higher standards of accountability and transparency. Sport integrity is a complex concept. By drawing on and adapting a number of strategies, sports administrators have the opportunity to leave a positive legacy for the next generation inspired to believe in the spirit of sport.

Notes

1   In a case of spot fixing as part of an alleged betting scam, three no balls were arranged to be bowled during a test match between Pakistan and England. The players involved

were convicted and jailed (see *R v. Amir*, 2011, EWCA Crim 2914; *Gardiner, S. 'R v Amir and Butt*, 2011 EWCA Civ 2914).

2   In 2011, Ryan Tandy of the Canterbury Bulldogs of the Australian NRL was charged and convicted of the criminal offence of 'attempting to dishonestly obtain a financial advantage by deception'. This involved a case of spot fixing where betting dividends of $100,000 could have been won had the first score in a match resulted from a penalty, which Ryan deliberately conceded (see Massoud, 2014).

3   In 2013, an elaborately planned match-fixing scandal orchestrated by an Asian betting ring engulfed the Victorian Premier League, a state-based association football competition which sat below the Australian national competition. The Southern Stars team had won only one of 21 matches, yet on 18 August 2013, the bottom-of-the-table club defeated the competition leader 1-0. Some specially imported players and the local ring leader were convicted of various criminal offences and life bans were issued (Portelli and Rolfe, 2014).

4   For example, Senator McCain introduced the bill which became the Amateur Sport Integrity Act into the U.S. Senate in 2001 (S. 718) and in Australia, the National Sport Integrity Unit was established by the Commonwealth Government in 2012 (Australian Government Department of Health, 2016).

5   Numerous cases have considered these violations. For more, see David (2013).

6   Ibid cl 3(i). For example, compare the coaching techniques of *blooding* (i.e., resting star players and giving an opportunity for junior athletes to play off the bench; Woolley, 2009) and *tanking* (i.e., deliberately losing towards the end of the season to be in a stronger position to select players in the following season draft process; Balsdon, Fong, Thayer, 2007).

7   The example of South African cricket captain, Hansie Cronje, is instructive (Forrest, 2012). For more, see Anderson, Duval, Van, and McArdle (2014).

8   Extortion is discussed further, for example, by Declan Hill (2002).

9   For example, following the December 2010 announcement that Russia would host the 2018 Men's World Cup and Qatar the 2022 Men's World Cup, Transparency International outlined a number of specific, concrete actions the international governing body of football, FIFA could take to repair its reputation (see, for example, 'England Miss Out', 2010).

10   ACLEI (n.d.-a) also refers to leaders setting the 'tone from the top' and 'regards managers and supervisors as the frontline of corruption control' ('Leadership and Culture' section, paras. 1–2).

11   With thanks to Caron Egle of Sage Thinking (www.sagethinking.com.au/) for her explanation of conscious leadership development.

12   The status of the FIFA Executive members who voted in the 2018 and 2022 men's World Cup tournaments (as at November 2015) are set out by New FIFA Now (n.d.-b).

13   Australian Sports Anti-Doping Authority hotline (www.asada.gov.au/anti-doping-programmes/intelligence) and confidential Report Doping webpage (www.asada.gov.au/report-doping); UK Anti-Doping, 'Report Doping in Sport' (www.ukad.org.uk/what-we-do/report-doping/); UCI (cycling) Professional cyclist help line (www.cyclingsa.com/anti-doping-press/2014/9/28/uci-launches-anti-doping-helpline-for-professional-riders); British Horseracing Authority, Race Straight hotline, *Integrity*, BHA, (www.britishhorseracing.com/resource-centre/integrity/)

14   For example, the British Horseracing Authority (n.d.) is currently undergoing a review involving 'the timeliness of investigations, case management and processing of applications; communication; participant engagement and education; internal processes

and performance monitoring; and technological threats and opportunities' ('Integrity Review' section, para. 3).

15 In 2000, the International Cricket Council launched their Anti-Corruption and Security Unit; however, only 1 per cent of their profit was budgeted and spent on the unit (Carpenter, 2012).

16 The International Tennis Federation reportedly spends 30 per cent of its worldwide development fund on its Integrity Unit (Gardiner and Naidoo, 2006).

17 On 11 February 2011, all Australian sports ministers endorsed on behalf of their governments, an updated National Anti-Doping Framework with the aim of aligning domestic anti-doping efforts in Australia through a set of agreed upon principles, alongside clearly identified areas for cooperation among Australian governments (Australian Government Department of Health, 2015).

18 This is in contrast to the approach taken in France, Italy and Germany where doping is decriminalised; for example, in 1998, vials of EPO were found in a French Festina team car following a police raid at the Tour de France. Several riders and team support crew were suspended ('WADA Against Jail', 2014).

19 In April 2014, Tandy was found dead from a reported drug overdose ('Former NRL Player', 2014; Massoud, 2014).

20 In ancient Greece, fines paid by athletes who broke the rules went to buy bronze statues of Zeus hurling thunderbolts like javelins. Called 'Zanes', they were set up along the road to the stadium, where the athletes could read on them warnings in couplets like this one ('Cheating in the Ancient Olympic', n.d.).

References

Alm, J. (ed.). (2013, April). *Action for good governance in international sports organisations*. Retrieved from Play the Game website: www.playthegame.org/fileadmin/documents/Good_governance_reports/AGGIS_Final_report.pdf

Amateur Sport Integrity Act of 2001, S. 718 107th Cong. (2001).

Andersen, J. S. and Alvad, S. (2015, January 6). Governments face global upgrade of their sports policies. *Play the Game*. Retrieved from www.playthegame.org

Anderson, J. (2012). Gambling-led corruption in international sport: An Australian perspective. *International Sports Law Journal, 1*(2), 3–6. Retrieved from www.springer.com/law/international/journal/40318

Anderson, P. M., Blackshaw, I. S., Siekmann, R. C. R. and Soek, J. (eds). (2012). *Sports betting: Law and policy*. The Hague: Asser Press.

Anderson, J., Duval, A., Van, R. B. and McArdle, D. (2014, July). *Study on risk assessment and management and prevention of conflicts of interest in the prevention and fight against betting-related match-fixing in the EU 28: Final Report*. Retrieved from http://ec.europa.eu/sport/news/2014/docs/study-asser_en.pdf

Ashenden, M. J. (2002). A strategy to deter blood doping in sport. *Haematologica, 87*, 225–232. Retrieved from www.haematologica.org/

Australian Commission for Law Enforcement Integrity. (n.d.-a). *Corruption prevention toolkit*. Retrieved from www.aclei.gov.au/Pages/Corruption-Prevention/Corruption-Prevention-Toolkit.aspx#leadership

Australian Commission for Law Enforcement Integrity. (n.d.-b). Key concepts. Retrieved from www.aclei.gov.au/Pages/Corruption-Prevention/Key-concepts.aspx

Australian Government Department of Health. (2013, October, 25). Role of the National Integrity of Sport Unit. Retrieved from www.health.gov.au/internet/main/publishing.nsf/Content/role-of-the-national-integrity-of-sport-unit

Australian Government Department of Health. (2014, February 11). *National policy on match-fixing in sport*. Retrieved from www.health.gov.au/internet/main/publishing.nsf/Content/national-policy-on-match-fixing-in-sport

Australian Government Department of Health. (2015, October 28). *Anti-doping framework*. Retrieved from www.health.gov.au/internet/main/publishing.nsf/Content/anti-doping-framework

Australian Government Department of Health. (2016, January 19). National Integrity of Sport Unit. Retrieved from www.health.gov.au/internet/main/publishing.nsf/content/national-integrity-of-sport-unit

Australian Olympic Committee. (2015, August 21). *Team membership agreement – athletes*. Retrieved from http://aoc-rio2016.s3.amazonaws.com/files/dmfile/ATHLETES%20-%202016%20Australian%20Olympic%20Team%20Membership%20Agreement%20-%20FINAL%20w%20Schedules_201015.pdf

Australian Sports Drug Agency Act of 1990, Act No. 18 (1991).

Australian Sports Commission. (n.d.). What is sport integrity? Retrieved from www.ausport.gov.au/supporting/integrity_in_sport/about/what_is_sport_integrity

Australian Transactions Reports and Analysis Centre. (2011). *Money laundering in Australia 2011*. Retrieved from www.austrac.gov.au/sites/default/files/documents/money_laundering_in_australia_2011.pdf

Balsdon, E., Fong, L. and Thayer, M. A. (2007). Corruption in college basketball? Evidence of tanking in postseason conference tournaments. *Journal of Sports Economics, 8*, 19–38. doi:10.1177/1527002505275095

Bang, S. (2013, June 1). Berlin Declaration: 137 countries call for enhanced effort against match-fixing and corruption. *Play the Game*. Retrieved from www.playthegame.org/

Barroso, O., Mazzoni, I. and Rabin, O. (2008). Hormone abuse in sports: The antidoping perspective. *Asian Journal of Andrology, 10*, 391–402. doi:10.1111/j.1745-7262.2008.00402.x

Beyerle, S. (2014). *Curtailing corruption: People power for accountability and justice*. Boulder, CO: Rienner.

British Horseracing Authority. (n.d.). Integrity review. Retrieved from www.british-horseracing.com/resource-centre/integrity/

Brown, B. C. (2013). The future of leadership for conscious capitalism. Retrieved from MetaIntegral Associates website: https://metaintegral.org/sites/default/files/MetaIntegral_Brown_The%20future%20of%20leadership%20for%20conscious%20capitalism.pdf

Carpenter, K. (2012, June 5). *Match-fixing – the biggest threat to sport in the 21st century?* Retrieved from www.lawinsport.com/articles/anti-corruption/item/match-fixing-the-biggest-threat-to-sport-in-the-21st-century-part-1

Carpenter, K. (2013). Global match-fixing and the United States' role in upholding sporting integrity. *Berkeley Journal of Entertainment and Sports Law, 2*, 214–229. doi:10.15779/Z38JS90

Carson, W. G. (2003, August). *Whole of government and crime prevention for Victoria*. Melbourne: University of Melbourne, Department of Criminology.

Chappelet, J.-L. and Mrkonjic, M. (2013). *Basic indicators for Better Governance in International Sport (BIBGIS): An assessment tool for international sport governing bodies* (IDHEAP Working Paper 1/2013). Retrieved from www.transparency.ch/de/PDF_files/Newsletter/201306_Newsletter_Publikation_Chappelet_und_Mrkonjic__2013__Basic_Indicators_for_Better_Governance_in_International_Sport.pdf

Cheating in the Ancient Olympics. Retrieved from the Hellenic World website: www.ancientworlds.net/aw/post/1273461

Cook-Greuter, S. R. (2004). Making the case for a developmental perspective. *Industrial and Commercial Training, 36*, 275–281. doi:10.1108/00197850410563902

Corrupt. (2001). In *The Macquarie dictionary: Federation edition*. New South Wales, Australia: Macquarie.

Council of Europe. (2014, July 9). *Convention Europe on the manipulation of sports competitions*. Retrieved from https://wcd.coe.int/ViewDoc.jsp?Ref=CM/Del/Dec(2014)1205/8.1& Language=lanEnglish&Ver=app9&Site=CM&BackColorInternet=DBDCF2&BackCol orIntranet=FDC864&BackColorLogged=FDC864

Cycling Independent Reform Commission. (2015, February). *Report to the President of the Union Cycliste Internationale*. Retrieved from www.uci.ch/mm/Document/News/ CleanSport/16/87/99/CIRCReport2015_Neutral.pdf

David, P. (2013). *A guide to the World Anti-Doping Code* (2nd ed.). Cambridge: Cambridge University Press.

Davis, S. (2015, June 11). FIFA may not be able to change the hosts of the 2018 and 2022 World Cups even if they want to. *Business Insider*. Retrieved from www.business insider.com/

Dubin, C. L. (1990). *Commission of Inquiry into the Use of Drugs and Banned Practices Intended to Increase Athletic Performance*. Retrieved from Government of Canada website: http://publications.gc.ca/collections/collection_2014/bcp-pco/CP32-56-1990-1-eng.pdf

Duggar, J. W. (2009, April 12). The role of integrity in individual and effective corporate leadership. *Journal of Academic and Business Ethics, 3*. Retrieved from www.aabri.com/ jabe.html

Edwards, M. and Clough, R. (2005, January). *Corporate governance and performance: An exploration of the connection in a public sector context* (Issues Series Paper No. 1). Retrieved from www.governanceinstitute.edu.au/magma/media/upload/publication/158_Issues PaperNo-1_Governance-PerformanceIssues.docx

England miss out to Russia in 2018 World Cup vote. (2010, December 2). *BBC News*. Retrieved from http://news.bbc.co.uk/sport2/hi/football/9250585.stm

Engelberg, T., Moston, S. and Skinner, J. (2015). The final frontier of anti-doping: A study of athletes who have committed doping violations. *Sport Management Review, 18*, 268–279. doi:10.1016/j.smr.2014.06.005

Fang, F. C. and Casadevall, A. (2013). Why we cheat. *Scientific American Mind, 24*(2). Retrieved from www.scientificamerican.com/

FIFA. (2011, May 9). *FIFA's historic contribution to INTERPOL in fight against match-fixing* [Press release]. Retrieved from www.fifa.com/governance/news/y=2011/m=5/ news=fifa-historic-contribution-interpol-fight-against-match-fixing-1431884.html

FIFA scandal: US seeks extradition of seven FIFA officials being held in Switzerland. (2015, July 2). *ABC Grandstand Sport*. Retrieved from www.abc.net.au/news/2015-07-03/ us-seeks-extradition-of-fifa-7-in-switzerland/6591696?section=sport

Forrest, D. (2012). The threat to football from betting-related corruption. *International Journal of Sport Finance, 7*(2), 99. Retrieved from https://ijsf.wordpress.com/

Former NRL player Ryan Tandy found dead from reported drug overdose. (2014, April 29). *ABC News*. Retrieved from www.abc.net.au/news/2014-04-28/ryan-tandy-dies/ 5416398

Franke, W. and Berendonk, B. (1997). Hormonal doping and androgenization of athletes: A secret program of the German Democratic Republic Government. *Clinical Chemistry, 43*, 1262–1279. Retrieved from www.clinchem.org/

Fridman, S. (1999). Conflict of interest, accountability and corporate governance: The case of the IOC and SOCOG. *University of New South Wales Law Journal, 22*(3). Retrieved from www.unswlawjournal.unsw.edu.au/

Gardiner, S. and Naidoo, U. (2006). On the front foot against corruption. *Sport and the Law Journal, 15*(2), 16–27. Retrieved from www.britishsportslaw.org/

Geeraert, A. (2014, July 11). Switzerland prepares stricter laws against sports corruption. *Play the Game.* Retrieved from www.playthegame.org/

Greenberg cleared over Tandy betting allegations. (2014, May 16). Retrieved from www.nrl. com/greenberg-cleared-over-tandy-betting-allegations/tabid/10874/newsid/78500/ default.aspx

Hanstad, D. V. and Loland, S. (2005). *What is efficient doping control?: A study of procedures and their justification in the planning and carrying out of doping control in sport.* Retrieved from http://idrottsforum.org/push/efficient_doping_control.pdf

Harcourt, P. R., Unglik, H. and Cook, J. L. (2012). A strategy to reduce illicit drug use is effective in elite Australian football. *British Journal of Sports Medicine.* doi:10.1136 /bjsports-2012-091329

Harding, L. (2005, November 17). Two years in jail for match-fixing German referee. *The Guardian.* Retrieved from www.theguardian.com

Heron, M. and Jiang, C. (2010). The gathering storm – organised crime and sports corruption. *Australian and New Zealand Sports Law Journal, 5,* 99–118. Retrieved from https://anzsla.com/content/australian-new-zealand-sports-law-journal

Hill, D. (2002, December 11). The Russian mafia and hockey. *Play the Game.* Retrieved from www.playthegame.org/

Hill, D. (2010, April). A critical mass of corruption: Why some football leagues have more match-fixing than others. *International Journal of Sports Marketing and Sponsorship, 11,* 221–235. Retrieved from www.imrpublications.com/journal-landing.aspx?volno=L& no=L

Hill, D. (2011, August 29). The Ten Commandments for anti-corruption [Blog post]. Retrieved from http://leastthing.blogspot.com/2011/08/declan-hills-ten-command ments-for-anti.html

Hill, D. (2013). *The insider's guide to match-fixing in football.* Toronto, Canada: McDermid.

Ings, R. (2007). Australia: Revolutionary model battles doping on all eight fronts of the code. *Play True, 1,* 10–11. Retrieved from www.wada-ama.org/en/resources/search?f [0]=field_resource_collections%3A12

Inquiry. (2001). In *The Macquarie dictionary: Federation edition.* New South Wales, Australia: Macquarie.

International Association of Athletics Federations. (1928, October). *Handbook of the International Amateur Athletic Federation, 1927–1928.* Västerås, Sweden: Author.

International Anti-Corruption Conference. (n.d.). Social entrepreneurs. Retrieved from http://16iacc.org/game-changers/social-entrepreneurs/

International Olympic Committee. (2014, November 18). *Grant programmes encouraging Olympic Movement related research.* Retrieved from www.olympic.org/Assets/OSC% 20Section/pdf/Grant_programmes_encouraging_OM_research.pdf

International Olympic Committee. (2015, August 2). *Olympic charter.* Retrieved from www.olympic.org/Documents/olympic_charter_en.pdf

International Criminal Police Organization. (n.d.). *Integrity in sport* [Brochure]. Retrieved from www.interpol.int/Crime-areas/Integrity-in-Sport/Integrity-in-sport

International Criminal Police Organization. (2013, September 23). *INTERPOL Global Complex for Innovation reaches new heights* [Press release]. Retrieved from www.interpol. int/News-and-media/News/2013/PR114

International Criminal Police Organization. (2015, May 11). *Boosting national efforts against match-fixing focus of INTERPOL-FIFA meeting in Canada* [Press release]. Retrieved from www.interpol.int/News-and-media/News/2015/N2015-055

International Criminal Police Organization and World Anti-Doping Association. (2009, February 2). *Cooperation Agreement between INTERPOL and WADA*. Retrieved from www.interpol.int/content/download/9287/68584/version/2/file/INTERPOL_WADA.pdf

Interpol opens new Singapore headquarters in bid to target cybercrime. (2015, April 13). *South China Morning Post*. Retrieved from www.scmp.com/news/asia/article/1765805/interpol-opens-new-singapore-base

Jacques Rogge: Corruption next fight. (2011, July 14). *ESPN*. Retrieved from http://espn.go.com/olympics/story/_/id/6768358/jacques-rogge-says-match-fixing-gambling-big-fights-sports

Jones, K. L. (2013). Compliance mechanism as a tool of prevention? In M. T. R. Haberfeld and D. L. Sheehan (eds) *Match-fixing in international sports: Existing processes law enforcement and prevention strategies* (pp. 199–228). New York: Springer.

Lane, S. (2011, July 27). Illegal betting, match-fixing as dangerous as doping, says IOC chief. *The Sydney Morning Herald*. Retrieved from www.smh.com.au/

Legal India. (2013, October 14). Sporting fraud prevention bill styled on laws in many countries. Retrieved from www.legalindia.com/news/sporting-fraud-prevention-bill-styled-laws-many-countries

Le Grand, C. (2015). *The straight dope*. Melbourne: Melbourne University Press.

Lord Woolf and PricewaterhouseCoopers. (2012, February 1). *An independent governance review of the International Cricket Council*. Retrieved from www.playthegame.org/fileadmin/documents/Good_governance_reports/DOC_6E43A6280C922ABC51A9C6AB55AA58E1_1328155148580_481.pdf

Lumpkin, A. (1983). Sport and human values. *Journal of Popular Culture, 16*(4), 4–10. doi:10.1111/j.0022-3840.1983.1604_4.x

Marriott-Lloyd, P. (2010). *International Convention against Doping in Sport* (Report No. SHS/2010/PI/H/2). Retrieved from UNESCO website: http://unesdoc.unesco.org/images/0018/001884/188405e.pdf

Massoud, J. (2014). *The penalty*. New South Wales: Allen and Unwin.

Moston, S., Engelberg, T. and Skinner, J. (2015). Self-fulfilling prophecy and the future of doping. *Psychology of Sport and Exercise, 16*, 201–207. doi:10.1016/j.psychsport.2014.02.004

Muhsin, M.V. (2013, December 8). Mandela the secret weapon in 1995 World Cup Rugby final. *The Sunday Observer*. Retrieved from www.sundayobserver.lk/

New FIFA Now. (n.d.-a). Guiding principles for FIFA reform. Retrieved from www.newfifanow.org/guiding-principles.html

New FIFA Now. (n.d.-b). Where are they now? Retrieved from www.newfifanow.org/where-are-they-now.html

New FIFA Now. (2015, January). Charter for FIFA reform. Retrieved from www.newfifanow.org/charter-for-fifa-reform.html

NRL reportedly investigating Todd Greenberg over knowledge of Ryan Tandy's gambling on rugby league games. (2014, May 9). *ABC News*. Retrieved from www.abc.net.au/news/2014-05-10/nrl-investigating-greenberg-over-tandy-allegations-report/5444154

Play the Game. (2015, November 12). *IOC to initiate independent audits of International Federations*. Retrieved from www.playthegame.org/news/news-articles/2015/0132_ioc-independent-audits-of-ifs/

Portelli, E. and Rolfe, P. (2014, April 24). Professional clown Segaran 'Gerry' Subramaniam jailed for role in Southern Stars match-fixing, as club loses points, cops $10,000 fine *Herald Sun*. Retrieved from www.heraldsun.com.au/

Richards, R. and Murphy, G. (2015, August). *Sport participation in Australia.* Retrieved from www.clearinghouseforsport.gov.au/knowledge_base/sport_participation/community_ participation/sport_participation_in_australia

Rooke, D. and Torbert, W. R. (2005, April). Seven transformations of leadership. *Harvard Business Review.* Retrieved from https://hbr.org/

Ruigrok, W., Peck, S. I. and Tacheva, S. (2007). National and gender diversity on Swiss corporate boards. *Corporate Governance: An International Review, 15,* 546–577. Retrieved from http://onlinelibrary.wiley.com/journal/10.1111/(ISSN)1467-8683

Salter, A. (2003). *Predators, pedophiles, rapists, and other sex offenders: Who they are, how they operate, and how we can protect ourselves and our children.* New York: Basic Books.

Schumacher, Y. O. and Pottgiesser, T. (2009). Performance profiling: A role for sport science in the fight against doping. *International Journal of Sports Physiology and Performance, 4,* 129–133. Retrieved from http://journals.humankinetics.com/ijspp

Shipley, A. (2007, October 5). Marion Jones admits to steroid use. *Washington Post.* Retrieved from www.washingtonpost.com/

Sigmund, S. (2004). The jurisprudence of Judge Kenesaw Mountain Landis. *Marquette Sports Law Review, 15,* 277–330. Retrieved from http://scholarship.law.marquette.edu/sportslaw/

Simons, J. W. (2015, June 3). How Interpol got into bed with FIFA. *Politico.* Retrieved from www.politico.eu/

Sports Governance Observer – a benchmarking tool to strengthen transparency and democracy in your sport. (2015). Retrieved from www.playthegame.org/theme-pages/the-sports-governance-observer/

Sweeney, G. (2015, April 9). Welcome to Transparency International's new 'Corruption in Sport Initiative' [Blog post]. Retrieved from http://blog.transparency.org/2015/04/09/welcome-to-transparency-internationals-new-corruption-in-sport-initiative/

Sydney Scoreboard. (n.d.). Global scoreboard. Retrieved from www.sydneyscoreboard.com/global-scoreboard/

Torbert, B. (2004). *Action inquiry: The secret of timely and transforming leadership.* San Francisco, CA: Berrett-Koehler.

Transparency International. (n.d.). What is corruption? Retrieved from www.transparency.org/what-is-corruption/#define

Transparency International. (2011, August 16). *Safe hands: Building integrity and transparency at FIFA.* Retrieved from www.transparency.org/whatwedo/publication/safe_hands_building_integrity_and_transparency_at_fifa

Transparency International. (2013, November 18). *Fair play: strengthening integrity and transparency in cricket.* Retrieved from www.transparency.org/whatwedo/publication/fair_play_strengthening_integrity_and_transparency_in_cricket

Transparency International. (2014a, April 7). *Policy Brief 01/2014: Gender, equality and corruption: What are the linkages?* Retrieved from www.transparency.org/whatwedo/publication/policy_position_01_2014_gender_equality_and_corruption_what_are_the_linkage

Transparency International. (2014b). *Staying on side: Education and prevention of match-fixing.* Retrieved from www.transparency.org/whatwedo/activity/staying_on_side_education_and_prevention_of_match_fixing

U.N. Office on Drugs and Crime. (2004). *United Nations convention against corruption.* Retrieved from www.unodc.org/documents/brussels/UN_Convention_Against_Corruption.pdf

UNESCO. (2005, October 19). International Convention against Doping in Sport. Retrieved from www.unesco.org/new/en/social-and-human-sciences/themes/anti-doping/international-convention-against-doping-in-sport/

UNESCO. (2013, May 30). *UNESCO conference in Berlin adopts roadmap to clean up sport and make it accessible for all* [Press release]. Retrieved from www.unesco.org/new/en/social-and-human-sciences/themes/physical-education-and-sport/sv14/news/unesco_con ference_in_berlin_adopts_roadmap_to_clean_up_sport_and_make_it_accessible_for_all /#.VjCa936rQgt

UNESCO. (2014, November 4). *Preliminary draft of the revised International Charter of Physical Education and Sport*. Retrieved from http://unesdoc.unesco.org/images/0023/002305/ 230547e.pdf

Unger, D. (2015, April 9). What made corruption a hot topic in sports [Blog post]. Retrieved from http://blog.transparency.org/2015/04/09/what-made-corruption-a-hot-topic-in-sports/

Ungerleider, S. (2001). *Faust's gold: Inside the East German doping machine*. New York: Dunne.

U.S. Anti-Doping Agency. (2012, October 10). *Report on proceedings under the World Anti-Doping Code and the USADA Protocol: USADA v. Armstrong*. Retrieved from https://d3epuodzu3wuis.cloudfront.net/ReasonedDecision.pdf

van der Walt, N. and Ingley, C. (2003). Board dynamics and the influence of professional background, gender and ethnic diversity of directors. *Corporate Governance: An International Review, 11*, 218–234. doi:10.1111/1467-8683.00320

WADA advances cooperation with Interpol, athlete passport development. (2008, November 23). Retrieved from International Sports Press Association website: www.aips media.com/index.php?page=news&cod=2803&tp=n#.Vc7Z9fmqqko

WADA against jail terms for athletes. (2014, November 17). *The Age*. Retrieved from www.theage.com.au/sport/wada-against-jail-terms-for-athletes-20141116-11o25a. html

Welch, D. (2014, May 8). Ryan Tandy: Disgraced NRL footballer's gambling led to his career, life unravelling. *ABC News*. Retrieved from www.abc.net.au/news/

Woolf, L. and PricewaterhouseCoopers. (2012, February 1). *An independent governance review of the International Cricket Council*. Retrieved from http://static.espncricinfo. com/db/DOWNLOAD/0000/0093/woolfe_report.pdf

Woolley, R. (2009). Commercialization and culture in Australian gambling. *Continuum: Journal of Media and Cultural Studies, 23*, 183–196. doi:10.1080/10304310802710520

World Anti-Doping Agency. (n.d.-a) Athlete biological passport. Retrieved from www.wada-ama.org/en/what-we-do/science-medical/athlete-biological-passport

World Anti-Doping Agency. (n.d.-b). INTERPOL Cooperation. Retrieved from www.wada-ama.org/en/what-we-do/investigation-trafficking/trafficking/interpol-cooperation

World Anti-Doping Agency. (n.d.-c). Research. Retrieved from www.wada-ama.org/ en/what-we-do/science-medical/research

World Anti-Doping Agency. (2005, May). *Planning doping control for the purpose of detecting, deterring and/or preventing the use of prohibited substances*. Oslo: World Anti-Doping Agency .

World Anti-Doping Agency. (2007, March 12). *WADA applauds actions targeting the illegal manufacture and distribution of doping substances: New era in anti-doping must involve coordination with law enforcement* [Press release]. Retrieved from www.wada-ama.org/en/media/ news/2007-03/wada-applauds-actions-targeting-the-illegal-manufacture-and-distribution-of

World Anti-Doping Agency. (2008, November 23). *Minutes of the WADA Foundation board meeting*. Retrieved from https://wada-main-prod.s3.amazonaws.com/resources/files/ wada_foundationboardminutes_200811_en.pdf

World Anti-Doping Agency. (2011a, January 5). *Guidelines for coordinating investigations and sharing anti-doping information and evidence*. Retrieved from www.wada-ama.org/

en/resources/world-anti-doping-program/coordinating-investigations-and-sharing-anti-doping-information

World Anti-Doping Agency. (2011b). Investigations. Retrieved from www.wada-ama.org/en/investigations

World Anti-Doping Agency. (2015). *World Anti-Doping Code*. Retrieved from www.wada-ama.org/en/what-we-do/the-code

Zulauf, R. and Weder D. (n.d.). Swiss corporate law tax reform III. Retrieved from www2.deloitte.com/ch/en/pages/tax/articles/corporate-tax-reform-III.html

5

MATCH-FIXING AND MANIPULATION IN SPORT

Markus Breuer and Sebastian Kaiser

A crucial element that contributes to the fascination for millions of spectators and fans of professional sport and sports promotion is the uncertainty of the outcome of a contest. The uncertainty of outcome was described in one of the first sport economic papers ever published (Rottenberg, 1956). Although in most contests one team or athlete is determined to be superior to their competitor(s), the result of the contest remains uncertain. Furthermore, fans and spectators often support the 'underdog', which is the team or athlete that is expected to lose. However, the elimination of uncertainty from sports contests, known as match-fixing, causes competitors to give up their integrity; further, fans become less engaged and less excited, thus decreasing their willingness to pay for events. In 2011, Hein Verbruggen, president of SportAccord, stated that integrity in professional organised sports is the most important commodity (Pitsch, Emrich and Pierdzioch, 2015). Similarly, McNamee (2013) pointed out that the basis of a sports contest has been undermined if the outcome is predetermined through match-fixing. Fans must believe that what they see on the field of play represents a true test of the competitor's skills, otherwise there is a real risk that they will stop watching the contests and the sport will lose sponsors and broadcasters (Carpenter, 2014).

According to Carpenter (2014), the Council of Europe Convention on the Manipulation of Sports Competition has experienced a significant increase in the number of cases of match-fixing, which can be attributed primarily to two factors: the proliferation of different types of betting and the development of a large market for illegal liquid betting, particularly in Europe. Carpenter (2014) provided a review of cases involving match-fixing that have gone to the Court of Arbitration for Sport: *FK Pobeda, Aleksandar Zabrcanec, Nikolae Zdraveski v. UEFA* (CAS 2009/A/192), *FC Carpaty and FC Metalist v. Football Federation of Ukraine* (unreported, 2 August 2013), *Besiktas Jimnastik Kulübü v. UEFA* (CAS 2013/A/

3258), *Fenerbahce Spor Kulübü v. UEFA* (CAS 2013/A/3256), and *Eskisehispor Kulübü v. UEFA* (CAS 2014/A/3628).

The current chapter will first explore the fundamentals of match-fixing, including brief descriptions of different kinds of match-fixing. Then, gambling related to match-fixing will be examined. Lastly, match-fixing induced by investors will be discussed using a simple model based on a profit-maximising individual investor who holds shares of more than one club at the same time. Due to the ongoing professionalisation of sports and large-scale investments by individual investors as well as multinational companies, multi-club ownership situations are becoming more relevant.

Fundamentals of match-fixing

Definition of match-fixing

Match-fixing refers to any activity that alters the uncertain outcome of a contest and destroys the integrity of sport, which includes both bribery (receiving benefits) and duress by threats (e.g., threats by criminals) and duress by circumstances. The current chapter shall also not limit match-fixing to a specific stakeholder group. Thus, athletes, trainers, patrons, investors or unrelated third parties such as gambling agencies can be considered as having the ability to influence the uncertain outcome of a sports event. Athletes who are neither bribed nor threatened yet intentionally perform below their skill level can be regarded as a special case. The focal question is if the integrity of the contest is compromised under these special circumstances. Although professional athletes are expected to make their best effort to win a competition, each individual is free to choose how to maximise their skills and contributions from several possible actions that include performing below their own best effort. Therefore, match-fixing will only be considered if two or more contestants and/or teams have agreed to a particular outcome prior to a contest.

Variations of match-fixing

A review of extant literature reveals that the term match-fixing has been applied to a variety of phenomena involved in compromising the integrity of professional sporting events. Figure 5.1 provides a general overview.

The first category in Figure 5.1 relates to match-fixing used by gamblers or gambling agencies to maximise their individual payoff from gambling or offering bets on sports events. The sharp increase in the global betting market is generally given as one of the main reasons for an increased significance of match-fixing. Carpenter (2014) differentiated sports gambling into three categories:

1   *Illegal sports betting*: Any gambling on sporting events that is not allowed by applicable laws. Gambling on illegal sports was recently estimated to have a value of £320 billion per year (McNamee, 2013; Singh, 2013).

2   *Irregular sports betting*: Any gambling on sporting events that is inconsistent with usual or anticipated patterns of the market.

3   *Suspicious sports betting*: Any gambling on sporting events that appears to be linked to a manipulation of the contest.

The second category in Figure 5.1 relates to match-fixing that is based on collusion, such as bilateral agreements between the parties involved. Incentives for match-fixing involving collusion often involve a tournament such as the FIFA World Cup. In one of the most notorious examples, it is widely believed that West Germany colluded with Austria to determine the result of their match against each other in the 1982 World Cup (Caruso, 2007). A win by Germany by one or two goals would ensure that both teams would qualify for the second round. After West Germany scored a goal, neither team scored again and both sides played passively and appeared to deliberately avoid scoring chances. West Germany won the match and both teams advanced to the next round of the tournament.

The 3-point rule used in European football leagues can be used to illustrate the importance of a tournament's setup on match-fixing. According to the rule, winning teams receive 3 points, losing teams receive no points, and both teams receive 1 point when a match ends in a draw. Under this system, two teams of the same quality that play each other twice a season would prefer having a sure-fire home win and an away loss rather than struggling in each game with a high probability of a draw and receiving 1 point for each game (2 points in total). In this scenario, the two teams could easily engage in collusion by agreeing that the home team would win each match, thus ensuring they would both receive 3 points and decreasing their chances of relegation (Shepotylo, 2005). In fact, some have suggested that the system of promotion and relegation employed by European football leagues is disposed to match-fixing via collusion (Caruso, 2007). However, strong incentives for collusion are mainly found in matches between balanced teams and not for matches in which one team is the odds-on favourite because betting behaviour could otherwise be easily detected as suspicious. Nevertheless,

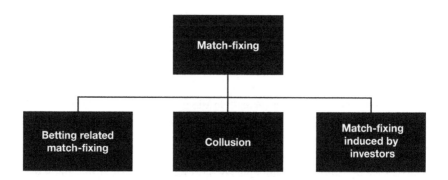

Figure 5.1 Overview of match-fixing

collusion can be difficult to detect as the threshold between match-fixing and a subpar performance by an athlete or team is often difficult to differentiate. Low-evaluation players could simply exert less effort than very motivated and well-paid players (Caruso, 2007). Caruso (2007) reviewed the extant literature and identified formal approaches for analysing the economics of match-fixing. Finally, match-fixing via collusion can occur when the same investors hold shares of more than one professional sports club at the same time.

In a general sense, any factor that has a strong influence on a club can be regarded as a potential threat to compromise the integrity of a match or contest. The next sections will further focus on betting-related match-fixing and multi-club ownerships situations. Collusion will not be further discussed since its economic impact appears to be smaller than other forms of match-fixing and is difficult to prove when suspected between two or more teams.

Betting-related match-fixing

Operational importance

Bozkurt (2012) performed a general analysis of match-fixing in European football contests using third-party data and found that 20 out of 28 current E.U. member states experienced match-fixing scandals in the past, and includes the following countries: Austria, Belgium, Bulgaria, Croatia, Cyprus, the Czech Republic, Estonia, Finland, France, Germany, Greece, Hungary, Italy, Latvia, Malta, Poland, Portugal, Slovenia, Spain and the United Kingdom. Furthermore, based on the assumption that match-fixing activities were often not monitored in the past, it can be assumed that problems occurred in other European countries that were not identified in Bozkurt's (2012) analysis.

Carpenter (2012) provided a detailed overview of match-fixing scandals across several different sports, including the following incidents:

1   Basketball: In 2011, ten people were indicted in the United States in connection with a scheme to fix multiple college basketball games from 2008 to 2011.
2   Cricket: In August 2010, three international Pakistani cricket players were implicated in a scandal related to intentionally bowling no-balls in certain situations, which is known as spot-fixing. The players were convicted and imprisoned.
3   Horseracing: In May 2011, the British Horseracing Authority charged 13 jockeys and owners with serious breaches of the rules in several races that occurred in 2009. Eleven individuals were found guilty and were temporarily banned from horseracing for varying lengths of time.
4   Snooker: In April 2010, John Higgins, who was the three-time world champion at the time, and his manager, Pat Mooney, who was a World Professional Billiards and Snooker Association (WPBSA) board member, were accused of

taking bribes. Higgins received a six-month suspension and was fined £75,000. Mooney was also suspended and resigned from his position on the WPBSA board.

5   Sumo wrestling: In 2011, the Japan Sumo Association cancelled a tournament after 13 veteran wrestlers were suspected of involvement in a match-fixing scandal.

6   Tennis: In 2007, Nikolay Davydenko was suspected of match-fixing when several bets – ten times the usual amount – were placed in favour of his opponent, despite Davydenko having just won the first set 6-2 and being the favourite to win the match. The bets were placed with the online British gambling company Betfair, which reported the activity as suspicious. Both players were cleared of any wrongdoing after a lengthy investigation. In 2011, top-100 player Daniel Koellerer from Austria was found guilty of three offences in relation to match-fixing.

Possible rules and regulations

Bozkurt (2012) provided a detailed overview of current criminal law provisions for all 27 E.U. member states. However, relying on national laws without considering multinational regulations is likely to fail since punters often use foreign gambling agencies to place bets on sports events. Since the laws regulating professional sports and gambling differ from country to country, the International Centre for Sport Security (ICSS, 2014) made several recommendations for principles to protect the integrity of sports competitions, including the following:

1   Recommendations for public authorities including betting regulatory authorities. In addition to the implementation of effective negotiation procedures and a stronger financial support, the ICSS proposed the centralisation of all national information regarding sports betting, a limitation of bets per person/period and stronger transnational cooperation.

2   Recommendations for sport organisations include good governance, and harmonization of disciplinary provisions, awareness, education and prevention. Sports actors (i.e., athletes, trainers) should not be able to bet on their own competitions.

3   Recommendations for sports betting operators focused on money laundering requirements.

Currently, sport organisations like the Union of European Football Associations (UEFA) have devised several strategies to deal with the increasing threat of betting-related match-fixing, such as appointing more than 50 integrity officers to operate within national organisations. The UEFA also implemented a system to monitor gambling patterns with informants in the field. Furthermore, the UEFA and European Club Association have agreed to a Memorandum of Understanding that establishes a partnership between football clubs and national associations (Bozkurt,

2012). However, these steps only affect the strongly regulated gambling market within Europe and not the illegal market, which might be a first step but will not save sports integrity in the long run. Additionally, the UEFA and FIFA have set up an early warning system for monitoring gambling patterns and working together with Interpol (Bozkurt, 2012).

Managerial effects) 0

According to Carpenter (2014), match manipulation that can be linked to organised crime often involves some form of money laundering. Since websites providing sports betting can be located anywhere in the world, criminal organisations shop for countries where there is least supervision and control from public authorities for their operations (Bozkurt, 2012). If we assume a strong level of match-fixing in a country or a league (e.g., Greece 2008–2011), the minimised uncertainty of outcome can lead to high levels of competitive imbalance. In the Greek example, the creation of 'rich' clubs and 'poor' clubs resulted from match-fixing activities (Manoli and Antonopoulos, 2015). It is common sense that a low competitive balance lowers the overall attractiveness of a league and thus, the customer's willingness to pay.

The extent of match-fixing in professional sports leagues is difficult to determine (although most discussions assume an increasing level). One of the few investigations was conducted for Germany by Pitsch, Emrich, and Pierdzioch (2012; see also, Pitsch et al., 2015). Whereas a quantitative analysis with the support of the German Football Association and a second approach using Internet forums and newsgroups failed, a third, e-mail-based approach was successful and resulted in a final set of 277 records. Due to the randomised nature of the responses, the results stand up to scrutiny: 22.7 per cent of the participants answered that they had experienced match-fixing,[1] while 14.8 per cent experienced match-fixing in the 2010–2011 season. Pitsch et al. (2012) concluded that match-fixing is not a top-league phenomenon in Germany, but is widely spread and a considerable number of players have already been involved in match-fixing. However, the demand for football was not affected negatively. Moreover, match-fixing is not always based on investing money as incentives. In many cases, players agreed to engage in unsports-manlike behaviour for non-monetary benefits like clothes or a crate of beer (Pitsch et al., 2012).

Case study: match-fixing in German professional football

Within the last ten years, the name 'Robert Hoyzer' has become a synonym for bribery in professional sports in Germany. Hoyzer was a young and talented referee who refereed matches in several minor leagues and the German Deutscher Fussball-Bund (DFB) Cup. In 2005, he admitted that he had received money and other benefits for privileging teams. According to German press reports, he received more than €10,000 from professional bettors from Croatia. In 2006, he was found guilty of supporting match-fixing and fraud and was imprisoned for more than two years according to German anti-corruption laws. In total, ten matches were found to be fixed. In the eight cases where Robert Hoyzer acted as referee, the remaining matches were refereed by another referee. Hamburger Sportverein received a compensation payment of €1.5 million from the German Football Association. The club dropped out of the DFB Cup (against a minor league opponent) based on several decisions made by Robert Hoyzer. Since the tournament had already finished when the scandal was made public, the match could not be repeated.

The Hoyzer scandal shocked German football fans. Hardly anyone had ever suspected the threat to sports integrity that results from bribing the referee. However, several changes have been implemented: Prior to the scandal, information on which referee will referee a certain match was made public long before the match. This setting facilitated bribery since professional bettors had plenty of time to place their bets and contact/bribe the referees. As a result of the Hoyzer scandal, the decision about the referee is now only made public two days prior to the match. Although this change cannot prohibit match-fixing all together, it has become more difficult for criminals since the preparation time is reduced significantly.

Match-fixing induced by investors

Private investors have gained more and more importance in international sports during the last decades. Whereas some leagues restrict the power of investors (e.g., the German Bundesliga and its '50% + 1' rule that ensures that the majority shareholder of any professional club has to be a non-profit organisation), most sport organisations welcome private as well as constitutional investors. Patrons from the Russian Federation and the Middle East have become especially popular in European football (e.g., in England and France).

The concept of multiple club ownerships

For our analysis, we consider the following structure as multiple club ownership. A single investor dominates at least two different sports clubs that are competing in the same league or tournament. Domination can result from different scenarios:

- A single investor might hold directly or indirectly more than 50 per cent of the shares of each club (majority shareholder).
- A single investor might have a dominating position in or against the club's management. This multi-club ownership situation might result from a minor stake in the club's shares and any additional fact that ensures the investor's influence. One might think of the minority shareholder as being the main sponsor of a club, owning the stadium, and so on.

Due to this differentiation, multi-club ownership situations in a wider sense might also appear in those sport leagues that restrict the power of single investors by rules and regulations like the German 50 per cent + 1 rule.

Up to now the operational importance of multi-club ownerships has been very limited. In European professional football, multi-club ownerships became relevant for the first time in the late 1990s. In these years, the English National Investment Company held shares of both Athlitiki Enosis Konstantinoupoleos (AEK) Athens and Slavia Prague, which had to play against each other in the UEFA cup (Müller, 2003). Outside Europe, the Anschutz Entertainment Group held a majority of three Major League Soccer clubs in the United States at the same time ('Zukunft der 50+1-Regel', 2008).

Formal analysis

In the following section, we will provide a simple analysis of multi-club ownerships in professional sport leagues. First, we act on the assumption of two different sports clubs named Team A and Team B. Both are dominated by a profit-maximising investor. The revenue is the only variable of the target function. Costs are not considered. Individual preferences for one of the two clubs, as they would be expected by a patron, are not assumed either. The revenues will be considered as R_A for Team A and R_B for Team B. They imply revenues from merchandising, sponsoring, ticketing and profits from selling TV rights, and so on. All of these aspects are strongly related to the athletic success of each team. The athletic success itself is represented by the individual position on the table at the end of a season. We act on the assumption of a situation where the final league table is determined by a single match between Team A and Team B on the last match day. This constellation is often used to deduct negative effects from multi-club ownership situations and is characterised by strong incentives to influence the result of this final match by an ex ante intervention regarding the result.

The turnovers are noted by the additions 'V' for a team's victory, and 'L' for a lost match. So we have R_A^V for Team A winning the match and R_B^L for Team B losing. The greater the athletic success, the greater the estimated turnover so that $R_A^V > R_A^L$ and $R_B^V > R_A^L$. From an economic point of view, the victory of Team A should be more attractive for the investor, implying a general incentive for an agreement that ensures Team A defeating its rival Team B in the final match. Formally, this incentive is given by the expression $R_A^V + R_B^L > R_A^L + R_B^V$. Considering the marginal revenues, this leads to $MR_A > MR_B$.

Without any ex ante agreement, the probability for Team A winning the final match is given by the expression q. A draw is excluded in this model so that the probability for Team B winning is given by $1 - q$. This simplification is acceptable because even a draw will help either Team A or B accomplish its objectives. The model covers two periods, T_0 and T_1, so that the revenues from both periods have to be considered as well an investor's point of view (see Figure 5.2 for a visual). Turnovers from the second period are discounted with the interest rate i. The investor's possibility to influence the outcome of the sports event is restricted to the final match day.

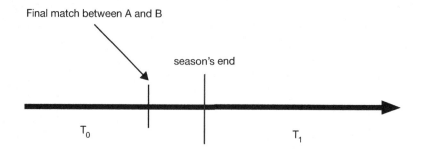

Figure 5.2 Timeline for match-fixing induced by investors

During the ongoing season, the consumers/spectators should have no possibility to react on a (real or assumed) match-fixing agreement. This is why revenues in T_0 are directly dependent on the result of the match between Team A and Team B and the final table. One possible arrangement is that Team A will become the champion if the team wins the match, whereas Team B will be located in the mid-field of the table. In T_1, consumers can sanction the investor by reducing their interest either in Team A, Team B or both. Declining attendance figures could be one sanction. Revenues from ticketing and merchandising would be affected directly; in the long run, reduced earnings from sponsoring and the sale of TV rights seem likely as well. Effects such as these would likely affect both clubs dominated by a single investor. If consumers presume an ex ante agreement, then we expect the turnover to be $R_{A/B}$; in the case of a match that has been recognised as upright where the stronger team is winning, the turnover should be $\bar{R}_{A/B}$. As sanctions have to lead to reduced earnings, we assume $\bar{R}_{A/B} > R_{A/B}$. The fact that the athletic success of Team A is more profitable than Team B, winning the match is valid for T_0 and T_1, as well as for the sum of revenues from both periods.

Moreover, we assume asymmetric information between consumers and investors in the following design: the consumers have no reliable information whether the outcome of the match has been fixed by the investor himself or not. In order to judge, they can only rely on public information (media) and an analysis of the match itself. On this basis, they can conclude that either the match was honest and fair (probability p), or it was the opposite and the result was arranged ex ante (probability $[1 - p]$). The consumers' conclusion does not have to reflect reality! It is possible that no arrangement was made, but it is assumed (e.g., if a single player – especially the goalkeeper – made more mistakes than in a 'standard' match). The other way around a fixed result could be not detected and the public assumes a fair tournament. On the basis of the structure presented here, the target function of the investor can be written as follows:

$$q(R_A^V + R_B^L) + (1-q)(R_A^L + R_B^V) +$$
$$\left[q(p(\bar{R}_A^V + \bar{R}_B^L) + (1-p)(\underline{R}_A^V + \underline{R}_B^L)) + (1-q)(p(\bar{R}_A^L + \bar{R}_B^V) + (1-p)(\underline{R}_A^L + \underline{R}_B^V)) \right](1+i)^{-1} \to \max.$$

The upper row gives the first period (T_0), while the lower row represents the estimated pay offs in the second period. All terms noted by a q represent pay offs for Team A winning the match. Those terms noted by $1 - q$ describe revenues caused by Team B winning the match; p indicates payoffs, which are realised by a match that has been identified as a fair game without any agreement. The other way around, terms connected to $1 - p$ indicate consumers considering the event as fixed.

First, a standard two-club situation should be analysed. From an investor's point of view, q is a binary variable. If he decides to influence the result of a match, it is $q = 1$. If there is no agreement on the match results, q is between 0 and 1 and can only be estimated (e.g., by analysing betting odds). The assumptions of the spectators and indirectly the revenues in T_1, too, are not directly influenced by the investor's choice. If there is no agreement on the result, there is uncertainty on the match itself as well as on the consumers' assumptions.

A detailed analysis leads to the conclusion that the additional payoffs in the case of match-fixing are bigger than the other way around (i.e., uncertainty of outcome, integrity). This is valid for every case in which both clubs are affected by the consumer's sanctions in the same way and intensity as long as the investor's interference is assumed. This presupposition is not obligatory in reality (e.g., fans of single clubs differ regarding their preferences for integrity), but from the model, no arguments against this assumption can be derived.

Hence, on the basis of the underlying model, a threat to the integrity of sports events can be derived. There are strong incentives driving a profit-maximising investor to influence the outcome of a fictional final match between Teams A and B. Consumers' abilities to sanction the clubs in the second season are not powerful enough to guarantee or push integrity under the current model restrictions.

So far, we have assumed that match-fixing (Team A wins the final match; no uncertainty for the investor) has no influence on the consumers' perception (if they perceive the event to be integer or not). In reality, it seems obvious that any actual investor's intervention should increase the probability that fans assume match-fixing (although we should not think of an automatism). The following aspects might play a role in this context:

- One or more players might contact the press and make the intervention public (whether for common reasons like problems with the club management or strong personal preferences for integrity).
- The match itself indicates an agreement because of an important individual failing.
- If there was a money transfer between Team A and Team B, this could be detected by the press or the league management (e.g., during the licensing process).

Within the structure of the model, these aspects can be considered by the introduction of a variable α $(0 < \alpha < p)$. Introducing α, the probability p (assumption of a fair sports event by the fans) is reduced to a certain degree. The other way around, the counter probability $(1 - p)$ increases by the same figure. Thus, the new estimated payoff can be derived as follows:

$$R = (R_A^V + R_B^L) + \left[(p - \alpha)((\overline{R}_A^V + \overline{R}_B^l) + (1 - p + \alpha)(\underline{R}_A^V + \underline{R}_B^l)\right](1+i)^{-1}$$

Depending on the value for α, it is possible to derive situations where an integer match (without any match-fixing) leads to higher revenues for the investor. In general, the higher the value for α, the higher the incentive for a fair sports event. If $\alpha = p$, the investor deciding on an intervention gains the smaller revenues in T = 1, which becomes relevant if the fans assume an agreement. Finally, this leads to an abstention from any intervention!

A detailed analysis leads to the following results: The difference between high revenues, in the case of the consumers' assumption of 'integrity', and low revenues, in the case of assumed match-fixing, shows the potential for spectators' sanctions. The higher the potential for consumers' sanctions, the higher the probability that a given α is above the critical value and thus, the investor abstains from influencing the outcome of the match.

Managerial effects

The outlined model shows that there are incentives for a profit-maximising invest-or to arrange the outcome of a match between two dominated teams under specific conditions (final match at the end of a season, league table effects). Con-sidering the fact that a real agreement normally increases the probability that this agreement is assumed by the consumers, too, the situation differs: The consumers' option to sanction single clubs or the complete league in the follow-up season can especially influence the investor's decision dominating at least two clubs. Heermann's (2007) general conclusion that there is always a threat to the integrity of professional sports if an investor owns more than a single team participating in a tournament is not supported by the results of this model.

Turning to the players, we must raise the question of how they are facing an investor's possible interventions. Especially for older players, match-fixing could be an incentivising alternative to an integer event. In addition to the owners and the athletes, the consumers are the most important stakeholders. Our model accepts explicitly that integrity is important for the consumer's individual utility. In reality, however, we have realised for decades that with events in professional wrestling, for instance, integrity does not seem to play an important role for the spectators of these contests. It is widely known that the outcomes of single fights are arranged by the federation. In some other sports, we have to accept that integrity does not seem to be as important as the victory of the supported team. The possible acceptance of fixed matches has to be assumed as quite high in those cases.

Conclusion

The current chapter examined the widespread occurrence of match-fixing and manipulation in professional sports, differentiating and describing several varieties of match-fixing. Whereas betting-related match-fixing has become an important topic in sports media coverage, the potential problems resulting from investors with ownership stakes in multiple clubs are widely disregarded by journalists as well as fans. The economic impact of match-fixing scandals varies from country to country. For example, the Hoyzer scandal in Germany had a minimal effect on the public's interest in football and fans' willingness to pay to watch the matches. Conversely, professional football leagues have collapsed due to match-fixing in Singapore, Malaysia, and Vietnam (Hill, 2010). Therefore, it is difficult to accurately assess the overall negative effects of match-fixing and manipulation because they vary across different countries and different sports. Consequently, general steps toward the fight against manipulation would likely be ineffective; instead, with each action taken, the specific and marginal costs and benefits on the individual market must be considered.

Note

1   *Match-fixing* was defined as the request to single or multiple players to act in an unsporting way. Moreover, the request had to be connected with individual benefits, including – but not limited to – money.

References

Bozkurt, E. (2012, September 17). *Match fixing and fraud in sport: Putting the pieces together.* Retrieved from the European Parliament website: www.europarl.europa.eu/document/activities/cont/201209/20120925ATT52303/20120925ATT52303EN.pdf

Carpenter, K. (2012). Match-fixing – the biggest threat to sport in the 21st century? *International Sports Law Review, 2,* 13–24. Retrieved from http://iasl.org/pages/en/sports_law_iasl_journals.php

Carpenter, K. (2014). Match-fixing: Framing the fight-back. *International Centre for Sports Security Journal, 2*(4), 62–69. Retrieved from http://icss-journal.newsdeskmedia.com/home

Caruso, R. (2007, May). *The economics of match-fixing* (MPRA Paper No. 3085). Retrieved from Munich Personal RePEc Archive website: https://mpra.ub.uni-muenchen.de/3085/1/MPRA_paper_3085.pdf

Heermann, P. W. (2007). Mehrheitsbeteiligung an einer deutschen Fußballkapitalgesellschaft im Lichte der sog. '50%+1-Klausel' [Majority stake in a German football corporation in light of the so-called '50%+1 Rule']. *Causa Sport, 4,* 426–436. Retrieved from www.causasport.ch/cas/show?id=00_CaS-2015-3_STARTSEITE

Hill, D. (2010). A critical mass of corruption: why some football leagues have more match-fixing than others. *International Journal of Sports Marketing and Sponsorship, 11*(3), 221–235. Retrieved from www.imrpublications.com/journal-landing.aspx?volno=L&no=L

International Centre for Sport Security. (2014, May). *Guiding principles for protecting the integrity of sports competitions.* Paris: Sorbonne-ICSS Research Program on Ethics and Sports Integrity.

Manoli, E.A. and Antonopoulos, G.A. (2015). 'The only game in town?': Football match-fixing in Greece. *Trends in Organized Crime, 18,* 196–211. doi:10.1007/s12117-014-9239-3

McNamee, M. (2013). The integrity of sport: Unregulated gambling, match fixing and corruption. *Sport, Ethics and Philosophy, 7,* 173–174. doi:10.1080/17511321.2013.791159

Müller, C. (2003). Wettbewerbsintegrität als oberziel des lizenzierungsverfahrens der deutschen fußball liga GmbH [Competitive integrity as overall objective of the licensing procedure of the German football league GmbH]. In K. Zieschang and C. Klimmer (eds) *Unternehmensführung im profifußball: Symbiose von sport, wirtschaft und recht* [Corporate management in professional football: Symbiosis of sport, business and law] (pp. 19–44). Berlin: Erich Schmidt Verlag GmbH and Co.

Pitsch, W., Emrich, E. and Pierdzioch, C. (2012). *Fixing im deutschen fußball: Eine empirische analyse mittels der randomized-response-technik* [Fixing in German football: An empirical analysis using a randomized-response technique] (Working Paper 120/2012). Hamburg: Helmut Schmidt University.

Pitsch, W., Emrich, E. and Pierdzioch, C. (2015). Match fixing im deutschen fußball [Match fixing in German football]. In E. Emrich, C. Pierdzioch and W. Pitsch (eds) *Falsches spiel im sport: Analysen zu wettbewerbsverzerrungen* [False play in sport: Analysis of distortions of competition] (pp. 157–171). Saarbrücken: Saarland University Press.

Rottenberg, S. (1956). The baseball players' labor market. *Journal of Political Economy, 64,* 242–258. Retrieved from www.journals.uchicago.edu/toc/jpe/current

Shepotylo, O. (2005, November 8). *Three-point-for-win in soccer: Are there incentives for match-fixing?* doi:10.2139/ssrn.755264

Singh, P. P. (2013, February 19). How does illegal sports betting work and what are the fears? *BBC Business News.* Retrieved from www.bbc.com/news/business

Zukunft der 50+1-Regel offen [Future of the 50+1-Rule under discussion]. (2008, May 3). *Kicker.* Retrieved from www.kicker.de/news/fussball/bundesliga/startseite/artikel/375897

Further reading

Anderson, P. M., Blackshaw, I. S., Siekmann, R. C. R. and Soek, J. (eds). (2012). *Sports betting: law and policy.* New York: Springer.

Brooks, G., Aleem, A. and Button, M. (2013). *Fraud, corruption and sport.* London: Palgrave Macmillan.

Haberfeld, M. R. and Sheehan, D. (eds). (2013). *Match-fixing in international sports: Existing processes, law enforcement, and prevention strategies.* New York: Springer.

6

DOPING CONTROL AND GLOBAL SPORT

Jules R. Woolf

Consider the following proposal: You could become the CEO of your favourite sports team for only five years, but then you will die. You can have your dream job for five years, but then your life will end. Are you interested?

This scenario is analogous to a proposal offered to elite athletes in 1982. Dr. Bob Goldman asked 198 world-class athletes if they would take a magic drug that would guarantee a victory in every competition they entered for the next five years. However, the drug would also kill them upon the conclusion of the five-year period. Over half of the athletes (52 per cent) were reported to have agreed to the proposal (Goldman, Klatz and Bush, 1984). Goldman reportedly repeated this survey every two years until the mid-1990s and always received similar responses (Bamberger and Yaeger, 1997). This scenario, and the results, became popularly known as the Goldman dilemma. So, why does this matter?

The results of the Goldman dilemma are generally taken as fact and perpetuate a narrative that athletes are willing to do absolutely anything for sporting glory – even sacrifice their own life. Indeed, a colleague of Goldman, Dr. Gabe Mirkin, reported that over 50 per cent of elite runners indicated that they would take a pill if it guaranteed they would become an Olympic champion, even if it caused their death within 1 year (Goldman *et al.*, 1984). The belief that athletes will trade death for short-term glory has often been repeated in academic literature (Ehrnborg and Rosen, 2009) and the popular press (Alderson, 2014; Fell, 2014). Some researchers have also found that the general public also perceives a drug problem in professional sport (Becker and Scheufele, 2008). Additionally, the results of the Goldman and Mirkin surveys imply that drug use among athletes is rampant. If 50 per cent of athletes were willing to die for Olympic success, then it would be reasonable to speculate that many more would use drugs if the consequences were not fatal. Furthermore, if winning is so attractive and drug use so prevalent, then sport managers may have to take drastic action in order to prevent drug use amongst athletes and ensure a level playing field.

A significant limitation of the Goldman dilemma was that the survey and methods utilised were not part of a rigorously performed research study. In fact, Goldman et al. (1984) reported only minimal information about the study design and methods used to conduct the survey and then analyse the data. In an effort to replicate the results of Goldman's survey using a more meticulous research design, Connor, Woolf, and Mazanov (2013) conducted a survey and found that only 0.93 per cent of contemporary elite athletes who participated agreed to accept a proposal similar to Goldman's original proposal. Additionally, approximately 6 per cent of respondents agreed to accept the proposal if the drug was legal but they would still die in five years' time, and 12 per cent of respondents would take an illegal drug if there were no consequences (i.e., they would not die or get caught). Although these numbers are still quite high, especially if you extrapolate these percentages to the world population of athletes, they are nowhere near as high as the numbers reported by Goldman. However, the results of the study conducted by Connor et al. do suggest that some athletes are willing to use drugs even if they harm their health. Furthermore, there have been periodic reports of professional athletes who have been caught using a banned substance, which confirm that some athletes do use illegal drugs to improve their performance. As such, sport managers are faced with the challenge of how to manage drug use amongst athletes.

The use of illicit or illegal drugs, also known as *doping*, is one method utilised by athletes to enhance their performance. The current chapter will examine issues related to doping, as well as anti-doping efforts. The first section will explore the meaning and complexities of doping. The following section will analyse the prevalence rate of doping. Then, the strategies and tactics used to prevent doping will be discussed, which will include an in-depth description of the structure, policies, procedures and activities of the leading anti-doping organisation, the World Anti-Doping Agency (WADA). The chapter will conclude with a short statement on how anti-doping policies are justified in sport.

The current chapter will enable readers to define doping, describe the prevalence of doping in sport, and critique media reports and popular stories of doping. Readers should also be able to summarise the governance structure of WADA and describe its role and activities in the global management of anti-doping efforts. Finally, readers should be able to discuss the primary reasons that have made doping into a contemporary sport management issue.

Doping

In general, most people think of steroids or performance-enhancing drugs when they hear reports of illegal or banned performance enhancement in sport. However, the issue is much more convoluted. The term *drug* is defined as 'chemical substances that, by interaction with biological targets, can alter the biochemical systems of the body' (Mottram, 2011, p. 3), which does not encapsulate all the different ways in which an athlete's performance may be artificially enhanced. For example, blood doping is a procedure whereby an athlete removes their own blood, and then stores it so that it can later be transfused back into their body. In a slightly different procedure that is still considered blood doping, an athlete will transfuse someone else's blood into their body, provided they have the same blood type. These methods are not drugs, but they have been shown to reliably improve athletic performance. Hence, the preferred term is *doping* as it includes not just drugs, but other material or means to enhance an athlete's performance outside the rules.

The word doping is derived from *dop*, the name of an alcoholic beverage used in South Africa to improve physical performance (Mottram, 2011). Alcohol consumption provides a feeling of well-being and can alleviate the sensation of fatigue. Stimulants, such as caffeine, strychnine (which is poisonous), and cocaine, have also been used to improve physical performance. For example, marathon runner Thomas Hicks was reported to have used brandy and strychnine in the 1904 Olympic Games. At the time, Hicks did not violate any rules since these types of stimulants were not banned from international athletics until 1928 (Dimeo, 2007). Thus, the list of prohibited substances and methods changes over time. For instance, the use of caffeine was prohibited until it was removed from the list of banned substances in 2004. However, it still remains on WADA's monitoring list to track trends in use and potential abuse. Sport managers therefore need to remain aware of the evolving definition of a doping offence.

Another issue that sport managers should consider is the complexity of doping in sports. A machine is a common metaphor used to describe the human body and understand its functions. However, the human body is an intricate organism and, as such, the use of substances to improve performance may not follow a simple input–output pathway. Popular phrases, such as, 'you are what you eat', may have some merit but are gross simplifications. For instance, the idea that athletes who take an increased amount of a substance will experience a linear effect on their performance (e.g., double the dosage will double the effect) may not necessarily be true. In contrast, the negative side effects associated with drugs may manifest or become more pronounced with extremely high doses (Mottram, 2011). Moreover, people may have different responses to drugs, and drugs taken in combination may interact and produce different effects. Consequently, sport managers should consult reliable sources for information when making decisions about doping rather than rely on common knowledge or intuition.

Although the negative side effects of drug use have been well documented, there have also been many instances of incorrect information accepted as truth, a lack of rigorous fact checking, and general hyperbole surrounding the dangers of doping substances. For example, the story of the death of Danish cyclist Knud Enemark Jensen during the 1960 Olympic Games in Rome is often cited as a cautionary tale about the risks of doping in sport. Although Jensen was reported to have died due to amphetamine use, an investigation into the circumstances of his death concluded that extreme heat and then a lack of medical attention were the most likely causes of his death (Møller, 2005). Moreover, Jensen used Roniacol, which is a vascular dilator and would likely inhibit his physical performance because it increases blood flow to both working and non-working muscles. Consequently, the Roniacol would have reduced Jensen's blood pressure, which was potentially exacerbated by extreme heat and suspected dehydration as Jensen fainted and fell while riding his bicycle. Møller (2005) argued that had Jensen taken amphetamines, they would have counteracted the effects of the Roniacol by restricting blood flow to the skin, which would have potentially improved his blood pressure and performance. Although Møller's explanation is problematic since it does not account for the heat stress that Jensen suffered, the investigation is important because it challenges the existing narrative that doping was the primary cause of his death. Furthermore, the official autopsy report attributed the primary cause of death to heatstroke and did not implicate amphetamines or any other drugs. Therefore, any stories or reports that state otherwise and attribute Jensen's death to doping are not based on the official autopsy report, and are likely to have originated from people who never had access to the actual medical records.

Similar to the Goldman dilemma, inaccurate stories, such as Jensen's death being caused by doping, become regarded as true when they are not thoroughly investigated, which in turn falsely makes them part of the narrative used to inform or justify anti-doping policy. In another investigation of doping-related deaths, López (2011) found no evidence to support the claim that erythropoietin (EPO) killed 18 Dutch and Belgian cyclists in the late 1980s and early 1990s. Nevertheless, this is another story that is often used to illustrate the dangers of drugs in sport. Moreover, López (2013) analysed the research literature and media coverage of human growth hormone (HGH) and similarly found little empirical evidence to support the claim that HGH is a highly dangerous (i.e., death inducing) drug.

Despite the results of the investigations conducted by Møller (2005) and López (2011, 2013), it would be incorrect to state that drugs and other doping methods are safe and should therefore be legalised. All drugs have negative side effects (Mottram, 2011). For example, EPO has been reported to cause nausea, joint pain, hypertension and thrombosis (Birzniece, 2015). HGH has been reported to cause fluid retention, muscular fatigue and pain, cardiomyopathy and increased risk of diabetes mellitus (Birzniece, 2015; Saugy et al., 2006). Moreover, medical research on health or performance-enhancing substances is generally restricted to the general public and is conducted in clinical settings. Additionally, medical research trials are often short in duration and involve lower dosages than those used by athletes.

Given the complexities of doping, sport managers have a duty to be adequately informed of the empirically supported evidence about doping-related issues, and should avoid hyperbole in order to remain credible to both athletes and fans. In light of this statement, the next section will examine the reasons for doping amongst athletes.

Doping amongst athletes

Researchers have shown significant interest in understanding the various factors involved in an athlete's decision to engage in doping that go beyond simple explanations such as the desire to win. Donovan, Egger, Kapernick, and Mendoza (2002) hypothesised that while athletes are making a decision about doping, they often consider the threat (i.e., potential for harm and detection), the benefits (i.e., performance enhancement), and their own personal morality. Other factors that have been shown to be involved in the athletes' decision-making process include the athlete's personality, influences from the athlete's reference group (e.g., senior athletes), and the availability and affordability of performance-enhancing drugs. Some scholars have suggested that personal values and emotions play a more dominant role than other personal or social factors (Moston, Engelberg and Skinner, 2015; Strelan and Boekmann, 2006). Doping has also been examined from a sociological perspective. For example, Stewart and Smith (2008) contextualised doping relative to society, which led them to identify nationalism, commercialism, and the sport culture (e.g., hyper-masculinity) as influential factors. Athletes may become socialised to the norms and rules of a specific sport culture that does not perceive doping as cheating, but instead as a necessary function of the job (Brissonneau and Ohl, 2010). In contrast, being surrounded by a majority of teammates who have negative views about doping may promote similar attitudes in other members of the team (Ohl, Fincoeur, Lentillon-Kaestner, Defrance and Brissonneau, 2013).

Clearly, doping is not a straightforward, black-and-white decision and may not occur in isolation. Even when an athlete decides to dope, it may not be an easy decision (Kirby, Moran and Guerin, 2011). Career stage, performance deterioration, and injury serve as critical periods for athletes to consider doping (Bloodworth and McNamee, 2010; Lentillon-Kaestner and Carstairs, 2010; Mazanov, Huybers and Connor, 2011; Petróczi and Aidman, 2008). Sport managers should be aware of these vulnerable time periods as they are windows of opportunity to provide needed support. There has also been increased awareness of the influence that an entourage (e.g., support staff, family and friends) may have on the athlete's decisions and actions (Mazanov and McDermott, 2009). For example, WADA's education outreach efforts incorporate group and social influences, and its anti-doping policies and procedures are also applicable to the members of an athlete's entourage (see Table 6.1).

Suspected prevalence

It is challenging to accurately gauge the prevalence of doping in sport. Athletes are unlikely to willingly divulge their proclivity to partake in illegal drug consumption. Strategies, such as athlete surveys, will in all likelihood be biased as the results from prior research studies indicate that survey respondents exhibit a tendency to provide socially acceptable answers (James, Nepusz, Naughton and Petróczi, 2013).

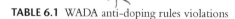

TABLE 6.1 WADA anti-doping rules violations

Violations
1   Presence of a prohibited substance or its metabolites or markers in an athlete's sample
2   Use or attempted use by an athlete of a prohibited substance or a prohibited method
3   Evading, refusing or failing to submit to sample collection
4   Whereabouts failures: Three missed tests and/or filing failures within 12-month period
5   Tampering or attempted tampering with any part of doping control – includes attempted intimidation of potential witnesses to ADRV
6   Possession of a prohibited substance or a prohibited method
7   Trafficking or attempted trafficking in any prohibited substance or prohibited method
8   Administration/attempted administration to any athlete (in or out of competition) of any prohibited substance or prohibited method
9   Complicity: assisting, encouraging, aiding, abetting, conspiracy to cover up or be complicit in any ADRV
10   Prohibited association – with any athlete or athlete support person who is ineligible to compete, or has been convicted of an offence that would constitute an ADRV

Note: ADRV = anti-doping rules violation.

Despite these difficulties, some researchers have collected data that could provide insights into the prevalence of doping behaviour.

For several decades, researchers have been surveying adolescent athletes and non-athletes about their use of drugs such as tobacco, cocaine, and anabolic androgenic steroids. In the United States, the Monitoring the Future (MTF) study and the Youth Risk Behavioral Surveillance programme have surveyed steroid consumption since 1989 and 1991, respectively. Results from the MTF study indicated that lifetime prevalence rates (i.e., ever used) in 2014 of steroid use for individuals aged 17 to 18 years was 1.9 per cent and the rate for individuals aged 19 to 28 years was 1.7 per cent (Miech, Johnston, O'Malley, Bachman and Schulenberg, 2015). The results of the MTF study also found that lifetime prevalence rates had steadily declined since 2002 (Miech *et al.*, 2015). In contrast, the percentage of students who considered steroids to be very harmful decreased: Just over 50 per cent of respondents reported that they believed steroids were very harmful (Miech *et al.*, 2015). The results of the Youth Risk Behavioral Surveillance studies were generally the same as the MTF study and demonstrated a steady decline of overall steroid use amongst adolescents, as well as greater lifetime prevalence in 2013 (3.2 per cent; Kann *et al.*, 2014). The European School Survey Project on Alcohol and Other Drugs conducted a similar series of studies in school-aged children from 36 European countries and reported a 1 per cent lifetime prevalence rate for steroid use amongst students aged 16 years (Hibell *et al.*, 2012). The issue of adolescent steroid use is a concern for policymakers because of the common belief that they may be influenced by steroid use amongst professional athletes (Woolf and Swain, 2014), despite evidence to the contrary (Woolf, Rimal and Sripad, 2014). Doping has also been recognised as a public health issue. For example, anti-doping efforts in Denmark have been extended to recreational gym users (Christiansen, 2009), and government officials in France recently followed suit by creating a 'charter of commitment' that targets fitness club chains (WADA, 2015c).

While there are genuine concerns about steroid use amongst adolescents and the general public, the media often focuses on the abuse of steroids by elite athletes. Periodically, athletes and sport commentators speculate on the prevalence of drug use in sport and often make estimates that are significantly higher than the actual rate. In 1986, former NFL player and member of the NFL Hall of Fame, Howie Long, stated that 75 per cent of offensive lineman, the largest athletes on the field, used steroids (Zimmerman, 1986). Recently, the Ultimate Fighting Championship (UFC) commentator, Joe Rogan, provided similar statistics about steroid use amongst mixed martial arts athletes (Rogan, 2015). However, athletes have also exhibited a tendency to estimate the prevalence of steroid use as higher for individuals who belong to groups that are dissimilar to their own group (e.g., athletes on other teams) than for individuals belonging to similar groups (Woolf et al., 2014). Furthermore, an athlete's own behaviour has been shown to influence his or her estimation on the prevalence of steroid use in sport (Petróczi, Mazanov, Nepusz, Backhouse and Naughton, 2008). This information does not suggest that Long or Rogan engaged in doping, but rather illustrates the frequent inaccuracy of speculation about the identity and number of athletes who do engage in doping.

A more concrete approach to determine the frequency of doping amongst professional athletes is to examine the prevalence of positive doping tests. From 1987 to 2013, WADA laboratories reported that adverse analytical findings (AAF) occurred in athlete doping tests at a rate of approximately 2 per cent (WADA, 2015b). It should be noted that an AAF does not automatically result in the athlete being sanctioned or suspended, as additional analyses are required to determine if it meets the anti-doping results violation (ADRV) criteria (see Table 6.1 for a list of ADRVs). WADA (2015b) reported that 2,540 AAFs occurred out of 207,513 samples; of these, 1,687 were confirmed as analytical ADRVs (i.e., positive tests) and the athlete was sanctioned. There were an additional 266 non-analytical ADRVs (e.g., athletes who refused to be tested). This indicates a prevalence rate of 0.81 per cent, which suggests a very low prevalence rate for doping offences (WADA, 2015b). Furthermore, the WADA testing results suggest that professional athletes and sports are relatively doping-free. In contrast, the results may also point to systemic failures to catch dopers, which resulted in an artificially low number of positive tests.

A recent review on the incidence of doping in international sport revealed a prevalence rate between 14 and 39 per cent for elite athletes (de Hon, Kuipers and van Bottenburg, 2015). De Hon et al. (2015) computed this range based on the results of a study that examined the prevalence of blood doping amongst elite track and field athletes (Sottas et al., 2011) and an anonymous survey of amateur and professional athletes in Germany who completed a sports doping questionnaire using a randomised response technique (RRT) design (Pitsch, Emrich and Klein, 2007). The RRT design used by Pitsch *et al.* (2007) created anonymity by de-identifying respondents' answers and then applying a mathematical formula to estimate the likelihood of a positive response to questions on sports doping. The RRT design has generally been found to provide a more valid estimate of self-reported doping behaviour compared to standard questionnaire formats (Striegel, Ulrich and Simon, 2010).

In summary, exceptionally high estimates made by athletes and sport commentators/journalists likely overestimate the prevalence of doping, while non-RRT questionnaire data and laboratory ADRV rates likely underestimate the prevalence since not every athlete who engages in doping will be caught or admit to it. As such, the results of the review conducted by de Hon *et al.* (2015) arguably provide a more accurate estimate of the true prevalence rate of doping in elite sport. The probability that 1 out of 5, or perhaps 2 out of 5 elite athletes engage in doping is a startling statistic and should be unsettling for those who favour doping-free sports. At this juncture, it is therefore appropriate to review the policies, procedures, and activities of the worldwide chief anti-doping organisation, WADA.

World anti-doping agency

WADA was formed in November 1999 as an independent international agency tasked with combating doping in sport. The independent status of WADA is a significant aspect of the organisation to mitigate potential conflicts of interest. Since the interests of sport organisations, such as the International Olympic Committee (IOC) and national and international sport federations, would be best served by minimising the number of doping scandals, these organisations have a compelling incentive to tamper with testing procedures and results to ensure ADRVs are not detected amongst their athletes. Therefore, the establishment of WADA as an independent agency circumvents the potential for anti-doping efforts to become only a façade. Kirkwood (2004) went further and argued that the creation of WADA was a strategy to protect the commercial aspects and brand of the IOC, and that anti-doping efforts have occurred primarily because doping is bad for business. To maintain its independence, WADA is funded by equal contributions made by the IOC and the governments of countries representing the five Olympic regions: Africa, the Americas, Asia, Europe and Oceania.

The creation of a single agency to coordinate and promote anti-doping efforts was an important milestone. The lack of consistent policies in different sport organisations provided opportunities to challenge the legitimacy of doping sanctions (WADA, 2015a). Consequently, a major initiative for WADA was to establish polices that promoted coordinated anti-doping efforts, a priority that is readily apparent in the agency's mission statement, 'to lead a collaborative world-wide movement for doping-free sport' (WADA, n.d.-b). To facilitate the coordination of anti-doping efforts, WADA created the *World Anti-Doping Code*, also known simply as *The Code*. WADA periodically revises *The Code*, and published the fifth and most recent version of in 2015. *The Code* is a comprehensive document that sets anti-doping policies, rules, and regulations. For example, *The Code* stipulates that an athlete who commits an ADRV is ineligible to compete for the next four years. All sport organisations that sign *The Code* have agreed to its policies. *The Code* also includes information on testing at events and rights for athletes to appeal against the results.

A common misperception of WADA is that it is directly involved in administering drug tests, when in fact it is primarily involved in setting policies, rules, and regulations. In order to establish and implement globally coordinated anti-doping policy and procedures, WADA performs several critical functions, such as oversight of the accreditation process for drug-testing laboratories, maintenance of standards used for testing samples, and conducting investigations and annual dissemination of the list of all prohibited substances and methods, both in and out of competition. These functions comprise three of the five international standards that WADA uses to coordinate technical areas related to its anti-doping efforts. The remaining standards used by WADA are the issuance of exemptions for the therapeutic use of a banned substance and ensuring the protection of athletes' privacy and personal information (see Table 6.2).

WADA has been generally successful in the global coordination of its anti-doping efforts. The area that remains as a major challenge is the realm of professional sport. Even professional sports that are associated with international sport federations and the IOC have come under criticism for their apparent lax enforcement of doping policies. For instance, WADA has called upon the Premier League in England to increase the number of times each player is tested, to include EPO testing and to use biological passports (Gibson, 2013). However, WADA does work with several professional sport leagues, such as the NFL, NHL, MLB, and NBA, to encourage consistent doping policies in line with *The Code*. A challenge that anti-doping agencies face when addressing professional sport leagues is that athletes form labour unions to represent their interests and to negotiate collective bargaining agreements with league management regarding working conditions, such as minimum salaries, free agency, and health benefits. The labour laws in many countries also typically require that drug-testing policies be negotiated by players'

TABLE 6.2 WADA international standards

Standards
1   Prohibited list
2   Testing and investigations
3   Laboratories
4   Therapeutic use exemptions
5   Protection of privacy and personal information

unions. Consequently, sport leagues are not legally allowed to unilaterally impose doping policies onto athletes without the consent of the players' union.

Recent negotiations between the NFL and the NFL Players Association regarding blood tests for HGH provide an example that demonstrates the negotiation process between a professional sport league and a players' union. Although the NFL Players Association agreed to include blood tests for HGH as part of the standard drug-testing procedures, they also negotiated an increase to the threshold of a positive test for marijuana and reclassified the terms and subsequent sanctions for amphetamine use in the offseason (Rosenthal, 2014). While it may seem that the players' union and the league have a shared interest in promoting a doping-free work environment, the union has a responsibility to represent its members. Even if both the league and union want the same outcome, a savvy union will use the negotiations as leverage to obtain something in return such as changes to other aspects of the NFL doping policy. Moreover, the union must protect its members' interests and ensure the players are treated fairly. Therefore, all doping policies must include safeguards that protect the athletes such as the right to due process, the right to appeal, and guidelines for how and when the public will be notified of a positive test. WADA takes into consideration the rights and interests of athletes by including an athlete's committee as part of its governance structure.

The governance structure of WADA

The governance structure of WADA is uniquely comprised of representatives from the Olympic movement and governments of the five Olympic regions. The inclusion of government representatives is important because governments can implement anti-doping initiatives in their respective countries that are beyond the scope of sport organisations, such as passing laws that impact the manufacturing and trafficking of drugs used in sports doping.

WADA has three levels of governance: (a) the foundation board, (b) the executive committee, and (c) several committees with various functions. The foundation board is the ultimate decision-making authority for WADA and is comprised of 38 members. The members from the Olympic movement come from a variety of sport-governing organisations (e.g., IOC, International Paralympic Committee, SportAccord), along with current athletes who serve on the IOC Athletes' Commission. The inclusion of athletes and representatives from different segments of the Olympic and non-Olympic sports world provides a diverse governing board. The government representatives on the foundation board consist of officials who are typically the sport minister for their home country. In many countries, the government office of the sport minister also represents different configurations of other related interests and/or groups such as youth, recreation, tourism, culture and education. The United States is amongst the few countries that does not have a government official responsible for sport promotion and is currently represented on the foundation board by an executive from the White House Drug Policy Office. The presidency of WADA alternates between representatives from the Olympic movement and the governments. Currently, the president is former British Olympic Association chairman, Sir Craig Reedie. Reedie's predecessor was John Fahey, a former Premier of New South Wales. The inaugural president was former Olympian and IOC member Dick Pound, who held the post for eight years.

While the foundation board serves as the main decision-making entity for WADA, the 12-member executive committee is responsible for the organisation's policies, execution, and organisational administration. Similar to the foundation board, the executive committee has equal representation from the Olympic movement and governments of the five Olympic regions.

Finally, there are several committees with specialised functions related to various administrative operations, such as the Finance and Administration committees, as well as committees dedicated to carrying out the overall mission of WADA, such as the Education Committee. Efforts to promote education and increase public awareness are hallmarks of the WADA anti-doping strategy. In particular, WADA has focused on developing a values-based education that frames doping as a moral issue. Additionally, WADA utilises two other primary anti-doping strategies: the Whereabouts programme and Athlete Biological Passport (ABP) programme.

The WADA Whereabouts programme

One challenge with testing athletes out of competition is locating them without giving prior notice of testing dates. The Whereabouts programme addresses this issue with the creation of the Registered Testing Pool (RTP), a select group of national and international athletes who are required to provide the time(s) and location(s) of their out-of-competition training activities, as well as other scheduled routine activities, such as familial or educational activities (WADA, n.d.-a). Athletes who are part of the RTP must also provide a 60-minute time period for each day during which they can be located and tested. While this may seem to be a cumbersome process and an invasion of the athletes' privacy, the use of online tools and mobile phone applications have made it easier for athletes to update representatives from their respective anti-doping agency. Although the out-of-competition testing is not limited to RTP athletes, the Whereabouts programme is designed to facilitate the testing of elite athletes out of competition.

The WADA athlete biological passport programme

Rather than relying on the detection of a banned substance or method to determine the occurrence of an ADRV, the ABP programme monitors select doping biomarkers to detect manipulation of an athlete's physiological variables (WADA, 2014). For example, a urine test for testosterone measures and compares the levels of testosterone and epitestosterone in an athlete's urine. The normal ratio of testosterone to epitestosterone is approximately 1:1, and an elevated ratio of 4:1 is indicative of an ADRV based on current testing standards. However, some individuals may naturally have a higher testosterone/epitestosterone ratio, which requires a longitudinal and comparative analysis to provide sufficient evidence of doping (Mottram, 2011). A consistently elevated ratio over time for these individuals may indicate that doping has not occurred, whereas a change in their ratio may indicate a doping violation (Mottram, 2011). The ABP programme has proven effective in real-life testing situations as a case was recently reported in which an ADRV would have been undetected without the use of ABP techniques (WADA, 2015c). In addition to urine samples, the ABP programme has also developed the capacity to examine blood for biomarkers of EPO use and other blood-doping methods (WADA, 2014).

Anti-doping rationale

A simple statement on the rationale for anti-doping regulations would be that doping substances and methods are prohibited because they constitute cheating or a violation of the rules. However, a sound rationale must be provided to justify the exclusion of specific substances and methods from a given sport. In order to be prohibited by WADA, a substance or method must meet at least two of the following three criteria: (a) the substance or method has to verifiably (i.e., supported scientifically) enhance performance, (b) the substance or method represents an actual or potential health risk and (c) the substance or method must violate the 'spirit of sport'. Although the last criterion can be considered as relatively subjective, WADA has outlined 11 criteria that constitute the spirit of sport (see Table 6.3). Furthermore, WADA (2015a) described the spirit of sport construct as the essence of *Olympism*, a philosophy of life based on the fundamental principles stated in the Olympic Charter, and as an ideal that invokes a celebration of the human spirit, body and mind.

TABLE 6.3 WADA spirit of sport criteria

Criteria
1 Ethics, fair play and honesty
2 Health
3 Excellence in performance
4 Character and education
5 Fun and joy
6 Teamwork
7 Dedication and commitment
8 Respect for rules and laws
9 Respect for self and other participants
10 Courage
11 Community and solidarity

WADA does not enjoy universal support and some scholars have questioned the legitimacy of the agency's mission (Strelan and Boekmann, 2006). Alternative policies, such as harm reduction, have been proposed (Kirkwood, 2009) wherein athletes are allowed to dope and compete provided they satisfy certain health markers (e.g., acceptable haematocrit range). The harm-reduction approach presents an alternative to the libertarian perspective that all drugs should be legalised and the decision to engage in doping is the exclusive responsibility and individual choice of each athlete. Despite the potential benefits, harm-reduction programmes are not a panacea for doping in sport, but sport managers should be aware of the strengths and weaknesses of alternative viewpoints.

Conclusion and future outlook

Doping in sport is a complicated area that is often reduced to simplistic arguments and unsubstantiated facts. Enacting anti-doping policy is likewise complicated. For example, the U.S. Anti-Doping Agency recently formed a relationship with the UFC to regulate doping in mixed martial arts. One issue that arose was the use of intravenous (IV) bags to rehydrate athletes after weighing in for a fight. The use of IV bags is traditionally considered an ADRV because they can easily mask various methods of blood doping. However, the use of IV bags in the UFC case appears to be legitimate. While rehydration will improve an athlete's performance, the primary effect and benefit is to maintain healthy body function rather than harm it. Therefore, the use of IV bags by the UFC is not against the spirit of sport. This scenario illustrates the inherent difficulties of implementing a globally coordinated anti-doping policy, since the application of it will necessarily vary depending on the unique environment and aspects of each sport.

In light of these difficulties, Sir Craig Reedie (WADA, 2015d) has proposed that drug testing must target and match specific procedures appropriate for each sport. Such efforts would make testing more efficient, and potentially more effective. Furthermore, cost-effective methods are necessary as doping has become a business enterprise that is largely managed by criminal organisations (Donati, 2007). WADA is aware of the involvement of criminal organisations and collaborates with the International Criminal Police Organisation to combat their role in illegal doping. Finally, with scientific advancements such as clustered regularly interspaced short palindromic repeats on the rise, athletes may soon be able to manipulate their own genetics through gene doping techniques.

Doping in sport is a complicated, ongoing, and ever-evolving issue. Sport managers should be well versed on the intricacy and details involved with this subject.

References

Alderson, A. (2014, February 8). Gene doping looms as the next big cheat. *The New Zealand Herald*. Retrieved from www.nzherald.co.nz

Bamberger, M. and Yaeger, D. (1997, April 14). Over the edge aware that drug testing is a sham, athletes to rely more than ever on banned performance enhancers. *Sports Illustrated, 86*(15), 60–70.

Becker, A. B. and Scheufele, D. A. (2008). Public perceptions of steroid use in sport: Contextualizing communication efforts. *International Journal of Sport Communication, 1,* 444–457. Retrieved from http://journals.humankinetics.com/ijsc

Birzniece, V. (2015). Doping in sport: Effects, harm and misconceptions. *Internal Medicine Journal, 45,* 239–248. doi:10.1111/imj.12629

Bloodworth, A. and McNamee, M. (2010). Clean Olympians? Doping and anti-doping: The views of talented young British athletes. *International Journal of Drug Policy, 21,* 276–282. doi:10.1016/j.drugpo.2009.11.009

Brissonneau, C. and Ohl, F. (2010). The genesis and effect of French anti-doping policies in cycling. *International Journal of Sport Policy and Politics, 2,* 173–187. doi:10.1080/19406940.2010.488063

Christiansen, A. V. (2009). Doping in fitness and strength training environments – politics, motives and masculinity. In V. Møller, M. McNamee and P. Dimeo (eds) *Elite sport, doping and public health* (pp. 99–118). Odense: University Press of Southern Denmark.

Connor, J., Woolf, J. and Mazanov, J. (2013). Would they dope? Revisiting the Goldman dilemma. *British Journal of Sports Medicine, 47,* 697–700. doi:10.1136/bjsports-2012-091826

de Hon, O., Kuipers, H. and van Bottenburg, M. (2015). Prevalence of doping in elite sports: A review of numbers and methods. *Sports Medicine, 45,* 57–69. doi:10.1007/s40279-014-0247-x

Dimeo, P. (2007). *A history of drug use in sport 1876–1976. Beyond good and evil.* New York: Routledge.

Donati, A. (2007). *World traffic in doping substances.* Retrieved from World Anti-Doping Agency website: https://wada-main-prod.s3.amazonaws.com/resources/files/WADA_Donati_Report_On_Trafficking_2007.pdf

Donovan, R. J., Egger, G., Kapernick, V. and Mendoza, J. (2002). A conceptual framework for achieving performance enhancing drug compliance in sport. *Sports Medicine, 32,* 269–284. doi:10.2165/00007256-200232040-00005

Ehrnborg, C. and Rosen, T. (2009). The psychology behind doping in sport. *Growth Hormone and IGF Research, 19,* 285–287. doi:10.1016/j.ghir.2009.04.003

Fell, L. (2014, June 3). Doping in sport – a science festival review. *Gloucestershire Echo.* Retrieved from www.gloucestershireecho.co.uk

Gibson, O. (2013, February 12). Wada calls for Premier League to up its game over testing for dopers. *The Guardian.* Retrieved from www.theguardian.com

Goldman, B., Klatz, R. and Bush, P. J. (1984). *Death in the locker room.* South Bend, IN: Icarus Press.

Hibell, B., Guttormsson, U., Ahlström, S., Balakireva, O., Bjarnason, T., Kokkevi, A. and Kraus, L. (2012). *The 2011 ESPAD report: Substance use among students in 36 European countries.* Retrieved from Swedish Council for Information on Alcohol and Other Drugs website: www.can.se/contentassets/8d8cb78bbd28493b9030c65c598e3301/the_2011_espad_report_full.pdf

James, R. A., Nepusz, T., Naughton, D. P. and Petróczi, A. (2013). A potential inflating effect in estimation models: Cautionary evidence from comparing performance enhancing drug and herbal hormonal supplement use estimates. *Psychology of Sport and Exercise, 14,* 84–96. doi:10.1016/j.psychsport.2012.08.003

Kann, L., Kinchen, S., Shanklin, S. L., Flint, K. H., Hawkins, J., Harris, W. A., Zaza, S. (2014). Youth risk behavior surveillance – United States, 2013. *Morbidity and Mortality Weekly Report Surveillance Summaries, 63*(SS-4). Retrieved from www.cdc.gov/mmwr/index.html

Kirby, K., Moran, A. and Guerin, S. (2011). A qualitative analysis of the experiences of elite athletes who have admitted to doping for performance enhancement. *International Journal of Sport Policy and Politics, 3*, 205–224. doi:10.1080/19406940.2011.577081

Kirkwood, K. (2004). Good as gold: Commercial aspects of WADA's development. In K. B. Wamsley, S. G. Martyn and R. K. Barney (eds) *Cultural relations old and new: The transitory Olympic ethos* (pp. 199–212). London, Canada: International Centre for Olympic Studies.

Kirkwood, K. (2009). Considering harm reduction as the future of doping control policy in international sport. *Quest, 61*, 180–190. doi:10.1080/00336297.2009.10483609

Lentillon-Kaestner, V. and Carstairs, C. (2010). Doping use among young elite cyclists: A qualitative psychosociological approach. *Scandinavian Journal of Medicine and Science in Sports, 20*, 336–345. doi:10.1111/j.1600-0838.2009.00885.x

López, B. (2011). The invention of a 'drug of mass destruction': Deconstructing the EPO myth. *Sport in History, 31*, 84–109. doi:10.1080/17460263.2011.555208

López, B. (2013). Creating fear: The social construction of human growth hormone as a dangerous doping drug. *International Review for the Sociology of Sport, 48*, 220–237. doi:10. 1177/1012690211432209

Mazanov, J., Huybers, T. and Connor, J. (2011). Qualitative evidence of a primary intervention point for elite athlete doping. *Journal of Science and Medicine in Sport, 14*, 106–110. doi:10.1016/j.jsams.2010.06.003

Mazanov, J. and McDermott, V. (2009). The case for a social science of drugs in sport. *Sport in Society, 12*, 276–295. doi:10.1080/17430430802673635

Miech, R. A., Johnston, L. D., O'Malley, P. M., Bachman, J. G. and Schulenberg, J. E. (2015). *Monitoring the Future national survey results on drug use, 1975–2014: Volume I, secondary school students* [Monograph]. Retrieved from http://monitoringthefuture.org/pubs/monographs/mtf-vol1_2014.pdf

Møller, V. (2005). Knud Enemark Jensen's death during the 1960 Rome Olympics: A search for truth? *Sport in History, 23*, 452–471. doi:10.1080/17460260500396319

Moston, S., Engelberg, T. and Skinner, J. (2015). Self-fulfilling prophecy and the future of doping. *Psychology of Sport and Exercise, 16*, 201–207. doi:10.1016/j.psychsport.2014.02. 004

Mottram, D. R. (2011). *Drugs in sport* (5th ed.). New York: Routledge.

Ohl, F., Fincoeur, B., Lentillon-Kaestner, V., Defrance, J. and Brissonneau, C. (2013). The socialization of young cyclists and the culture of doping. *International Review for the Sociology of Sport, 50*, 865–882. doi:10.1177/1012690213495534

Petróczi, A. and Aidman, E. (2008). Psychological drivers in doping: The life cycle model of performance enhancement. *Substance Abuse Treatment, Prevention, and Policy, 3*, Article 7. doi:10.1186/1747-597X-3-7

Petróczi, A., Mazanov, J., Nepusz, T., Backhouse, S. H. and Naughton, D. P. (2008). Comfort in big numbers: Does over-estimation of doping prevalence in others indicate self-involvement? *Journal of Occupational Medicine and Toxicology, 3*, Article 19. doi:10.1186/1745-6673-3-19

Pitsch, W., Emrich, E. and Klein, M. (2007). Doping in elite sports in Germany: Results of a www survey. *European Journal for Sport and Society, 4*, 89–102. Retrieved from www.ejss.ch/

Rogan, J. (Producer). (2015, February 10). *The Joe Rogan experience* [Audio podcast]. Retrieved from http://podcasts.joerogan.net/podcasts/

Rosenthal, G. (2014, September 12). NFLPA approved new drug policy; HGH testing included. *Around the NFL*. Retrieved from www.nfl.com/news

Saugy, M., Robinson, N., Saudan, C., Baume, N., Avois, L. and Mangin, P. (2006). Human growth hormone doping in sport. *British Journal of Sports Medicine, 40*(Suppl. 1), i35–i39. doi:10.1136/bjsm.2006.027573

Sottas, P. E., Robinson, N., Fischetto, G., Dollé, G., Alonso, J. M. and Saugy, M. (2011). Prevalence of blood doping in samples collected from elite track and field athletes. *Clinical Chemistry, 57*, 762–769. doi:10.1373/clinchem.2010.156067

Stewart, B. and Smith, A. C. T. (2008). Drug use in sport: Implications for public policy. *Journal of Sport and Social Issues, 32*, 278–298. doi:10.1177/0193723508319716

Strelan, P. and Boekmann, R. J. (2006). Why drug testing in elite sport does not work: Perceptual deterrence theory and the role of personal moral beliefs. *Journal of Applied Social Psychology, 36*, 2909–2934. doi:10.1111/j.0021-9029.2006.00135.x

Striegel, H., Ulrich, R. and Simon, P. (2010) Randomized response estimates for doping and illicit drug use in elite athletes. *Drug and Alcohol Dependence, 106*, 230–232. doi:10.1016/j.drugalcdep.2009.07.026

Woolf, J. and Swain, P. (2014). Androgenic anabolic steroid policy and high school sports: Results from a policy Delphi study. *International Journal of Sport Policy and Politics, 6*, 89–106. doi:10.1080/19406940.2013.767852

Woolf, J., Rimal, R. and Sripad, P. (2014). Understanding the influence of proximal networks on high school athletes' intentions to use androgenic anabolic steroids. *Journal of Sport Management, 28*, 8–20. doi:10.1123/jsm.2013-0046

World Anti-Doping Agency. (n.d.-a). Whereabouts. Retrieved from www.wada-ama.org/en/questions-answers/whereabouts

World Anti-Doping Agency. (n.d.-b). Who we are. Retrieved from www.wada-ama.org/en/who-we-are

World Anti-Doping Agency. (2014). *Athlete biological passport: Operating guidelines and compilation of required elements*. Retrieved from https://wada-main-prod.s3.amazonaws.com/resources/files/wada_abp_operating_guidelines_2014_v5.0_en.pdf

World Anti-Doping Agency. (2015a, January 1). *World anti-doping code 2015*. Retrieved from www.wada-ama.org/en/resources/the-code/world-anti-doping-code

World Anti-Doping Agency. (2015b, May 15). *2013 anti-doping rules violations (ADRVs) report*. Retrieved from https://wada-main-prod.s3.amazonaws.com/wada-2013-adrv-report-en.pdf

World Anti-Doping Agency. (2015c, May 20). *WADA Foundation Board meeting – 16 November 2014, Paris, France* [Meeting minutes]. Retrieved from www.wada-ama.org/en/resources/governance/foundation-board-meeting-minutes

World Anti-Doping Agency [wadamovies]. (2015d, June 25). *WADA talks with Sir Craig Reedie* [Video file]. Retrieved from www.youtube.com/watch?v=9j1eEfX-mxQ

Zimmerman, P. (1986, November 10). The agony must end: As injuries in the NFL continue at an unacceptable rate, a longtime student of pro football tells what has to be done. *Sports Illustrated, 65*(20), 17–21.

Further reading

Albergotti, R. and O'Connell, V. (2014). *Wheelmen: Lance Armstrong, the Tour de France, and the greatest sports conspiracy ever*. New York: Penguin.

Hoberman, J. (2006). *Testosterone dreams: Rejuvenation, aphrodisia, doping*. Berkeley, CA: University of California Press.

Møller, V. (2010). *The ethics of doping and anti-doping: Redeeming the soul of sport?* New York: Routledge.

Mottram, D. R. (2011). *Drugs in sport* (5th ed.). New York: Routledge.

7

HEAD INJURIES AND CONCUSSION ISSUES

Annette Greenhow and Lisa Gowthorp

I think as a footballer, you expect to have knocks … you expect maybe to
have arthritis later on in years. You do not expect to die of brain damage
aged 59.

(Dawn Astle[1] in Webb, 2014)

Sports-related concussion is an important and complex issue, but it is not a new
phenomenon. Meehan and Bachur (2009) traced early forms of sports-related
concussion to 776 B.C. in the sports of wrestling and fist fighting. The physical risks
of contact and collision sports (Luntz, 1980) and challenges of managing injuries
(Mitten, 1993), particularly return-to-play or practice decisions, are reoccurring
themes across sport, across jurisdictions and across disciplines. However, the recent
growth of public awareness regarding sports-related concussion – fuelled by
litigation, concussion-related deaths and links to long-term degenerative brain
disease – raises questions about the adequacy of the decisions made by rule-makers,
including their roles, responsibilities and assessments of risk. It also exposes tensions
that arise in balancing the interests of player health and welfare on the one hand,
with commercial interests and spectator demands on the other.

From a management and governance perspective, it is important to consider the
role of international and national sporting organisations in determining where
responsibilities lie and in determining who is responsible for setting rules regarding
sports-related concussions. For the purposes of this chapter, the organisation with
the greatest responsible for rule-making (i.e., ultimate rule-maker) for the sport
will be referred to as the *sport governing body*. Key issues for consideration include
whether the relevant sport governing body has recognised the issue, the emphasis
it places on the risks involved (and where it sits on its risk agenda) and whether
the sport governing body has promulgated rules and implemented appropriate
policies and procedures to limit or reduce risk.

From a legal perspective, considerations include whether the sport governing body has taken reasonable care over the years to protect and enhance the safety of participants in their sport, and whether the particular sport has kept abreast of evolving science and research on sports-related concussion. A retrospective analysis of research demonstrates that this issue has been dominated by scientific efforts to establish the epidemiology of sports-related concussion. Perhaps equally important is the overarching consideration of whether the regulatory system is properly equipped to respond to the actual or potential risks associated with sports-related concussion. In other words, it is critical to identify which governing body is ultimately responsible for developing appropriate rules and protocols; who determines whether those rules have been implemented and enforced at the relevant level and, finally, whether appropriate and consistent sanctions for non-compliance have been applied. This chapter will also examine the ethical question of whether, as custodian of the sport, the sport governing body has an obligation to invest in research and education for participants across the relevant constituency and across different levels of the sport.

The first part of this chapter will briefly outline the clinical understanding of sports-related concussion, the symptoms and sequelae, and provide an overview of the evolving state of medical art and scientific knowledge. The second part examines the legal vulnerabilities arising from the concussion litigation commenced in the United States by retired NFL players. In 2015, in a court-ordered settlement, the NFL allocated an estimated US $1 billion towards compensating retired NFL players for certain medical conditions attributable to their participation in the sport at the professional level. Finally, the third part of this chapter will consider the regulation and governance of sports-related concussion and the implications for sport managers and their organisations.

Medical considerations

Since 776 B.C., athletes have participated in sports that exposed them to risks for concussion (Echemendia, 2006; Meehan and Bachur, 2009). Discussions of symptoms associated with concussion can be traced to the time of Hippocrates; however, it was not until the twentieth century that symptoms were examined in scientific studies. The first studies of concussion in a sporting context were of boxers in the 1920s; studies identified the possible neurological effects of repetitive head trauma and *dementia pugilistica* later, literally meaning 'dementia of a fighter' (Martland, 1928; see also Geddes, Vowles, Robinson and Sutcliffe, 1996; Sait, 2013). Pathologist Harrison Martland (1928) conducted post-mortem examinations in 23 cases and discovered neurological lesions in the brains of boxers. Martland is credited as having discovered 'punch drunk syndrome' in 1928. Between late 1930s and the late 1940s, with the growing recognition that this syndrome could be associated with other sports, the term *progressive traumatic encephalopathy* became the preferred term, leading to what is now described as *chronic traumatic encephalopathy* (CTE; Cantu, 2007; McKee *et al.*, 2013).

In contemporary times, sports-related concussion, particularly in contact and collision sports, has become a common occurrence and commonly recognised as an inherent risk associated with participation. It is estimated that two to three players per team will suffer from concussion per season. Australian football injury surveillance data estimate the number of reported concussions to be six to seven per team per year (Orchard, Seward and Orchard, 2013; Richards, 2015a). Based on Magnusson and Opie's (1995) classification system, the codes of Australian football, rugby league and rugby union are classified as contact sports, with the primary objective of scoring goals or tries. Contact sport has been described as 'the mid-point between fighting and the milder sports' (*R v. Donovan*, 1934, 2 KB 498). In the pursuit of the primary object, physical contact between participants is permitted and occurs continuously at a high impact and often at an aggressive level throughout the game. Soccer, on the other hand, is classified as a collision sport where direct physical contact between players is not permitted, but concussion is still an inherent or inevitable outcome (Magnusson and Opie, 1995). Football players in these contact and collision sports are at a high risk of sustaining concussive and sub-concussive injuries throughout their playing careers.[2]

Clinical understandings of sports-related concussion

Described as a 'sacrosanct anatomical structure', the brain is the epicentre of human behaviour and vitally important to the maintenance of long-term quality of life (Gardner, 2013). Altering the brain will in turn alter a person. Assessing the true extent of alterations to brain function in a living patient is not without its difficulties. Challenges – including those faced by earlier researchers whose experimental subjects included monkeys, heartless frogs and mice – are due to the very subjective nature of symptoms, which continue to hamper an accurate diagnosis in the twenty-first century (Dashnaw, Petraglia and Bailes, 2012; Gardner, 2013; Symonds, 1962).

Concussion is a brain injury caused by a direct or indirect blow to the head, face, neck or other part of the body, with an impulsive force transmitted to the head, causing the brain to 'slosh' inside the skull and disturbing brain function (McCrory et al., 2013). Since Hippocrates, the definition of concussion has continued to evolve, aligning with scientific discoveries and technological advances in diagnostic methods. However, despite these advances, there remains no universally accepted definition of concussion, thus presenting a number of challenges and limitations to this field of study (McCrory, 2001; McCrory et al., 2013). Risks associated with the effects of sub-concussive injuries – blows to the head that do not meet the threshold for diagnosis as a concussion – are not fully understood (Dashnaw et al., 2012). For the purposes of this chapter, the term *concussion* will include both concussive and sub-concussive head trauma.

A football player who has sustained a concussive or sub-concussive injury is thought to be at a greater risk of sustaining another injury if returned to play or practice before asymptomatic. Despite the evolving state of epidemiological certainty and developments in scientific knowledge, consensus in the medical literature is for conservative concussion management, which is critical to ensure that a player is not further exposed to brain trauma whilst being in an 'injury-induced vulnerable state' with a stepwise process for the management and return-to-play decisions (McCrory et al., 2013; Wojtys et al., 1999). In professional sports, time is a luxury; players face pressure to remain competitive and often are unable to allow the brain enough time to fully recover.

Moving towards consensus

Collaboration across a number of international sporting federations and among medical experts with an interest in sports-related concussion first occurred in 2001 with the convening of the inaugural Concussion Conference in Vienna and the establishment of the Concussion in Sport Group (CISG). The symposium was organised by the governing body of the contact sport of ice hockey, the International Ice Hockey Federation in partnership with FIFA and the International Olympic Committee. One of the aims of this conference was to provide recommendations to improve the safety of those athletes who suffer concussive injuries in high-impact sports, such as ice hockey and football (Aubry, 2002). Since 2001, three other symposia have convened to revise the consensus statements issued by the CISG. Revisions were reflective of the evolving state of medical art and scientific knowledge. In 2012, the fourth International Conference of Concussion in Sport described injury constructs to include the rapid onset of short-lived impairment of neurological function that usually resolves spontaneously, but may evolve, and a graded set of clinical symptoms that may or may not involve loss of consciousness, some of which may be prolonged (McCrory et al., 2013).

Symptoms and sequelae

The latent nature of concussion and the subjective elements of its sequelae contribute greatly to the difficulties associated with measuring the nature and scope of the risks it presents. One of the areas of complexity involves the plethora of symptoms and variability of the presentation of these symptoms. A list of symptoms and the differing clinical manifestations in sports-related concussion was developed at the first meeting of the CISG in 2001. In 2012, this list was expanded to include 22 possible symptoms, as outlined in the Sport Concussion Assessment Tool (3rd ed.; McCrory et al., 2013). Symptoms are categorised as somatic (e.g., headaches), cognitive (e.g., fogginess) and emotional (e.g., mood lability). Physical signs include loss of consciousness, amnesia, behavioural changes such as irritability and cognitive impairment, such as slowed reaction times and sleep disturbance (McCrory et al., 2013). However, loss of consciousness is not a precursor to a diagnosis of concussion. To make diagnosis more complex, the symptoms can evolve and those that present in the first few minutes can differ from those presenting many hours later, and beyond (Meeuwisse, 2013). Each case is different owing to an evolving and variable range of symptoms and their sequelae.

If managed properly, symptoms in 80 to 90 per cent of adult patients resolve in a short period, typically seven to ten days (McCrory *et al.*, 2013). The more complex cases are those in which symptoms continue beyond this timeframe. However, as described, if concussion is not managed properly, there is a greater risk of further injury or serious damage due to the brain being in an injury-induced vulnerable state. It is this vulnerability that supports the requirement for physical and cognitive rest until the patient is asymptomatic (Wojtys *et al.*, 1999). It is difficult to determine when a patient is asymptomatic, given to the absence of a visible marker, so either a routine MRI or CT scan may be of limited diagnostic value (McCrory *et al.*, 2013).[3] Currently, the science is evolving to develop a reliable diagnostic method or tool to determine when a patient is asymptomatic. Typically, symptoms are more commonly identified in the first instance through the use of neuropsychological tests such as the Sport Concussion Assessment Tool.

Chronic traumatic encephalopathy (CTE) and concussion

> CTE is caused by repetitive brain trauma.... The number or type of hits to the head needed to trigger degenerative changes is unknown.... It is likely that other factors, such as genetics, may play a role in the development of CTE, as not everyone with a history of repeated brain trauma develops this disease. However, these other factors are not yet understood.
>
> *(Boston University CTE Center, n.d.-a, para. 2)*

Perhaps one of the most contentious issues in medical literature about sports-related concussion is the nature and extent of the association between repetitive concussive/sub-concussive injuries and CTE. As previously indicated, what is now known as CTE was first discovered in boxers in 1928. CTE is a progressive and degenerative disease of the brain. It has been linked to a history of repetitive concussion, triggering progressive degeneration of the brain tissue and leading to the build-up of abnormal tau protein. Brain degeneration is associated with memory loss, confusion, impaired judgment, paranoia, impulse control problems, aggression, depression and, eventually, progressive dementia (Boston University CTE Center, n.d.-b).

Over the past decade, public awareness of CTE has heightened following reports in the United States, where researchers have found a high incidence of CTE in former NFL players. This has subsequently led to a class action suit from retired players against the NFL. At the 2009 Congressional Hearing on NFL Player Head Injuries, the Director of the Boston University CTE Center, Dr. Ann McKee provided testimony based on her research on the nature of CTE and concussion and relationship to engagement in American football (*Legal Issues Relating to Football*, 2009, 2010). McKee's testimony included references to 11 cases involving professional and college footballers, all of which, in her opinion, had exhibited clear evidence of CTE. Her testimony included reference to her observations during her 23-year career, where she had examined 'thousands of brains, from individuals of all walks of life, of all ages', concluding that she had 'only seen this unique pattern with this severity in individuals with repetitive head trauma, and that has included football as well as boxing' (*Legal Issues Relating to Football*, 2009, 2010, p. 154).

Since the 2009 Congressional Hearing, a 'brain bank' has been established to undertake post-mortem examinations to determine the prevalence of CTE. McKee *et al.* (2013) reported that post-mortem examinations of 34 out of 35 former professional American football players had shown clear evidence of CTE. The first Australian case of CTE was reported in February 2014 when a diagnosis was reported by the CTE Centre in the post-mortem examination of a 79-year-old former rugby union player ('Brain Disease CTE', 2014).

CTE has been identified as a medical condition qualifying for compensation under the NFL court-ordered settlement in the United States, yet the nature, extent, and scope of the long-term risk is an area that has polarised views in the scientific research community. In 2012, the CISG, in the fourth Consensus Statement, indicated that the 'cause and effect relationship' between CTE and concussions or exposure to contact sport had not been demonstrated (McCrory *et al.*, 2013, p. 258). The CISG also observed that 'the *speculation* that repeated concussion or sub-concussive impact causes CTE remains unproven' (emphasis added) (McCrory *et al.*, 2013, p. 258). In summary, there are, and continue to be, significant differences of opinion regarding the association between the cumulative effects of sports-related concussion and CTE. Despite these differences, legal vulnerabilities have been exposed in court proceedings testing the roles and responsibilities of sports managers and administrators.

Legal vulnerability associated with sports-related concussion

This part of the chapter will examine the allegations made against the NFL, the NHL, and FIFA and the potential legal issues pertaining to negligence in the context of the role of the governing body. These issues are highlighted in the case studies involving players who sued for negligence associated with sports-related concussion. Albeit allegations, the case studies highlight legal vulnerabilities and have led to monumental changes within the management of sports-related concussion and associated policies.

Sport does not operate in a 'law-free zone' and is not a protected domain or immune from issues associated with harmful conduct against others. In the Australian High Court decision of *Agar v. Hyde* (2000), Justice Callinan referred to rugby union as a 'notoriously dangerous sport' and considered it reasonable to assume that an adult football player was expected to know that there was a risk of injury and a reasonable likelihood of being subjected to fierce, deliberate and harmful contact within the parameters of the rules of the game. In the context of football, depending on the particular code and the playing position, players are at risk of sustaining concussive and sub-concussive injuries across their playing careers (Orchard *et al.*, 2013; Richards, 2015a). Despite these obvious and inherent risks associated with participating in contact and collision sports, the primary focus of this chapter is on more latent risks – those risks associated with the consequences of mismanaging concussion and the exposure to the risk of more serious and long-lasting damage. A concern for the sport manager and the organisation is the potential for litigation and allegation of negligence in failing to provide a safe environment for their players.

Sports-related concussion litigation

With debate around CTE and football continuing in the medical and scientific research communities, legal proceedings were initiated in 2011 in the United States to test the legal vulnerabilities surrounding the issue of sports-related concussion. An Australian court has yet to test the legal vulnerabilities associated with the mismanagement of sports-related concussion. However, it is possible to draw from allegations made in recent litigation claims, primarily from the United States, based on the tort of negligence against the sports' governing body, the national sporting organisations, the employer club, the team doctor, and the school administrator.

Claims against a sport governing body and administrator. The NFL, the NHL, and FIFA have all been sued in respect to their roles as sports administrators responsible for sports-related concussion. The first claim against the NFL was filed in July 2011 in *Vernon Maxwell v. National Football League et al.*, with many claims following, involving an estimated 5,000 players. The claims were consolidated on 31 January 2012. Case Study 1 outlines the facts of the case, the central allegations and the terms of the medical monitoring and compensation settlement for brain injuries allegedly caused by head impacts experienced in NFL football.

Case Study 1: The NFL. The central allegation against the NFL in the court proceedings issued since 2011 was that it owed, and failed to discharge, a duty of care to protect players from the hazards of head knocks and repetitive concussions sustained during their playing careers. In some cases, allegations of fraudulent concealment of information were made, with accusations of inherent conflicts of interest in the way the NFL-funded scientific research was managed. The NFL's initial response was a vehement denial of the allegations that it knew and concealed the risks associated with repetitive concussion – a position it has maintained throughout proceedings.

An early chapter in the NFL's concussion narrative began in 2002 when Dr. Bennet Omalu, a forensic pathologist in Pittsburgh, conducted a routine autopsy on the body of deceased NFL footballer and subsequently published the paper entitled 'Chronic Traumatic Encephalopathy in a National Football League Player' (Omalu *et al.*, 2005). The response from the NFL was immediate. They denied the validity of the research, dismissing the suggested link by Omalu *et al.* (2005), and published the results of their own research, concluding that in their view, there was no increased risk of repetitive concussion in football. Some suggested that the NFL embarked upon a campaign to minimise the issue by discrediting the quality of the emerging independent research (Heiner, 2012). The debate that ensued polarised both the football and scientific communities. Allegations of conflict and competing interests were also made against the NFL.

With the body of independent scientific research questioning the link between repetitive concussions and football, forensic journalists continued in their pursuit of the NFL, with the media applying the moniker 'a concussion crisis'. In 2009 and 2010, a Congressional Hearing was convened to investigate the actions of the NFL and to test the substance of the allegations that the NFL was putting commercial interests ahead of its players' health and welfare. Coincidentally, the NFL undertook significant reforms within its sport, following the Congressional Hearings. These reforms included rule changes that were aimed to make the game safer, development of mandatory return-to-play directives, and a strong commitment to fund more research, acknowledging this as a serious issue. The NFL, after detailed public examination at the Congressional Hearing, was heavily criticised for failing to regulate its sport for and in the best interests of its players and the public (*Legal Issues Relating to Football*, 2009, 2010).

Litigation was commenced against the NFL, with the first claim filed in July 2011 that involved 75 retired NFL players. Within a relatively short period of time, 252 other complaints were filed against the NFL that represented over 4,800 NFL players. The common allegation made by the complainants was that the NFL owed a duty of care to protect its players – to inform, educate and warn players about the possible links of football to CTE (*Easterling et al. v. National Football League*, 2011; *Evans et al. v. National Football League*, 2012; *Vernon Maxwell v. National Football League et al.*, 2011). These allegations were based on the NFL's primary role as rule-maker in the sport of American football.

Following the Congressional Hearing, and perhaps influenced by the concussion litigation, the NFL has continued to take reformative steps by engaging in open self-regulation, permeable to government, stakeholder, and community expectations. Examples include the provision of unrestricted research funds to support concussion medical research, support of youth concussion legislation across each state within the United States, and collaboration with the U.S. military by working on common platforms of concussion and head injuries, both in football and the military.

Rule changes have been made to fundamentally prevent, manage, and treat players who sustain concussion and head injuries during play and training. Independent neurologists have been assigned to games to add an additional layer of scrutiny to a team doctor diagnosis and return-to-play decisions. In 2012, the NFL announced a US $30 million commitment to support independent studies of neurological diseases, representing a sign of the commitment to meet high government, stakeholder, and community expectations.

In July 2014, a mediated settlement of the NFL concussion litigation was reached between the parties and finally approved by the court in May 2015. The large part of NFL's settlement involved an unrestricted Injury Compensation Fund

to pay monetary awards to retired NFL players (which currently includes approx- ~~#14~~
imately 21,000 eligible former players) who show symptoms of severe cognitive $765 mill
impairment, dementia, Alzheimer's disease, CTE, or amyotrophic lateral sclerosis
(ALS).

The settlement is monumental, both in terms of quantum and significance, despite being wrapped in the usual 'no admission of liability' packaging and justified on a basis of the immediate needs of the claimants and the desire to avoid protracted and expensive litigation. Therefore, the question of whether the NFL breached its duties referred to in the litigation remains moot.

In August 2014, a number of amateur soccer players and parents sued FIFA as the sport's governing body, together with the U.S. Soccer Federation, the U.S. Youth Soccer Association, American Youth Soccer Organisation, the U.S. Club Soccer and the California Youth Soccer Association. Case Study 2 outlines allegations against FIFA and other soccer administrators in the United States in the case of *Mehr et al. v. Fédération Internationale de Football Association et al.* (2014).

Case Study 2: FIFA, U.S. soccer and other soccer administrators. Proceedings were filed in the United States against FIFA and a number of other sporting associations in the organisational hierarchy responsible for the management of concussion in youth soccer in the United States (*Mehr et al. v. Fédération Internationale de Football Association et al.*, 2014). Two former junior soccer players and three parents have brought the complaint seeking class action certification. Unlike the NFL and NHL litigation, which involved allegations of mismanagement at the professional level, the FIFA proceedings involve claims of mismanaging concussion at the junior level and alleging that FIFA had a duty to protect players at all playing levels.

[The allegations include failure by the governing authorities responsible for soccer in the United States to take the appropriate steps to reduce concussion-related injuries. The FIFA complaint relies heavily on the consensus statements issued by the CISG (McCrory *et al.*, 2013) and academic publications seeking to establish the state of the medical art and science at the relevant times (*Mehr et al. v. Fédération Internationale de Football Association et al.*, 2014).] ╎5

The FIFA complaint alleges negligence against the governing body and organisations within the junior soccer hierarchy for failing to educate and warn players, disclose risks, promulgate rules, and concealing and misrepresenting important facts (*Mehr et al. v. Fédération Internationale de Football Association et al.*, 2014). This complaint alleges that the defendants knew or ought to have known of the dangers associated with concussion by heading the ball or attempting to head the ball. Comparisons have been made to other sports where changes to the rules were made to minimise the risk associated with concussion. The central allegation here is that the defendants failed to take the necessary steps to alter the rules and that this failure caused the injuries to the claimants.

Further, this complaint alleges a breach of a voluntary undertaking by each defendant that it assumed the role of supervisor, regulator, monitor, and provider of appropriate rules to minimise the risk of injury. Unlike the NFL and NHL litigation, the FIFA complaint is not seeking monetary damages, but rather changes to align concussion management policies to those of other sports. It is also seeking medical monitoring to detect the manifestation of post-injury symptoms (*Mehr* et al. *v. Fédération Internationale de Football Association et al.*, 2014).

Case study discussion points and key themes. The following threshold issue is raised in light of the case studies presented above. Who is ultimately responsible for the design, implementation, and enforcement of rules around sports-related concussion?

If it is the role and responsibility of the sport's governing body, the following questions arise from the case studies:

1   Did the governing body know or ought to have known that participants who sustained repetitive concussive events, sub-concussive events, and/or brain injuries were at significantly greater risk for chronic neurological diseases and disabilities during their playing careers or later in life?
2   Did the governing body assume a voluntary duty of care through the creation of its concussion management programmes and policies to inform its players of the risks of concussive events, sub-concussive events, and/or brain injuries?
3   Did the governing body actively and purposely conceal information from its players regarding the severe risks of concussive events, sub-concussive events, and/or brain injuries?
4   Do sport administrators owe duty of care to protect players and inform, educate, and warn them about CTE in light of the evolving science in this area?

Another high profile sport and governing body was sued in a case similar to that of the NFL concussion cases. In November 2013, proceedings were issued against the NHL by a number of retired professional ice hockey players (*Leeman et al. v. National Hockey League et al.*, 2014). Further claims have been filed and now consolidated into one action. The litigation has yet to be finalised, with the NHL seeking unsuccessfully to dismiss the action.

The regulator of American football at the collegiate level, the National Collegiate Athletic Association, was sued in 2011 for allegedly breaching its duty of care owed to college football players in the United States (*Arrington et al. v. National Collegiate Athletic Association,* 2011). A settlement of US$70 million for medical monitoring was reached in 2014, but it has yet to be approved.

The clubs employing the players have also been sued in legal proceedings with allegations of mismanaging concussion and causing harm to former professional players as employees. In 2013, the Kansas City Chiefs NFL club was sued by former players in *Cooper et al. v. Kansas City Chiefs Football Club, Inc.* (2013). Shortly after this claim was filed, proceedings were issued by former players against NFL team, the Arizona Cardinals, in *Green v. Arizona Cardinals Football Club LLC.* These claims have yet to be finalised.

Claims against other parties. In 2000, a former professional football player sued the team doctor for negligence in failing in his duty of care owed to the player when sustaining multiple concussions while playing in the NFL (*Hoge v. Munsell,* 2002). More recently, a claim was filed against a high school and hospital in Dublin, by a former student, alleging mismanagement of sports-related concussion in school rugby union.

The primary litigation involving the rule-makers has also led to a series of consequential litigation involving insurance companies and questions around indemnity claims. Insurers and the NFL and the NHL have also been involved in litigation, in attempts to define responsibility for indemnifying against the risks referred to in the NFL litigation (see, for example, Dolmetsch, 2014; *TIG Insurance Co. v National Hockey League,* 2014).

There is yet to be a court ruling on the specific roles and responsibilities around the regulation of sports-related concussion. Despite the absence of a clear precedent, the legal claims that have been issued demonstrate that there are genuine legal vulnerabilities and risks associated with the mismanagement of concussion in a sporting context. Litigation in and of itself only provides recompense to those directly involved in proceedings or captured through class action certifications. However, what can be inferred from the litigation is that at the very least, a sport manager will need to ensure that formal concussion policies and protocols are in place, with active enforcement, compliance policies, and preventive measures for the long-term good of the sport and well-being of participants.

Regulation and governance in Australia

Within the Australian context, allegations such as those contained in the NFL, FIFA, and NHL litigation would likely constitute a novel case and would very much depend on the particular circumstances and merits of each case. An overarching consideration is whether, at the relevant time, reasonable care was taken to protect and enhance the safety of participants in the sport. This would also require a determination of whether concussion protocols reflected the state of medical art and scientific knowledge in sports medicine at the particular time. From a regulatory perspective, questions arise concerning the implementation and enforcement of the protocols by sport governing bodies, requiring appropriate and consistent sanctions for non-compliance.

There are relatively few cases in Australia involving claims for personal injuries sustained in contact or collision sport, and only a small number of cases involving claims directly against the sports administrators in failing to protect participants (*Agar v. Hyde,* 2000; *Green v. County Rugby Football League of NSW,* 2008; *Haylen v. New South Wales Rugby Union Ltd.,* 2002). There are no cases that examine legal responsibility of a governing body in Australia in relation to sports-related concussion and negligence involving claims for personal injuries suffered by a professional player. At the elite level, compensation associated with career-ending concussive injuries have, thus far, been determined in accordance with the terms of the player contract and the collective bargaining agreements.[4]

This chapter does question the role of sport managers in regard to player health and safety. Operating within a self-regulated system, governing bodies are expected to promulgate rules to ensure their sport is safe. The nature and effect of these rules and the methods of self-regulation by the governing body are of vital importance to preserve the integrity of the sport. As a rule-maker, the governing body also has a responsibility to ensure that rules reflect the current safety standards and that they are modified to reflect the current health practices, and enforced consistently and vigorously to achieve the objectives of providing a safe sport system for all participants at every level.

The relationship between the governing body and the participant needs to be examined when considering the existence of a duty of care and when evaluating where the responsibility lies with respect to the prevention and management of sports-related concussions. At the professional level, this will depend upon the varying degrees of influence and practical control over aspects of the particular sport, clubs, and players. Apart from the CISG medical diagnostic tool, the SCAT3, there is currently no standard or uniform management policy or government-mandated concussion policy for implementation within and across sport. The only policies available are guidelines developed by those within the self-regulated system, such as those designed and implemented by the individual governing bodies including the National Rugby League and the Australian Football League (AFL).

To demonstrate the role of the sport's governing body, the AFL is the rule-maker and principal controller in the promotion, organisation, and regulation of Australian football (for more details, see the *AFL Annual Report*; AFL, 2014a). It has the exclusive authority to grant licences and rights to participate in the competition and has the power to design, implement and enforce policies, rules and promulgates the Laws of the Game. The standard player contract in the AFL is a triparted agreement among the AFL, a licensed club and a player, with the club recognised as the employer of the player, but the governing body exerting a significant degree of influence over the playing environment. Therefore, who is ultimately responsible for mandating compulsory concussion regulation and enforcement within this sport? Currently, the AFL's concussion policy is focused on medical diagnosis and the medical management of a player's concussive injury. A number of changes in response to concerns about potential long-term effects of concussion have been made within the sport. These include the introduction of rule changes to protect the head, a standard concussion assessment tool and new concussion substitutes rules (AFL, 2014b). But the question remains, who is responsible for regulating the concussion changes and what, if any, are the consequences for clubs or players not adhering to the changes in policy?

The ultimate rule-maker is either the international or national governing body for the particular sport. The organisation is in the best position, as rule-maker, to take responsibility and provide clear guidelines and policies in relation to the management of concussion within their sport, while also adhering to a national or international standard of concussion management practices. However, a national or international standard has yet to be developed.

Ethical considerations

Sports-related concussion raises numerous medical and legal issues, but is it fundamentally an ethical issue? Does a governing body have an ethical obligation as custodian or 'guardian' of the game to protect participants across all playing levels?[5] The important health benefits associated with participation link sport and society.[6] Sport is a neutral instrument itself, but societies often expect it to produce champions and elite athletes, and thus encourage mass participation for the health and development of communities (Greenhow and East, 2014). Society also typically expects through this process that risk assessments will be made on a continuum of benefit/harm to public interests.

The provision of a safe sporting environment?

Sports-related concussion should be considered in a social context and not taken lightly by the management of sport governing bodies. Across all playing levels, there is an expectation that a safe sporting environment will be provided to all participants, regardless of age or ability. At the community level, parents, caregivers, and families allow their children to participate in sport and entrust others to provide and enforce rules that support and promote a safe sporting environment. The sustainability and future success of professional sport is said to be heavily dependent on the participation of children from a young age, with the children of today being said to be the 'stars and fans of tomorrow' (Cornelius and Singh, 2011, p. 294). Children have a right to protection and should be afforded the full opportunity to play, which promotes their general development and well-being (U.N. General Assembly Resolution 45/25; U.N. International Charter of Physical Education and Sport, 1978).

At the professional level, the risk of concussion has been viewed, to some extent, as an occupational hazard when perusing the objectives of the game – a dangerous occupation, considered, by some, to be analogous to soldiers in armed conflict or police officers on duty.[7] There are, however, significant and obvious differences, not the least of which is the underlying motivation for entering the occupation and the safety net provided by a state-regulated compensation regime to protect against the short- and long-term impact of work-related injuries.

Drawing from sports management literature, the financial and non-financial investments made in sport places higher levels of expectations on those who ultimately regulate it (Sherry, Shilbury and Wood, 2007). The commercialisation of sport has created a heightened expectation and duty on the governing body to maximise safety and reduce injury risk across all levels of participation. Assessed on the basis of having significant public benefit, the Australian Sports Commission directs government funding and support to national sporting organisations.[8] As publicly funded non-government organisations, the public expects that sporting organisations will allocate and responsibly utilise resources to promote policies that enhance a safe sporting system. Arguably, this includes investment in research and education regarding important safety issues in sport.

Costs associated with concussion

Incidence rates of concussive and sub-concussive injuries are high. So too are related health care costs to treat these injuries. According to Finch, Clapperton, and McCrory (2013), there were 47,450 hospitalisations resulting from sports-related concussions over a nine-year period, costing the Victorian community around A\$20 million annually. In addition to health care costs, there are also other costs associated with concussions due to decreased productivity. Although difficult to quantify and measure, the Australian Sports Commission has identified that these additional costs arise from time lost to employment, education and home activities, future sporting activities, and long-term physical, psychological and/or emotional damage (Richards, 2015b).

The national governing body as custodian

Within the Australian context, sport governing bodies are responsible for the long-term development and sustainability of their particular sport, providing a wide range of public benefits through a self-funding business model. It is expected that a significant portion of revenue will be allocated towards enhancing, promoting, and developing sport for all Australians both at the national and grassroots level (Coalition of Major Professional and Participation Sports, 2013).

Sport governing bodies occupy a unique position of control in the democratic process, particularly when performing the crucial function of rule-maker. It is this element of control that arguably justifies a responsibility to a broader constituency in order to ensure that their actions are of a sufficient standard to meet community expectations and, moreover, to evaluate the tensions that might arise in reconciling competing interests from the range of stakeholders. It is fair to assume that the public has a heightened expectation that governing bodies will effectively utilise appropriate regulatory and governance tools when faced with problems that have associated 'public interest' elements and be more permeable to external influences.

The 'cascade-effect' of decisions made by the governing body and how these decisions are implemented at the elite level of professional sports have a significant impact on community and grassroots sport. In 1994, the Head and Neck Injury Panel of the Australian National Health and Medical Research Council (NHMRC, 1994) published a report identifying concussion as an important issue in the four professional codes of football. The report identified illegal play as being as a major contributor to head injuries and recognised the importance of 'example-setting' by strongly recommending that illegal conduct be 'severely punished'.[9] The expectation would be consistent enforcement and sanctions for non-compliance.

Cultural 'machismo'

In identifying the distinguishing features of elite athletes, Murthy, Dwyer, and Bosco (2012) described professional players as unique patients with an inherent 'will to win'; they are driven to perform and pursue the extremes of physical capacity in order to compete. Long-term health impacts are sometimes regarded as a secondary consideration. Another dimension arises in male-dominated team sport, which is described as the 'machismo' effect – a form of societal glorification of footballers, whereby participation in sport sets the boundaries for masculine behaviour and hierarchy, thus relegating personal health and safety as secondary issues (Hecht, 2002). When suffering injury such as a concussion, a player will face the pressure and the desire to return to the game as soon as possible. This is exactly where the ethical dilemma arises and where the strength of the concussion management policies and the resolve of the governing body will be tested (Panahi, 2014).

Conclusion

Until recent times, there has been little collaboration in sport for concussion management.[10] Each respective football code has responded in different ways, at different times, and is subject to its organisational structures to make rule changes and to develop strategies for the enforcement and compliance of concussion policies. In 1994, the NHMRC recommendations suggested a coordinated and consistent approach across the codes on matters pertaining to concussion management, prevention, research, and education. Opportunities for cross-sport collaboration were identified, particularly in the area of data collection and research funding initiatives, but much more remains to be done in these areas (NHMRC, 1994).

Sport governing bodies should be driving the concussion agenda and should integrate mechanisms to ensure that community expectations are met by making their respective sport safer for all participants. Initially, the quest for scientific certainty appears to have been the platform upon which decision-makers have relied, which ultimately may have delayed measures aimed at reducing risk in contact and collision sports. Without disputing the importance of the scientific and medical dimensions of sports-related concussion, other perspectives are important. Doherty (2012) explained that concussion in sport includes many other perspectives including social and cultural, legal, regulatory, governance and marketing perspectives, to name a few. The legal perspective gained momentum with the filing of the concussion litigation in the United States in 2011. This litigation (and the final settlement of the class action litigation) exposed potential legal vulnerabilities of sport governing bodies. In recent times, and perhaps motivated by the experiences of the NFL in the United States, the issue has moved higher up the risk agenda ladder.

Despite jurisdictional differences, U.S. concussion litigation serves as a valuable case study of both private and public expectations regarding the role of the governing body as custodian or guardian. Upon reflection, the Congressional Hearing appeared to be the cornerstone of the NFL's reconfigured response, and demonstrated that the power of public scrutiny still remains an important driver of change. When sports-related concussion is framed in a wider social context, social responsibility is equally applicable. It is this dimension that should be considered by all contact or collision sport administrators in the future design of sports-related concussion policies and regulations.

Notes

1 Dawn Astle, daughter of late Jeff Astle, former England and West Bromwich Albion soccer player, died at age 59 from a brain trauma caused by repeatedly heading the ball (Webb, 2014).

2 Incidence rates of concussion have increased in Australian football due, in part, to the increased awareness and concussion management protocols implemented for the sport (see Orchard *et al.*, 2013). The probability of concussion is estimated at approximately 1 in 7 (Richards, 2015).

3 Functional MRI scans can detect chemical changes in the brain, but these are not currently part of the routine assessment at the present time. PET scans are in the early stages of development.

4 An early case in the AFL involved the retirement of Dean Kemp and compensation payment for career-ending concussive injuries in 2001. Since that time, a number of other players have been awarded compensation for concussive injuries (Lane, 2011).

5 FIFA describes itself as 'guardian' of the game (*Mehr et al. v. Fédération Internationale de Football Association et al.*, 2014).

6 In addition to the physical health benefits of sport participation, recent studies found that keeping adolescents in sport is fundamental to mental health. Adolescents who drop out of organised sport are 10 to 20 per cent more likely to be diagnosed with a mental health problem during the next three years than their peers who stay in organised sport. The Australian First Study uses sport to reduce depression and suicide rates in young men ('Australian First Study', 2014).

7 It is no coincidence that the NFL has partnered with the U.S. military to research the effects of traumatic brain injury. The International Professional Sports Concussion Research Think Tank included the U.S. military as part of the research collaboration (Hackney, 2014). The comparison drawn between war and sport was made by George Orwell (1945) when he compared serious sport to war, minus the shooting.

8 Established under the Australian Sports Commission Act 1989, the Australian Sports Commission is empowered to make grants, lend money, and provide scholarships or like benefits. The powers are outlined in s 8(1)(d) of the Australian Sports Commission Act 1989. An investment of A$134-million taxpayer dollars was made during the 2011–2012 financial year (Australian Sports Commission, 2012).

9 An example of this can be found in NHMRC (1994) report whereby the power of the sport governing body to penalise illegal behaviour would reflect the severity of concussion.

10 The first Concussion in Sport conference was held in March 2013, where the four codes of football presented their approaches to concussion management.

References

Agar v. Hyde, 201 CLR 552 (2000).

Arrington et al. v. National Collegiate Athletic Association, Northern District of Illinois District Court, Eastern Division, Case No. 11-cv-0656 (2011).

Aubry, M. (2002). Summary and agreement statement of the First International Conference on Concussion in Sport, Vienna 2001. Recommendations for the improvement of safety and health of athletes who may suffer concussive injuries. *British Journal of Sports Medicine, 36*, 6–10. doi:10.1136/bjsm.36.1.6

Australian First Study uses sport to reduce depression and suicide rates in young men. (2014, September 10). Retrieved from http://medianet.com.au/releases/release-details?id=811940

Australian Football League. (2014a). *AFL annual report*. Retrieved from www.afl.com.au/afl-hq/annual-reports

Australian Football League. (2014b, September 14). *Concussion* [Video file]. Retrieved from www.afl.com.au/respectandresponsibility/concussion

Australian Sports Commission. (2012). *Annual report 2011–2012*. Retrieved from www.ausport.gov.au/__data/assets/pdf_file/0019/502804/ASC_Annual_Report_2011-12.pdf

Boston University CTE Center. (n.d.-a). Frequently asked questions. Retrieved from www.bu.edu/cte/about/frequently-asked-questions/

Boston University CTE Center. (n.d.-b). What is CTE? Retrieved from www.bu.edu/cte/about/what-is-cte/

Brain disease CTE found in former Manly rugby player Barry Taylor. (2014, February 18). *The Courier Mail*. Retrieved from www.couriermail.com.au/sport/rugby/brain-disease-cte-found-in-former-manly-rugby-player-barry-taylor/story-fnii0ksb-1226840201898

Cantu, R. C. (2007). Chronic traumatic encephalopathy in the National Football League. *Neurosurgery, 61*, 223–225. doi:10.1227/01.NEU.0000255514.73967.90

Coalition of Major Professional and Participation Sports. (2013, May 31). *COMPPS response to the inquiry into the practice of sports science in Australia*. Retrieved from www.compps.com.au/submissions/COMPPS-2013-05-31-practice-of-sports-science.pdf

Cooper et al. v. Kansas City Chiefs Football Club, Inc., No. 1316-CV30043 (Mo. Cir. Ct. 2013).

Cornelius, S. and Singh, P. (2011). Protection of young athletes. In J. A. R. Nafziger and S. F. Ross (eds) *Handbook on international sports law* (pp. 294–310). Cheltenham, UK: Edward Elgar.

Dashnaw, M. L., Petraglia, A. L. and Bailes, J. E. (2012). An overview of the basic science of concussion and subconcussion: Where we are and where we are going. *Neurosurgery Focus, 33*, 1–9. doi:10.3171/2012.10.FOCUS12284

Doherty, A. (2012). 'It takes a village': Interdisciplinary research for sport management. *Journal of Sport Management, 26*, 1–10. Retrieved from http://journals.humankinetics.com/jsm

Dolmetsch, C. (2014, April 16). NHL sued by insurer over defense of concussion lawsuits. *Bloomberg News*. Retrieved from www.bloomberg.com/

Easterling et al. v. National Football League, No. 11-cv-05209-AB (E.D. Pa. 2011).

Echemendia, R. (2006). *Sports neuropsychology: Assessment and management of traumatic brain injury*. New York: Guilford Press.

Evans et al. v. National Football League, No. 2:12-cv-02682 (E.D. Pa., 2012).

Finch, C. F., Clapperton, A. J. and McCrory, P. (2013). Increasing incidence of hospitalisation for sport-related concussion in Victoria, Australia. *Medical Journal of Australia, 198*, 427–430. doi:10.5694/mja12.11217

Gardner, A. (2013). The complex clinical issues involved in an athlete's decision to retire from collision sport due to multiple concussions: A case study of a professional athlete. *Frontiers in Neurology, 4*, 141. doi:10.3389/fneur.2013.00141

Geddes, J. F., Vowles, G. H., Robinson, S. F. D. and Sutcliffe, J. C. (1996). Neurofibrillary tangles, but not Alzheimer-type pathology, in a young boxer. *Neuropathology and Applied Neurobiology, 22*, 12–16. doi:10.1111/j.1365-2990.1996.tb00840.x

Green v. Arizona Cardinals Football Club LLC, No. 4:14CV461 CDP (E.D. Mo. 2014).

Green v. Country Rugby Football League of New South Wales, No. NSWSC 26 (2008).

Greenhow, A. and East, J. (2014). Custodians of the game: Ethical considerations for football governing bodies in regulating concussion management. *Neuroethics, 8,* 65–82. doi:10.1007/s12152-014-9216-1

Hecht, A. N. (2002). Legal and ethical aspects of sport-related concussions: The Merril Hoge story. *Seton Hall Journal of Sport Law, 12,* 17. Retrieved from http://scholarship.shu.edu/sports_entertainment/

Hackney Publications. (2014, August 26). *A Report from the International Professional Sports Concussion Research Think Tank.* Retrieved from http://concussionpolicyandthelaw.com/2014/08/26/a-report-from-the-international-professional-sports-concussion-research-think-tank/

Haylen v. New South Wales Rugby Union Ltd., No. NSWSC 114 (2002).

Heiner, J. A. (2012). Concussion in the National Football League: *Jani v. Bert Bell/Pete Rozelle NFL Player Ret. Plan* and a Legal Analysis of the NFL's 2007 Concussion Management Guidelines. *Seton Hall Journal of Sports and Entertainment Law, 18,* 225. Retrieved from http://scholarship.shu.edu/sports_entertainment/

Hoge v. Munsell, 328 Ill. App.3d 1239 (2002).

Lane, S. (2011, April 1). Head injury payouts revealed. *The Age.* Retrieved from www.theage.com.au/afl

Leeman et al. v. National Hockey League et al., No. 1:13-cv-01856 (D.C. 2014).

Legal Issues Relating to Football Head Injuries (Part I and II), 111th Cong. 1 and 2 (2009, 2010).

Luntz, H. (1980). Compensation for injuries due to sport. *Australian Law Journal, 54,* 588. Retrieved from http://sites.thomsonreuters.com.au/journals/category/the-australian-law-journal/

Magnusson, R. S. and Opie, H. (1995). HIV and hepatitis in sports: An Australian legal framework for resolving hard cases. *Monash University Law Review, 20,* 214–222. Retrieved from www.monash.edu/law/about-us/publications/monlr

Martland, H. S. (1928). Punch drunk. *Journal of the American Medical Association, 91,* 1103–1107. doi:10.1001/jama.1928.02700150029009

McCrory, P. (2001). What's in a name? *British Journal of Sports Medicine, 35,* 285–286. doi:10.1136/bjsm.35.5.285-a

McCrory, P., Meeuwisse, W. H., Aubry, M., Cantu, R. C., Dvoák, J., Echemendia, R. J., … Turner, M. (2013). Consensus statement on concussion in sport: The 4th International Conference on Concussion in Sport, Zurich, November 2012. *Journal of Athletic Training, 48,* 554–575. doi:10.4085/1062-6050-48.4.05

McKee, A. C., Stein, T. D., Nowinski, C. J., Stern, R. A., Daneshvar, D. H., Alvarez, V. E., … Cantu, R. C. (2013). The spectrum of disease in chronic traumatic encephalopathy. *Brain: A Journal of Neurology, 136,* 43–64. doi:10.1093/brain/aws307

Meehan, W. P., Bachur, R. G. (2009). Sport-related concussion. *Pediatrics, 123,* 114–123. doi:10.1542/peds.2008-0309

Meeuwisse, W. (2013, April). *Professor Winne Meeuwisse on concussion in sport* [Podcast]. Retrieved from https://soundcloud.com/bmjpodcasts/professor-winne-meeuwisse-on

Mehr et al. v. Fédération Internationale de Football Association et al., No. 3:14-cv-03879 (N.D. Ca., 2014).

Mitten, M. J. (1993). Team physicians and competitive athletes: Allocating legal responsibility for athletic injuries. *University of Pittsburgh Law Review, 55,* 129. Retrieved from http://lawreview.law.pitt.edu/ojs/index.php/lawreview

Murthy, A. M., Dwyer, J., Bosco, J. A. (2012). Ethics in sport medicine. *Bulletin of New York University Hospital for Joint Diseases, 70,* 56–90. Retrieved from www.nyuhjdbulletin.org/

National Health and Medical Research Council. (1994, June). *Report of the 117th Session Sydney* (Report No. SESS117). Retrieved from www.nhmrc.gov.au/guidelines-publications/sess117

Omalu, B., DeKosky, S. T., Minster, R. L., Kamboh, M. I., Hamilton, R. L. and Wecht, C. H. (2005). Chronic traumatic encephalopathy in a National Football League player. *Neuro-surgery, 57*, 128–134. doi:10.1227/01.NEU.0000163407.92769.ED

Orchard, J. [John], Seward, H. and Orchard, J. [Jessica]. (2013). *Australian Football League injury report 2013*. Retrieved from Australian Football League website: www.aflcommuni-tyclub.com.au/fileadmin/user_upload/Play_AFL/Multicultural/2013_AFL_Injury_Report.pdf

Orwell, G. (1945, December 14). *The sporting spirit*. Retrieved from www.orwell.ru/library/articles/spirit/english/e_spirit

Panahi, R. (2014, September 20). AFL players are cheating concussion tests to stay on the field, players' association fears. *Herald Sun*. Retrieved from www.heraldsun.com.au/

Richards, R. (2015a, August 31). *Sport concussion and head trauma*. Retrieved from the Clearinghouse for Sport website: www.clearinghouseforsport.gov.au/knowledge_base/sport_participation/sport_injuries_and_medical_conditions/sports_concussion_and_head_trauma

Richards, R. (2015b, October 15). *Cost of sport injuries*. Retrieved from the Clearing house for Sport website: www.clearinghouseforsport.gov.au/knowledge_base/sport_participation/sport_injuries_and_medical_conditions/sports_injuries

Sait, K. (2013, March). *Football, head injuries and the risk of dementia*. Retrieved from Alzheimer's Australia website: https://nsw.fightdementia.org.au/sites/default/files/AlzNSW_Football_head_injuries__the_risk_of_dementia_final_130313_web.pdf

Sherry, E., Shilbury, D. and Wood, G. (2007). Wrestling with 'conflict of interest' in sport management. *Corporate Governance, 7*, 267–277. doi:10.1108/14720700710756544

Sport Concussion Assessment Tool – 3rd Edition (SCAT3™). Retrieved from www.bjsm.bmj.com/

Symonds, C. (1962). Concussion and its sequelae. *The Lancet, 279*(7219), 1–5. Retrieved from www.thelancet.com/

TIG Insurance Co. v. National Hockey League, No., 651162/2014 (Ny. 2014).

U.N. General Assembly Resolution 44/25 (1989, November).

U.N. International Charter of Physical Education and Sport (1978, November 21).

Vernon Maxwell et al. v. National Football League, No. 2:11-cv-08394 (Ca. 2011).

Webb, J. (2014, September 11). Sports concussion 'breathalyser' proposed. *BBC News*. Retrieved from www.bbc.com/news

Wojtys, E. M., Hovda, D., Landry, G., Boland, A., Lovell, M., McCrea, M. and Minkoff, J. (1999). Current concepts. Concussions in sport. *American Journal of Sports Medicine, 27*, 676–687. Retrieved from http://ajs.sagepub.com/

PART 2

Globalisation

8

GLOBALISATION AND PROFESSIONAL SPORT

Geoff Dickson and João M. C. Malaia Santos

Globalisation is almost a buzzword. Its use was once so common in the latter part of the twentieth century, that it almost became meaningless. Nonetheless, there has been renewed interest in globalisation given recent events – a global financial crisis, the rise of nationalism, and religious extremism (Wójcik, 2014). *Globalisation* is 'a process through which space and time are compressed by technology, information flows and trade and power relations, allowing distant actions to have increased significance at the local level' (Miller, Lawrence, McKay and Rowe, 2001, p. 131). Globalisation features two main processes (Brannagan and Giulianotti, 2014). First, there is the increasing interconnectedness amongst nations and regions. The reach of social media, the global financial system, the proliferation of international governmental organisations and global cultural events (e.g., Olympics) all exemplify this connectedness. Second, there is increasing recognition and understanding that the world is a single place, not a collection of disparate, independent nations. Examples of this include international political diplomacy and the transnational environmental movement. These processes are reflected in Robertson's (1992) assertion that globalisation is 'both the compression of the world and the intensification of consciousness of the world as a whole' (p. 8).

Globalisation, and more specifically, the emergence of transnational corporations has profoundly impacted professional sports (Mason and Duquette, 2005). Within transnational corporations, also known as multinational enterprises or multinational corporations, the world is viewed as a single market. National corporations (e.g., McDonalds) have expanded internationally and today, are global in scope. Sport appeals to consumers of transnational corporations with global strategic interests (Maguire, 1999). Foreign direct investment (FDI) is the controlling ownership in a business in one country by an entity based in another country. Increases in FDI have resulted in greater global economic integration (Baldwin and Martin, 1999). FDI is 'the single most important factor contributing to the globalization of the international economy' (Henley, Kirkpatrick and Wilde, 1999, p. 223).

Globalisation is not a one-way street. *Glocalisation* refers to 'the processes and practices – some intended, others unintended – whereby the specificities of the local culture generatively interpenetrate the contingencies of global networks and flows' (Andrews, Batts and Silk, 2014, p. 261). Within glocalisation, there is the presence of 'both universalizing and particularizing tendencies' and, by extension, 'homogenization and heterogenization' (Giulianotti and Robertson, 2007a, p. 134). The terms *glocal* and *glocalisation* are used with different meanings in different academic disciplines (Giulianotti and Robertson, 2012). In marketing and business, glocalisation involves the adaptation of global commercial practices to better fit local markets. Here, at the global–local nexus, global or transnational corporations are said to negotiate local structures, regulations, and cultures (Kobayashi, 2012). In cultural studies, glocalisation is adaptation of global styles and trends to produce distinctive cultural movements and trends. Put simply, global and local are not dichotomous. Rather, local cultures can adapt and redefine global cultural products to suit their particular needs, beliefs, and customs (Robertson, 1995). For example, Huang (2013) argued that the NBA's growing presence in China has 'remoulded' Chinese basketball and sport culture. Local resistance prevented a complete homogenisation of the Chinese professional basketball league. Instead, the NBA 'accommodated and reconstructed indigenous norms' (Huang, 2013, p. 267).

Grobalisation refers to the 'imperialistic ambitions of nations, corporations, organisations, and the like and their desire, indeed need, to impose themselves on various geographic areas' (Ritzer, 2003, p. 192). The term implies that these entities grow their power, influence, and profitability.

Sport is 'one of the most dynamic, sociologically illuminating domains of globalization' (Giulianotti and Robertson, 2004, p. 545). Globalisation of professional sport is evidenced by the following:

1   international scouting and recruitment of talent,
2   broadcasting of games and other media content (online),
3   scheduling of games in foreign markets,
4   sales of team/player merchandise around the world, and
5   cross-border investing in team ownership.

International scouting and recruitment of talent

The participation of foreign-born players in professional leagues is a strong symbol of globalisation (Chen, Gunter and Zhang, 2012). Player migration preceded other manifestations of globalisation in sport. As far back as the 1920s, professional football clubs in Europe recruited amateur South American footballers. Professionalism would soon emerge in these South American countries. Professional sport organisations are recruiting more foreign athletes, especially from developing countries. These organisations establish academies in foreign countries or recruit foreign players from the transfer market. Clubs are motivated by a desire to recruit the best talent. Athletes are motivated by a desire to enhance their economic and social status.

A consequence of this migration is an increase in competitive balance at the international level. For developing nations, their capacity is enhanced because their athletes are exposed to otherwise unavailable development opportunities. For established sporting nations, foreign players take the place of local players, thus restricting the opportunities for local athletes to develop into quality national-team athletes.

Athlete salaries have increased because of the global demand for their services. For example, Rugby Union players in Australia and New Zealand sell their services to the Australian Rugby Union and New Zealand Rugby Union, respectively. In more recent times, these organisations have had to compete with offers from professional clubs in Japan and Europe. Many athletes have migrated to Middle Eastern countries, lured by financial incentives and the opportunity to participate in World Championships and the Olympics. For instance, foreign-born players with Qatari citizenship comprised more than two-thirds of the Qatar's 16-man squad at the 2015 World Championships. While Qatar's team selection conformed to the rules, there was considerable debate regarding whether it was in the spirit of competition. Whether it is individual or team sports, national and international sport organisations have well-defined policies on citizenship and eligibility. Athletes become eligible to represent another country through normal citizenship processes, residence, and family history (i.e., birthplace of parents and/or grandparents).

Broadcasting and media

Maguire (2011) described elite sport competitions as 'global media spectacles' (p. 965). Whilst globalisation was in effect prior to the advent of the Internet and associated technologies, these technologies heralded a massive acceleration and strengthening of globalisation and professional sport. For Falcous and Maguire (2006,), global sport is inseparable from global media. Similarly, sport is a key strategic platform for global media organisations (Grainger and Andrews, 2005). The global broadcasting of leagues such as the NBA or English Premier League (EPL) exemplify the transnationalisation of local sport (Grainger and Andrews, 2005). Media globalisation 'necessitates deconstructing the national boundaries of sport' (Chung, Hwang and Won, 2015, p. 484).

Under the heading 'World's Most Watched League', the EPL website proclaims that the EPL is broadcast into 212 territories, a number which exceeds the member states of the United Nations. EPL matches are broadcast in a variety of languages: English, Arabic, French, Mandarin, Cantonese, Japanese, Mongolian, Korean, Indonesian, Malay, Burmese, Thai, Vietnamese, Hindi, Spanish, Portuguese, German, Azerbaijani, Russian, Dutch, Bosnian, Serbian, Croatian, Bulgarian, Greek, Czech, Danish, Estonian, Finnish, Georgian, Hungarian, Icelandic, Hebrew, Italian,

Albanian, Latvian, Lithuanian, Montenegrin, Norwegian, Polish, Romanian, Slovak, Slovene, Swedish, Turkish and Ukrainian.

Though not necessarily global in their reach, other professional sports leagues are broadcast into other geographic markets. The Brazilian Championship and the São Paulo Regional Championship are broadcast throughout Asia and Europe. Both the São Paulo and the Brazilian championships have scheduled games as early as 11:00 a.m. local time to accommodate the demands of Chinese broadcasters.

The global broadcasting of professional sport has been fuelled by the Internet and related digital technologies. There are many websites offering online broadcasts live. These can be broadcast to television or to mobile devices (e.g., phones or tablets) and can be either legally or illegally distributed. The same technologies that have allowed for broadcasting have underpinned the availability of news (from traditional news organisations). Websites for professional teams are global in their reach and are often available in multiple languages. Social media allows fans from all corners of the globe to interact on matters of mutual interest. Technologies such as Twitter and Instagram allow fans to communicate with players.

In summary, the broadcasting of live games worldwide and other media content is modifying sports globally and the way that spectators can watch and interact with their favourite organisation or player. There are almost no limits for a sports fan. One can watch almost any kind of sport live in any part of the world. All one needs is an Internet connection.

Scheduling of games in foreign markets

Many organisations have responded to globalisation by increasing the international scope of their sales activity and developing an international network of subsidiaries (Bowen, Baker and Powell, 2015). Discontent with the mere broadcasting of games into other countries, sport organisations are scheduling events in foreign markets.

No single theory can explain the full complexity of international expansion (Akhter and Machado, 2014). The resource-based view of the firm suggests that firms internationalise when they possess resources that enable them to present a value proposition to a market that local suppliers cannot easily match (Barney, 1991). Industrial-organisational theory suggests that internationalisation occurs because firms capitalise on product and market factor imperfections (Akhter and Machado, 2014). When expanding internationally, transaction cost analysis considers what combination of asset specificity and environmental uncertainty will dictate the firm's decision to either internalise operations or use markets. In addition to the above, *psychic distance* – or the cultural and business gap between the home market and foreign market – is also important (Evans and Mavondo, 2002).

International expansion is clearly evident within Formula 1 (F1). F1 was traditionally a Western European sport (Gezici and Er, 2014). Since 2000, the circuit has expanded considerably. In 2015, more than half the races were held outside Europe. F1 expansion is driven by the emergence of new economies in Asia and the Middle East. F1 has employed a two-tier approach: (a) promoting native drivers and

(b) awarding an event to a host nation (Jensen, Cobbs and Groza, 2014). Tennis, another traditionally Western sport, has also expanded its international footprint. Shanghai replaced Hamburg as host of a Masters 1000 tournament, and Rio de Janeiro replaced Memphis as a host of an ATP 500 tournament. Non-ATP events, popularly known as exhibition events, are played in New Delhi and Kuala Lumpur. Mixed martial arts (MMA), has its roots in United States, Brazil, and Japan. Nowadays, the most important MMA event producer is Ultimate Fighting Championship (UFC). UFC once focused on the American market, but now also produces events in Canada, Mexico, Brazil, England, Germany, Russia, Japan and the United Arab Emirates.

In 2008, the EPL proposed playing a '39th Game', whereby clubs would play a competitive match in international cities. Cities would pay for the privilege of hosting these matches. The extra match is important, as it would not reduce the number of matches available for local fans. FIFA strongly opposed the initiative; additionally, other football associations expressed concern and local fan response was 'almost unanimously negative' (Rookwood and Chan, 2011, p. 906). The initiative was not pursued, but has still not been dismissed by the EPL ('Premier League Chief Scudamore', 2014). This initiative should not be confused with friendly or pre-season matches. EPL clubs have been playing these for many years. The Premier League Asian Trophy – the only Premier League-affiliated competition to have been held outside of England – is a more formalised pre-season tournament. Four EPL teams participate in the biennial competition. In 2014, the Spanish La Liga and the Spanish government's sports agency initiated the LFP World Challenge. The aim is to promote the brand 'Spain' through sport. La Liga teams play friendly matches in Europe, North and South America, and Asia.

Sales of team/player merchandise around the world

In addition to scheduling matches in and broadcasting into distant markets, sport organisations have also been licensing their logos and names all over the world. Licensing conveys the right to use another organisation's intellectual properties for commercial purposes (Fullerton, 2010). Licensed products can be found in a number of sectors including entertainment, movies, and fashion. Sports licensing covers licensing of teams' or leagues' trademarks such as logos, symbols, and images of team players. These items are owned by sports properties (licensors) that lease the rights to licensees in return for royalties. These logos are applied to various products or merchandise (Kwak, Kwon and Lim, 2015). For licensors, licensing provides opportunity for both revenue generation and brand awareness. For consumers, the consumption of team-licensed merchandise reflects team identification (Menefee and Casper, 2011). The net effect of team-licensed merchandise is a strengthening of the fan–team relationship (Fisher and Wakefield, 1998). Licensed merchandise provides opportunities for people to feel part of a brand and/or consumption community (Hedlund, 2014), no matter how geographically remote they may be from the point of attachment.

In 2014, the NBA partnered with Jabong, an Indian fashion and lifestyle e-commerce portal, to create the first NBA online store in India. A number of teams and leagues have also entered into a similar arrangement with Alibaba, the Chinese e-commerce giant. In 2007, São Paulo FC, one of the major professional football teams in Brazil, signed a three-year agreement with Warner Bros. Consumer Products. They developed more than 100 licensed products to sell in Brazil and other non-Brazilian markets.

Cross-border investing in team ownership

The final manifestation of globalisation and sport is the cross-border ownership of professional sport teams. This cross-border ownership is a clear manifestation of FDI controlling ownership in a business enterprise in one country by an entity based in another country. FDI promotes knowledge transfer, fills savings gaps, creates jobs, improves technology, increases the quantity and the quality of capital, and adds to competition in domestic markets (Jones and Cook, 2015).

Despite the view that FDI generates spillovers that benefit local firms in the host country, research on this topic has yielded mixed results: positive effects, negative effects, marginal effects and nonlinear relationships (Yi, Chen, Wang and Kafouros, 2015). The authors concluded that the occurrence and magnitude of FDI spillovers are contingent upon many factors, and that positive FDI effects are never guaranteed.

Multinational corporations look for markets with economic growth, evidence of other FDIs to take advantage of agglomeration effects, and impeccable levels of physical infrastructure development (Jakobsen, Solberg, Halvorsen and Jakobsen, 2012). Cross-border ownership of professional sport teams is clearly evident in the EPL. By 2015, EPL teams were in the minority: 11 of the 20 clubs were in foreign hands. Nauright and Ramfjord (2010) outlined three factors underpinning the 'explosion' (p. 431) of foreign ownership within the EPL. The first involves the increased value of selling licensed products and television broadcasts internationally. Second, the economic structure of the EPL teams allows for majority owners, unlike other European countries where only minority holdings have been allowed. Third, there are opportunities for cross-marketing sporting brands and other products in large-scale investment portfolios.

The cross-border ownership of professional sport teams can be divided into two types. The first is a diversification acquisition. In these circumstances, a company purchases a controlling interest in another to expand its product and service offerings. This type of acquisition allows the acquiring organisation to operate in a fundamentally different type of business. For example, Russian businessman and oligarch Roman Abramovich purchased a controlling interest in Chelsea FC after making a considerable fortune in other industries, namely manufacturing, oil, and aluminium. Similarly, Red Bull, the Austrian-based energy drink manufacturer, has purchased or established football teams in the United States, Brazil, Ghana, and Germany, as well as an ice hockey team in Germany.

The second type of cross-border ownership is when a sport organisation acquires a financial interest in another sport organisation. The City Football Group – more popularly known as Manchester City – established the New York City Football Club and became the twentieth Major League Soccer team. City Football Group acquired 80 per cent of the Melbourne Heart, which was immediately rebranded as Melbourne City, and acquired a minority share in the J-League's Yokohama F. Marinos. The geographic complexity is further complicated, given that City Football Group is a holding company under the Abu Dhabi United Group.

Despite the growth of cross-border ownership, some professional sports leagues resist or prohibit foreign ownership. For instance, the ownership structure of Bundesliga clubs does not allow for any private sector investment, regardless of their nationality (Franck, 2010). Additionally, the J-League has recently revised its foreign ownership policies. While previously, foreign owners were restricted to 49 per cent ownership, the policy now allows for majority ownership by a non-Japanese entity through the creation of a Japanese subsidiary.

As is evident, cross-border ownership of professional sports teams is a contentious topic. Nauright and Ranfjord (2010) captured key elements underpinning fan opposition to foreign ownership:

> Hostility to American owners appears greater than for others due to the widely held perception – rightly or wrongly held – that Americans do not really know or care about football but that investment in English clubs is purely for profit taking and not long-term club development.
>
> *(p. 437)*

Indeed, FDI is often associated with consumer animosity (Fong, Lee and Du, 2015). Nauright and Ranfjord described the relationship between Liverpool fans and the club's first American owners as 'uneasy'; fans were both 'skeptical' and 'disillusioned' (Nauright and Ranfjord, 2010, p. 438). Teams were originally 'community institutions', but were 'transformed by the logic of the marketplace'; although teams would 'routinely appeal to civic (and national) sentiments ... the languages of communal tradition and loyalties are increasingly supplanted by corporate images and by the discourse of consumer choice' (Whitson, 2000, p. 59).

Concepts related to globalisation

The terms *McDonaldisation*, *Disneyisation*, and *Americanisation* all relate to globalisation. The key link between these concepts and globalisation is that they all imply homogenisation of production and consumption. Ritzer (2015) described McDonaldisation as 'the process by which *the principles* of the fast-food restaurant are coming to dominate more and more sectors of American society as well as of the rest of the world' (p. 1). The key features of McDonaldisation are efficiency, calculability, predictability, and control. Similarly, Disneyisation refers to the principles and characteristics of the Disney theme parks (Bryman, 1999). The key features of Disneyisation include theming, differentiation of consumption, merchandising, and emotional labour. In one investigation, Duke (2002) used both McDonaldisation and Disneyisation to examine recent changes in English professional football. Duke argued that both processes are infiltrating professional football in England. However, this is not a one-way process (or a process without resistance) and football fans have demanded more attention to local customs. For Carlsson and Backman (2015), Americanisation captures both a central and peripheral perspective whereby the United States uses economic and political power to export its culture throughout the world. Embedded within the concept of Americanisation, Dyreson (2013) introduced the term *Californisation* to refer to the global growth of 'California cool' (p. 258) and sports like beach volleyball, sailboarding, mountain-biking, and triathlon.

Concerns about globalisation

The ongoing, perhaps even unrelenting globalisation of sport is not without its criticisms. Kobayashi (2012) wrote the following:

> Discussions and debates about the nature, impact and consequences of globalization are now a fundamental part of academic, political, economic and popular discourse.
> … The dominant discourses about globalization have often been equated with modernization, Westernization or Americanization, thereby marginalizing or even destroying local/national systems, traditions and values in the non-West.
>
> *(p. 725)*

Indeed, the diffusion of sports is often perceived as Western cultural and/or economic imperialism (Chen *et al.*, 2012). The specific concern is that local cultures and their underlying values and traditions will be changed – perhaps even annihilated – by Western approaches to leisure, lifestyle, and commerce.

Local sport organisations are likely casualties of the globalisation of sport. Thibault (2009) argued that the internationalisation of leagues has detrimentally affected domestic leagues in certain countries (Thibault, 2009). Additionally, George Ritzer's concept of globalisation predicts that the effects of globalisation will result in all clubs becoming increasingly similar (Sondaal, 2013). Globalisation may therefore result in cultural homogeneity and loss of diversity.

Managerial implications

The managerial implications of globalisation vary according to both sector and region (Rao, 2001). Masteralexis and McDonald (1997), for example, outlined the case for sport managers with international business capabilities. The internationalisation of the sport industry has resulted in a demand for integration of international perspectives into the sport management higher education curriculum (de Haan and Sherry, 2011). De Haan and Sherry argued (2011) that this can take one of two forms. In the first form, international abroad requires the movement of people or programmes to international environments. The second, internationalisation at home, promotes and supports international/intercultural understanding through campus-based activities.

Still in the context of education, there is encouragement for international internships, research collaborations and the redesign of curriculum at both the programme and course level to better facilitate an understating of the international business environment (Danylchuk, 2011). There are explicit calls for second language and cultural training (Masteralexis and McDonald, 1997). Further, Danylchuk (2011) encouraged faculty to internationalise themselves through exchanges, visiting scholars' programmes, engaging in study abroad programmes and participation in international conferences.

For leaders and managers, globalisation creates tensions between global and local, between differentiated and integrated, especially given the possibility of multiple cultures within a single organisation (Thomas, Bellin, Jules and Lynton, 2012). Thomas et al. (2012) suggested that global leadership teams need to (a) establish a clear purpose and operating principles to ensure focus and a consistent message, (b) be capable of adjusting the way they think and the persons involved in the decision-making process, and (c) be able to change ahead of the curve and even ahead of the rest of the organisation.

A global workforce creates greater demand for staff with cross-cultural sensitivities and skills (Burke and Ng, 2006). These sensitivities will relate not just to staff, but also consumers. For example, there are concerns that women and other underrepresented socio-demographic and geo-political groups may be further marginalised in global organisations, unless there are customised approaches to understanding motivation, emotional ties, procedural justice, and psychological ownership (Choi and Kim, 2007).

Further, there are increasing concerns that the world's hyper-connectivity creates the 'butterfly effect', whereby a small, innocuous change in one place leads to major changes in distant locales (Goldin and Mariathasan, 2014).

Conclusion

The globalisation genie is out of the bottle. Efforts to put globalisation back in the bottle are futile, and the future of globalisation will continue to be a battle between the local and global. The local will rarely win out; a draw might be the most optimistic of outcomes for local cultures. Life in the twenty-first century will become more uncertain. Upheavals are likely as resources, money, and space become even scarcer. The world will become smaller, and the sport you see, no matter which corner of the world you wake up in, will be increasingly familiar.

References

Akhter, S. H. and Machado, M. (2014). Internationalization dilemma for Brazilian firms: China vs. the Greater Mercosur region. *European Business Review, 26*, 514–530. doi:10. 1108/EBR-03-2013-0063

Andrews, D. L., Batts, C. and Silk, M. (2014). Sport, glocalization and the new Indian middle class. *International Journal of Cultural Studies, 17*, 259–276. doi:10.1177/1367877913487531

Baldwin, R. E. and Martin, P. (1999). Two waves of globalisation: Superficial similarities, fundamental differences. In J. C. B. Mohr (ed.) *Globalisation and labour* (pp. 3–59). Tubingen, Germany: Kiel Institute of World Economics.

Barney, J. (1991). Firm resources and sustained competitive advantage. *Journal of Management, 17*, 99–120. doi:10.1177/014920639101700108

Bowen, H. P., Baker, H. K. and Powell, G. E. (2015). Globalization and diversification strategy: A managerial perspective. *Scandinavian Journal of Management, 31*, 25–39. doi:10.1016/j.scaman.2014.08.003

Brannagan, P. M. and Giulianotti, R. (2014). Soft power and soft disempowerment: Qatar, global sport and football's 2022 World Cup finals. *Leisure Studies.* Advance online publication. doi:10.1080/02614367.2014.964291

Bryman, A. (1999). The Disneyization of society. *Sociological Review, 47*, 25–47. doi:10. 1111/1467-954X.00161

Burke, R. J. and Ng, E. (2006). The changing nature of work and organizations: Implications for human resource management. *Human Resource Management Review, 16*, 86–94. doi:10.1016/j.hrmr.2006.03.006

Carlsson, B. and Backman, J. P. (2015). The blend of normative uncertainty and commercial immaturity in Swedish ice hockey. *Sport in Society, 18*, 290–312. doi:10.1080/17430437. 2014.951438

Chen, K., Gunter, C. and Zhang, C. (2012). How global is U.S. Major League Baseball? A historical and geographic perspective. *GeoJournal, 77*, 429–444. doi:10.1007/s10708-011-9406-x

Choi, C. J. and Kim, S. W. (2007). Women and globalization: Ethical dimensions of know-ledge transfer in global organizations. *Journal of Business Ethics, 81*, 53–61. doi:10.1007/s10551-007-9480-7

Chung, J., Hwang, S. and Won, D. (2015). Globalization, media imperialism and South Korean sport. *International Journal of the History of Sport, 32*, 484–498. doi:10.1080/09523367.2015.1004887

Danylchuk, K. (2011). Internationalizing ourselves: Realities, opportunities, and challenges. *Journal of Sport Management, 25*, 1–10. Retrieved from http://journals.humankinetics.com/jsm

de Haan, D. and Sherry, E. (2011). Internationalisation of the sport management curriculum: Academic and student reflections. *Journal of Studies in International Education, 16*, 24–39. doi:10.1177/1028315311403487

Duke, V. (2002). Local tradition versus globalisation: Resistance to the McDonaldisation and Disneyisation of professional football in England. *Football Studies, 5*(1), 5–23. Retrieved from http://footballstudiesgroup.iwarp.com/

Dyreson, M. (2013). The republic of consumption at the Olympic Games: Globalization, Americanization, and Californization. *Journal of Global History, 8*, 256–278. doi:10.1017/S1740022813000211

Evans, J. and Mavondo, F. T. (2002). Psychic distance and organizational performance: An empirical examination of international retailing operations. *Journal of International Business Studies, 33*, 515–532. doi:10.1057/palgrave.jibs.8491029

Falcous, M. and Maguire, J. A. (2006). Imagining 'America': The NBA and local-global mediascapes. *International Review for the Sociology of Sport, 41*, 59–78. doi:10.1177/1012 690206066961

Fisher, R. J. and Wakefield, K. (1998). Factors leading to group identification: A field study of winners and losers. *Psychology and Marketing, 15*, 23–40. doi:10.1002/(SICI)1520-6793(199801)15:1%3C23::AID-MAR3%3E3.0.CO;2-P

Fong, C.-M., Lee, C.-L. and Du, Y. (2015). Consumer animosity and foreign direct investment: An investigation of consumer responses. *International Business Review, 24*, 23–32. doi:10.1016/j.ibusrev.2014.05.005

Franck, E. (2010). Private firm, public corporation or member's association governance structures in European football. *International Journal of Sport Finance, 5*, 108–127. Retrieved from https://ijsf.wordpress.com/

Fullerton, S. (2010). *Sports marketing* (2nd ed.). New York: McGraw-Hill Irwin.

Gezici, F. and Er, S. (2014). What has been left after hosting the Formula 1 Grand Prix in Istanbul? *Cities, 41*, 44–53. doi:10.1016/j.cities.2014.05.004

Giulianotti, R. and Robertson, R. (2004). The globalization of football: A study in the glocalization of the 'serious life'. *British Journal of Sociology, 55*, 545–568. doi:10.1111/j.1468-4446.2004.00037.x

Giulianotti, R. and Robertson, R. (2007a). Forms of glocalization: Globalization and the migration strategies of Scottish football fans in North America. *Sociology, 41*, 133–152. doi:10.1177/0038038507073044

Giulianotti, R. and Robertson, R. (2007b). Sport and globalization: Transnational dimensions. *Global Networks, 7*, 107–112. doi:10.1111/j.1471-0374.2007.00159.x

Giulianotti, R. and Robertson, R. (2012). Glocalization and sport in Asia: Diverse perspectives and future possibilities. *Sociology of Sport Journal, 29*, 433–454. Retrieved from http://journals.humankinetics.com/ssj

Goldin, I. and Mariathasan, M. (2014). *The butterfly defect: How globalization creates systemic risks, and what to do about it.* Princeton, NJ: Princeton University Press.

Grainger, A. and Andrews, D. L. (2005). Resisting Rupert through sporting rituals?: The transnational media corporation and global-local sport cultures. *International Journal of Sport Management and Marketing, 1*, 3–16. doi:10.1504/IJSMM.2005.007118

Grant, N., Heere, B. and Dickson, G. (2011). New sport teams and the development of brand community. *European Sport Management Quarterly, 11*, 35–54. doi:10.1080/16184742.2010.537364

Hedlund, D. P. (2014). Creating value through membership and participation in sport fan consumption communities. *European Sport Management Quarterly, 14*, 50–71. doi:10.1080/16184742.2013.865775

Henley, J., Kirkpatrick, C. and Wilde, G. (1999). Foreign direct investment (FDI) in China: Recent trends and current policy issues. *World Economy, 22*, 223–243. doi:10.1111/1467-9701.00201

Huang, F. (2013). Glocalisation of sport: The NBA's diffusion in China. *International Journal of the History of Sport, 30*, 267–284. doi:10.1080/09523367.2012.760997

Jakobsen, J., Solberg, H. A., Halvorsen, T. and Jakobsen, T. G. (2012). Fool's gold: Major sport events and foreign direct investment. *International Journal of Sport Policy and Politics, 5*, 363–380. doi:10.1080/19406940.2012.717099

Jensen, J. A., Cobbs, J. and Groza, M. D. (2014). The niche portfolio strategy to global expansion: The influence of market resources on demand for Formula One racing. *Journal of Global Marketing, 27*, 247–261. doi:10.1080/08911762.2014.909554

Jones, A. and Cook, M. (2015). The spillover effect from FDI in the English Premier League. *Soccer and Society, 16*, 116–139. doi:10.1080/14660970.2014.882819

Kobayashi, K. (2012). Globalization, corporate nationalism and Japanese cultural interme-diaries: Representation of bukatsu through Nike advertising at the global-local nexus. *International Review for the Sociology of Sport, 47*, 724–742. doi:10.1177/1012690211 420202

Kwak, D. H., Kwon, Y. and Lim, C. (2015). Licensing a sports brand: Effects of team brand cue, identification, and performance priming on multidimensional values and purchase intentions. *Journal of Product and Brand Management, 24*, 198–210. doi:10.1108/JPBM-05-2014-0579

Maguire, J. A. (1999). *Global sport: Identities, societies, civilizations.* Cambridge, UK: Polity.

Maguire, J. A. (2011). The global media sports complex: Key issues and concerns. *Sport in Society: Cultures, Commerce, Media, Politics, 14*, 965–977. doi:10.1080/17430437.2011. 603552

Mason, D. S. and Duquette, G. H. (2005). Globalisation and the evolving player-agent relationship in professional sport. *International Journal of Sport Management and Marketing, 1*, 93–109. doi:10.1504/IJSMM.2005.007123

Masteralexis, L. P. and McDonald, M. A. (1997). Enhancing sport management education with international dimensions including language and cultural training. *Journal of Sport Management, 11*, 97–110. Retrieved from http://journals.humankinetics.com/jsm

Menefee, W. C. and Casper, J. M. (2011). Professional basketball fans in China: A comparison of National Basketball Association and Chinese Basketball Association team identifi-cation. *International Journal of Sport Management and Marketing, 9*, 185–200. doi:10.1504/ IJSMM.2011.041571

Miller, T., Lawrence, G. A., McKay, J. and Rowe, D. (2001). *Globalization and sport: Playing the world.* London: Sage.

Nauright, J. and Ramfjord, J. (2010). Who owns England's game? American professional sporting influences and foreign ownership in the Premier League. *Soccer and Society, 11*, 428–441. doi:10.1080/14660971003780321

Premier League Chief Scudamore still in favour of '39th game'. (2014, August 13). *BBC News.* Retrieved from www.bbc.co.uk/sport/0/football/28770356

Rao, C. P. (2001). *Globalization and its managerial implications.* London: Quorom.

Ritzer, G. (2003). The globalization of nothing. *SAIS Review, 23*, 189–200. doi:10.1353/ sais.2003.0053

Ritzer, G. (2015). *The McDonaldization of society* (8th ed.). Thousand Oaks, CA: Sage.

Robertson, R. (1992). *Globalization: Social theory and global culture.* London: Sage.

Robertson, R. (1995). Glocalization: Time-space and homogeneity-heterogeneity. In M. Featherstone, S. Lash and R. Robertson (eds) *Global modernities* (pp. 25–44). London: Sage.

Rookwood, J. and Chan, N. (2011). The 39th game: Fan responses to the Premier League's proposal to globalize the English game. *Soccer and Society, 12*, 897–913. doi:10.1080/ 14660970.2011.609688

Sondaal, T. (2013). Football's grobalization or globalization? The lessons of Liverpool Football Club's evolution in the Premier League era. *Soccer and Society, 14*, 485–501. doi:10.1080/14660970.2013.810432

Thibault, L. (2009). Globalization of sport: An inconvenient truth. *Journal of Sport Management, 23*, 1–20. Retrieved from http://journals.humankinetics.com/jsm

Thomas, R. J., Bellin, J., Jules, C. and Lynton, N. (2012). Global leadership teams: Diagnosing three essential qualities. *Strategy and Leadership, 40*(3), 25–29. doi:10.1108/1087857 1211221185

Whitson, D. (2000). Circuits of promotion: Media, marketing and the globalization of sport. In L. A. Wenner (ed.) *MediaSport* (pp. 57–72). London: Routledge.

Wójcik, D. (2014). Review of the book *The butterfly defect: How globalization creates systemic risks, and what to do about it. Journal of Economic Geography, 15*, 250–252. doi:10.1093/jeg/lbu043

Yi, J., Chen, Y., Wang, C. and Kafouros, M. (2015). Spillover effects of foreign direct investment: How do region-specific institutions matter? *Management International Review, 55*, 539–561. doi:10.1007/s11575-014-0235-2

Further reading

Dickson, G. and Schofield, G. (2005). Globalisation and globesity: The impact of the 2008 Beijing Olympics on China. *International Journal of Sport Management and Marketing, 1*, 169–179. doi:10.1504/IJSMM.2005.007128

Giulianotti, R. (2015). The Beijing 2008 Olympics: Examining the interrelations of China, globalization, and soft power. *European Review, 23*, 286–296. doi:10.1017/S1062798714000684

Hallinan, C. and Burke, M. (2005). Transition game: Globalisation and the marketing of a suburban "nationalised" basketball team in Australia. *International Journal of Sport Management and Marketing, 1*, 127–140. doi:10.1504/IJSMM.2005.007125

Maguire, J. A. (2011). The global media sports complex: Key issues and concerns. *Sport in Society, 14*, 965–977. doi:10.1080/17430437.2011.603552

Thibault, L. (2009). Globalization of sport: An inconvenient truth. *Journal of Sport Management, 23*, 1–20. Retrieved from http://journals.humankinetics.com/jsm

9

SOCIO-ECONOMIC IMPACTS OF SPORTS MEGA-EVENTS

More unintended than intended?

Wolfram Manzenreiter and John Horne

This chapter takes a critical approach to understanding the socio-economic impacts of mega-events. As Rojek (2013) suggested, a critical approach to events and event management asks searching questions about 'event power' to get an idea of *who* defines events, *how* they are managed and *what* they achieve' (pp. xi–xii). Professional event literature usually takes a *technocratic view*, focusing 'on the nuts and bolts in the machine and when and where to oil the parts' (Rojek, 2013, p. xii). Further, critical discourse on events asks questions about 'who owns the machine, who controls it and what is its purpose' (Rojek, 2013, p. xii). This chapter will elucidate why the socio-economic impact of sports mega-events is a critical issue, not only because of the vast sums of money involved and the potential risks to a city's, region's, or entire nation's prestige or reputation should things go wrong, but also given the possibility of unexpected or unintended potential impacts. First, we will critically reflect on the language used to frame the consequences of sports mega-event hosting. Further, we will explore the interrelatedness of both intended and unintended impacts of sports mega-events. Finally, we will present a case study of the London 2012 Olympic Games to illustrate these impacts. The final section will also feature a short conclusion and suggestions on managerial implications.

Impacts, legacy, heritage and leverage: clarifying concepts

Since the 1990s, mega-event hosting and its impacts have been discussed at great length. The preparation and staging of a sports mega-event such as the Olympic Games or the FIFA World Cup undoubtedly impacts the lives of people on site. Yet, it is not always clear what it is that is being claimed when impacts are discussed or claimed more generally. Academic debates have pointed out four broad areas of interest: (a) the potential for economic development impacts from hosting mega-events, (b) the political impacts in terms of image management by 'branding' the cities, regions and nations that host mega-events, (c) the social impact of bringing people together as participants, volunteers, and audiences, and (d) the cultural–ideological impacts in terms of providing citizens of hosting nations with opportunities to positively identify with their host nation or city. Impacts can be tangible and material or intangible and symbolic, and economists and urban planners have tended to focus their research attention on the former (Gratton, Shibli and Coleman, 2006), whereas sociologists, political scientists, and social geographers have often been more interested in the intangible, symbolic, and representational outcomes (Manzenreiter, 2014).

Whereas *impact* has a more neutral connotation – permitting the discovery of both negative and positive outcomes – the softer and warmer term of *legacy* is most often used nowadays to discuss the repercussions of sports mega-events, albeit not uncontested (Hiller, 2003; MacAloon, 2008). The emergent usage of legacy in relation to sports mega-events coincided with the spectacular growth in the size of the Olympic Games, which generated an increasing number of *white elephant*[1] constructions – a fear of gigantism and growing concern about environmental damages. The Samaranch era was also fuelled by corruption scandals that dogged the International Olympic Committee (IOC) in the 1990s. Seeing the image of the Olympic Games and its sales value seriously at risk, the IOC actively foresaw the increased desire to develop a legacy, including detailed operational plans about how legacy would be implemented, how operations could be monitored, and how a post-Games legacy implementation could be evaluated. Acknowledging the utility of hosting as a tool in achieving a range of sport and non-sport policy objectives, governments were complicit with IOC demands (Cashman and Horne, 2013).

By reframing debates on the costs and benefits of hosting sports mega-events in terms of legacy planning, its proponents unintentionally raised awareness about potentially negative outcomes resulting from a lack of proper legacy management, and about positive as well as negative outcomes being unevenly distributed among different social groups. 'Leverage' that shifts the focus away from the actual event, its immediate impacts and legacy to the strategic implementation of larger and longer-lasting economic or social goals of the hosting society, is one type of solution. According to De Lisio, Derom, and Van Wynsberghe (2015), leverage studies 'are more longitudinal in nature and focus on the organisational processes and strategies that are associated in the planning as well as the long-term legacies related to the event' (p. 175), while 'impact studies are defined as those, which are invested in the evaluation of the immediate fallout associated to the event' (p. 175). Our discussion is more in line with the latter statement, as we will consider economic impacts via increasing revenues and income 'through tourism and/or (international, national or local) private and public contracting/collaboration' (De Lisio *et al.*, 2015, p. 176), and social impacts 'to appease people living within local communities whilst distracting from the mega-cost affiliated to the event itself' (De Lisio *et al.*, 2015, p. 176).

The intentional impacts of hosting sports mega-events

Since the 1980s, *rent-seeking behaviour* – 'seeking control of assets and resources that can be used to extract rent from users' (Sayer, 2014, p. 53) – has become the economic imperative in global capitalism. This has had implications for elite sport, and in particular, its flagship mega-events: the Olympic Games and the men's football World Cup. Further, these events' proprietary rights holders have turned into business-oriented, international, non-government organisations. The massive growth in the involvement of commercial interests in sport has created a 'global media sports cultural complex' (Rowe, 2011, p. 34), in which the role of corporate media and sponsors has especially gotten bigger and bigger. At the same time, several features of the sports mega-events that these bodies oversee have become attractive and have been used by states for a variety of non-sporting ends. As Barrie Houlihan (2002) noted, the 'willingness of governments to humble themselves before the IOC and FIFA through lavish hospitality and the strategic deployment of presidents, prime ministers, royalty and supermodels is a reflection of the value that governments place on international sport' (p. 194).

Economists and social scientists (e.g., Manzenreiter, 2008; Preuss, 2004; Whitson and Horne, 2006) have assessed the costs and benefits of sports mega-events which, as an iron law of mega-projects, are usually 'over budget, over time, over and over again' (Flyvbjerg, 2011, pp. 321ff.). As a response to citizens' protest movements and investigations of shortcomings in the operations of sports mega-events (Jennings, 2006; Simson and Jennings, 1992; Sugden and Tomlinson, 1998, 2003; Tomlinson, 2014), demands for regulatory systems, greater transparency and accountability in governance have emerged in line with the legacy debate outlined above.

Strategies associated with economic and political liberalisation, economic growth and social development, nation-building and nation-signalling are the core categories of intended impacts. However, behind these labels there are a number of 'known unknowns' that have remained part of the political debate about these sports mega-events (Horne, 2007). Effectually, these known unknowns are a mixture of the intended and unintended impacts of sports mega-events as shifting perspectives inevitably lead to different answers to the critical questions of who benefits, who controls, and who loses out. These impacts include the following:

- Economic regeneration by increased business opportunities, new markets, new customers, increasing consumptions and new marketing opportunities due to a more appealing brand image. However, public sector funds – often quite extensive – are used to enhance private corporate sector gain and the local host sites. Further, spaces benefit global flows of capital, trade and finance – rather than local actors – notwithstanding that the economic impact is highly spatially concentrated and benefiting only a relatively small sector.
- Attracting tourist flows – though event tourists usually just replace 'non-sport' tourists who defer their visit to the usually well-established destination for the time of the event.

- Employment stability and growth for local labour markets – though these effects are usually of limited duration and rather in low-end sectors of the labour market.
- Urban regeneration and the improvement of public infrastructure that often leads to the gentrification of specific areas being regenerated, the 'zoning' of urban areas and the displacement (and subsequent 'replacement') of poor and less powerful communities of people.
- Changes in sport participation rates of the host population, with evidence for this claim largely wanting.
- 'Action politics' – though rather than being in charge, politicians often appear to be driven by private actors to make use of a 'state of emergency' as a particular way of manufacturing consent of local and national publics to gain their agreement about staging the event.

Unintended impacts

As we have indicated, the social forces unleashed by sports mega-events and their capabilities to impact social life often develop as a result of the pursuit of intended impacts and are quite varied. They include (a) the potential destabilisation of employment and the labour market, (b) the housing market and availability of homes in the areas hosting an event, (c) the amenities and infrastructure that remain after city restructuring, (d) the impacts on the leisure sector and in particular tourism, (e) the depoliticisation of local democratic processes and, moreover, (f) the huge ecological costs. Addressing the first of these, producing a sports mega-event involves full-time paid workers, part-time workers, unpaid volunteers, and an executive 'circus' moving from one event to the next. Critics have suggested that mega-events should only create short-term employment opportunities with limited benefits to the host population. As Preuss (2004) noted, 'the jobs required to host and organize the Olympics are temporary from the start' (p. 252). Their duration depends on the schedule for preparing and staging the sports mega-event. In addition, as volunteerism has become a crucial input factor for organisers, there is an associated depressing in the cost of labour.

13

The unintended social impacts of sports mega-events can take at least four forms. First, they include changes in conceptions of freedom and democracy; for example, accepted practices and conceptions of security can be altered as a result of increased surveillance that leads to lasting changes in the control of space and crowds beyond the actual event period. Second, the commodification of sport has been accelerated by the practices adopted at sports mega-events with respect to what it means to 'follow' or support elite sport as a fan or, increasingly, as a consumer. This raises the question about who the Games are for: the locals, the tourists, the media audience or the sponsors? Generally, the hosting of a mega-event stimulates the spread of market relations among all parties involved, clearly demonstrating that, as an unintended impact, sports mega-events work as a steering tool for consumption-based development rather than for social redistribution.

14

Third, the utilisation of the liminality of the festival mood that characterises the cultural framing of sports mega-events, and that has been discussed as the basis for the strengthening of collective identities, community feelings or national pride, often leads to concerns about the exclusionary or even xenophobic impact of an event's power in forging effective communities. Further, sports mega-events enable the diffusion of 'global standards'. Each sports mega-event serves as benchmark for the following one, thereby defining standards of world-class events not only for the flagship events, but also for second- or third-tier events, too. A related aspect of this is the growth of a mega-event *consultocracy* that travels with the global event circuit and operates according to global standards, with norms and procedures no longer merely defined nationally or by locally operating traditions.

One unintended impact factor that increasingly demands attention is the ecological impact of sports mega-events. Granting protection of the environment and claims of sustainability have become central requirements in bid books. However, 'zero carbon' or 'zero waste' promises are never realistic and are actually part of the greenwash public relations that surrounds the events. Environmental organisations have documented in virtually all cases of previous sports mega-events the devastating impact on green land, wildlife, protection policies, and climate change. It must be noted that the tensions that appear in a host region are affected by the competing agendas of organising committees and local authorities, by primary and secondary impacts, by intended and unintended impacts, and by short-term and long-term impacts. For example, local organisers often refuse to acknowledge that the ecological footprint of their event is exceeding the number of weeks during which it takes place. However, who is responsible for the impacts generated over the years of preparation and construction work, including illegal waste dumping, the destruction of green land, even in protected areas, and the irreversible loss of endangered species and biodiversity, and who should account for the heightened CO_2 emission due to all the people flying to the event? While some of the unintended impacts listed above may have even been secretly intended by some actors, other impacts, such as the environmental impact, are unintentional. All of these developments can also lead to the growth of opposition event coalitions, opposed to the event, as another unintended result (see Gruneau and Horne, 2016, for further discussion of these issues).

A case study of London 2012

The presently enforced emphasis on legacy as 'the value of sport facilities and public improvements that are turned over to communities or sports organizations after the … games' (Gratton and Preuss, 2008, p. 1923) has a lasting and altering impact on the temporality of sports mega-events. The period of holding the sports mega-event is just a minor fraction of four extended, overlapping, and interpenetrating time cycles. The first stage starts with the bidding process and probably much earlier with feasibility studies, excessive lobbying, and the creation of a rationale and its narrative, until the bid is eventually awarded. During the run-up period, cities and a country are mobilised for frantic infrastructure construction and the complete preparation of the Games. The event period itself is followed by the legacy period in which the books are closed, reports are published, and a retrospective theme is fashioned to engage broadly in the culminating project of legacy making (Kelly, 2011). Now that legacy concerns have become part of the entire event temporality, the orientation to future outcomes, post-event usage, and public memory are colouring each and every step of managerial planning, designing, implementing, and recording. This has been most explicitly and arguably only the case thus far in the London Summer Olympics. London's surprising win of the bid in 2005 was largely attributed to the explicit focus on legacy and urban regeneration, for which the Games were merely declared a 'housewarming party'.

The London bid was given UK Government approval in May 2003, submitted in 2004, and then gained the IOC's vote of support on 6 July 2005 (Horne and Whannel, 2012). In this respect, London was the first true legacy Olympics, as it became mandatory for a city to articulate at the bid stage both a vision of how the host city and country would benefit from the staging of the Games, and how its operational plans about the realisation of legacy would be implemented only after the first IOC conference on legacy in 2002 (De Moragas, Kennett and Puig, 2003). It has been suggested that one of the reasons why London won its bid was that it had attractive legacy plans in key areas: sport, youth, and the regeneration of a part of East London. Specific legacy plans were incorporated into the city's bid, and an ambitious range of objectives was identified. The UK Government committed to five, followed by six, legacy outcomes for the 2012 Games that collectively came to be referred to as the 'London 2012 Legacy Promises'. The sixth legacy promise was added in December 2009, belatedly mindful that London 2012 referred to both the Olympic and Paralympic Games. The following are 'plans for impact' (University of East London and Thames Gateway Institute for Sustainability, 2010, p. 15):

- To make the United Kingdom a world-class sports nation: elite success, mass participation, and school sport.
- To transform the heart of East London.
- To inspire a new generation of young people to take part in local volunteering, cultural, and physical activity.
- To make the Olympic Park a blueprint for sustainable living.
- To demonstrate that the United Kingdom is a creative, inclusive, and welcoming place to live in, to visit and for business.
- To develop opportunities and choices for disabled people.

These impact promises reflected the potential Games legacies identified by De Moragas *et al.* (2003) following the IOC legacy conference: (a) urban and environmental; (b) sporting, economic, and tourism-related; (c) political, cultural, social, and communication-related and (d) educational. Broadly speaking, the London bid included an increase in grassroots sports participation – particularly among youth

– the development of the London Olympic Park that would drive the regeneration of East London, promotion of economic growth and community engagement with the Games. Legacy governance was, however, initiated well before the Games took place in 2012. For example, the Olympic Park Legacy Company in London was established in 2009. Baroness Margaret Ford, Chair of the company, suggested that the true legacy of the London 2012 Olympic Games would be seen over a 20- to 25-year timescale as the newly named Queen Elizabeth Olympic Park and surrounding infrastructural changes mature (Ford, 2010).

Writing three years since London 2012, it is possible to briefly review three of the key legacy promises: (a) sport participation and volunteering, (b) urban regeneration, and (c) rebranding the United Kingdom as a place to do business. While there is little robust evidence that elite sport inspires participation through a 'demonstration effect' (Weed, 2009) or a 'trickle-down effect' (Sotiriadou, Shilbury and Quick, 2008), caution is needed before the potential for a participation legacy is dismissed out of hand. This caveat notwithstanding, most research challenges the assumption that hosting mega-events will stimulate increased participation (e.g., Girginov and Hills, 2008; Veal, Toohey and Frawley, 2012).

In July 2005, then-UK Prime Minister Tony Blair had told the IOC, gathered in Singapore, to choose the hosts of the 2012 Games and that the London Olympic bid vision was 'to see millions more young people in Britain and across the world participating in sport, and improving their lives as a result of that participation' (Williams, 2015, p. 12). Despite the lack of supporting evidence, the London Olympic organisers set specific legacy targets for participation aiming to get at least 1 million people more active and 1 million people doing more sport as a result of the Games. After the Conservative–Liberal Democrat coalition government came to power in 2010, however, many commitments were dropped (Hughes, 2012) and replaced by the vaguer objective published in the 2010 Legacy Action Plan (Department for Culture, Media and Sport, 2010): 'To increase grass roots participation, particularly by young people – and to encourage the whole population to be more physically active' (p. 1).

In assessing the extent to which the participation legacy has been delivered, the problem is not only disentangling the impact of the Olympics from other socio-economic factors, but also determining an appropriate timescale over which legacy should be judged. As is the case in many policy interventions, there is a time lag between the intervention and the impact. Therefore, a key factor to consider is exactly when to 'draw the line' about impact. Hence, with respect to sport participation, the evidence suggested in 2013 that there had been a steady increase in the number of people aged 16 and over taking part in sport at least once per week for at least 30 minutes. From a baseline figure of 13.9 million in 2005–2006, there had been an increase of 1.4 million to 15.3 million people in April 2013. According to Sport England (2013), if the period from just before the Olympic year (October 2011) was compared to April 2013, 'there are now over 530,000 more people playing sport regularly' (p. 1). If the overall assessment of the impact of the Games on participation in 2013 was one of cautious optimism, by 2015 after two successive reporting periods when statistics showed a considerable fall in participation, it was declared a 'disaster' by the opposition (i.e., Labour) sports minister (Gibson, 2015b). In June 2015, it was reported that the number of British people over 16 playing sport at least once a week had declined by 222,000 in six months. The figures also showed that the number of people playing no sport had increased by 1.2 million in the previous year. The trend was firmly a decline in participation, with 391,000 fewer people swimming in the year since June 2014 (Gibson, 2015b).

Additionally, according to the Active People survey, there was another significant cause for concern: Increases in participation were significantly skewed in favour of upper income groups. Moreover, data from the previous Active People report (Sport England, 2013) showed that while a statistically significant increase in participation (2006–2012) was evidenced in the 26+ age group, no increase was evident in the 16–25 age group. A legacy, which relies on older and more affluent people for its delivery, would be, at best only a partial success.

A related element of the participation legacy was the aim to increase the number of volunteers. Indeed, with 240,000 people applying to be 'Games Makers' in London, the hope was that many of the approximately 70,000 volunteers would continue in sport volunteering and that their presence at the heart of the Games would inspire others to do the same. However, there is some scepticism about the degree to which volunteering at a major event can be converted into regular, long-term volunteering in local sports organisation. Ritchie (2000) and Downward and Ralston (2006) suggested that the conversion rate is modest and that volunteer enthusiasm dissipates quite rapidly following the end of an event. This scepticism was reinforced by a recent survey of sports clubs, which reported that 78 per cent had noticed no change in the number of people volunteering at their club since the Games (Sport and Recreation Alliance, 2012).

A second key impact of the legacy for East London was economic development or regeneration (Davies, 2012). Although it was acknowledged that much of the infrastructure development would have taken place anyway, it was also accepted that the Games had accelerated the process. The government's 2010 Legacy Plan suggested that the redeveloped Olympic Park would generate between 8,000 and 10,000 jobs. The House of Lords Select Committee (House of Lords, 2013) acknowledged that substantial progress had been made towards the target figure for employment, but questioned the 'extent to which local residents are benefiting' (para. 309), particularly given the focus on high technology jobs. Additionally, though regeneration plans also included improving the availability of affordable housing for the local community, the House of Lords (2013) repeated concerns that the number of homes available for poorer local residents should aim to meet a target of 35 per cent.

Disputes over the future use of the Olympic Stadium have also marred developments of the Olympic Park post-Games. For instance, while much of the construction work on the Olympic site has been seen as a triumph of engineering and organisation, questions have been raised about the planning for the post-Games legacy, given the failure to secure a tenant for the Olympic Stadium. Initially, the

Olympic Stadium's future was to be as a scaled-down athletics venue. When that was judged economically uncertain, bids were invited from football clubs. West Ham United emerged as the preferred bidder, but both Tottenham Hotspur and Leyton Orient challenged the decision. With the legacy of London's Olympic stadium heading for the law courts, the government decided to intervene, retain the stadium in public ownership, and lease the stadium to a bidder. The decision to allow West Ham to lease the stadium has left taxpayers to cover the cost of its conversion for football- and stadium-running costs after the Games. These costs have now increased to £272 million, taking the total cost of the stadium to more than £700 million, from an originally estimated £280 million (Gibson, 2015a).

As well as the physical regeneration of East London, the government had the further ambition that hosting the Games would have economic impacts and 'demonstrate that the UK is a creative, inclusive and welcoming place to live in, to visit and for business' (see aforementioned 'plans for impact' No. 5; University of East London and Thames Gateway Institute for Sustainability, 2010, p. 15). This legacy objective was reinforced by the Department for Culture, Media, and Sport (2011), which noted the importance of 'exploiting to the full the opportunities for economic growth offered by hosting the Games' (p. 17). At the heart of the strategy for delivering the business legacy was the use of the Games to project a brand image of the United Kingdom in general and London in particular as a modern, knowledge-based, business-friendly environment. The Foreign and Common-wealth Office asserted that 'London 2012 will have a profound impact on the UK's international reputation' (House of Commons, 2011, Ev 19) and developed an 'engagement strategy' designed to 'cement Britain's reputation as a ... vibrant, open and modern society, a global hub in a networked world' and 'to bolster the UK economy, increase commercial opportunities for British business in target countries and secure high value inward investment' (House of Commons, 2011, Ev 39).

A central element of the government's Foreign and Commonwealth Office (FCO) strategy was marketing the United Kingdom's organisational expertise related to the delivery of sports mega-events, particularly to countries such as Brazil and Russia. According to then-FCO minister Jeremy Browne, London 2012 was seen as a major opportunity to contribute to the economic objective of the FCO to make the United Kingdom 'attractive' for trade and inward investment. As Browne pointed out 'the Olympic Games is not only the greatest sporting event but also the biggest corporate networking event in the world' (House of Commons, 2011, Ev 39). The London Olympics was one of the clearest recent examples of the use of hosting as an opportunity for enhancing a nation's brand. Hosting the Olympics, with huge global audiences, was clearly seen by the British government as an important opportunity to project a particular identity and an ideal vehicle for showcasing a vision of modern Britain. In the 2013 Nation Brand Index, Britain ranked third behind the United States and Germany – a position that it held in 2012, but an improvement from fourth in 2009.[2] Apart from the survey data from the Nation Brand Index, there is a substantial volume of qualitative data that strongly suggests that the London Games had a positive impact on Britain's international brand. A survey of international newspapers (Grix and Houlihan, 2012) indicated an almost universally positive perception of Britain projected by the opening ceremony and by the overall Games and one that corresponded with the objectives of the government.

Conclusion

This brief chapter has attempted to raise three issues with respect to the socio-economic impacts of sports mega-events. First, we have identified and tried to clarify some of the conceptual muddle that surrounds terms such as impact, legacy, heritage, and outcome in the discourse surrounding sports mega-events. Second, we have argued that there remains the need to consider a distinction between intended and unintended impacts. Though not all intended, mega-events may nonetheless profoundly impact everyday life in host cities, communities, and populations. Third, we have illustrated some of the gaps between the intended and unintended impacts of hosting a sports mega-event with reference to London 2012. London 2012 delivered impacts, but not quite what was intended or stated as the intention.

International non-governmental organisations in sports have recognised the importance of gaining impacts as part of the legacy and as a means of staging a sustainable event and have sought to move such developments from the periphery to centre stage in the past decade. We have demonstrated that sports mega-events are highly political affairs, surrounded by sports, urban, and corporate interests. One significant lesson from all this is that sports mega-event managers have to take into consideration that a clear differentiation of impacts must be made according to the stage of the event cycle. Further, mega-event managers cannot avoid negative outcomes, mainly because they are a surrogate of the cultural, political form of the mega-event. In that regard, there have been some welcomed new initiatives in the past decade to attempt to monitor and further encourage host cities to take legacy-impact management seriously.

Finally, we point out the difficulty for indiscriminate use of the legacy concept. On the one hand, legacy creates a tension between management of the sport association and management of the sports mega-event over who will be responsible for acknowledging that there can be negative legacies (although somewhat oxymoronic) emerging from Games. In contrast, widespread use of the term in bid documents and in publicity can amount to 'overkill' and excessively raise local host and national population expectations. In this respect, legacy is both a blessing and curse. It is certainly part of the risky nature of hosting a sports mega-event and requires considerable management if expectations are not to be too high. *Symbolic politics* – the politics of promotional culture via public diplomacy, 'soft power' and/or propaganda – are thus fundamental features of the contemporary risks of managing sports mega-events (on the concept of *soft power*, developed to describe the ability to attract and co-opt rather than coerce, use force, or give money as a means of persuasion, see Nye 1990). Whether or not competing with other cities or nations to host an event, winning the right to do so or actually hosting an event, the potential for symbolic power plays, or pitfalls, is real. All such exercises in promotional politics – nation-branding, city-branding, image alteration – run the danger of heightening reputational risk to the bidders – and the eventual hosts – involved. Legacy promises remain one of the most politically charged features of hosting an Olympic Games or other sports mega-event.

Notes

1   *White elephants* refers to facilities and stadiums built for the event but that are more costly to use and maintain in the long run than they are worth.
2   Nation Brand Index findings for 2013 are available online (www.gfk.com/news-and-events/press-room/press-releases/pages/nation-brand-index-2013-latest-findings.aspx).

References

Cashman, R. and Horne, J. (2013). Managing legacy. In S. Frawley and D. Adair (eds) *Managing the Olympics* (pp. 50–65). London, United Kingdom: Palgrave.

Davies, L. (2012). Beyond the games: Regeneration legacies and London 2012. *Leisure Studies, 31*, 309–337. doi:10.1080/02614367.2011.649779

De Lisio, A., Derom, I. and Van Wynsberghe, R. (2015). Reimagining the urban citizen: Leveraging physical cultural legacies. In J. Baker, P. Safai and J. Fraser-Thomas (eds) *Health and Elite Sport* (pp. 174–186). London: Routledge.

De Moragas, M., Kennett, C. and Puig, N. (eds). (2003). *The legacy of the Olympic Games, 1984–2000: International symposium, Lausanne, 14–16 Nov. 2002.* Lausanne: International Olympic Committee.

Department for Culture, Media and Sport. (2010). *Plans for the legacy from the 2012 Olympic and Paralympic Games.* Retrieved from www.gov.uk/government/uploads/system/uploads/attachment_data/file/78105/201210_Legacy_Publication.pdf

Department for Culture, Media and Sport. (2011, February). *Government Olympic Executive: London 2012 Olympic and Paralympic Games* [Annual report]. Retrieved from www.gov.uk/government/uploads/system/uploads/attachment_data/file/77633/DCMS_GOE_annual_report_february_2011.pdf

Downward, P. M. and Ralston, R. (2006). The sports development potential of sports event volunteering: Insights from the XVII Manchester Commonwealth Games. *European Sport Management Quarterly, 6*, 333–351. doi:10.1080/16184740601154474

Flyvbjerg, B. (2011). Over budget, over time, over and over again: Managing major projects. In P. W. G. Morris, J. K. Pinto and J. Söderlund (eds) *The Oxford handbook of project management* (pp. 321–344). Oxford: Oxford University Press.

Ford, M. (2010, December 6). Living in the Olympic park: Will dreams become reality? *BBC News.* Retrieved from www.bbc.co.uk/news/uk-11842550

Gibson, O. (2015a, June 20). Final bill for revamped Olympic Stadium will exceed £700m. *The Guardian.* Retrieved from www.theguardian.com/

Gibson, O. (2015b, June 12). Olympic legacy ends in lethargy and now anger. *The Guardian.* Retrieved from www.theguardian.com/

Girginov, V. and Hills, L. (2008). A sustainable sports legacy: Creating a link between the London Olympics and sports participation. *International Journal of the History of Sport, 25*, 2091–2116. doi:10.1080/09523360802439015

Gratton, C. and Preuss, H. (2008). Maximizing Olympic impacts by building up legacies. *International Journal of the History of Sport, 25,* 1922–1983. doi:10.1080/0952336080 2439023

Gratton, C., Shibli, S. and Coleman, R. (2006). The economic impact of major sports events: A review of ten events in the UK. In J. Horne and W. Manzenreiter (eds) *Sports mega-events: Social scientific analyses of a global phenomenon* (pp. 41–58). Oxford: Blackwell.

Grix, J. and Houlihan, B. (2012). Sports mega-events as part of a nation's soft power strategy: The cases of Germany (2006) and the UK (2012). *British Journal of Politics and International Relations, 16,* 572–596. doi:10.1111/1467-856X.12017

Gruneau, R. and Horne, J. (eds). (2016). *Mega-events and globalization: Capital and spectacle in a changing world order.* London: Routledge.

Hiller, H. (2003). Toward a science of Olympic outcomes: The urban legacy. In M. De Moragas, C. Kennett and N. Puig (eds) *The legacy of the Olympic Games, 1984–2000* (pp. 102–109). Lausanne: International Olympic Committee.

Horne, J. (2007). The four 'knowns' of sports mega-events. *Leisure Studies, 26,* 81–96. doi:10. 1080/02614360500504628

Horne, J. and Whannel, G. (2012). *Understanding the Olympics.* London, United Kingdom: Routledge.

Houlihan, B. (2002). Political involvement in sport, physical education and recreation. In A. Laker (ed.) *The sociology of sport and physical education: An introductory reader.* London: Routledge.

House of Commons. (2011, February 6). *FCO public diplomacy: The Olympic and Paralympic Games 2012* (Report No. HC 581). Retrieved from www.publications.parliament. uk/pa/cm201011/cmselect/cmfaff/581/581.pdf

House of Lords. (2013, September 11). *Select committee on Olympic and Paralympic legacy* [Audio transcript]. Retrieved from www.parliament.uk/documents/lords-committees/ olympic-paralympic-legacy/copl240713ev18wh.pdf

Hughes, K. H. (2012). *Sport mega-events and a legacy of increased sport participation: An Olympic promise or an Olympic dream?* (Doctoral thesis, Leeds Metropolitan University, Leeds, United Kingdom). Retrieved from www.kh2.org.uk/wp-content/uploads/2013/11/ Thesis-Kate-Hughes.pdf

Jennings, A. (2006). *Foul! The secret world of FIFA: Bribes, vote rigging and ticket scandals.* London: HarperSport.

Kelly, W. (2011). East Asian Olympics, Beijing 2008, and the globalisation of sport. *International Journal of the History of Sport, 28,* 2261–2270. doi:10.1080/09523367.2011. 626679

MacAloon, J. J. (2008). 'Legacy' as managerial/magical discourse in contemporary Olympic affairs. *International Journal of the History of Sport, 25,* 2060–2071. doi:10.1080/095233 60802439221

Manzenreiter, W. (2008). The 'benefits' of hosting: Japanese experiences from the 2002 Football World Cup. *Asian Business and Management, 7,* 201–224. doi:10.1057/abm. 2008.1

Manzenreiter, W. (2014). Magical thought and the legacy discourse of the 2008 Beijing Games. In J. Grix (ed.) *Leveraging legacies from sports mega-events: Concepts and cases* (pp. 119–129). Basingstoke, UK: Palgrave.

Nye, J., Jr. (1990). Soft power. *Foreign Policy, 80,* 153–171. doi:10.2307/1148580

Preuss, H. (2004). *The economics of staging the Olympics: A comparison of the games 1972–2008.* Cheltenham, UK: Edward Elgar.

Ritchie, J. (2000). Turning 16 days into 16 years through Olympic legacies. *Event Management, 6,* 155–165. doi:10.0000/096020197390239

Rojek, C. (2013). *Event power: How global events manage and manipulate.* London: Sage.

Rowe, D. (2011). *Global media sport: Flows, forms and futures.* London, UK: Bloomsbury Academic.

Sayer, A. (2014). *Why we can't afford the rich.* Bristol: Policy Press.

Simson, V. and Jennings, A. (1992). *The lords of the rings: Power, money and drugs in the modern Olympics.* London: Simon and Schuster.

Sotiriadou, P., Shilbury, D. and Quick, S. (2008). The attraction, retention/transition and nurturing process of sport development: Some Australian evidence. *Journal of Sport Management, 22,* 247–272. Retrieved from http://journals.humankinetics.com/jsm

Sport and Recreation Alliance. (2012, October 16). *Olympic legacy survey: Topline results.* London: Sport and Recreation Alliance.

Sport England. (2013). *Active People Survey: Sport Participation Factsheet,* available online at http://archive.sportengland.org/research/active_people_survey/active_people_survey_7.aspx [last accessed 12 November 2015].

Sugden, J. and Tomlinson, A. (1998). *FIFA and the contest for world football: Who rules the peoples' game?* Cambridge: Polity.

Sugden, J. and Tomlinson, A. (2003). *Badfellas: FIFA family at war.* Edinburgh: Mainstream Publishing.

Tomlinson, A. (2014). *FIFA (Fédération Internationale de Football Association): The men, the myths and the money.* London: Routledge.

University of East London and Thames Gateway Institute for Sustainability. (2010, October) *Olympic Games impact study – London 2012 pre-games report.* Retrieved form www.uel.ac.uk/geo-information/documents/UEL_TGIfS_PreGames_OGI_Release.pdf

Veal, A., Toohey, K. and Frawley, S. (2012). The sport participation legacy of the Sydney 2000 Olympic Games and other international sports events hosted in Australia. *Journal of Policy Research in Tourism, Leisure and Events, 4,* 155–184. doi:10.1080/19407963.2012.662619

Weed, M. (2009, October). *The potential of the demonstration effect to grow and sustain participation in sport.* Retrieved from http://archive.sportengland.org/about_us/sport_england_conferences/idoc.ashx?docid=b97bc095-eb32-4c20-91d4-5943b85e9462&version=2

Whitson, D. and Horne, J. (2006). Underestimated costs and overestimated benefits? Comparing the outcomes of sports mega-events in Canada and Japan. In J. Horne and W. Manzenreiter (eds) *Sports mega-events: Social scientific analyses of a global phenomenon* (pp. 73–89). Oxford: Blackwell.

Williams, R. (2015, June 20). Failure of Olympic legacy shows we are not all in it together. *The Guardian.* Retrieved from www.theguardian.com/

10

SOCIAL MEDIA, FAN ENGAGEMENT AND GLOBAL SPORT

Olan Scott, Michael Naylor and Katherine Bruffy

This chapter is a discussion of social media and fan engagement from an international perspective. It draws on existing literature of these two topics, while also including more recent research on consumer/fan segmentation in the online space (Bruffy, Scott, Naylor and Beaton, 2014; Scott, Pegoraro and Watkins, 2015). Social media has never been more 'personalized, individualized, and made pleasurable to use' (Booth, 2010, p. 2). Further, the rise of social media outlets, such as Facebook, Twitter, Instagram, and Snapchat, has provided consumers with new opportunities to communicate and interact online (Chao, Parker and Fontana, 2011). Social media consumers also produce and consume media content simultaneously (Mahan and McDaniel, 2006), suggesting that consumers are actively engaged in mass media (Booth, 2010).

Social media platforms enable users to create and maintain 'social networks' and help individuals connect with others based on common interests (Boyd and Ellison, 2007). Social media platforms are typically:

> Web-based services that allow individuals to (1) construct a public or semi-public profile within a bounded system, (2) articulate a list of other users with whom they share a connection, and (3) view and traverse their list of connections and those made by others within the system.
>
> *(Boyd and Ellison, 2007, p. 211)*

Similarly, Kaplan and Haenlein (2010) described these platforms as 'application[s] that enable users to connect by creating personal information profiles' (p. 63). Further, a user's connections can be made available for others to view, which connects social media users (Boyd and Ellison, 2007). Security measures allow profiles to be made public or semi-public on the Internet. The individual user's online social network allows the user to tailor the information he or she receives.

The personalisation of content provides a unique user experience catered to individual interests.

These modern communication opportunities have allowed sport teams, sport leagues, and athletes to enhance their global brands. Sport brands are, therefore, able to reach new markets with the use of social media because fans from all over the world have access to the social media channels of their favourite sport brands. For example, a sport fan's online social network connects him or her with favourite teams, athletes, and media sources. Sport organisations are able to provide consumers with new information that was not readily available in the past using traditional marketing strategies. Organisations can now deliver unique information to consumers about teams, players and coaches in real time, such as behind-the-scenes and insider stories, #QandA sessions with key stakeholders, and targeted sales/discounts.

Social media is most effective for organisations when the majority of staff understand and help contribute to online content. However, adapting social media into an organisation's branding approach is not easy. Departments within an organisation need to work together, sufficient resources need to be allocated to support the social media strategy, and employees need to be equipped with the knowledge and technology in order for social media to be successful. When organisations get past these barriers, social media can enhance brand equity by creating additional opportunities to connect with the sport consumer and/or other key stakeholders, such as sponsors and mass media members.

In this chapter, an overview of social media is first provided, followed by a discussion of how social media can facilitate engagement between fans and organisations within a relationship-marketing framework. Further, a number of examples of how sport organisations use social media are provided, in order to illustrate best international practices. The overall objective of the chapter is to provide the reader with an overview of the effective use of social media to engage fans in a variety of settings around the globe.

Social media and sport

In Australia and New Zealand, over 50 per cent of the population has a Facebook account (Adcorp, 2013). Because social media use is quite high in these nations, the potential for sport organisations to reach fans (and potential fans) through these channels is significant. Although sport comprises just a small proportion of television content, nearly 50 per cent of all Twitter content is related to sports (Nielsen Holdings, 2013). The rise in popularity of social media has drastically changed the ways in which sport organisations communicate with their key stakeholders (Pedersen, Miloch and Laucella, 2007). It is increasingly important for sport organisations to prioritise social media platforms in their overall communication, public relations, and marketing strategies.

Social media has changed how consumers get information and what information consumers can access. For example, it has given sport organisations, athletes, celebrities, and consumers an unfiltered voice in an increasingly cluttered media marketplace, and it should come as no surprise that sport organisations have been quick to embrace the opportunities that the digital environment provides (Evans and Smith, 2004). Traditionally, sport content has been vetted by journalists, producers, or editors who have decided whether or not it would be made available to fans. The adoption of social media platforms, however, has enabled users to have complete control over their message (Scott, Hill and Zakus, 2014). Social media also allows sport consumers to communicate directly with one another across the world and with their favourite teams and/or players (Tapp and Clowes, 2002). The ability to facilitate a myriad of interactions in the online space sets social media apart from any other form of communication that has ever existed (Watkins, Pegoraro and Scott, 2015) while also enabling sport organisations to add value to the fan experience and potentially add value to sport consumption (Williams and Chinn, 2010). As such, sport organisations have responded by incorporating these platforms into their approaches to communications, promotions, and marketing strategies. As this relatively new approach to communication with consumers evolves, it is vital for those involved in the management and marketing of sport to understand some of the issues related to social media.

There has been extensive social media research in many areas, such as public relations, marketing, as a communication platform, and numerous others. However, scholars have argued that some of these studies have not been sufficiently theoretically driven (Hardin, 2014). Other scholars have welcomed its inherent disruptiveness on legacy media, which was traditionally a one-to-many medium and noted that it is appropriate for new perspectives to emerge (Pegoraro, 2014). Hutchins (2014) cautioned against exploring Twitter-based strategy using simple analytics alone, such as counting the number of likes or followers an organisation has on its various social media platforms. In addition, Billings (2014) argued that the power of social media does not lie in the content that is posted, but rather in the proliferation of content, which leads to increased reach of the message.

Given that the sports industry has been an early adopter of social media – and particularly Twitter – a number of scholars have carried out research projects specifically exploring the use of that platform (Blaszka, Burch, Frederick, Clavio and Walsh, 2012; Frederick, Lim, Clavio, Pedersen and Burch, 2014; Hambrick, Frederick and Sanderson, 2015). Many of the studies on Twitter have focused on self-presentation, parasocial interaction, relationship marketing, crisis management and use of Twitter as a public relations tool. Studies examining Twitter have also included a number of foci: athletes, teams, leagues, and events. For example, Hull and Lewis (2014) analysed professional golfers' Tweets during the U.S. Masters Golf Tournament and found that golfers were able to give fans a more intimate view of their life through Twitter than they would normally receive through traditional news media. In terms of self-presentation, which is characterised as the creation of an online identity, golfers used both frontstage and backstage performances when using social media. Self-presentation enables an individual to craft an identity reflecting how one wishes to be seen (Hull and Lewis, 2014). *Front stage performances* are those that occur when other people are present, which suggests that individuals are concerned with the image they portray to the public. In contrast, *backstage performances* take place when there is either nobody else around or there are people with whom the performer is familiar, such as family and friends (Geurin-Eagleman and Burch, 2015). During backstage performances, individuals tend to be more open and candid. In another study on athlete presentation on Twitter, Frederick *et al.* (2014) found that athletes from major North American sports (i.e., football, baseball, basketball, and ice hockey) attempted to develop both social and parasocial relationships with consumers on Twitter. *Parasocial relationships* are characterised as being one-sided and interaction is mediated by a media person with a media user. Further, the message is controlled by the media person.

Social media as a tool in sport fan engagement

Connecting to and interacting with consumers is essential for the long-term success of any business. This is certainly true of sport – a setting in which cultivating relationships with fans over many seasons is often the key to sustainability. The term *engagement* has been used to characterise the iterative nature of communication between consumers and firms. Engagement can be thought of as a consumer's 'spontaneous, interactive and co-creative behaviours' (Yoshida, Gordon, Nakazawa and Biscaia, 2014, p. 400). Though cognitive, affective and behavioural aspects of fan engagement have been studied, engagement is most typically conceptualised in terms of behaviour (Yoshida *et al.*, 2014). In other words, for engagement to occur, a consumer must actually do something (e.g., enter a contest, invite a friend along to an event, or provide market insight to firms through a questionnaire), not just have an attitude or preference. For example, an engaged social media user may comment on a post or share a video on his or her social network.

Another key aspect of consumer engagement is that it is typically non-transactional in nature. Yoshida *et al.* (2014) theorised a typology of sport consumers' engagement based on activity (i.e., transactional or non-transactional) and role (i.e., in-role or extra-role). *Transactional behaviours* are either both sport-related and in-role (e.g., attending matches) or relational and extra-role (e.g., participating in membership/season ticket holder initiatives). On the other hand, *non-transactional behaviours* can be characterised as either impression-management or fan-engagement behaviours. Therefore, when sport organisations are engaging consumers, facilitating an exchange process is not usually part of the direct sales strategy, as in traditional marketing tactics (e.g., when purchasing a good or service).

Many sport organisations are now employing specialists in order to facilitate non-transactional, social media-based engagement with fans. For example, the organisation behind Great Britain's Olympic Games involvement is known as 'Team GB'. In the early stages of Team GB's preparation for the 2016 Games in Rio de Janeiro, the organisation sought to hire a Fan Engagement and Customer Relationship Management Manager ('Team GB Fan Engagement and CRM

Manager', 2015). The job description that was put forth by the organisation provides insight into the nature of fan engagement and the types of activities associated with it. Two of the areas of focus were database development and consumer insight generation. The common theme is the fact that neither are transaction-based, and both can be considered stepping stones towards the exchange processes that marketers covet.

The following question, however, needs to be asked. If engaging fans will not always lead directly to transaction (i.e., ticket purchase, merchandise purchase), then why should a sport organisation bother? In short, engagement between customer and organisation is right at the heart of relationship marketing – the approach widely believed to be the most effective for fostering the long-term sustainability of an organisation. *Relationship marketing* can be described as 'the attraction, development, and retention of customers' (Bee and Kahle, 2006, p. 103). Engaging fans in a non-transactional way might, therefore, lead to long-term relationships with fans. This is consistent with the way in which Morgan and Hunt (1994), among others, have characterised relationship marketing.

One reason for a sport team to engage with its fans is that a return on investment may be more widespread than just what the individual fan consumes at a later date. In addition to buying merchandise and watching games live/on television, it is also expected that a highly engaged fan will facilitate similar desirable outcomes from fellow fans through extra-role behaviours (Ahearne, Bhattacharya and Gruen, 2005), such as word-of-mouth communication and other personal influence. In other words, engaged fans are likely to benefit the organisation beyond the financial exchange for goods and services, which is a consumer's traditional role.

Social media is the ideal platform to facilitate the non-transactional spontaneity, interaction and co-creative behaviours that sport organisations seek from fans. With handheld, Internet-capable devices and data plans now widespread, social media provides the opportunity for organisations to connect with fans wherever they are throughout the day; this can deepen consumer brand relationships (Ashley and Tuten, 2015).

Another key benefit of having an engaged fan base relates to their response to a team's poor performance. In their study of Japanese football fans, Yoshida *et al.* (2014) suggested that engaged fans were likely to continue to attend games and wear team apparel, even during a losing season. Social media, therefore, facilitates ongoing content sharing and engagement with fans beyond just scores, standings, and otherwise focusing on the performance of the team itself.

One anecdotal criticism of social media is that it provides nothing more than an additional means for a sport organisation to connect with fans that are already loyal, highly engaged, and connecting at a deep psychological level. According to Funk and James' (2001) psychological continuum model (PCM), highly engaged fans fit into the *allegiance stage*, which is the stage at which fans exhibit the highest degree of psychological connection. However, Bruffy *et al.* (2014) suggested that less connected fans (i.e., those in preliminary PCM stages known as *attraction* and *attachment*) were also active members of a professional basketball team's social media community. This appears to support the utility of social media in linking, and ultimately fostering more intimate connections, with less fervent fans.

One example of best practice in social media fan engagement is that displayed by the Los Angeles Kings of the NHL who have creatively encouraged the development of a relationship between the team and fans (Armstrong, Delia and Giardina, 2014) through creative and non-transactional content. However, for a professional sport team, sometimes facilitating access is just as important as driving the engagement itself. For example, acknowledging that baseball is not the most fast-paced sport, the San Francisco Giants installed 1,300 network access points to free Wi-Fi for fans to use during breaks in the action (Lelinwalla, 2015). During the first part of the 2015 season, fans were using 1.14 TB of data per game or the equivalent of 3.2 million social media updates.

Sponsors can also engage with sport fans through social media. In advance of the All Blacks test match against Argentina during the 2015 Rugby Championship, Air New Zealand – the airline sponsor of the All Blacks – offered free tickets to those willing to upload and tag a video of themselves dancing a tango. This shows how organisations can engage their fan base no matter where in the world they are by fostering user-generated content in their online communities.

However, the use of social media is far from a magic bullet in terms of engaging fans. In fact, despite the best of intentions, some sport managers fail miserably. Usually, failed attempts of social media fan engagement are the result of a transparent sponsor leverage or an overt attempt at securing a sale, such as the overt posting of a sponsorship advertisement. These activities can be characterised as transactional in nature, as indicated by Yoshida et al. (2014), and perhaps not the engagement to which social media is most suited. As of yet, there is no template for non-transactional social media initiatives that will drive iterative communication between fans and organisations or among fans themselves. As with any creative initiative, some attempts will not resonate with the online community. The old refrain, 'try, try, again', is sound advice for those using social media to engage fans, as learning about and ultimately understanding a team's social media community will improve the success rate.

Global sport and social media

Modern media channels have increased the ability of sport brands to become globally recognised. Social media enables brands to transcend their local environments, bringing sport to all corners of the globe. For example, the NBA consumer market is no longer solely based in North America. International fans of the NBA, its teams and its players follow their favourite brands through social media, allowing them to connect with sport brands despite their geographic location. As the world continues to 'shrink', allowing for real-time communication in sporting and other contexts, the role of social media is becoming increasingly important and is a marketing tactic that sport managers cannot ignore. Several modern global social media cases are highlighted in this section.

There are dozens of professional tennis events staged around the world each year, but none draws interest from the masses like the four Grand Slams: Australian Open, Roland Garros (French Open), Wimbledon, and the U.S. Open. The Grand Slams have been leaders in the social media community, always inventing new ways to share and enhance the tennis experience with fans. During Wimbledon 2015, several unique and creative social media strategies or stories were utilised. First, tournament organisers used Vine, a service that is used to create short looping videos that can be embedded into other social media platforms. The tournament used the hashtag '#14VinesForWimbeldon' to showcase a different video each day. Short videos are an excellent way to share content with time-pressed consumers while they are on the go. Further, Vine videos seamlessly integrate into other social media platforms, which means that Facebook and Twitter Wimbledon followers were exposed to the content regardless of whether or not they were Vine users. Another successful social media strategy implemented over the course of the event was to create beautiful, non-traditional photos and post them to Instagram, a prominent photo-sharing, social media platform. Importantly, the photos were not simply another way of reporting match scores, but rather captured more human moments, thereby expanding the focus and catering to alternative audiences. Although there is limited academic research exploring successful Instagram usage in sport settings, findings so far suggest that alternative images of everyday life, or life behind the scenes, drive engagement most effectively (Geurin-Eagleman and Burch, 2015; Smith and Sanderson, 2015). A third element that was unique about Wimbledon's 2015 social media approach was the incorporation of play-by-play commentary. Social media has been shown to enhance second-screen viewing (i.e., the simultaneous consumption of television programming while also using a second device, such as a computer, tablet, or mobile device) among consumers during sport viewing (Watkins *et al.*, 2015). However, bland play-by-play commentary can fill up a person's timeline (Smith, 2015); therefore, photos were often used instead, in conjunction with minute-to-minute score updates, which added to the story and broadened the appeal of each tennis match.

Social media has created the opportunity for teams to engage with fans outside the domestic marketplace and around the globe. Clubs can now actively engage with fans leading up to and during away matches. Two examples of professional sport teams with global fan followings are Liverpool Football Club in England's Premier League, and Super Rugby's Brumbies, based in Canberra, Australia. The Brumbies have sought to develop opportunities for their fans to get together and create fan communities not only in Australia, but also overseas in South Africa and New Zealand, where they regularly play away matches during the season (S. Chester, personal communication, 11 September 2014). Further, custom merchandise, social gatherings and fan groups have all been featured in the Brumbies' social media global engagement strategy.

Customising social media content is another strategy that a sport team may use to engage with fans outside their local market. For example, Liverpool FC has 27 local websites in a variety of languages, 13 local language Twitter accounts, five international Twitter accounts, 14 Facebook accounts, and other social media accounts with Weibo, QQ and Instagram (www.liverpoolfc.com). Liverpool FC is able to create storylines and content that caters to the local market. Further, it is able to engage with the fan base in its local language, which strengths consumers' engagement with the brand. Liverpool FC is also able to engage its fan base when it travels overseas to play in exhibition tours, such as the 2015 tour to Asia and Australia. Liverpool FC highlights its tours on a special website (www.liverpoolfc. com) and on all social media accounts to engage with the locals who may be able to see the team for the first and, perhaps, only time in their lives.

Managerial implications

The adoption and use of social media is important for sport organisations and is key to developing and maintaining relationships with modern sport consumers. When done well, brands can grow to become globally recognised. Consumers, many of whom are loyal fans, will offer benefits to the organisation beyond simply selling merchandise and/or tickets as they engage with sport organisations online. Both loyal and casual fans can engage with a brand online, so it is important for sport organisations to cater its social media content to all fan types, not simply their most loyal fans (Bruffy et al., 2014). Non-transactional behaviours, such as spontaneous discussion, interaction with and between fans, and the co-creation of content are key facets of social media that organisations should harness. Additionally, it is important for sport managers to ensure that social media posts do not 'feel' to the consumers like an advertisement to reach a sale (Yoshida et al., 2014). Content that is purely transactional in nature will not foster engagement from fans, but sport managers need to balance the needs of the organisation (i.e., profit through sales) with the wants of its social media consumers (i.e., engaging content).

Conclusion

Social media is increasingly being woven into marketing strategies by sport organisations around the world. Scholars and practitioners are largely learning 'as they go' with aggregated insights into best practice just starting to trickle in. There is little doubt that social media usage will continue and potentially even expand further because of the degree to which technology is intertwined with daily lives of sport fans.

References

Adcorp. (2013, October 1). Social media statistics October 2013, Australia and New Zealand [Blog post]. Retrieved from www.adcorp.com.au/news-blog/Social-Media-Statistics-October-2013,-Australia-an

Ahearne, M., Bhattacharya, C. B. and Gruen, T. (2005). Antecedents and consequences of customer-comparny identification: Expanding the role of relationship marketing. *Journal of Applied Pyschology, 90,* 574–585. doi:10.1037/0021-9010.90.3.574

Armstrong, C. G., Delia, E. B. and Giardina, M. D. (2014). Embracing the social in social media: An analysis of the social media marketing strategies of the Los Angeles Kings. *Communication in Sport*. Advance online publication. doi:10.1177/21674795 14532914

Ashley, C. and Tuten, T. (2015). Creative strategies in social media marketing: An exploratory study of branded social content and consumer engagement. *Psychology and Marketing, 32*, 15–27. doi:10.1002/mar.20761

Bee, C. C. and Kahle, L. R. (2006). Relationship marketing in sports: A functional approach. *Sport Marketing Quarterly, 15*, 102–110. Retrieved from www.sportmarketingassociation. com/journal/

Billings, A. C. (2014). Power in the reverberation: Why Twitter matters, but not the way most believe. *Communication and Sport, 2*, 107–112. doi:10.1177/2167479514527427

Blaszka, M., Burch, L. M., Frederick, E. L., Clavio, G. and Walsh, P. (2012). #WorldSeries: An empirical examination of a Twitter hashtag during a major sporting event. *International Journal of Sport Communication, 5*, 435–453. Retrieved from http://journals.human kinetics.com/ijsc

Booth, P. (2010). *Digital fandom: New media studies*. New York: Lang.

Boyd, D. and Ellison, N. B. (2007). Social network sites: Definition, history, and scholarship. *Journal of Computer-Mediated Communication, 13*, 210–230. doi:10.1111/j.1083-6101. 2007.00393.x

Bruffy, K., Scott, O., Naylor, M. E. and Beaton, A. (2014). *Segmentation of a professional sport team's social media community*. Paper presented at the Sport Management Association of Australia and New Zealand Conference, Melbourne, Australia. Abstract retrieved from www.academia.edu/9055988/Segmentation_of_a_professional_sport_team_s_social_ media_community

Chao, J. T., Parker, K. R. and Fontana, A. (2011). Developing an interactive social media based learning environment. *Issues in Informing Science and Information Technology, 8*, 323–334. Retrieved from www.informingscience.org/Journals/IISIT/Overview

Evans, D. and Smith, A. (2004). Internet sports marketing and competitive advantage for professional sports clubs: Bridging the gap between theory and practice. *International Journal of Sport Marketing and Sponsorship, 6*, 86–98. Retrieved from www.imr publications.com/journal-landing.aspx?volno=L&no=L

Frederick, E., Lim, C. H., Clavio, G., Pedersen, P. M. and Burch, L. M. (2014). Choosing between the one-way or two-way street: An exploration of relationship promotion by professional athletes on Twitter. *Communication and Sport, 2*, 80–99. doi:10.1177/ 2167479512466387

Funk, D. C. and James, J. D. (2001). The psychological continuum model: A conceptual framework for understanding an individual's psychological connection to sport. *Sport Management Review, 4*, 119–150. doi:10.1016/S1441-3523(01)70072-1

Geurin-Eagleman, A. N. and Burch, L. M. (2015). Communicating via photographs: A gendered analysis of Olympic athletes' visual self-presentation on Instagram. *Sport Management Review*. Advance online publication. doi:10.1016/j.smr.2015.03.002

Hambrick, M. E., Frederick, E. L. and Sanderson, J. (2015). From yellow to blue: Exploring Lance Armstrong's image repair strategies across traditional and social media. *Communication and Sport, 3*, 196–218. doi:10.1177/2167479513506982

Hardin, M. (2014). Moving beyond description: Putting Twitter in (theoretical) context. *Communication and Sport, 2*, 113–116. doi:10.1177/2167479514527425

Hull, K. and Lewis, N. P. (2014). Why Twitter displaces broadcast sports media: A model. *International Journal of Sport Communication, 7*, 16–33. Retrieved from http://journals. humankinetics.com/ijsc

Hutchins, B. (2014). Twitter: Follow the money and look beyond sports. *Communication and Sport, 2,* 122–126. doi:10.1177/2167479514527430

Kaplan, A. M. and Haenlein, M. (2010). Users of the world, unite! The challenges and opportunities of social media. *Business Horizons, 53,* 59–68. doi:10.1016/j.bushor. 2009.09.003

Lelinwalla, M. (2015, June 26). The data usage numbers per game at the San Francisco Giants' AT&T Park will astound you. *Tech Times.* Retrieved from www.techtimes.com/

Mahan, J. E., III and McDaniel, S. R. (2006). The new online arena: Sport, marketing, and media converge in cyberspace. In A. A. Raney and J. Bryant (eds) *Handbook of sports and media* (pp. 409–434). Mahwah, NJ: Erlbaum.

Morgan, R. M. and Hunt, S. D. (1994). The commitment-trust theory of relationship marketing. *Journal of Marketing, 58,* 20–38. doi:10.2307/1252308

Nielsen Holdings. (2013). *Year in sports media report 2013.* Retrieved from www.nielsen.com/ content/dam/corporate/us/en/reports-downloads/2014%20Reports/year-in-sports-media-report-2013.pdf

Pedersen, P. M., Miloch, K. S. and Laucella, P. C. (2007). *Strategic sport communication.* Champaign, IL: Human Kinetics.

Pegoraro, A. (2014). Twitter as disruptive innovation in sport communication. *Communication and Sport, 2,* 132–137. doi:10.1177/2167479514527432

Scott, O. K. M., Hill, B. and Zakus, D. (2014). Framing the 2007 National Basketball Association finals: An analysis of commentator discourse. *International Review for the Sociology of Sport, 49,* 728–744. doi:10.1177/1012690212466852

Scott, O. K. M., Pegoraro, A. and Watkins, J. (2015, June). *Analysing the water cooler: Conversation analysis of the University of Canberra Brumbies' social media users.* Paper presented at the North American Society for Sport Management Conference, Ottawa, Canada. Abstract retrieved from www.nassm.org/files/conf_abstracts/2015-016.pdf

Smith, J. (2015, July 11). Four solid social media ideas from Wimbledon [Blog post]. Retrieved from http://socialnsport.com/four-ideas-from-wimbledon/

Smith, L. R. and Sanderson, J. (2015). I'm going to Instagram it! An analysis of athlete self-presentation on Instagram. *Journal of Broadcasting and Electronic Media, 59,* 342–358. doi:10.1080/08838151.2015.1029125

Tapp, A. and Clowes, J. (2002). From 'carefree casuals' to 'professional wanderers': Segmentation possibilities for football supporters. *European Journal of Marketing, 56,* 1248–1269. doi:10.1108/03090560210445164

Team GB Fan Engagement and CRM Manager. (2015, June 26). Retrieved July 12, 2015, from www.globalsportsjobs.com/job/956629/team-gb-fan-engagement-and-crm-manager/

Watkins, J., Pegoraro, A. and Scott, O. K. M. (2015, July). '*My feckin heart!!': Differences in cross-platform sports fan conversation.* Paper presented at the Refereed Proceedings of the Australian and New Zealand Communication Association Conference: Rethinking Communication, Space and Identity, Queenstown, New Zealand.

Williams, J. and Chinn, S. J. (2010). Meeting relationship-marketing goals through social media: A conceptual model for sport marketers. *International Journal of Sport Communication, 3,* 422–437. Retrieved from http://journals.humankinetics.com/ijsc

Yoshida, M., Gordon, B., Nakazawa, M. and Biscaia, R. (2014). Conceptualisation and measurement of fan engagement: Empirical evidence from a professional sport context. *Journal of Sport Management, 28,* 399–417. doi:10.1123/jsm.2013-0199

Further reading

Numerous journals have a strong focus on social media and frequently post new articles. We suggest reading the following journals: *International Journal of Sport Communication, Communication and Sport* and *Sport Management Review*. Further, we recommend two recent review articles on social media:

Abeza, G., O'Reilly, N., Séguin, B. and Nzindukiyimana, O. (2015). Social media scholarship in sport management research: A critical review. *Journal of Sport Management, 29*, 601–618. doi:10.1123/jsm.2014-0296

Filo, K., Lock, D. and Karg, A. (2015). Sport and social media research: A review. *Sport Management Review, 18*, 166–118. doi:10.1016/j.smr.2014.11.001

It is important to remember that the field of social media and sport is constantly changing as new platforms emerge and new ways of using older platforms develop; therefore, it is best to follow various research journals for the newest publications.

11

MANAGING FOOTBALL HOOLIGANISM

Joel Rookwood

Football (often known as 'soccer' in countries with a more dominant national variant) is the most popular participation and spectator sport in the world. Football contests have been organised, regulated, participated in, observed and followed in a wide range of contexts, adopting varying degrees of significance for those involved (Goldblatt, 2014). It is not only the performances of teams and players that help explain the global importance of the game therefore, but also the significance of its supporters (Rookwood and Chan, 2011). Football has become a sphere of social action in which fan relations and identities are shaped, expressed, and contested. This occurs partly through the meanings attached to football teams, and the associated attitudes and conduct of football supporters.

The violent and disorderly behaviour of football fans has often been referred to as *football hooliganism*, which has been a prevailing concern in many countries where the sport has been played for decades. The phenomenon is often thought to comprise of key elements, which are detailed in this chapter; however, transnational dissimilarities complicate the process of formulating a global conceptualisation of football hooliganism (Spaaij, 2014). Popular perspectives on 'football disorder' have been shaped in part by related media coverage, reflecting fluctuating degrees of proportionality and sensationalism (Cleland, 2015). Football disorder has produced consequences of varying severity, and the reputation of some national and regional football cultures have become closely intertwined with hooliganism. For instance, the phenomenon is sometimes referred to as the 'English disease', reflecting its perceived prevalence in England (Green and Simmons, 2015). In order to manage the problem, legislation has been introduced in countries such as the Netherlands, Germany, and England, enabling authorities to impose stiffer penalties to deter and punish football hooligans (Hopkins and Hamilton-Smith, 2014).

Although football hooliganism is a relatively recent term, instances of spectator violence long precede the expression. Factions of chariot racing, for instance, engaged in violent altercations in ancient Greece and Rome (Goldblatt, 2014). The contemporary phenomenon often proves more diverse and encompassing than it has been presented (Young, 2012). There are also variations in the targets of fan violence, ranging from fellow fans to players, police, bystanders, coaches, and officials. The term *hooligan* is of uncertain origin with inconclusive etymological studies. It might derive from Patrick Hooligan, an Irishman who gained notoriety for committing acts of violence and theft in London during the 1890s. Alternatively, hooligan may be a reference to the surname of a fictional rowdy Irish family in a popular music hall song from the same decade (Rookwood, 2014a). Nevertheless, hooligan was adopted into common usage in the English language from the end of the nineteenth century, although it was not applied in relation to English football until the early 1960s, and is considered to be a phrase of media invention. Reflecting the extent of the connection since the 1960s, the terms football hooligan and hooligan have often become virtually interchangeable in some contexts. Regarding related terminology, *football disorder* is perhaps best considered here as an umbrella term, which includes acts of football hooliganism as well as various non-violent but illegal football-related offences that may include pitch invasions and ticket touting. As a reference to another related phenomenon, the term *ultra movement* in Italy and elsewhere often has violent connotations, although the often necessary political connotations prevent the term from being employed as an unambiguous synonym for hooligan.

In the United Kingdom, the National Criminal Intelligence Service frames football hooliganism in number of ways – in terms of the degree of organisation, discipline, hierarchy, criminality and involvement. Perhaps as a consequence, there is no precise definition of football hooliganism, and the term lacks both a legal definition and precise demarcation of membership. The label is often applied to various actions which transpire in football-related contexts. Jewell, Simmons, and Szymanski (2014) defined the term in relation to 'episodes of crowd trouble inside and outside football stadiums on match days' (p. 429). However, some of the most notable consequences of football violence occur on adjacent days, particularly regarding modern European contests in which fan excursions can spread across several days. For instance, the deaths of two Leeds United fans following clashes with Galatasaray supporters in Istanbul in 2000 occurred the night before the UEFA Cup semi-final match between the teams.

To clarify some of the main features of football hooliganism, Spaaij (2014) suggested that a distinction should be drawn between the spontaneous, relatively isolated incidents of spectator violence and the behaviour of socially organised or institutionalised hooligan groups (sometimes known as *firms*) who engage in competitive violence, primarily against other hooligan groups. Existing football hooligan legislation in the United Kingdom includes references to various offences including vandalism, ticket touting, and pitch invasions (Hopkins and Hamilton-Smith, 2014); however, as Spaaij (2014) noted in a transnational context, such behaviours should be conceptualised as distinct from the violent form of fandom that many consider to be hooliganism. Another debated issue concerns the confusion between fandom and hooliganism, and whether the former should be treated as a direct synonym for the latter. Some researchers differentiate fans from hooligans; others use the terms interchangeably. It is also important to note that in applied contexts, many hooligans will themselves claim to be fans (Rookwood and Pearson, 2012). Hooliganism is, therefore, perhaps best considered a distinct variant of rather than a synonym for fandom. The terms *supporters*, *spectators*, and *fans* are, however, used interchangeably here.

Regarding the demography of hooligans, it has been noted that 'the gender of football hooligans is strikingly homogenous' (Spaaij, 2014, p. 334). Most football hooligans are male and aged between 15 and 50; however, given the additional demographic variance associated with the phenomenon, many scholars are not able to provide a typical profile or a precise definition of a hooligan. Nevertheless, it is important to offer a definitional framework when undertaking research of this nature. Consequently, the following working definition was adopted:

> An individual who attends football matches with the intention of becoming involved in violence with rival supporters (whether or not s/he achieves that aim) or a fan who becomes involved in violence (but not other disorder or criminal activity) even if this was not his/her initial aim.
>
> *(Rookwood, 2014a, p. 347)*

Rival supporters in this context can include those who follow the same club or national team, but is more commonly a reference to those who support opposing teams.

Despite notable disagreement among scholars about its seriousness, causes, and solutions and how it should be defined, some researchers have suggested that football hooliganism has been over-researched (Kurland, Tilley and Johnson, 2014). Understanding football hooliganism has been subject to much debate in both legal and cultural contexts, and, therefore, this chapter briefly outlines some methodological challenges before examining some key definitional positions. It is important to address methodology in this context, as the phenomenon has often proven difficult to research, access, and understand. The present chapter adopts English football as an integrated case study in order to demonstrate key developments in football fan culture, examining some notable causes of football violence and addressing the severity and impact of disorderly fan behaviour. Then, the chapter addresses some connected managerial implications, focusing on how football hooliganism has been prevented and controlled.

Conducting meaningful research about football hooliganism has often proved a complex and even dangerous undertaking. In a management context, it is possible to examine aspects of the severity, impact, and response to fan violence by focusing on arrest statistics, legislative critique, and crowd control strategies, for instance (Havelund, Joern and Rasmussen, 2015). However, investigating the causes of disorderly behaviour may require overt research approaches, perhaps interviewing hooligan protagonists or facilitating focus groups with fans involved in or otherwise affected by football disorder. Alternatively, covert participant observation research has been conducted in such contexts, although the subculture can prove difficult to penetrate (Rookwood and Pearson, 2012). Examining football hooliganism, therefore, can present researchers with certain methodological challenges, as well as both moral and ethical dilemmas associated with interacting with proponents of violent disorder.

The development, severity and causes of hooliganism in English football

Versions of football are thought to have been played by various ancient civilisations, some of which spread with imperial expansion along networks of trade routes (Goldblatt, 2014). Lisi (2011) argued that during conquests, Roman armies imported some games to Great Britain, one of which later surfaced as a popular pastime of the masses, known as *mob football*. There were several attempts to ban this game due to its violent nature and the damage caused to property (Curry, 2014). In contrast, during the early nineteenth century, folk antecedents of modern football emerged in English public schools during a period of behavioural reform, with organised sports facilitating moral and physical development (Watson and Parker, 2014). The history of modern football is, therefore, intertwined with both connections to violent behaviour, and attempts to eradicate it. Football was subsequently diffused throughout British society, as rules were established, clubs were formed, and competitions were introduced. Football also gained increasing significance, with many emergent organisational and cultural practices adopted throughout and beyond Europe, including football hooliganism.

Until the late 1950s, match attendance in English football was primarily confined to relatively localised support (Goldblatt, 2014). Subsequent alterations in employment conditions enabled increasing numbers (primarily – although not exclusively – working-class males) to travel to matches as 'away fans', often in groups. Benkwitz and Molnar (2012) consider football to be rooted in binary oppositions and rivalries, which are informed by and shaped from the internal/external dialectic of identification. Framed in the context of social identity, interactions between the collective (i.e., internal 'us') and opposing supporters (i.e., external 'them') modified the dynamics of fandom and the behaviours, experiences, and impact of supporters at matches. This presents authorities with the challenge of managing instances of increasingly problematic fan conduct. One of the most significant responses involved the segregation of supporters in stadiums. The spatial demarcation of football grounds and the separation of partisan spectators helped to control some aspects of the emerging phenomenon of football violence. However, this may also have sharpened distinctions and enhanced hostilities between supporters. Football grounds became increasingly territorialised as some rivalries became more problematic and violence became a recurrent manifestation (Rookwood, 2009).

During this period, some British journalists began to report on the conduct of football fans, eventually giving rise to the term football hooliganism. Such representations (including some sensationalist and disproportionate coverage) began to reshape what had previously been the popularly held view that English football supporters were self-controlled, with their Latin, continental, and Celtic counterparts considered more disorderly (Rookwood, 2014a). The moral panic that ensued resulted in demands for football hooliganism to be managed, which subsequently led to developments in legislation and policing. Broadcasting the problem effectively advertised football stadiums as sites to engage in violence, which exacerbated the issue, reinforcing and glamorising hooligan behaviour (Poulton, 2014). Conversely, many who were unlikely to engage in disorderly conduct might have been dissuaded from attending matches, which perpetuated the problem and demographic of football supporters (Rookwood, 2009).

Football hooliganism has produced injuries, fatalities, and damage to property both inside and outside stadiums, in England and elsewhere. However, not all football tragedies can be directly attributed solely to fan violence, as causes also include the structure of grounds, the conditions for fans (e.g., safety of terracing and fences, accessibility of exits) and the movement and control of supporters. Two hundred seventy-six football fans lost their lives in British sporting disasters during the twentieth century (Johnes, 2005); however, the 1980s are often most readily associated with football disasters in the United Kingdom. As part of the legacy of these disasters, resultant changes have helped revolutionise stadiums, fandom, legislation, and policing, impacting connected industries, communities and cultures. In May of 1985, the Bradford fire claimed the lives of 56 supporters who were unable to escape a stand that had accidentally caught on fire during an English league game. Then, at the European Cup final in Brussels, the 60-year-old Heysel stadium was unable to withstand a fatal stampede of Liverpool supporters towards their Juventus counterparts in a 'neutral' section (i.e., where fans are not segregated); a wall collapsed and many spectators were crushed, resulting in 39 deaths. The memory of such tragedies continues to resonate with supporters in contemporary football, particularly in Italy (Doidge, 2015) and England (Rookwood, 2009).

In April 1989, 96 Liverpool supporters died at the FA Cup semi-final against Nottingham Forest at Hillsborough in Sheffield. Although some authors of popular and academic works have connected this tragedy to hooliganism, Scraton (2013) found Hillsborough to have been caused by stadium neglect, the penning of fans and the compromising of crowd safety. The disaster also exposed ingrained organisational complacencies and mismanagement (Cocking and Drury, 2014). The metal fences erected at football grounds such as Hillsborough (against which fans were crushed to death) in the aftermath of Heysel were considered representative of a UK governmental 'obsession with secure containment' (Scraton 2009, p. 196). The intended management of football hooliganism, therefore (addressed in the subsequent section of this chapter), has actually contributed to the escalation of problems for fans.

Although English football offers some useful insight, fan violence has been prevalent elsewhere to varying degrees of severity. In Europe, domestic and international competitions have been affected by hooliganism, including Poland, Germany, the Netherlands, and Russia (Duke and Crolley, 2014). Several disasters have resulted from crowd disturbances in South America and Africa. Often configured like paramilitary task groups, hooligan gangs known as *barras bravas* (i.e., tough gangs) in Latin America conduct illegal acts through violence and compulsion; they are often employed and utilised by political and sporting leaders (Spaaij, 2014). In February of 2012, 74 people were killed after an Egyptian league match between Al-Masry and Al-Ahly in Port Said. Most fatalities were caused by stab wounds, concussion, and suffocation following a pitch invasion. Twenty-one fans were later sentenced to death, which led to violent protests. Most episodes of football disorder are far less severe however, and on a global level, the vast majority of contemporary football matches transpire without fan violence. Its historical significance, ingrained cultural resonance, continued prevalence in some contexts and the requirement to manage the problem renders the phenomenon worthy of continued academic scrutiny, but its severity should not be overstated.

Football hooliganism might have multiple causal links and both academic and popular perspectives have emerged. Representing the latter category for example, Brimson (2002) noted that various explanations have been offered, relating to factors including social class, intellectual capacity, education, family background, political affiliation and socio-psychological experience. Though each of these components have been featured in various explanations of hooliganism, this does not encapsulate the essence of related academic research. Dunning, Murphy, and Waddington (2002) offered another suggestion about the cause of football hooliganism: 'Hooliganism occurs simply due to having an allegiance to opposing football clubs' (p. 2). Though this theory has limitations, collective identifications with particular football clubs – as well as associated communities and nationalities – and disdain for those perceived to be in opposition offer key contexts for understanding acts of hooliganism.

Spaaij (2014) framed engagement in football violence relative to individual, interpersonal, situational, environmental, and socio-structural components. On an individual level, hooliganism has been attributed to factors such as unemployment, substance abuse, aggression, frustration, enjoyment and coping with a sense of marginalisation or alienation (Piotrowski, 2006). Contemporary research often places greater emphasis on interpersonal contexts. For example, Collins's (2008) interactionist theory emphasises confrontation, tension, and emotional flow in relation to interpersonal violence. He highlights three necessary emotional dynamics: collective effervescence in the build-up of dramatic tension, emotional resonance, and emotional energy. Some instances of inter-group football violence may feature these ingredients; however, it is important not to detach references to individual motivations. Hooliganism can often be understood as a violent manifestation of hatred, jealousy, or bitterness towards an 'enemy'. Football rivalries have developed across various intersecting levels: geographical areas (e.g., Newcastle and

Sunderland), religion (e.g., Glasgow Rangers and Glasgow Celtic), and socio-political grounds (e.g., Red Star Belgrade and Dinamo Zagreb). In the case of the latter, a riot during a televised Yugoslav league match between the clubs in 1990 helped instigate the Bosnian War, in which associated hooligan gangs formed paramilitary groups responsible for genocide and rape between 1992 and 1995 (Mills, 2012).

On an environmental level, one of the most significant factors contributing to the escalation of football violence is the interaction between supporters and the police. Attempts to manage football hooliganism can lead to further outbreaks of violence, particularly when police forces are tasked with controlling supporters in an unfamiliar context (e.g., visiting supporters in European competitions). Trans-national variations in hooligan conduct and police response can inhibit the effectiveness of crowd management. That is, police may demonstrate a lack of understanding regarding what causes and exacerbates football violence, and hooligans may perceive police presence as an unnecessary act of aggression. Management tactics can indicate that the police perceive themselves to be facing a uniformly violent crowd; however, this is rare in most instances.

The correlation between environmental and interpersonal dynamics can also be relevant in football violence, particularly regarding the attitude and approach of the police and the response of supporters. The psychology of crowds can be trans-formed by what is collectively perceived as indiscriminate or disproportionate policing, just as when supporters sense provocation from rival hooligans. In such circumstances, those with no initial intention to engage in football violence may reframe such conduct as legitimate or even necessary (Rookwood, 2009). Social psychologists such as Hoggett and Stott (2010) have developed more dynamic approaches to understanding the interactions between police officers and football fans – focusing more on the ways in which behaviours develop in context, rather than explaining hooliganism in relation to the macro-social origins of conflictual norms.

Further, a consistent weakness of many existing scholarly examinations of hooliganism is the tendency to under-represent the significance of situational triggers, and their connection to cultural references and inter-group dynamics. The combination of these elements can spark seemingly spontaneous instances of football violence, and can also shape the ingrained patterns of disorder. For example, the relationship between some supporter groups of Juventus and Fiorentina in Italy has been shaped by the latter's manipulation of the events involving the former at the Heysel tragedy (Doidge, 2015). Goading rival supporters in match contexts, by 'celebrating' their disasters through chanting, gesticulations, symbolism and verbal abuse can lead to violent confrontations, as has been the case regarding this and other football disasters. In such contexts, a chain of revenge reprisals can ensue, shaped by a burgeoning legacy of antagonism (Scraton, 2013).

In conclusion, the causes of individual involvement in football hooliganism is rarely devoid of interpersonal contexts. Moreover, a broad array of circumstances may shape the likelihood to abstain from or engage in violent acts. Whether violence is premeditated or spontaneous, a hooligan's decisions are often informed by perceptions of history, ideology, conflict and behavioural norms. Causes of hooligan confrontations should be understood with reference to the wider social context and the structural conditions that prevent or facilitate football hooliganism – the influence of which is likely to be mediated by interpersonal connections and environmental characteristics (Spaaij, 2014).

Managerial implications: preventing and controlling football hooliganism

Football hooliganism has been ingrained in the sporting culture of many countries for over half a century. Consequently, various attempts to manage the problem have developed over the decades. A number of measures have been introduced to curb football disorder, including the segregation of supporters and the erection of fences to prevent pitch invasions, as examined in the previous section. Closed-circuit television, identity card schemes, and intelligence gathering have also been proposed and/or operationalised to differing degrees in order to monitor fan behaviour and facilitate the prosecution of hooligans. Football tragedies and publicised incidents of disorder (particularly in high-profile matches, international fixtures, and at sports mega events) have resulted in successive developments in punishments, policy, policing, and legislation. For instance, English clubs were banned from European competition for five years following the Heysel tragedy, restricting the threat of English hooliganism on the continent as a result. During this period, the Hillsborough disaster provided the most significant catalyst for change in the history of English football culture (Scraton, 2013).

Policing operations became increasingly focused on keeping rival fan groups apart, with escorts put in place if deemed necessary and special measures often operationalised for high-risk fixtures. Football intelligence offers were, for example, assigned to professional clubs in England, who travel to home and away matches to gather intelligence, identify banned or potential offenders, and liaise locally with relevant law agencies (Hoggett and Stott, 2010). Further, various laws were passed, such as the 1985 Sporting Events Act, which implied a causal connection between alcohol and hooliganism as indicated in the title, which includes the term *control of alcohol.* The 1989 Football Spectators Act made distinctions between football supporters and fans of other sports. Following these legislative acts, entering a football stadium drunk, being found in possession of alcohol in or on the way to a ground, throwing objects at or towards the pitch or supporter areas, pitch invasions, racist or indecent chanting, and ticket touting were among the behaviours criminalised, and those convicted of football-related offences were to be banned from attending football matches at home and abroad for a minimum of three years (Hopkins and Hamilton-Smith, 2014). Various subsequent pieces of legislation have been applied to football fans. This includes the 2003 Criminal Justice Act, Section 60, which stipulates that police can confine people in a given area and conduct basic searches, whilst taking names, addresses, and photographs.

The *Taylor Report*, conducted after the Hillsborough tragedy, included 76 recommendations, among which was the call for the conversion to all-seater facilities – the legacy of which helped transform English football and altered the participatory nature of fandom (Millward, 2011). Clubs also concentrated efforts on attracting and catering to new types of supporters in order to increase revenue and to alienate or dilute violent supporters (Rookwood and Chan, 2011). Such changes represented significant shifts from traditional patterns, interests and priorities, as many clubs increasingly gained autonomy from their communities in terms of finances and fan support. Although the phenomenon continues to exist, hooliganism and terrace culture have become marginalised in the modern era, facilitated in part by inflated ticket prices and behavioural restrictions.

Football hooliganism has been referred to as an English disease (Green and Simmons, 2015), a dysfunction of British society and sporting culture typically manifest in deviant behaviours. Continuing the pathology analogy, the disease has spread through interpersonal contact, as fans travelling within and across borders in international competitions demonstrate and imitate symptoms such as violent conduct. Some attempts to manage the disease and 'cure' the patient are successful, such as some of the aforementioned measures and strengthening of police controls. In many cases, however, treatment is resisted, as illustrated when hooligans fight with the police. Some go into 'remission' and periodically 'relapse', perhaps for a derby or grudge match against a rival club. Additionally, new 'strains' of the disease evolve, often with modified symptoms. In response to heightened surveillance and draconian measures, for instance, hooligan protagonists have developed contacts with one another to arrange confrontations away from stadiums in locations where fights might remain undetected. In cases where hooliganism becomes culturally ingrained, some supporters engage in football violence across different contexts, such as domestic and international football. Subsequently, where a clash of two 'viruses' meet in an 'infected' person, recombinants can prove more or less aggressive than the strains from which they developed. The various strains of the disease have spread, as attempts to prevent further infections also advance, shaping its status within popular consciousness. Similarly, English football developed a reputation for fan violence, yet hooliganism is typically considered more aggressive and emblematic of South American and Eastern European fandom. Search 'The Animals of Sofia' to watch my film on football hooliganism in the Balkans as an example (Rookwood, 2014b).

Conclusion

Football hooliganism, like many other sporting cultures, is not static, but is comprised of various complex and fluid subcultures that develop relative to contemporary conditions and experiences. Media coverage of football violence has often sensationalised fan cultures, with some instances of disorder misleadingly presented as reflective of all fans. However, the vast majority of supporters in contemporary Britain and throughout the world do not engage in football hooliganism. Team affiliations, personal identifications, individual attributes and exposure to typical football-related experiences do not inspire violent behaviour in most supporters. Match attendances diminished from the 1960s to 1980s partly due to football violence. However, English football has since undergone extensive alterations, with many hooligan elements marginalised or diluted as a consequence. The large crowds of the modern Premier League typically feature markedly different fan demographics.

Developments in policing and legislation have been designed to both deter and punish offenders in football contexts. Lawmakers and enforcers may assert the legitimacy and benefits of these alterations. Critics might claim that the sanctions imposed – often for some relatively innocuous, non-violent offences – represent legislative disproportionality, with some banning orders unjustly restricting the civil liberties of citizens. Spectator violence does occur in other sports, but football has been singled out, reflected in the focused legal response. The strategic and comprehensive attempts to manage English football hooliganism have certainly not eradicated the phenomenon. Although it has become severely restricted, hooligan culture has nevertheless become ingrained in most English league clubs. Some traditional links to cultural and behavioural norms remain. Compared with contemporary English football, hooliganism remains more prevalent in other parts of the world, particularly in Eastern Europe and Latin America. This chapter offers an overview of the causes, severity and management of football hooliganism. Many research perspectives have not been examined here because of the depth and complexity of football hooliganism, including notable regional and transnational variations. Future work could focus on interdisciplinary causal explanations, transnational variations, and legislative applications.

References

Benkwitz, A. and Molnar, G. (2012). Interpreting and exploring football fan rivalries: An overview. *Soccer and Society, 13*, 479–494. doi:10.1080/14660970.2012.677224

Brimson, D. (2002). Fans for a change. In M. Perryman (ed.) *Hooligan wars: Causes and effects of football violence* (pp. 198–204). Edinburgh: Mainstream.

Cleland, J. (2015). *A sociology of football in a global context*. London: Routledge.

Cocking, C. and Drury, J. (2014). Talking about Hillsborough: 'Panic' as discourse in survivors' accounts of the 1989 football stadium disaster. *Journal of Community and Applied Social Psychology, 24*, 86–99. doi:10.1002/casp.2153

Collins, R. (2008). *Violence: A micro-sociological theory*. Princeton, NJ: Princeton University Press.

Curry, J. (2014). The origins of football debate: Comments on Adrian Harvey's historiography. *International Journal of the History of Sport, 31*, 2158–2213. doi:10.1080/09523367.2014.913573

Doidge, M. (2015). 'If you jump up and down, Balotelli dies': Racism and player abuse in Italian football. *International Review for the Sociology of Sport, 50*, 249–264. doi:10.1177/1012690213480354

Duke, V. and Crolley, L. (2014). *Football, nationality and the state*. Abingdon, UK: Routledge.

Dunning, E., Murphy, P. and Waddington, I. (2002). Towards a sociological understanding of football hooliganism. In E. Dunning, P. Murphy, I. Waddington and A. Astrinakos (eds) *Fighting fans, football hooliganism as a world phenomenon* (pp. 1–22). Dublin: University College Dublin Press.

Goldblatt, D. (2014). *The game of our lives*. London: Penguin.

Green, C. and Simmons, R. (2015). The English disease: Has football hooliganism been eliminated or just displaced? In P. Rodríguez, S. Késenne and R. Koning (eds) *The economics of competitive sports* (pp. 39–55). Northampton, MA: Edward Elgar.

Havelund, J., Joern, L. and Rasmussen, K. (2015). A qualitative examination of police officers' perception of football supporters. *Police Practice and Research, 16*, 65–78. doi:10.1080/15614263.2013.865184

Hoggett, J. and Stott, C. (2010). Crowd psychology, public order police training and the policing of football crowds. *Policing: An International Journal of Police Strategies and Management, 33*, 218–235. doi:10.1108/13639511011044858

Hopkins, M. and Hamilton-Smith, N. (2014). Football banning orders: The highly effective cornerstone of a preventative strategy? In M. Hopkins and J. Treadwell (eds) *Football hooliganism, fan behaviour and crime* (pp. 222–247). Basingstoke, UK: Palgrave Macmillan.

Hopkins, M. and Treadwell, J. (eds). (2014). *Football hooliganism, fan behaviour and crime.* Basingstoke: Palgrave Macmillan.

Jewell, R. T., Simmons, R. and Szymanski, S. (2014). Bad for business? The effects of hooliganism on English professional football clubs. *Journal of Sports Economics, 15*, 429–450. doi:10.1177/1527002514535169

Johnes, M. (2005). Heads in the sand: Football, politics and crowd disasters in twentieth century Britain. In P. Darby, M. Johnes and G. Mellor (eds) *Soccer and disaster: International perspectives* (pp. 10–27). London: Routledge.

Kurland, J., Tilley, N. and Johnson, S. (2014). The football 'hotspot' matrix. In M. Hopkins and J. Treadwell (eds) *Football hooliganism, fan behaviour and crime* (pp. 21–48). Basingstoke, UK: Palgrave Macmillan.

Lisi, C. A. (2011). *A history of the World Cup*. Plymouth: Scarecrow Press.

Mills, R. (2012). Commemorating a disputed past: Football club and supporters' group war memorials in the former Yugoslavia. *History, 97*, 540–577. doi:10.1111/j.1468-229X.2012.00564.x

Millward, P. (2011). *The global football league: Transnational networks, social movements and sport in the new media age.* Basingstoke, UK: Palgrave Macmillan.

Piotrowski, P. (2006). Coping with football-related hooliganism: Healing symptoms versus causes prevention. *Journal of Applied Social Psychology, 36*, 629–643. doi:10.1111/j.0021-9029.2006.00022.x

Poulton, E. (2014). The hooligan film factory: Football violence in high definition. In M. Hopkins and J. Treadwell (eds) *Football hooliganism, fan behaviour and crime* (pp. 154–175). Basingstoke, UK: Palgrave Macmillan.

Rookwood, J. (2009). *Fan perspectives of football hooliganism: Defining, analysing and responding to the British phenomenon.* Saarbrücken: VDM Publishing House.

Rookwood, J. (2014a). Hooliganism. In H. Copes and C. Forsyth (eds) *Encyclopaedia of social deviance* (pp. 347–351). Thousand Oaks, CA: Sage.

Rookwood, J. [JoelRockwood]. (2014b). *The animals* [Video file]. Retrieved from www.youtube.com/watch?v=oDqHBixrP2Y

Rookwood, J. and Chan, N. (2011). The 39th game: Fan responses to the Premier League's proposal to globalise English football. *Soccer and Society, 12*, 897–913. doi:10.1080/14660970.2011.609688

Rookwood, J. and Pearson, G. (2012). The hoolifan: Positive fan attitudes to football 'hooliganism'. *International Review for the Sociology of Sport, 47*, 147–162. doi:10.1177/1012690210388455

Scraton, P. (2009). *Hillsborough: The truth*. Edinburgh: Mainstream.

Scraton, P. (2013). The legacy of Hillsborough: Liberating truth, challenging power. *Race and Class, 55*, 1–27. doi:10.1177/0306396813499488

Spaaij, R. (2014). Sports crowd violence: An interdisciplinary synthesis. *Aggression and Violent Behavior, 19*, 146–155. doi:10.1016/j.avb.2014.02.002 1359-178

Watson, N. J. and Parker, A. (2014). *Sport and the Christian religion: A systematic review of literature*. Newcastle-upon-Tyne: Cambridge Scholars.

Young, K. (2012). *Sport, violence and society*. New York: Routledge.

Further reading

Relative to its prominence in other sport-related academic disciplines, football hooliganism has not been featured heavily in recent sport management research. However, there are a number of relevant studies that readers may find useful; for example, Jewell *et al.* (2014) studied the economic impact of hooliganism in the context of revenue generation at football clubs. In addition, Spaaij's (2014) research on sport crowd violence offers helpful structured analyses, transnational examples and interdisciplinary connections across different sports. Finally, the various chapters of Hopkins and Treadwell's (2014) edited collection on hooliganism and crime explore issues pertaining to sectarianism and violence and illuminate how hooliganism is both manifest and managed, focusing on policing, legislation, and banning orders.

12

FAREWELL TO THE HOOLIGAN?

Modern developments in football crowd management

Geoff Pearson and Clifford Stott

Within sports and stadium–development industries, recent debates on the management of football crowds have focused on *security* – providing technological and structural crowd control systems designed to prevent spectators from undermining crowd control and safety by engaging in violence or disorderly behaviour. Numerous trade magazines, exhibits at sports industry conferences, and private consultancy firms emphasise the need for innovative monitoring and control mechanisms to regulate crowd movement, thereby providing 'solutions' to crowd misbehaviour, disorder, and violence. The limited focus of these proposals ties in with the normalisation of crime and disorderly behaviour by neoliberal modes of governance and the move towards preventative rather than reactive approaches to criminal justice (Garland, 2002; Zedner, 2009). However, while we have learnt from the disasters at Heysel, Hillsborough, and Ellis Park that it is vital that football stadiums are fit-for-purpose, a narrow focus on merely reconfiguring stadiums or adding surveillance systems to reduce the opportunity for violence and disorder fails to address the wider issues; there is much more involved when it comes to managing football crowds and reducing the risk of violence and disorder connected to the sport.

Security-driven approaches to football crowd and stadium management do not cast light on why football spectators have historically been considered disorderly, give sufficient importance to the numerous subcultures that exist amongst a team's match-going support, acknowledge the ability of supporters of rival teams to engage in meaningful and peaceful interaction, or give sufficient weight to the importance of the relationship between spectators and those managing them. Fundamentally, approaches to football crowds that limit themselves to reducing the opportunity for 'troublemakers' to engage in criminal activity or antisocial behaviour at or around football stadiums provide no long-term solution given that much 'football-related disorder' occurs far away from stadiums, and spectators are able to follow their teams internationally, encountering different legal and policing systems. This chapter casts a critical eye upon the limited progress that has been made to understand why football crowds can become disorderly, the influence of 'hooligan' fans, and the role of crowd management outside as well as inside stadiums. The chapter also consists of a discussion of the new debates – particularly in Europe – about fan culture and human rights, and puts forward solutions that can be applied internationally to help develop the policing of football crowds in a way that will enhance the legitimacy of those managing football crowds and reduce the risk of disorder on a sustainable basis.

Assessing the causes of football crowd disorder

Football crowd violence, disorder and/or criminality – most often couched in terms of 'hooliganism' – has been the focus of academic research in the social sciences since the 1970s. Based on sociological, criminological, socio-historical, socio-legal, and social psychological studies initially carried out in the United Kingdom – the supposed birthplace of 'the English disease' (Pearson, 1998) – but increasingly also in Continental Europe, we can be relatively certain of the following:

- Football crowd disorder and violence existed long before the moral panic (Cohen, 2002; Hall, 1978) about hooliganism that developed in the late 1960s and 1970s (Dunning, Murphy and Williams, 1988).
- The label 'football hooliganism' came from media reporting of instances of football crowd disorder and does not have an accepted definition in law or elsewhere (Coenen, Pearson and Tsoukala, in press; Pearson, 1998; Redhead, 1993).
- Groups of fans exist who attend matches with the intention of engaging in violence; however, the extent to which these are organised, and the seriousness of violence is usually exaggerated (Armstrong, 1998; Giulianotti, 1994; Marsh, Rosser and Harré, 1978).
- Football crowd violence is irregular, often spontaneous, and arising from the dynamics of the situation within which it occurs (Armstrong, 1998; King, 1995; Stott, Hutchison and Drury, 2001; Stott and Reicher, 1998).
- Individuals who have not attended matches with the intention of engaging in violence, or had any prior motivation towards violence, take part in football crowd violence and disorder (Millward, 2009; Pearson, 2012; Stott et al., 2001; Stott and Pearson, 2007; Stott and Reicher, 1998).

However, less is known about why large-scale football crowd disorder occurs, or equally importantly, why it does not happen more regularly. The lack of research on causal explanations of football crowd disorder might be explained by the narrow focus on those identified by the state – or self-identified – as hooligans, at the expense of other football spectator subcultures that can on occasion engage in disorder, violence, criminality, and/or antisocial behaviour. This focus has not only been criticised in restricting a wider understanding of football culture (Free and Hughson, 2003; Redhead, 1997; Richards, 2015), but it also fails to account for why violence or disorder occurs involving those without prior motivation.

Both media and legislative responses to instances of football rioting in the United Kingdom and across Europe have implicated predisposition as a causal factor of large-scale football crowd disorder, criminality, or antisocial behaviour. For example, arguably the biggest football riot involving England supporters, in Marseilles at the 1998 FIFA World Cup, was understood by the media to be the result of 'thugs', 'troublemakers', and hooligan 'ringleaders ... heard issuing orders' (Stott and Pearson, 2007, pp. 133–135). Similarly, large-scale disorder in Charleroi at the 2000 European Championships was considered to be the result of English hooligans, troublemakers ('Football Hooligans', 2000) and thugs (Hattersley, 2000; Syal, Alderson and Cobain, 2000).

Influence of alcohol is another suggested causal factor in football crowd disorder and violence, as evidenced by media reportage of most incidents of disorder involving British fans (e.g., England fans in Albufeira 2004, Manchester United fans in Rome 2007, and Glasgow Rangers fans in Manchester 2008). As the BBC claimed in their first report of the developing disorder in Marseilles during France 1998, 'Only a small number of English supporters were involved – probably those who had drunk the most' (BBC, 1998). Drunken fans were, the media claimed, easily led by hooligans who intended to cause trouble (see Stott and Pearson, 2007, for a critique of the media explanation of the disorder in Marseilles and Charleroi).

The media construction of the nature and cause of football crowd riots – if it does not reflect the reality of the situation – is in and of itself problematic, but even further exacerbated when it is used to inform potential legislative and policing solutions to the problem, which has occurred in the United Kingdom. The overall consensus among both government and police, influenced in no small part by the media portrayal of the 1998 and 2000 disorders, was that tougher action needed to be taken. If the presence of hooligans orchestrating riots amongst drunken England fans was the cause of football crowd disorder, then the obvious solution was to ban those identified as hooligans and reduce the availability of alcohol to the rest of the crowd. Consequently, the French authorities attempted to create an 'alcohol-free' zone stretching 70 miles between the Channel ferry ports and the venue for England's final group-stage game at France 1998, and reduced-strength beer was sold to England fans at the 2000 UEFA European Championships. Across all UEFA club and national matches in Europe, the sale of alcohol is now prohibited to those outside corporate hospitality areas.

However, the United Kingdom's legislative response was even more significant. Banning orders to prevent those convicted of football-related offences were extended following the Marseilles disorder. Further, within a matter of weeks following the events in Charleroi, the U.K. government enacted the Football Disorder Act 2000, which permitted magistrates to ban fans from attending matches domestically and abroad where they believed that (a) they had been involved in previous football violence or disorder and (b) that imposing a ban would be 'helpful' in reducing the likelihood of such violence or disorder in the future. These bans, which impose serious restrictions on liberty and on attending matches, can now be imposed without any conviction for a football-related offence (James and Pearson, 2015). Furthermore, this type of media stigmatisation coupled with reactionary legislative action – arguably a 'panic law' – is not limited to the United Kingdom. Studies of legislative and administrative responses to football violence across Europe have found a similar trend. Legal and policing powers are being extended to a level that threatens both civil and human rights of fans, often in the absence of any proof – to a criminal legal standard – of engagement in violence or disorder (Coenen *et al.*, in press; Tsoukala, 2009).

Considering the importance placed upon incidence of football violence and disorder by the media, and the desire of governments, police authorities, sports bodies, and clubs to reduce it, it is vital that we gain a solid evidence-based under-standing of the nature and causes of the phenomenon. We must first acknowledge that we cannot hope to gain an understanding of the phenomenon that is based wholly or mainly on media reports of instances of disorder, as these have been shown to be inaccurate, sensationalist (Armstrong, 1998; Giulianotti, 1994; Hall, 1978; Weed, 2001) and in some cases, deliberately misleading (Stott and Pearson, 2007). Similarly, we should be highly suspicious of the claims of 'self-confessed hooligans', who may exaggerate or downplay violence – or their engagement in it – for self-serving reasons, simply by mistake or in order to deliver what they believe their audience wishes to hear (Marsh *et al.*, 1978; Pearson, 2012). It is, therefore, essential that solutions to football crowd disorder be proposed on the basis of sustained and systematic research which allows both its methodology and findings to be the subject of rigorous peer review and testing.

Such research has been carried out in an increasingly systematic manner through utilisation of ethnographic methods based on observational techniques and immersion in the field of football crowds. Our own research into football crowd behaviour and management began at the 1990 World Cup in Italy and has incorporated all the major European tournaments since, along with British club matches domestically and across Europe from 1995 and a number of other European club fixtures. Combined with a number of other significant ethno-graphic studies into fan behaviour (most notably, Armstrong, 1998; Giulianotti, 1991, 1995; Rookwood, 2009), as well as similar studies conducted elsewhere in Europe (e.g., Coenen *et al.*, in press; Spaaij, 2006) a number of important lessons can be drawn in terms of the best approach to managing football crowds. These take us far beyond simply looking to introduce structural, technological or legal measures to enhance security in and around football stadiums.

The first important step in understanding football fan behaviour is the reali-sation that the football crowd cannot be understood as a homogeneous group. Fans from a particular country or supporting a particular team are often discussed in terms of a single social category. An alternative description of football crowds is a distinction between hooligans and 'ordinary supporters' (Giulianotti, 1999) or – as now dominates policing handbooks and guidance in Europe – 'risk' and 'non-risk' fans. However, within every single team's match-going support there are dozens of different identifiable subgroups and subcultures, and within these groups, individuals with very different objectives for their match-day experience and interpretations of the immediate social environment around them. It is simply not the case that entering into a crowd environment makes individuals lose their identity and develop a 'mob mentality' (Reicher, 1987). Understanding the expectations of both individuals and subgroups within a crowd and what they consider to be legitimate and illegitimate modes of policing and security interventions, are essential to effective crowd management practices.

The role of the hooligan

Connected to this, we maintain that there is a need to put aside the clumsy labels football hooligan and football hooliganism. The latter is virtually meaningless when applied to football as it incorporates a wide range of different behaviours depending on who is applying the label (Pearson, 1998) and in what geographical context (Coenen *et al.*, in press). Behaviour labelled hooliganism has included subcriminal antisocial behaviour (e.g., urinating in a street), regulatory criminal offences committed in a football context (e.g., unauthorised sale of tickets), spontaneous interpersonal violence, and serious conspiratorial inter-group violence. These are significantly varying problems with completely different causes and solutions. In contrast, if we choose to adopt a very narrow definition of hooliganism, by including only non-spontaneous gang violence, then we need to be careful not to let our analysis of why wider crowd disturbances become hooligan-driven; it is easy to overestimate the power and influence that hooligan gangs (or 'firms') have on the crowd around them by their mere presence. Even when hooligan gangs travel to match events with the intention of engaging in violence, they do not necessarily engage in violence or disorder and even if they do, we should not assume that this will escalate into wider-scale disorder or rioting involving other crowd members.

Research into both the presence and absence of major crowd disorder at the 1998 FIFA World Cup and the 2000 UEFA European Championships suggested that the existence of so-called hooligan groups was largely incidental. Contrary to the media reports, there is no evidence that these riots were orchestrated by hooligans (Stott and Pearson, 2007). The presence of those labelled hooligans within football crowds does not necessarily lead to widespread crowd disorder. Further, individuals engaging in crowd disorder do not usually possess prior motivation towards this behaviour. This was illustrated in part by the arrest rate among England fans at the 2000 European Championships, where fewer than 3 per cent of the 965 England fans arrested were known or suspected hooligans.[1] A similar pattern could be seen in research from Italia 1990, France 1998, the 2004 European Championships in Portugal and the 2006 World Cup in Germany (Stott and Pearson, 2007). This is not to suggest that individuals attending matches with the intention of engaging in violence do not pose a risk of violence, disorder or criminality, or that they do not require a sophisticated policing response; however, the low number of these individuals generally limits their ability to escalate low-level violence or disorder into wide-scale rioting, if appropriate crowd management approaches are adopted.

The role of alcohol

As we have seen, alcohol consumption has been identified by many commentators as a major factor in the development of football crowd disorder.[2] A number of European states have made legislative interventions to prevent fans consuming alcohol in stadiums or entering stadiums while drunk (Coenen *et al.*, in press), usually with very limited success. In addition, some clubs and governing bodies have also curtailed access to alcohol in a bid to reduce the risk of disorder. We suggest, however, that the connection between alcohol consumption and crowd disorder is much more complex than has been suggested and the role of alcohol in the development of football crowd disorder has been overstated. First of all, there is no scientifically proven psychopharmacological 'smoking gun' that alcohol consumption leads to individual or collective violence (see Pearson and Sale, 2011, for more on these issues). This is supported by what can be observed in terms of the relationship between football crowds and disorder. There are numerous examples of situations in which football crowds who have not been consuming alcohol engage in disorder or violence – usually where alcohol is not available or where particular fan cultures are not reliant upon alcohol consumption. More significantly, there are even more examples of highly drunken football crowds not engaging in disorder even under provocation and some fan cultures have a reputation for heavy drinking but also a reputation for not engaging in disorder (e.g., supporters of Scandinavian national teams, the Irish national team and Scotland's 'Tartan Army').

However, the persistence in isolating alcohol consumption as a cause of football crowd violence has led to some unintended consequences that have increased the risk of disorder. Given that match-going fan culture is based upon heavy social consumption of alcohol, attempts to restrict access to alcohol are likely to be resisted (Pearson, 2012; Pearson and Sale, 2011), whereby the risk of confrontation and disorder is increased. For example, denying the opportunity to drink alcohol in sight of a football pitch – a criminal offence in Britain – leads to congestion in stadium concourses around bars, which in turn can lead to instances of disorder in narrow confines that are difficult for the police to manage. Similarly, restrictions on the sale of alcohol in stadiums can lead to fans binge drinking in bars and pubs prior to matches meaning they are likely to arrive later and more heavily intoxicated. This, in turn, can lead to congestion at turnstiles and stairwells and public order/safety problems. Finally, restrictions on the sale of alcohol in city centres or on public transport, can push fan groups who wish to consume alcohol out of sight of the police, which makes them more difficult to manage (Pearson and Sale, 2011; Stott, Hoggett and Pearson, 2012).

The role of policing

Having challenged the dominant largely-flawed accounts for large-scale football crowd riots, how can we explain why crowds on occasion engage in disorder? The increasing body of data gathered from numerous studies of football crowd behaviour and management indicates that while individuals and subgroups within crowds may at the beginning of a football event have varying interpretations, understandings, and motivations, under certain circumstances shared social identities within crowds can change and develop depending on the experiences of individuals within it (Schreiber and Stott, 2015; Stott, Adang, Livingstone and Schreiber, 2007; Stott *et al.*, 2001; Stott and Reicher, 1998). [In practical terms, this means that a football crowd, constituted by various subcultures, that is subjected to disproportionate and indiscriminate policing or other security measures, or unprovoked attacks from opposing fans, may cease to be a loose gathering of individuals and groups and become united psychologically in opposition to their treatment] Such psychological unity creates empowerment, enabling many of the participants to confront other groups of fans. It is when this dynamic of inter-group interaction occurs that disorder can escalate from small incidents of confrontation or antisocial behaviour into a large-scale collective disorder involving hundreds of fans.

Research into crowd behaviour at a number of European-hosted international tournaments has identified numerous examples of how crowds developed a shared oppositional identity through coming under attack from local fans (Stott and Pearson, 2007) or through heavy-handed and indiscriminate policing. Importantly, such a theoretical account indicates how some football crowd riots have developed, and can also provide an explanation for arrest statistics and police statements regarding crowd disorder, indicating that the majority of those involved were not known to the police as suspected 'risk supporters' (Stott and Pearson, 2007). In other words, the conflict is less about predisposition than it is about the social psychological dynamics of the situations in which disorder and violence occur – dynamics of which the security measures are often a major contributory factor.

From this, we can see that preventing collective disorder in the football context is far from straightforward and not just a matter of monitoring, controlling, and banning hooligans. Further, it is also not a matter of restricting access to alcohol or improving physical security measures. Our research suggests that reducing the number and severity of incidents requires creating a complex and nuanced security approach that might actually involve reducing the level of riot control police tactics and instead focusing on the facilitation of human rights. If the problem is perceived illegitimacy of police intervention, then the solution is to increase police legitimacy amongst the crowd (or the legitimacy of other security interventions). Our research has shown that this can be achieved through increased communication, non-coercive interaction, and engagement between police officers – or, where appropriate, security personnel – and crowd members before any instances of criminality or disorder occur. The early introduction of small numbers of *dialogue officers* into a football crowd has been shown to enable the police to be seen in a more positive light. Dialogue officers have as their primary aim the facilitation of meaningful two-way communication between crowd members and the police.[3] Referred to in the United Kingdom as *police liaison officers*, these dialogue officers can and do act as a buffer between the crowd and public order police, passing information both ways, resolving minor problems, and otherwise working towards negotiated solutions where tensions arise (Havelund *et al.*, 2011; Stott, Scothern and Gorringe, 2013). This 'graded' tactical approach also allows tolerance levels to be established amongst fans, which in turn reduces the risk of incidents requiring forceful police intervention. It also means that senior officers or other crowd management officials maintain an accurate and dynamic understanding of the actual risk posed by those within the crowd as the event progresses. The intended outcome of this liaison-based strategy is that incidents of unacceptable behaviour – by police standards – will be reduced, and when they do occur, the police will be able to manage them in a differentiated way without being seen as illegitimate and without the need for indiscriminate mass riot control interventions, which have been demonstrated to exacerbate rather than quell crowd disturbances.

Such liaison-based graded tactical approaches to football policing have been successfully trialled, developed, and rolled out in domestic football in the United Kingdom, Germany, the Netherlands, and Sweden in particular, and also at international tournaments such as the 2004 European Championships in Portugal, the 2006 World Cup in Germany, and the European Championships in Poland/Ukraine in 2012. They were also specifically identified as good practice in the 2010 edition of the *European Union Handbook on International Police Cooperation and Measures to Prevent and Control Violence and Disturbances in Connection with Football Matches With an International Dimension* (Council of Europe, 2010). In the United Kingdom, the development of police liaison teams in football follows the successful roll out of these tactics to manage political and environmental protests engaged in by groups previously considered high risk, such as the 'Black Bloc' and the 'English Defence League'. Such approaches also improve police capacity to adhere to obligations created by the European Convention on Human Rights (e.g., the rights of Freedom of Assembly and Association and Freedom of Expression; Stott and Gorringe, 2013). Such rights almost certainly apply to football crowds throughout Europe (Coenen *et al.*, in press; James and Pearson, 2015), in addition to domestic civil rights and liberties that football fans should be able to rely on. The marriage of best practice between policing strategies designed to reduce the risk of football crowd disorder and those that protect human and civil rights of fans is no coincidence, but instead arises from the central role that police legitimacy plays in the behaviour of football crowds.

Conversely, more traditional and reactionary 'show-of-force' styles of policing continue to result in disorder around the world and also raise serious concerns about the extent to which fans' human rights are protected. In much of Eastern Europe, Africa, and South America, the management of football crowds remains couched in terms of 'hooligan threat', 'crowd control', and security. Furthermore, high regulation, 'zero tolerance' and deterrence are likely to be the key tenets of the crowd management operations at the 2016 European Championships in France and the 2018 World Cup in Russia, irrespective of the lack of evidence base for these approaches and their failure at previous football mega events.

Conclusion

The move towards more progressive and evidence-based policing and management of football crowds entails more than a simple move away from discredited theories of football crowd behaviour and counterproductive policing strategies and regulatory interventions. It also requires the involvement of the police themselves with crowd scientists and academics in an ongoing and long-term co-production of research and knowledge exchange on football crowd and fan behaviour, and the development of crowd management techniques that work in both the immediate and long term.

The start for such a process is the engagement of police, football clubs, governing bodies/event organisers, and fan groups with peer-reviewed academic research and the move towards using this research to inform major policing and security decisions. Only with the implementation of genuine evidence-based policing and an institutional reliance upon this, over more traditional ideas of police knowledge and 'know-how', can strategies that have been long discredited in academic circles be completely discounted. However, this should not be a one-way process, and police and other stakeholders in football crowd security have a role to play in terms of testing and developing more progressive and effective models of crowd and spectator management – in turn, adding to their own evidence base. Our contention is that this process also needs to entail the building of both methodological and theoretical expertise into the training and pedagogical development of public order police, internationally embedding evidence-based policing within forces, and ensuring that football crowds are both understood and managed in a way fit for the twenty-first century.

Notes

1   These statistics were also unbalanced by a number of mass and indiscriminate arrests of fans who did not engage in any kind or disorder or criminality.
2   Increasingly, the use of drugs, in particular cocaine, has also been identified as a factor behind football crowd disorder. There is little doubt that in the United Kingdom at least, drugs such as cocaine and mephedrone are being taken by some fans (particularly risk supporters) and may in some cases also have connection with the development of violence or anti-social behaviour (see Ayres and Treadwell, 2012). However, in at least Northern Europe, drug use does not yet have the cultural significance for wider football support that alcohol consumption possesses (Pearson, 2012) and – in contrast to alcohol – has not yet been the target for football-specific legal or regulatory intervention.
3   In Sweden, these officers (*Evenemangs Polis*) have been used to form specialised units for football crowds. In Denmark, dialogue-based units are referred to as *event police*.

References

Armstrong, G. (1998). *Football hooligans: Knowing the score*. Oxford: Berg.

Ayres, T. and Treadwell, J. (2012). Bars, drugs and football thugs: Alcohol, cocaine use and violence in the night time economy among English football firms. *Criminology and Criminal Justice: An International Journal, 12*, 83–100. doi:10.1177/17488958114 22949.

BBC. (1998, June 14). *BBC six o'clock news*. Retrieved from www.bbc.co.uk/programmes/p00fprd5

Coenen, P., Pearson, G. and Tsoukala, A. (in press). *Legal responses to football hooliganism in Europe: A comparative human rights analysis of legislation, policy and strategies designed to regulate football crowds*. The Hague: TMC Asser Press.

Cohen, S. (2002). *Folk devils and moral panics*. London: Routledge.

Council of Europe. (2010). *European Union handbook on international police cooperation and measures to prevent and control violence and disturbances in connection with football matches with an international dimension*. Strasbourg: Council of Europe.

Dunning, E., Murphy, P. J. and Williams, J. (1988). *The roots of football hooliganism*. London: Routledge.

Football hooligans: Merciful deceit. The grotesque behaviour of English football supporters in Europe is causing some agonised navel-gazing back home. (2000, June 22). *The Economist*. Retrieved from www.economist.com/node/81198

Free, M. and Hughson, J. (2003). Settling accounts with hooligans: Gender blindness in football supporter subculture research. *Men and Masculinities, 6*, 136–155. doi:10.1177/1097184X03255849

Garland, D. (2002). *The culture of control: Crime and social order in contemporary society*. Chicago, IL: University of Chicago Press.

Giulianotti, R. (1991) Scotland's tartan army in Italy: The case for the carnivalesque. *Sociological Review, 39*, 503–527. doi:10.1111/j.1467-954X.1991.tb00865.x

Giulianotti, R. (1994). Taking liberties: Hibs casuals and Scottish law. In R. Giulianotti, N. Bonney and M. Hepworth (eds) *Football, violence and social identity* (pp. 229–261). London: Routledge.

Giulianotti, R. (1995). Football and the politics of carnival: An ethnographic study of Scottish fans in Sweden. *International Review for the Sociology of Sport, 30*, 191–223. doi:10.1177/101269029503000205

Giulianotti, R. (1999). Hooligans and carnival fans: Scottish football supporter cultures. In G. Armstrong and R. Giulianotti (eds) *Football cultures and identities* (pp. 29–40). London: Palgrave Macmillan.

Hall, S. (1978). The treatment of 'football hooligans' in the press. In R. Ingham, S. Hall, J. Clarke, P. Marsh and J. Donovan (eds) *Football hooliganism: The wider context* (pp. 15–37). London: Inter-Action Inprint.

Hattersley, R., (2000, June 22). Catastrophe at Charleroi. *The Guardian*. Retrieved from www.theguardian.com

Havelund, J., Ilum, J., Jensen, M., Nielsen, B. P., Rasmussen, K. and Stott, C. (2011, Winter) Event policing – dialogue in the policing of mass events in Denmark. *CEPOL European Police Science and Research Bulletin, 4*, 3–7. Retrieved from www.cepol.europa.eu/science-research/european-police-science-and-research-bulletin/how-contribute

James, M. and Pearson, G. (2015). Public order and the rebalancing of football fans' rights: Legal problems with pre-emptive policing strategies and banning orders. *Public Law, 3*, 458–475. Retrieved from www.sweetandmaxwell.co.uk/Catalogue/ProductDetails.aspx?recordid=469

King, A. (1995). Outline of a practical theory of football violence. *Sociology, 29*, 635–651. doi:10.1177/0038038595029004005

Marsh, P., Rosser, E. and Harré, R. (1978). *The rules of disorder.* London, United Kingdom: Routledge.

Millward, P. (2009). Glasgow Rangers supporters in the city of Manchester: The degeneration of a 'fan party' into a 'hooligan riot'. *International Review for the Sociology of Sport, 44*, 381–398. doi:10.1177/1012690209344658

Pearson, G. (1998). The English disease? The socio-legal construction of football hooliganism. *Youth and Policy, 60*, 1–15. Retrieved from www.youthandpolicy.org/

Pearson, G. (2012). *An ethnography of football fans: Cans, cops and carnivals.* Manchester: Manchester University Press.

Pearson, G. and Sale, A. (2011). On the lash: Revisiting the effectiveness of alcohol controls at football matches. *Policing and Society, 21*, 1–17. doi:10.1080/10439463.2010.540660

Redhead, S. (1993). *The passion and the fashion: Football fandom in new Europe.* Aldershot: Avebury.

Redhead, S. (1997). *Post-fandom and the millennial: The soccer culture.* London: Routledge.

Reicher, S. (1987). Crowd behaviour as social action. In J. C. Turner, M. A. Hogg, P. J. Oakes, S. D. Reicher and M. S. Wetherell (eds) *Rediscovering the social group: A self-categorization theory* (pp. 171–202). Oxford: Blackwell.

Richards, J. (2015). 'Which player do you fancy then?' Locating the female ethnographer in the field of the sociology of sport. *Soccer and Society, 16*, 393–404. doi:10.1080/14660970.2014.961379

Rookwood, J. (2009). *Fan perspectives of football hooliganism: Defining, analysing and responding to the British phenomenon.* Saarbrücken: VDM Publishing House.

Schreiber, M. and Stott, C. (2015). Policing international football tournaments and the cross-cultural relevance of the social identity approach to crowd behavior. In J. F. Albrecht, M. C. Dow, D. Plecas and D. K. Das (eds) *Policing major events: Perspectives from around the world* (pp. 41–58). Boca Raton, FL: CRC Press.

Spaaij, R. (2006). *Understanding football hooliganism: A comparison of six Western European football clubs.* Amsterdam: Amsterdam University Press.

Stott, C., Adang, O., Livingstone, A. and Schreiber, M. (2007). Variability in the collective behaviour of England fans at Euro2004: 'Hooliganism', public order policing and social change. *European Journal of Social Psychology, 37*, 75–100. doi:10.1002/ejsp.338

Stott, C. and Gorringe, H. (2013). From Sir Robert Peel to PLTs: Adapting to liaison based public order policing in England and Wales. In J. Brown (ed.) *The future of policing: papers prepared for the Steven Independent Commission Into the Future of Policing in England and Wales* (pp. 239–251). London: Routledge.

Stott, C., Hoggett, J. and Pearson, G. (2012). Keeping the peace: Social identity, procedural justice and the policing of football crowds. *British Journal of Criminology, 52*, 381–399. doi:10.1093/bjc/azr076

Stott, C., Hutchison, P. and Drury, J. (2001). 'Hooligans' abroad? Inter-group dynamics, social identity and participation in collective 'disorder' at the 1998 World Cup Finals. *British Journal of Social Psychology, 40*, 359–384. doi:10.1348/014466601164876

Stott, C. and Pearson G. (2007). *Football hooliganism: Policing and the war on the English disease.* London: Pennant.

Stott, C. and Reicher, S. (1998). How conflict escalates: The inter-group dynamics of collective football crowd 'violence'. *Sociology, 32*, 353–377. doi:10.1177/0038038598032002007

Stott, C., Scothern, M. and Gorringe, H. (2013). Advances in liaison based public order policing in England: Human Rights and negotiating the management of protest? *Policing, 7*, 212–226. doi:10.1093/police/pat007

Syal, R., Alderson, A. and Cobain, I. (2000, June 18). Thugs mar England's night of triumph. *The Telegraph*. Retrieved from www.telegraph.co.uk/

Tsoukala, A. (2009). *Football hooliganism in Europe: Security and civil liberties in the balance.* London: Palgrave Macmillan.

Weed, M. (2001). ING-GER-LAND AT EURO 2000: How 'handbags at 20 paces' was portrayed as a full-scale riot. *International Review for the Sociology of Sport, 34*, 407–424. doi:10.1177/101269001036004003

Zedner, L. (2009). *Security*. London: Routledge.

Further reading

Stott, C., Hoggett, J. and Pearson, G. (2012). Keeping the peace: Social identity, procedural justice and the policing of football crowds. *The British Journal of Criminology, 52*, 381–399. doi:10.1093/bjc/azr076

Stott, C., Hutchison, P. and Drury, J. (2001). Hooligans abroad? Inter-group dynamics, social identity and participation in collective 'disorder' at the 1998 World Cup Finals. *British Journal of Social Psychology, 40*, 359–384. doi:10.1348/014466601164876

Stott, C. and Pearson G. (2007). *Football hooliganism: Policing and the war on the English disease.* London: Pennant.

Stott, C. and Reicher, S. (1998). How conflict escalates: The inter-group dynamics of collective football crowd 'violence'. *Sociology, 32*, 353–377. doi:10.1177/0038038598032002007

13

GLOBAL SPORT-FOR-DEVELOPMENT

Nico Schulenkorf, Emma Sherry and Katie Rowe

Since the start of the new millennium, an increased focus has been placed on the field of sport-for-development (SFD). This attention has come from non-governmental organisations, government agencies, sport practitioners, and sport academics around the world, with each stakeholder group exploring the potential contribution that sport can make to communities across the globe. *Sport-for-development* has been defined as the 'use of sport to exert a positive influence on public health, the socialisation of children, youths and adults, the social inclusion of the disadvantaged, the economic development of regions and states, and on fostering intercultural exchange and conflict resolution' (Welty Peachey, Cohen, Borland and Lyras, 2011, p. 311). The popularity of SFD stems from its ability to attract a large number of people – particularly those with an interest in sport and physical activity – and use sport and physical activity as strategic vehicles to communicate, implement, and achieve non-sport development goals including those related to social, cultural, educational, psychological, and health-related aspects of (community) life.

In this chapter, we aim to familiarise students with SFD by providing a review of the SFD literature. We base this chapter on a recently conducted integrated literature review that synthesised all SFD research studies published between 2000 and 2014. In referring to some of the key findings from this extensive review (for further details, see Schulenkorf, Sherry and Rowe, in press), we will present in this chapter the status quo of SFD activity in relation to the research foci, authorship, journal outlets, dates of publication, geographical contexts, thematic areas, sport activities, and research methodologies. Based on this review, we will reflect on the implications of SFD as an emerging area of research and provide recommendations for future work in the field.

Reviewing the field of sport-for-development

Before presenting the findings of our SFD literature review, it seems important to highlight two central points that underpin our investigation. First, we should highlight why literature reviews are an important aspect of scholarly work; and second, we need to explain how we conducted our integrative literature review on SFD. In essence, the value of review articles lies in their capacity to bring together extensive amounts of published material related to a specific topic and summarise relevant findings while also drawing relevant conclusions (Cooper, 1998; Jones, 2004; Keller, Fleury, Gregor-Holt and Thompson, 1999). Researchers can apply a range of methods to synthesise findings on a particular topic. The four most relevant methods are (a) meta-analysis, (b) systematic review, (c) qualitative review, and (d) integrative review.

While these approaches overlap and share commonalities in the processes employed to strategically gather and evaluate existing research, Whittemore and Knafl (2005) provided an overview of the purpose, strengths, and weaknesses of each of these analysis techniques. For the purposes of this chapter, we have high-lighted the key differences between the approaches, as summarised in Table 13.1. Based on the purpose of our investigation and the context of the literature (i.e., an emerging field with a range of qualitative and quantitative studies), we decided to use an integrative review to examine the state of research in the field of SFD.

TABLE 13.1 Forms of literature analysis

Form of Analysis	Description
Meta-analysis	Combine the evidence of multiple primary sources through statistical methods; similar to systematic reviews, meta-analyses focus on quantitative studies.
Systematic review	Aim to identify all studies that address a specific (often clinical) question and to utilize a methodology that ensures rigor in both the article selection and data extraction processes (Hiller *et al.*, 2011). Systematic review is, arguably, the most comprehensive and well-known form of literature analysis, but its quantitative focus presents issues for disciplines in which qualitative research is prominent.
Qualitative review	Qualitative reviews have been used to synthesize the findings of qualitative studies, which tends to be limited by sample size and the generalisability of findings.
Integrative review	The broadest type of literature review. Integrative reviews combine both qualitative and quantitative data, as well as different types of research approaches and designs. They are increasingly forming the foundation of policy development and have the potential to advance science, inform research, and develop practice.

Note: This table is based on Whittemore and Knafl's (2005) definitions of different forms of literature review

How we conducted the SFD review

We sought to provide a comprehensive, explicit, and transparent overview of SFD scholarship. With this in mind, we drew on the work of Whittemore and Knafl (2005) and applied their five-step process for conducting integrative reviews: (a) problem identification, (b) literature search, (c) data evaluation, (d) data analysis, and (e) presentation. We will now briefly explain the process that was followed with respect to the final four steps, given that problem identification was addressed in the introduction section.

Whittemore and Knafl (2005) clearly defined the parameters of the literature search, a distinguishing element of integrative reviews compared to alternative approaches. In exploring the SFD literature, two search terms, *sport* and *development*, were used to define two of the three key boundaries of the literature search. These two search terms provided a solid search frame which enabled us to collate all articles related to the topic of interest (SFD) whereby there was convergence and a distinct – albeit contested – theory of 'development', as well as the emergence of 'sport' as a social construct. The third boundary was the limitation of study inclusion criteria to material that was peer-reviewed and published in academic journals. As such, book publications and grey literature – including opinion pieces, editorials, newspaper articles, and any unpublished works – were not included.

Two key databases, SPORTDiscus and Scopus, were searched for peer-reviewed journal articles that were published between January 2000 and February 2014. The year 2000 was chosen as a starting point because, with the exception of early pioneering work (see, for example, Sugden, 1991), dedicated and focused research in the SFD field began in the early twenty-first century (Schulenkorf and Adair, 2013). The selected databases were deemed to provide sound coverage of the relevant literature. SPORTDiscus provided sport-specific material, while Scopus enabled us to explore a range of social sciences articles and delve into papers related to SFD published in journals beyond the sport domain (e.g., in community development or health journals). The literature search included the terms *sport* (NOT *transport*) AND *develop*. These search terms were applied to the domains of title, abstract and/or keywords as it was agreed that if *sport* and *develop* did not feature in any of the three key domain areas, then there was insufficient focus on the topic to warrant consideration.

The data evaluation process involved all three authors in different capacities. One author first screened each of the database hits (over 15,000 across the two databases) to exclude those articles that did not specifically relate to the topic of SFD/development through sport. The article title and abstract were the sources of information used to determine the relevance of the article in the context of the research problem. The second and third authors were involved in the process of checking the shortlisted articles and ensuring their relevance to the research topic. This resulted in the inclusion of 437 articles for the analysis stage.

The data analysis process involved examining the 437 articles included in the study and extracting information related to specific categories drawn by the authors from journal meta-data (see Table 13.2). The details of each article were recorded and a comprehensive SFD research literature database was developed. Once established, this database was examined and analysed for patterns, themes, and anomalies. The authors remained open to emerging patterns and trends throughout the analysis process, which resulted in the development of additional categories, such as *sport as a concept*.

After completing the data analysis, the researchers engaged in the final step of Whittemore and Knafl's (2005) integrative review process: presentation of research findings. The remaining sections of this chapter will now explore, present, and discuss the findings from this integrative literature review.

TABLE 13.2 Inclusion/exclusion criteria

Inclusion Criteria *Articles were* included *if they focused primarily on any (or a combination) of the following*	*Exclusion Criteria* *Articles were* excluded *if they focused primarily on any (or a combination) of the following*

• Sport as a vehicle to achieve developmental outcomes related to individuals and their communities. Major examples include:
   – Disease prevention/management
   – Improved physical or mental health outcomes
   – Development of life skills related to teamwork and cooperation (or otherwise)
   – Building confidence or self-esteem
   – Social inclusion
   – Education
   – Gender equality
   – Livelihoods
   – Reconciliation
   – Peace-building/peacekeeping
 • Physical education (PE) as a means to develop children or adolescents as people (rather than sport or general outcomes)
 • Physical activity and health promotion programs if a clear reference was made to sport/recreational activities (i.e., not clinical exercise interventions)
 • Disability sport (where elite outcomes were not a focus)
	• Influences on/determinants of participation, such as gender, race, geographic location
	 • Sport specific motor skill development (if no links made to fundamental life skills)
	 • Sport tourism and/or events (unless a very clear links with community development outcomes)
	 • Preventing sport dropout/discontinuation
	 • Elite athletes, umpires, coaches, or volunteers
	 • Studies on injury risk prevention/ management
	 • Virtual forms of sport (video games)
	 • Corporate social responsibility
	 • Historical accounts of sport issues
	 • Exercise prescription interventions (treadmill programs etc.), and yoga/fitness specific activities

Note: The themes for inclusion were largely similar to the thematic categories identified by the *Journal of Sport for Development*.

Sport-for-development: the *status quo*

As the title of this section suggests, the findings presented will essentially map the 'status quo' of the SFD literature. Frequency tables and graphs have been used to provide a clear summary of research undertaken in the SFD field. Where our findings have required interpretation or a summary, we have included a statement or overview of key themes because simple 'counting' techniques would not have provided the specific insights required to make sense of the data. In presenting these findings, we seek to provide an overarching view of the SFD field of research, as opposed to focusing specifically on the minutiae of individual articles.

Article titles

NVivo 10 was used to identify the 50 most frequently used words in article titles. This is also represented graphically in a word cloud (see Figure 13.1). As seen in Figure 13.1, *sport* and *develop(s)* were the two most common words used in article titles, which is a logical finding given that these were the two search terms used. The top ten terms also included: *social, youth, physical, community activity, health, educators* and *participation*. By reviewing these terms, students can start to appreciate some of the current areas that are central to SFD research. One key observation is the prevalence of social and youth sport initiatives. We also found it interesting to note that football (soccer) was the only sport-specific activity identified in the top 50 terms. This perhaps highlights the relevance of this sport in the context of SFD programmes and initiatives.

Figure 13.1 Article title word cloud (top 50 condensed words)

Dates of publication

A clear trend was observed with respect to the growth of SFD publications over the last decade, reaching a peak of 96 in 2013 (see Figure 13.2). As we only included articles published before February 2014 in our analysis, we decided not to list 2014 publications in Figure 13.2.

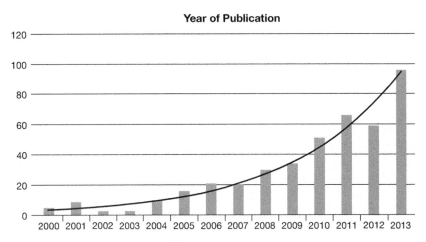

Year of Publication

Figure 13.2 Year of publication by number of articles

Journal outlets

In order to establish where SFD literature is published, the data set was analysed to identify the ten journals with the highest number of SFD manuscripts published between January 2000 and February 2014 (see Table 13.3). It was interesting to note that the two leading outlets in which SFD literature had been published were journals that specifically focus on the social aspects of sport (sociology discipline); however, the three leading sport management journals closely followed, rounding

TABLE 13.3 Top 10 journal outlets

Journal Title	Frequency
Sport in Society	29
International Review for the Sociology of Sport	26
Sport Management Review	21
Journal of Sport Management	16
European Sport Management Quarterly	13
Physical Education and Sport	13
Third World Quarterly	12
International Journal of Sport Policy	10
Journal of Sport for Development	10
Sport Education and Society	10

out the top five journal outlets. The *Journal of Sport for Development*, which was established in 2013, was also a strong target for SFD journal publications, also making the top ten journal outlets. Its ranking is expected to increase in the future due to its specific focus on SFD research.

Thematic areas

In order to explore the focus of SFD journal articles, seven specific thematic areas of SFD practice and research, identified by the *Journal of Sport for Development*, were used as a framework for data analysis. The categories include disability, education, gender, health, livelihoods, peace and social cohesion (for descriptions see http://jsfd.org/). With the caveat that research in some of these areas can overlap, we attempted to assign articles to the most relevant area in order to provide a general picture of the current focus of SFD work. Figure 13.3 shows that while some thematic areas were well-covered in the sample of journal articles (i.e., social cohesion and education), others were found less frequently in the SFD literature (i.e., gender, disability, and livelihoods). With this finding, we wish to point out that one-fifth of the literature analysed was classified as cross-disciplinary, meaning that it spanned different thematic areas.

Geographic representation: researchers and location of research

To explore the location of researchers and research studies, author details and the location of the research (SFD programme or initiative), as outlined in the study description, were captured for each of the included articles. We found that the majority of the 383 total researchers were based in Europe (37 per cent), North

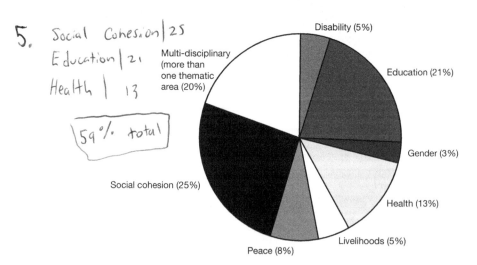

Figure 13.3 Thematic areas

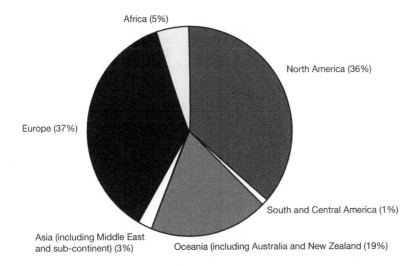

Figure 13.4 Researcher location (by continent)

America (36 per cent), or Oceania (predominantly Australia and New Zealand; 19 per cent), as seen in Figure 13.4. Yet, the location of the research was more evenly distributed, despite the strong representation of SFD research conducted on programmes or initiatives in North America (see Figure 13.5).

We further examined the data, breaking it down by country of researcher and research location (see Table 13.4). It was observed that much of the SFD research

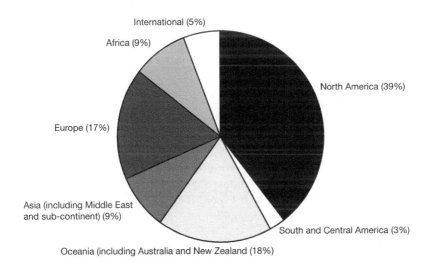

Figure 13.5 Location of research (by continent)

TABLE 13.4 Researchers and research sites (greater than five publications)

Research Site		Researcher Location	
USA	88	USA	128
Australia	49	UK	113
UK	47	Australia	87
Canada	33	Canada	69
South Africa	24	South Africa	22
Israel	6	Sweden	9
Zambia	6	Denmark	8
Denmark	5	NZ	7
Germany	5	Finland	6
Sri Lanka	5	Greece	6
		Norway	6
		Switzerland	6
		Belgium	5
		Germany	5
		Holland	5
		New Zealand	5

work to date had been undertaken in the researchers' 'home countries'. Table 13.4 shows that the top five nations for academics undertaking SFD research (United States, United Kingdom, Australia, Canada, and South Africa) were also the top five research sites. This would suggest that a large proportion of the published SFD research has been conducted in close proximity to the location of the researcher's institution. Few studies included in-country programme staff as part of the research team; only 28 journal articles mentioned the inclusion of in-country staff. Thus, we concluded that contributors from the countries under investigation were often not represented in the research team.

Sport programmes and initiatives

In approximately half of the articles analysed, sport was discussed as a 'concept' as opposed to a specific activity or intervention. In the remaining articles that did focus on a specific sport activity or intervention, many sport and physical activity programmes were identified. General physical activity (as opposed to sport-specific activities) and football (soccer) were the most commonly reported activity forms (see Table 13.5). There was a substantial body of research investigating SFD in the context of mega-events; the majority of these articles focused on the benefits and challenges of SFD in relation to the Olympics ($n = 14$) or FIFA World Cup ($n = 8$).

Research methodologies

In the articles analysed, qualitative research approaches were the most commonly utilised (see Figure 13.6); there was also a large number of conceptual studies.

TABLE 13.5 Sports activity

Sport Activity	Tally
General physical activity	108
Football	102
Basketball	35
Multi-sport programs	17
Mega-events (Olympics)	14
Volleyball	12
Swimming	10
Mega-events (FIFA)	8
Cricket	7
Athletics	7
Netball	6
Running	6
Tennis	6
Cycling	6
Baseball	5

Studies using quantitative and mixed method approaches were less frequently found within the data set.

Discussion

This integrated literature review sought to provide a snapshot of the current landscape of SFD research, with a particular emphasis on the development of the field more generally. Having presented the key findings, we will now discuss the factors potentially contributing to our results and the *status quo* of the field. We also identify gaps in SFD research and suggest opportunities for further scholarly enquiry.

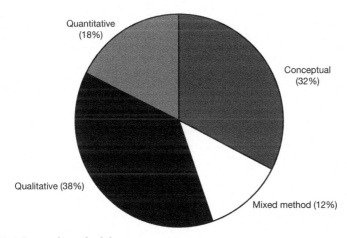

Figure 13.6 Research methodology

Publication outlets

Based on study findings, we conclude that scholarship in SFD has been growing significantly since the start of the new millennium. In contextualising these findings, it should be noted that official recognition, awareness, and legitimacy was brought to the field by initiatives such as the 2001 establishment of the United Nations Office for Sport for Development and Peace and the 2003 Magglingen Declaration (Schulenkorf and Adair, 2013). Since then, research in SFD has continued to gain momentum annually, with a peak of close to 100 published articles in 2013 alone. Academics are increasingly conducting SFD research and journals seem to be becoming more open to including SFD research in their repertoire (the *Journal of Sport for Development* was even established specifically for SFD research). Taken together, this would suggest that the growth of SFD literature is likely to continue into the future.

Based on our findings, it seems that sport sociology journals remain the dominant publication outlet. However, it was interesting to observe the growing trend towards the publication of SFD articles in mainstream sport management journals. In these publications, the focus often shifts away from examining the social and cultural issues surrounding SFD initiatives to the strategic design and management of SFD projects for wider community benefit (see, for example, Frisby and Millar, 2002; Kellett, Hede and Chalip, 2008; O'Brien, 2007; O'Brien and Gardiner, 2006; Sawrikar and Muir, in press; Schulenkorf, 2010, 2012; Schulenkorf and Edwards, 2012; Skinner, Zakus and Cowell, 2008; Thomson, Darcy and Pearce, 2010; Vail, 2007).

Article titles and research foci

In examining article titles we were not surprised to find that in SFD literature, *sport* and *development* were the most frequently used terms. Yet, the frequent use of the terms *social* and *youth* was an unexpected finding. This perhaps suggests that much of SFD research to date has emphasised social development outcomes, rather than physical or economic development (see 'Thematic Areas' section below). Similarly, youth-oriented programmes were more commonly reported on than programmes for adults. It could be argued that this was the case because programmes attempt to engage and positively influence the younger generation through sport. Future studies could attempt to target parents, particularly mothers, given the important role they play as supporters and role models for their children (Meier and Saavedra, 2009; Sawrikar and Muir, in press; Siefken, Schofield and Schulenkorf, 2014).

Thematic areas

In our view, the findings related to the thematic areas addressed by SFD programmes are of particular relevance. Initiatives aimed at creating social cohesion and providing opportunities for education, often to members of disadvantaged communities, have been a strong focus in the literature to date. However, our findings also identify gaps with respect to the coverage of topics such as disability, gender equality, and livelihoods. Arguably, disability research in SFD is still in its infancy because of the limited amount of funding and relatively small number of projects focused specifically on disabled community members. A number of articles identified in the initial literature search were focused on the Paralympics and elite athletes with disabilities. Grassroots disability sport studies with a clear focus on improving health outcomes or achieving specific SFD targets were few and far between. Similarly, the advancement of access and rights for girls and women were also inadequately covered in the literature identified.

Most surprising, perhaps, was the lack of research emphasising the concept of livelihoods. Research suggests that financial independence – a key aspect of what was described as livelihoods – plays a central role in improving living conditions and generating associated social benefits (Coalter, 2010; Portes and Landholt, 2000). Yet, this was not a strong focus in the research identified. Therefore, we encourage scholars to focus on SFD programmes that promote job skills training, employability, rehabilitation, and the creation of social enterprises; in particular, we believe that the SFD sector would benefit from collaborative research between social scientists and economists regarding new approaches, innovative strategies, and creative tactics to improve the livelihoods of disadvantaged people around the world.

Authors and research teams

In recent years, the field of SFD has been criticised for the practice of international implementers from high-income countries conducting research in low- and middle-income countries (Levermore, 2009; Lindsey and Grattan, 2012). In some cases, accusations of the misuse of 'bio-power' or the application of neo-colonialist tactics have been made (Coalter, 2013; Darnell and Hayhurst, 2012). Our review further stresses the divide between local and international actors in SFD, both on the ground and in the research context. On the ground, only one in two SFD projects described in the articles used local (in-country) staff, which means that a remarkable 50 per cent relied solely on 'international experts' to implement programmes. Negative consequences resulting from such a 'helicopter approach' can be significant, particularly regarding community support, empowerment, and ownership, as well as the wider sustainability of projects (Hayhurst and Frisby, 2010; Schulenkorf and Adair, 2013). Given that a helicopter approach may lead to disastrous outcomes for local communities, the 50 per cent figure should give aid programmes, funding bodies, sport managers, NGOs, and policymakers something to think about.

Similarly, very few SFD studies were conducted by authors from low- and middle-income countries. Whether this imbalance results from a lack of qualified researchers in these countries or inadequate opportunities for local researchers to lead or cooperate in research projects, the trend is certainly worrying and deserves more attention and scholarly investigation in the future. In regards to geographical background, a staggering 92 per cent of researchers were from North America, Europe and Australia. Authors from Africa accounted for only 5 per cent of contributors (with the majority from South Africa) and contributors from Asia, Latin America, and the Pacific Islands were hardly represented at all. These figures are remarkable, especially when taking into account that more than 20 per cent of SFD studies were actually conducted in the latter regions (9 per cent in Africa, 9 per cent in Asia, and 3 per cent in Latin America). Moreover, according to the Swiss Academy for Development (www.sportanddev.org), over half of all SFD projects worldwide are implemented and delivered in Africa, Asia, and Latin America.

Methodology and presentation of findings

Researchers have used a broad range of research approaches and methods to analyse SFD initiatives. Qualitative approaches currently seem to hold dominance over quantitative modes of enquiry. Given the significant number of publications in sociology and development journals – areas that are traditionally known for qualitative work – this outcome is hardly surprising. Similarly, the health-specific journals have a much higher number of quantitative studies and intervention/evaluation studies, which is reflective of research conducted in the health science disciplines. It is interesting to see, however, that publication outlets are increasingly interested in publishing research that applies 'non-traditional' approaches. In this context, non-traditional not only relates to the methods themselves but also to the presentation of research findings. For example, more accessible, innovative and user-friendly ways of presenting research have increasingly been encouraged (Garbutt, 2009); this seems particularly important for the SFD community, which by nature has a very close practitioner–scholar link. For instance, in the context of sport-for-health, researchers have recently attempted to go beyond statistics, presenting findings as posters and word clouds (Siefken, Schofield and Schulenkorf, in press). However, the SFD community is only starting to see the benefits of alternative approaches and could perhaps learn from other fields in which research findings have been presented more creatively (e.g., as pictures and poems; see Carroll, Dew and Howden-Chapman, 2011). Such visual communication of research is likely to assist SFD practitioners and participants on the ground, particularly if they come from disadvantaged communities and lack an academic background or the research qualifications necessary to understand complex statistical presentations.

Conclusion

Integrative reviews are used to examine, criticise, and synthesise representative literature on a particular topic; they are intended to highlight the *status quo* and yield provocative, new perspectives on key issues in a particular field (Torraco,

2005). We believe that our integrated review on SFD has done exactly that; it has provided a rigorous review and a strong synthesis of SFD literature, providing an encompassing panorama of current SFD research.

In this chapter, we have presented some of the key findings of our review. In doing so, we were able to highlight the increasing trend of journal publications in the field since the new millennium. We have also shown that scholars have predominantly focused on social and educational outcomes related to youth sport, with football (soccer) as the most common sport activity. Current SFD research is dominated by qualitative approaches to enquiry and studies are often published in sport sociology or sport management journals. Finally, the geographical context of authorship and study location presents an interesting paradox: Despite the fact that the majority of SFD projects were carried out in Africa, Asia, and Latin America, a remarkable 90 per cent of SFD authors were based in North America, Europe, and Australia. In other words, there is a clear practitioner–scholar divide in SFD and a significant need for capacity building not only in sport management, but also in the research domain.

References

Australian Department of Foreign Affairs and Trade. (2013). *Development-through-sport: A joint strategy of the Australian Sports Commission (ASC) and the Australian Agency for International Development (AusAID), 2013–2017.* Retrieved from www.ausport.gov.au/__data/assets/pdf_file/0007/529837/DTS_joint_strategy_FINAL_Logo_Black.pdf

Carroll, P., Dew, K. and Howden-Chapman, P. (2011). The heart of the matter: Using poetry as a method of ethnographic inquiry to represent and present experiences of the informally housed in Aotearoa/New Zealand. *Qualitative Inquiry, 17,* 623–630. doi:10.1177/1077800411414003

Coalter, F. (2010). The politics of sport-for-development: Limited focus programmes and broad gauge problems? *International Review for the Sociology of Sport, 45,* 295–314. doi:10.1177/1012690210366791

Coalter, F. (2013). *Sport for development: What game are we playing?* London: Routledge.

Cooper, H. M. (1998). *Synthesizing research: A guide for literature reviews* (3rd ed.). Thousand Oaks, CA: Sage.

Darnell, S. C. and Hayhurst, L. (2012). Hegemony, postcolonialism and sport-for-development: a response to Lindsey and Grattan. *International Journal of Sport Policy and Politics, 4,* 111–124. doi:10.1080/19406940.2011.627363

Frisby, W. and Millar, S. (2002). The actualities of doing community development to promote the inclusion of low income populations in local sport and recreation. *European Sport Management Quarterly, 2,* 209–233. doi:10.1080/16184740208721923

Garbutt, R. (2009). Is there a place within academic journals for articles presented in an accessible format? *Disability and Society, 24,* 357–371. doi:10.1080/09687590902789537

Hayhurst, L. and Frisby, W. (2010). Inevitable tensions: Swiss and Canadian sport for development NGO perspectives on partnerships with high performance sport. *European Sport Management Quarterly, 10,* 75–96. doi:10.1080/16184740903554140

Hiller, C. E., Nightingale, E. J., Lin, C.-W. C., Coughlan, G. F., Caulfield, B. and Delahunt, E. (2011). Characteristics of people with recurrent ankle sprains: a systematic review with meta-analysis. *Br J Sports Med 2011, 45,* 660-672 doi:10.1136/bjsm.2010.077404

Jones, M. L. (2004). Application of systematic review methods to qualitative research: practical issues. *Journal of Advanced Nursing, 48*, 271–278. doi:10.1111/j.1365-2648.2004.03196.x

Keller, C., Fleury, J., Gregor-Holt, N. and Thompson, T. (1999). Predictive ability of social cognitive theory in exercise research: An integrated literature review. *Journal of Knowledge Synthesis in Nursing, 5*, 6–8. doi:10.1111/j.1524-475X.1999.00019.x

Kellett, P., Hede, A.-M. and Chalip, L. (2008). Social policy for sport events: Leveraging (relationships with) teams from other nations for community benefit. *European Sport Management Quarterly, 8*, 101–121. doi:10.1080/16184740802024344

Levermore, R. (2009). Sport-in-international development: Theoretical frameworks. In R. Levermore and A. Beacom (eds) *Sport and international development* (pp. 26–54). Basingstoke: Palgrave Macmillan.

Lindsey, I. and Grattan, A. (2012). An 'international movement'? Decentring sport-for-development within Zambian communities. *International Journal of Sport Policy and Politics, 4*, 91–110. doi:10.1080/19406940.2011.627360

Meier, M. and Saavedra, M. (2009). Esther Phiri and the Moutawakel effect in Zambia: An analysis of the use of female role models in sport-for-development. *Sport in Society, 12*, 1158–1176. doi:10.1080/17430430903137829

O'Brien, D. (2007). Points of leverage: Maximising host community benefit from a regional surfing festival. *European Sport Management Quarterly, 7*, 141–165. doi:10.1080/16184740701353315

O'Brien, D. and Gardiner, S. (2006). Creating sustainable mega-event impacts: Networking and relationship development through pre-event training. *Sport Management Review, 9*, 25–48. doi:10.1016/S1441-3523(06)70018-3

Portes, A. and Landholt, P. (2000). Social capital: Promise and pitfalls of its role in development. *Journal of Latin American Studies, 32*, 529–547. doi:10.1017/S0022216X00005836

Sawrikar, P. and Muir, K. (in press). The myth of a 'fair go': Barriers to sport and recreational participation among Indian and other ethnic minority women in Australia. *Sport Management Review.*

Schulenkorf, N. (2010). The roles and responsibilities of a change agent in sport event development projects. *Sport Management Review, 13*, 118–128. doi:10.1016/j.smr.2009.05.001

Schulenkorf, N. (2012). Sustainable community development through sport and events: A conceptual framework for sport-for-development projects. *Sport Management Review, 15*, 1–12. doi:10.1016/j.smr.2011.06.001

Schulenkorf, N. and Adair, D. (2013). Temporality, transience and regularity in sport-for-development: Synchronizing programs with events. *Journal of Policy Research in Tourism, Leisure and Events, 5*, 99–104. doi:10.1080/19407963.2012.678600

Schulenkorf, N. and Edwards, D. (2012). Maximizing positive social impacts: Strategies for sustaining and leveraging the benefits of inter-community sport events in divided societies. *Journal of Sport Management, 26*, 379–390. Retrieved from http://journals.humankinetics.com/jsm

Schulenkorf, N., Sherry, E. and Rowe, K. (in press). Sport-for-development: An integrated literature review. *Journal of Sport Management.* doi:10.1123/jsm.2014-0263

Siefken, K., Schofield, G. and Schulenkorf, N. (2014). Laefstael jenses: An investigation of barriers and facilitators for healthy lifestyles of women in an urban Pacific Island context. *Journal of Physical Activity and Health, 11*, 30–37. doi:10.1123/jpah.2012-0013

Siefken, K., Schofield, G. and Schulenkorf, N. (in press). Process evaluation of a walking programme delivered through the workplace in the South Pacific island Vanuatu. *Global Health Promotion.* doi:10.1177/1757975914539179

Skinner, J., Zakus, D. and Cowell, J. (2008). Development through sport: Building social capital in disadvantaged communities. *Sport Management Review, 11*, 253–275. doi:10.1016/S1441-3523(08)70112-8

Sugden, J. (1991). Belfast United: Encouraging cross-community relations though sport in Northern Ireland. *Journal of Sport and Social Issues, 15*, 59–80. doi:10.1177/019372359101500104

Thomson, A., Darcy, S. and Pearce, S. (2010). Ganma theory and third-sector sport-development programmes for Aboriginal and Torres Strait Islander youth: Implications for sports management. *Sport Management Review, 13*, 313–330. doi:10.1016/j.smr.2010.01.001

Torraco, R. J. (2005). Writing integrative literature reviews: Guidelines and examples. *Human Resource Development Review, 4*, 356–367. doi:10.1177/1534484305278283

Vail, S. (2007). Community development and sports participation. *Journal of Sport Management, 21*, 571–596. Retrieved from http://journals.humankinetics.com/jsm

Welty Peachy, J., Cohen, A., Borland, J. and Lyras, A. (2011). Building social capital: Examining the impact of Street Soccer USA on its volunteers. *International Review of the Sociology of Sport, 48*, 20–57. doi:10.1177/1012690211432068

Whittemore, R. and Knafl, K. (2005). The integrative review: Updated methodology. *Journal of Advanced Nursing, 52*, 546–553. doi:10.1111/j.1365-2648.2005.03621.x

14

SPORT AND INTERNATIONAL DIPLOMACY

Robert E. Baker and Pamela H. Baker

Sport is a visible and viable option as a diplomatic tool to enhance international peacemaking, intercultural understanding, and both personal and community development. The relationship between sport and international development, peace-building and diplomatic endeavours reveals the complex intersections among international sport-based programming concepts that include subtle distinctions in emphases and terminologies. For example, emphases such as sport for development (SFD) and sport for peace (SFP) are distinct from sport diplomacy, yet all are interrelated and fall within the broader sport for development and peace (SDP) agenda (Baker, Baker, Evmenova and Esherick, 2012; Baker and Esherick, 2009; Welty Peachey, Cunningham, Lyras, Cohen and Bruening, 2014). While included as a component of the SDP sector, sport diplomacy is a unique concept in that it serves as a mechanism utilised by governmental and non-governmental organisations (NGOs) to advance their predetermined political, social, and civic agendas. Giulianotti (2011) noted the 'diverse political actors and ideologies' (p. 1) in the SDP sector often drive the specific agendas.

Diplomatic goals are reflected in numerous agendas, including peace-building and conflict resolution, the enhancement of cross-cultural understanding, and community development (Baker and Esherick, 2009). Multi-track diplomatic initiatives enhance the ability to address varied agendas across multiple levels of society (Broome and Hatay, 2006). The utility of sport to improve individual and collective understanding of diverse individuals and cultures makes it valuable in diplomatic endeavours. Sport is also a useful mechanism for building intercultural relationships, reducing conflict and bringing diverse individuals and cultures together.

Diplomacy through sport occurs at broad levels, such as the United Nations Office on Sport for Development and Peace (UNOSDP), which focuses efforts at the governmental, national, and international level. The UNOSDP serves as secretariat for Sport for Development and Peace International Working Group

(SDPIWG), an inter-governmental policy initiative that promotes the integration of sport-related policy recommendations into the strategies of national governments. Clearly a diplomatic undertaking, the SDPIWG further 'promotes and supports the adoption of policies and programmes by national governments to harness the potential of sport to contribute to the achievement of development objectives … and peace' (UNOSDP, n.d., para. 2).

Sport diplomacy also occurs at the local level through people-to-people programmes such as intercultural exchanges. Some sport-related diplomatic endeavours, such as the Olympic Games, function at both the global and local levels. On a broad international level, to be accomplished through governmental and inter-governmental policies, the Olympic Movement aims to 'contribute to building a peaceful and better world by educating youth through sport practised in accordance with Olympism and its values' (International Olympic Committee, 2014, p. 15). On a local level, this is achieved through the interaction of individual athletes, administrators, and spectators involved with the Olympics.

Theoretical framework

The aforementioned diplomatic efforts in sport are grounded in established theoretical underpinnings. In observing the role of sport in public diplomacy, Sanders (2011) noted that sport is 'a gigantic and powerful medium for the international spread of information, reputations and relationships that are the essence of public diplomacy' (para. 1). Acknowledging the global influence of the enormous economic impacts and the extent of popular interest in sport, he continued, 'the audience's level of interest exceeds those of any other subject matter, including political news and the movies' (Sanders, 2011, para. 1).

Given the popular interest in sport, Murray and Pigman (2014) described two types of sports diplomacy. The first involves governmental use of sport as a diplomatic tool, such as the U.S. Department of State's SportsUnited Sports Visitors Program, which involves exchanges among non-elite coaches and athletes as well as professional athletes, such as figure skater Michelle Kwan, travelling internationally as a sport envoy. The second type of diplomacy that Murray and Pigman identified was 'international-sport-as-diplomacy', which involves diplomatic interactions between NGOs and non-state actors that facilitate international sport, such as the International Olympic Committee and FIFA. In fulfilling both types of sport diplomacy, Manchester United is a vehicle of English government for diplomacy through international matches and diplomatic receptions. Additionally, Manchester United's participation in the Union of European Football Association's Champions League requires international cooperation that is akin to international-sport-as-diplomacy (Murray and Pigman, 2014; Rofe, 2014). Diplomatic agendas can be pursued both in and through sport.

Sport conveys its own inherent messages, but can also serve as an instrument through which diplomatic agendas can be pursued. Sanders (2011) suggested that 'a well-conceived public diplomacy strategy could capitalise on the opportunities that sport presents' (para. 1). For example, the use of sport-based diplomatic efforts can advance either an inclusive social justice agenda or a conflict resolution agenda. Sport is, therefore, a valuable mechanism in any diplomatic agenda aimed at fostering peace and social justice, by increasing popular support of global liberalism – a dominant political ideology (Ben-Porat, 2007; Jones, 2004). Kuriansky (2007) contended that interpersonal interactions and intergroup interventions are essential in diplomatic endeavours in order to facilitate peace and resolve conflicts.

Beer and Nohria (2000) offered a theoretical foundation for the use of sport as a diplomatic instrument through Theory E and Theory O. *Theory E,* or top-down change, can be more economically efficient and implemented more quickly, but can yield results that are not highly sustainable. *Theory O,* or bottom-up change, while generally longer and more expensive, can produce more sustainable results. Top-down initiatives are more commonplace and often receive the desired attention and necessary funding. While top-down diplomatic initiatives more regularly attract resources, bottom-up initiatives are essential in humanising the engaged stakeholders and fostering mutual understanding (Beer and Nohria, 2000). Bottom-up approaches enhance perceptual accuracy, thereby reducing misconceptions, and can even be a unifying force among stakeholders (Baker and Esherick, 2009). Efficacy in achieving diplomatic initiatives is enhanced through bottom-up, grassroots changes. Regardless of approach, diplomatic change is a long-term process (Simpson, Hamber and Scott, 2001).

Allport's (1954) contact hypothesis promoted the facilitation of interactive contact among culturally diverse stakeholders. Direct interaction lessens antagonism, debunks stereotypes, and stimulates more tolerant attitudes. Interactive contact with disparate individuals or groups fosters new awareness, while also diminishing the accompanying trepidation (Allport, 1954). Sports result in forced proximity among stakeholders and require interaction among participants. In alignment with contentions of the contact hypothesis, forced interactions through sport must be meaningful in order to optimise grassroots change.

Engagement in sport experiences commonly reflects Allport's (1954) hypothesis wherein collaborative interaction can transform stakeholder attitudes. For example, common interests among diverse stakeholders can influence their acceptance of an array of individual and cultural differences. Intercultural experiences in sport-based diplomatic programmes encourage cooperation, which can result in enhanced understanding and camaraderie. Meaningful interactions among grassroots stakeholders contribute to an empathetic and accepting atmosphere. Allport (1954) also noted,

> The effect is greatly enhanced if this contact is sanctioned by institutional supports (i.e., by law, custom or local atmosphere), and provided it is of a sort that leads to the perception of common interests and common humanity between members.

(p. 281)

Top-down support of bottom-up diplomatic initiatives is, therefore, most likely to yield desired, sustainable results. Chufrin and Saunders (1993) concluded that, 'while governments negotiate around interests and issues, citizens play a crucial role in changing behavior and relationships, for it is in the public political arena … that issues are reframed, comparable interests recognised, perceptions changed, fears allayed' (p. 158).

Grassroots sport diplomacy initiatives underpinned by the principles of Allport (1954) and Beer and Nohria (2000) can effect change. These local interpersonal interactions are the keystone for broader intercultural change. Broad diplomatic outcomes can be a result of engaged individuals within specific cultures (Baker, Baker, Evmenova and Harris-Hayes, 2015). While sport alone provides a mechanism, sport-for-development theory suggests that sport should be paired with cultural and educational components to successfully address many of the aims of sport diplomacy initiatives (Lyras, 2007; Lyras and Welty Peachey, 2011). Diplomatic interests occur at the global and local level. The universality of sport affords an opportunity to pursue these diverse global and local diplomatic interests.

In the pursuit of both global and local diplomatic interests, the concept of *glocalisation* becomes central. Glocalisation can be considered global or local globalisation. The term glocalisation itself suggests a seemingly dichotomous concept involving the interplay of homogeneity and heterogeneity. This balance between sameness and difference among stakeholders in a diplomatic initiative yields glocalisation that reflects local applications in global agendas and global interests in local programmes (Robertson, 1995). In business, differentiating global brands for particular markets is an aspect of glocalisation. In diplomacy, accomplishing global diplomatic agendas through local actions is reflective of the concept.

Sport diplomacy often involves an international agenda, pursued through localised actions. Sport-based *glocal* approaches connect global and local interests and engagements (Svensson, 2001). The use of sport as a diplomatic change agent requires an awareness of local interests and intercultural sensitivity among stakeholders (Lyras, 2008). Local interactions are, therefore, the foundation for broader cultural and intercultural change.

Case study

Examples of sport diplomacy efforts take multiple forms ranging from envoys who are sent abroad to offer clinics in-country to exchanges in which foreign visitors come to a host country to gain perspectives for implementation upon their return home. Regardless of delivery format, the intent is to advance an agenda reflective of both diplomatic and social goals via a grassroots movement based upon the development of one's network (Allport, 1954; Beer and Nohria, 2000). The Sport Diplomacy Initiative (SDI) is a funded cooperative agreement between the Center for Sport Management at George Mason University and the SportsUnited Sports Visitors Program at the U.S. Department of State's Bureau of Educational and Cultural Affairs. It should be noted that a partnership with a funding agent who has access to the participant groups and can sponsor programme activities is essential for the programme to succeed in attaining its goals. To date, this partnership has led to more than 50 exchanges during which groups of athletes, coaches, and/or sport leaders come to the United States for approximately two weeks. In all cases, it has been the sponsor who has selected the participants based upon embassy-based connections in countries targeted for diplomatic development through sport. The role of the Center for Sport Management has been to provide programming and logistics for events when groups of foreign athletes and coaches, referred to as sport visitors, are in the United States. It is also the Center's responsibility to evaluate programme efficacy – both short-term and long-term.

Participants from numerous countries across six continents represent a wide variety of team, individual and disability sports. As a diplomatic effort, the programme is designed to facilitate mutual respect between the participants and their American counterparts. The overarching goals of SDI are to create a combination of experiences that help participants to (a) cultivate an understanding of American culture in order to counteract negative stereotypes; (b) develop leadership skills such as conflict resolution, team building, and inclusiveness of diversity; (c) establish partnerships and networks to enable the sharing of knowledge and skills in their home communities; and (d) create positive change through sport. The programmes vary based upon the needs and ages of the participants. In general, all groups engage in active experiences in sport-specific skill development (e.g., on-court or on-field clinics), alternative sport skill development (e.g., yoga, rock climbing), inclusive sport awareness (e.g., Special Olympics, wheelchair basketball), and leadership skills development (e.g., ropes course). They also attend a variety of sporting events and participate in passive activities in classroom settings to examine topics such as sport psychology, injury prevention, and conflict resolution. Participants also engage in a variety of cultural activities to help them to better understand the American culture and people in an effort to build cultural tolerance. Each group is hosted by an American family for a home hospitality dinner, tours key landmarks and/or museums in the location(s) they visit, attends cultural events (e.g., circus, rodeo), and goes shopping at least once.

The programme of events for each group is an intensive immersion experience during their entire visit. Many days are 12 to 14 hours long with a variety of activities scheduled to maximise the chance for progress toward programme goals during the visit. However, programme delivery is complex due to serving a range of participants (e.g., teenage athletes, adult coaches), many of whom do not speak English, thus requiring constant use of interpreters to convey core concepts. The programme provides participants with all lodging, food, educational materials, and experiences, as well as transportation during their stay. An example itinerary can be found in Table 14.1. In an effort to prepare participants to share their experience with others upon returning home, each individual receives a flash drive with a logistics book of programme details and contact information, numerous photographs and a summary video of the visit.

TABLE 14.1 Sample itinerary for a basketball program with athletes and coaches

Day 1	Day 2	Day 3	Day 4	Day 5
International Arrival	Teambuilding Skills on Ropes Course	Strength Training Clinic	Injury Prevention and Sport Nutrition Sessions	Washington, D.C. Tour
Opening Session for General Orientation with Pre-program Assessment	Conflict Resolution and Sport Psychology Sessions	High School Visit, Lunch with Players and Coaches, Facilities Tour	Footwork Clinic	Selected Museums and Monuments Visits
Lodging Orientation and Group Activities	Rock Climbing	Attend Men's High School Basketball Game	Attend Women's High School Basketball Game	Embassy Visit and Dinner

Day 6	Day 7	Day 8	Day 9	Day 10
Shooting Clinic	Sport Leadership and Gender Equity in Sport	Defensive Drills Clinic	Exercise and Conditioning Sessions	Teambuilding Basketball Clinic
Therapeutic Recreation and Disability Sport Sessions	Offensive Drills Clinic	University Visit and Facilities Tour (secure waiver from NCAA)	Recreational Youth League Scrimmage	Shopping at Mall
Attend Special Olympics Unified Basketball Game	Wheelchair Basketball	Attend University Basketball Game	Attend Circus	Home Hospitality

Day 11	Day 12	Day 13	Day 14	
Sport in the U.S. and Sport Management Sessions	Youth Sport Development Session	National Basketball Association (NBA) Clinic	Wrap-up Session with Post-Program Assessment	
Tour of Community Sport Facility and Swimming	Action Plan Development	Tour NBA Arena with Shoot Around on court pre-game	Certificate Presentation	
Amateur Athletic Union Scrimmage	Yoga Class	Attend NBA Game	International Departure	

Note: All meals are provided but are not noted here to avoid repetition.

Part of working with a sponsoring agency is providing evidence that the programme is making an impact. In order to do this, an evaluation system that addresses both short-term progress and the more long-term reach of the programme is important. Due to the complexities noted previously regarding the age, language and cultural differences among participants, the evaluation system must be culturally sensitive and simple. For the SDI, the assessment measures are a pre-programme survey administered during orientation, a post-programme survey given during the wrap-up session, an action plan, and a follow-on survey sent to participants who are at least six months removed from the experience. All of the aforementioned measurement components of the evaluation system have been subjected to external review. The pre-programme and post-programme surveys have seven objective prompts and one open-ended item aligned with the programme objectives. The action plan focuses on post-programme multiplier effect efforts and is directly aligned with the follow-on survey design, which is a series of 17 objective items with an option for qualitative comments at the end to minimise the need for translation of responses upon completion. The short-term measures are translated during the designated sessions by interpreters and the follow-on survey is distributed via email in five languages (e.g., English, Russian, Spanish, French, and Arabic).

Managerial implications

Both macro- and micro-managerial implications become evident in the conduct of sport-based diplomatic initiatives. Macro-implications revolve around policies, procedures, and governance structures related to sport diplomacy; micro-implic-ations, on the other hand, centre on management applications directed toward implementation and operations involved in sport diplomacy.

Sport-based diplomatic endeavours, while dependent upon individual engage-ment, are most commonly supported by governments and NGOs. Policies, such as the stakeholders to be targeted, the goals to be pursued and the mission to be upheld, are often centrally derived and guide the diplomatic initiative. These policies, supported by specific procedures, such as proposal deadlines, and quarterly and budgetary restrictions, are intended to maintain the integrity of the diplomatic efforts. Governance structures dictate how initiatives are organised, where the efforts are located, how objectives are prioritised, and are typically a determinant in funding.

Managing the operational aspects of a funded project (e.g., SDI) requires a wide range of skills, such as grant writing, programme evaluation, events management, fiscal competence, and curriculum development. Programme evaluation requires the ability to not only collect and analyse data, but also to utilise the analytics to inform decisions regarding the sport diplomacy project. In some cases, languages skills or access to interpreters is central to the success of the diplomatic activities. Organisational and communication skills are also essential in order to balance the complications associated with managing so many different stakeholders in multiple locations. Designing the programme and navigating the bureaucracy associated with implementation require two very different skill sets. It is essential that sponsor/funding agency rules are followed, even though they may change during the course of the project. For example, planning to provide a banquet for networking of participants with American athletes and coaches requires an awareness of purchasing procedures of both the sponsor and any internal oversight system. Obtaining funds in advance of programme implementation is important for sustaining the programme, rather than incurring out-of-pocket expenses that may not be reimbursed. Examining ways to provide for unexpected expenses, such as lost luggage, and establishing preventative procedures to keep incidental expenses from being added to the hotel costs (e.g., locking of minibars, restriction of pay-per-view movies) reflect the attention to detail that is also important. Management of a project such as this goes far beyond planning the programme content and arranging guest speakers or space for clinics. Essentially serving as a travel agent responsible for logistics requires specific skills when arranging for transportation, accommodation, and meals. Further, managing finances requires an ability to serve as an accountant responsible for budget planning, purchasing, reconciliation, and reporting. Hiring and managing support personnel, each of whom contributes a unique set of specialised skills to the implementation of the programme, is critical as they provide invaluable service. For example, support personnel are able to escort the group, facilitate the completion of the evaluation assessments, collect photographs and video data, and troubleshoot any logistical issues that emerge. The demands of sport-based diplomatic initiatives commonly necessitate administrative support behind the scenes.

Furthermore, branding the sport-based diplomatic programme through utilising a program logo will enhance recognition and affiliation among stakeholders. For example, a banner with the programme logo as a backdrop for group pictures in key locations or at meaningful events, enhances identification of the programme. Providing the participants with logo items to take home, such as a t-shirt, water bottle, or flash drive, enhances affiliation and thereby contributes to the multiplier effect when the participants share their experiences – hopefully in a positive way – upon their return home.

Conclusion

The future direction of sport diplomacy remains uncharted. There are identifiable trends that will presumably persist in the foreseeable future. For example, most sport-based diplomatic endeavours are not financially self-sufficient; while some sport business enterprises engage in diplomatically significant activities, the majority of grassroots sport diplomacy programmes are dependent upon governments and NGOs for the bulk of their funding. Direct government funding and grant-based funding will remain crucial in the immediate future for the ongoing implementation of sport diplomacy initiatives. As the conduct of sport diplomacy programmes improves, these funding sources will become increasingly stressed. Further, the available resources will become progressively more difficult to acquire as their distribution becomes increasingly competitive. As government and NGO resources remain central to sport diplomacy activities, it will become increasingly important for sport diplomacy programmes to demonstrate their efficacy.

There is ample scepticism as to the effectiveness of sport diplomacy, in part due to what some view as exaggerated claims regarding the benefits of sport-based programming (Coalter, 2010; Kidd, 2008; Levermore, 2011; Whitley, Forneris and Barker, 2014). Levermore (2011) noted that 'the lack of convincing large-scale evaluation might contribute to the doubt that some development agencies have shown for the sport-for-development movement as a remedy' (p. 340). Rigorous and reliable programme evaluation is essential to demonstrate whether alleged diplomatic outcomes are achieved through sport-based initiatives. Calls to enhance the quality and quantity of evaluative activities and sport diplomacy research, are echoed in concerns expressed with regard to the challenges of conducting diplomatic programme evaluation, especially in underserved and diverse communities (Baker et al., 2015; Whitley et al., 2014). Coalter (2010) suggested that the lack of funding, resources, and expertise needed to conduct the work contributes to the dearth in reliable evaluation.

As funding for sport diplomacy initiatives becomes extremely competitive, funding agencies (e.g., governments and NGOs) have begun to specifically request more quantifiable data to demonstrate the efficacy of sport diplomacy programmes (Kidd, 2008; Levermore, 2011; Whitley et al., 2014). Funding agencies have, therefore, expected the implementation of rigorous evaluation techniques. Evaluative analytics and empowerment evaluation will serve as tools for sport diplomacy initiatives (Baker et al., 2015; Federman, Kaftarian and Wandersman, 2015). Already prominent in sport, analytics will continue to evolve in sport-based diplomatic evaluations in an effort to provide data that document programme effectiveness and efficiency. Evaluative analytics will also inform future decisions regarding sport-based diplomatic programming. However, the progression toward quantifiable analytics will not likely reduce the use of qualitative analyses in programme evaluation. Pictures, videos, testimonials, and ethnographies provide valuable, rich insights into the impacts of sport diplomacy. Empowerment evaluation, conceptualised and implemented to foster improvement and self-determination, focuses on increasing stakeholder capacity toward achieving desired outcomes (Federman et al., 2015).

References

Allport, G. W. (1954). *The nature of prejudice*. Reading, MA: Addison-Wesley.

Baker, R. E., Baker, P. H., Evmenova, A. and Esherick, C. (2012, November). *Implementation and evaluation of international sport development, peace, and diplomacy programs*. Symposium conducted at the meeting of the annual conference of the Sport Management Association of Australia and New Zealand, Sydney, Australia.

Baker, R. E., Baker, P. H., Evmenova, A. and Harris-Hayes, L. (2015). Perceptions of international sport exchange participants regarding inclusive sport. *International Journal of Sport Management, 16*, 417–436. Retrieved from http://journals.humankinetics.com/jsm-contents

Baker, R. E. and Esherick, C. (2009). Sport-based peace initiatives: Playing for peace. In E. Ndura-Ouédraogo and R. Amster (eds) *Building cultures of peace: Transdisciplinary voices of hope and action* (pp. 102–124). Newcastle-upon-Tyne: Cambridge Scholars.

Beer, M. and Nohria, N. (2000). *Breaking the code of change*. Boston, MA: Harvard Business School Press.

Ben-Porat, G. (2007). *Global liberalism, local populism: Peace and conflict in Israel/Palestine and Northern Ireland*. Syracuse, NY: Syracuse University Press.

Broome, B. J. and Hatay, A. J. (2006). Building peace in divided societies. In J. G. Oetzel and S. Ting-Toomey (eds) *The SAGE handbook of conflict communication* (pp. 627–662). Thousand Oaks, CA: Sage.

Chufrin, G. I. and Saunders, H. H. (1993). A public peace process. *Negotiation Journal, 2*, 155–177. doi:10.1111/j.1571-9979.1993.tb00698.x

Coalter, F. (2010). Sport-for-development: Going beyond the boundary? *Sport in Society, 13*, 1374–1391. doi:10.1080/17430437.2010.510675

Federman, D. M., Kaftarian, S. J. and Wandersman, A. (2015). *Empowerment evaluation* (2nd ed.). London, United Kingdom: Sage.

Giulianotti, R. (2011). The sport, development and peace sector: A model of four social policy domains. *Journal of Social Policy, 40*, 757–776. doi:10.1017/S0047279410000930

International Olympic Committee. (2014). *Olympic charter*. Retrieved from www.olympic.org/Documents/olympic_charter_en.pdf

Jones, C. (2004). Global liberalism: Political or comprehensive? *The University of Toronto Law Journal, 54*, 227–248. Retrieved from www.utpjournals.press/loi/utlj

Kidd, B. (2008). A new social movement: Sport for development and peace. *Sport in Society: Cultures, Commerce, Media, Politics, 11*, 370–380. doi:10.1080/17430430802019268

Kuriansky, J. (2007). *Beyond bullets and bombs: Grassroots peacebuilding between Israelis and Palestinians*. Portsmouth, NH: Praeger.

Levermore, R. (2011). Evaluating sport-for-development approaches and critical issues. *Progress in Development Studies, 11*, 339–353. doi:10.1177/146499341001100405

Lyras, A. (2007). *Characteristics and psycho-social impact of fan inter-ethnic educational sport initiative on Greek and Turkish Cypriot youth*. Available from ProQuest Dissertations and Theses database. (UMI No. 3265785)

Lyras, A. (2008). Organizational change theory: Sport for peace and development. *The Chronicle of Kinesiology and Physical Education in Higher Education, 2*, 14–16. Retrieved from www.nakhe.org/ChronicleQuest

Lyras, A. and Welty Peachey, J. (2011). Integrating sport-for-development theory and praxis. *Sport Management Review, 14*, 311–326. doi:10.1016/j.smr.2011.05.006

Murray, S. and Pigman, G. A. (2014). Mapping the relationship between international sport and diplomacy. *Sport in Society, 17*, 1098–1118. doi:10.1080/17430437.2013.856616

Robertson, R. (1995). Glocalization: Time-space and homogenity-heterogeneity. In M. Featherstone, S. Lash and R. Robertson (eds) *Global modernities* (pp. 25–44). London: Sage.

Rofe, J. S. (2014). It is a squad game: Manchester United as a diplomatic non-state actor in international affairs. *Sport in Society, 17*, 1136–1154. doi:10.1080/17430437.2013.856610

Sanders, B. (2011). Sports as public diplomacy. *CPD Monitor, 2*(6). Retrieved from http://uscpublicdiplomacy.org/pdin_monitor_article/international_sport_as_public_diplomacy

Simpson, G., Hamber, B. and Scott, N. (2001, February). *Future challenges to policy-making in countries in transition*. Paper presented at the meeting of the Comparative Experiences of Policy Making and Implementation in Countries in Transition Workshop, Derry/Londonderry, Northern Ireland. Retrieved from www.csvr.org.za/docs/international/futurechallenges.pdf

Svensson, G. (2001). 'Glocalization' of business activities: A 'glocal strategy' approach. *Management Decision, 39*, 6–18. doi:10.1108/EUM0000000005403

United Nations Office for Sport for Development and Peace. (n.d.). Sport for Development and Peace International Working Group. Retrieved from www.un.org/wcm/content /site/sport/home/unplayers/memberstates/pid/6229

Welty Peachey, J., Cunningham, G., Lyras, A., Cohen, A. and Bruening, J. (2014). The influence of a sport-for-peace event on prejudice and change agent self-efficacy. *Journal of Sport Management, 29*, 220–244. doi:10.1123/jsm.2013-0251

Whitley, M.A., Forneris, T. and Barker, B. (2014). The reality of evaluating community-based sport and physical activity programs to enhance the development of underserved youth: Challenges and potential strategies. *Quest, 66*, 218–232. doi:10.1080/00336297. 2013.872043

PART 3

Technology and social media

15

ANALYTICS, TECHNOLOGY AND HIGH-PERFORMANCE SPORT

Bill Gerrard

Performance analysis is at the core of the coaching process in sport at all levels of performance. Coaches attempt to facilitate improvements in the future perform-ance of their athletes by investigating the key factors involved in the outcomes of recent games. This performance analysis involves analysing the observed outcomes of performances to understand the underlying causal mechanisms. Understanding the deeper structure of performances, particularly identifying the *controllables* – the key factors that are under the control of the athlete – is crucial in order for the coach to decide on the optimal intervention strategy to facilitate improved future performance. For example, what should be the training priorities in preparation for the next contest? What is the best tactical plan for the next contest? In the case of team sports, who should be selected to participate in the next contest? These are all critical decisions for a coach that may have a significant impact on the outcome of the next contest in which their athletes compete, and all of these coaching decisions can be informed by performance analysis.

This chapter explores how technological developments have revolutionised the collection of performance data with profound consequences for performance analysis. It is shown how the advent of video recording and then digital technology has had two effects on the type of performance data collected. First, there has been a widening of the range of observed actions on which data can be collected. Second, there has also been a deepening of the nature of the data collected with techno-logical advances providing the means to capture data on more fundamental aspects of performance. Performance analysis not only includes frequencies of different types of actions that have been performed, but also data on the more fundamental dimensions of performance underlying the observed actions. These more fundamental aspects of performance can be summarised as the four As: *ability* (i.e., technical), *athleticism* (i.e., physical), *attitude* (i.e., psychological), and *awareness* (i.e., tactical). Recent technological developments have particularly impacted the

5

collection of tracking data on distances covered and speed of an athlete's movement. The impact of technology on performance data collection is discussed in this chapter using a three-stage schema: (a) paper-and-pencil methods, (b) video recording, and (c) digital technology. The enhanced possibilities for greater use of expert data to assess the more fundamental aspects of performance are also considered.

The impact of technology on data collection in high-performance sport has not only led to an exponential growth in the quantity of data collected, but has also massively increased the scope for statistical analysis of performance data. There has been a parallel development in the type of data analysis – qualitative to quantitative – used in high-performance sport. Qualitative analysis based on video replays and the reconstruction of critical incidents has been supplemented by quantitative analysis – initially the reporting of summary performance statistics and, more recently, the use of statistical analysis and other related quantitative techniques – to analyse patterns across performances. Sport analytics depends on the use of statistical and other quantitative analytical techniques to inform the decision-making of elite coaches. The growth in sports analytics is surveyed in this chapter with particular emphasis on the distinction between statistical reporting and analytics.

Throughout the chapter the focus is on the specific context of team sports; however, we argue that the managerial implications are transferable to all sports and, indeed, to the management of non-sporting performance. Of particular importance is the distinction between the striking-and-fielding team sports, such as cricket and baseball, and the invasion-territorial team sports, such as the various codes of football. Further, we argue that the technological developments in data collection, for studies on performance, have impacted most significantly the invasion-territorial sports with the widespread use of count data in these sports only really possible with the advent of digital technology. We conclude the chapter with a summary of the key points and some thoughts on the outlook for perform-ance analysis and sports analytics.

The impact of technology on performance analysis

A useful way of understanding the impact in recent years of technological develop-ments on the collection and analysis of performance data is to consider three broad stages, starting with the use of paper-and-pencil methods and then progressing to the impact of video recording and digital technology. A key aspect in this evolution of performance analysis is that the impact of video recording and digital tech-nology has been much greater in the invasion-territorial sports, such as football.

Stage 1: paper-and-pencil methods

Striking-and-fielding sports – primarily cricket and baseball – are structurally very simple games; at the core of cricket and baseball is a sequence of head-to-head contests between the batsman/hitter and the bowler/pitcher. The structure of striking-and-fielding sports has two very important implications for performance analysis; for example, the performance of athletes in striking-and-fielding sports is highly separable such that the major contributions of individual players can be easily identified and separated from the contributions of other players. Further, there is a very direct link between the contributions of individual players and match outcomes. Indeed, match outcomes are largely driven by the performances of the batsman/hitter and the bowler/pitcher. The defensive contributions of fielders in preventing runs and getting players out through catching or returning the ball to the wicket/base ahead of a running player are relatively minor in comparison to the contributions of the bowler/pitcher; however, the interdependence of bowling/pitching and fielding remains an issue in evaluating defensive contributions, particularly in baseball.

The structure of striking-and-fielding sports as a sequence of individual contests has facilitated the collection of key-performance data during games; play is naturally broken up between bowls/pitches as the ball is returned to the bowler/ pitcher in preparation for the next delivery, giving time for the basic details of each play to be recorded on a scorecard. These scorecards are of a 'double-entry' form, with each play recorded from the perspectives of both the batsman/hitter and the bowler/pitcher. In cricket, the batting team's scorecard shows the outcome for each batsman for every ball faced as well as how the batsman's innings ended while the bowling team's scorecard shows the outcome of every delivery by each of their bowlers. The natural delay between deliveries indicates sufficient time to record these outcomes. From the scorecards basic count data of runs scored by each batsman, wickets taken and runs conceded by each bowler can be calculated easily and these, in turn, can be used to generate batting averages (i.e., runs scored per innings) and bowling averages (i.e., runs conceded per wicket taken) for comparisons across games. Cross-checking for internal consistency between the batting and bowling scorecards and the match score should ensure that the data collected are accurate and free from recording errors. The scorecards should provide an objective record of a match since the data report the outcomes as adjudicated and signalled by the umpire. A similar scoring system was developed for baseball with the format of box scores being originally adapted from the cricketing scorecard by Henry Chadwick in the 1860s, albeit allowing for the additional complexities in baseball for how runs are scored, particularly runs batted in, as well as whether or not a pitch is judged by the umpire as a strike or a ball, given that three strikes is an out whereas four balls advances the hitter to first base on a walk (Schwartz, 2004).

Stage 2: video recording

Paper-and-pencil methods, although highly effective for data collection in striking-and-fielding sports, are of much more limited use in invasion-territorial sports. These are the team sports, such as the various codes of football, hockey, and basketball, that attempt to replicate the battlefield with teams scoring by moving an object (e.g., a ball or puck) to designated locations (e.g., between posts, across a line, or through a hoop) defended by the opposing team. In addition to being territorial, these games are also time-dependent, with the match outcome determined by the cumulative scores within a specified playing time. Invasion-territorial sports by their very nature are highly tactical; the game cannot be reduced easily to a sequence of head-to-head contests between individual players, as in striking-and-fielding sports. All players on the field are potentially involved in every play and, to be effective, all players in a team must coordinate their actions. Therefore, players need to be tactically and spatially aware in their decision-making during games and this becomes a key aspect in the analysis of player performance (see Section 3 below).

Invasion-territorial sports are much more complex in structure than striking-and-fielding games, which create greater challenges for both data collection and data analysis. There is a much more indirect link between the individual contributions of players, scoring, and match outcomes. Attacking and defending are much more interdependent, since possession of the ball, or puck, by the attacking team also has a defensive function by denying attacking opportunities to the opposing team as well as running down the clock. Possession and time are the ultimate scarce resources in invasion-territorial games. Attacking and defending are also interdependent in the sense that in most invasion-territorial games, possession has to be won by the defending team before an attacking play can instigate. Within attacking plays, different actions are also highly interdependent; in order to score, the ball must be moved forward into areas of the pitch in which scoring opportunities can be created, and these opportunities must in turn be converted into scores. This structural hierarchy of interdependent player actions in invasion-territorial sports creates a real separability issue for the performance analyst of how to weight the importance of different individual contributions and becomes even more complicated when certain contributions involve joint actions, such as lineouts and scrums in rugby union.

The nature of invasion-territorial sports complicates the data collection process. For example, in striking-and-fielding sports, games need to be coded principally in regard to two dimensions – players (Who?) and actions (What?) – while in invasion-territorial games, there are four basic dimensions: players (Who?), actions (What?), position (Where?), and time (When?). But not only is the data collection process made more demanding by the need to gather a greater amount of information both in terms of the number of dimensions and the variety of possible alternatives within each dimension, there is also much greater time pressure. Unlike striking-and-fielding sports, there is often little or no natural delay between individual plays, with teams switching continuously between attacking and defending as possession changes.

Not surprisingly, paper-and-pencil methods can only capture very limited amounts of performance data during invasion-territorial games. Historically, the only data consistently recorded in invasion-territorial sports have been appearances, scores, disciplinary warnings, and player ejections (e.g., sin-bins and sending-offs).

The advent of the video recorder in the 1970s – with the ability to pause, rewind, and fast forward game videos – greatly facilitated the ability to collect performance data in invasion-territorial sports. Although coaches had, for many years, watched films of games to review performances and analyse future opponents, the use of game films had been restricted by their limited availability, the need for projection facilities to watch these games, and the difficulties in replaying specific critical moments. The explosion in the TV coverage of sport from the 1960s onwards combined with the development of video recording technology in the 1970s resolved all of these issues and opened up the opportunity for detailed video analysis of games. Rather than being restricted to in-game data collection, teams could now compile performance data by applying paper-and-pencil methods to video replays of the games. The process was slow and time-consuming, so, as a consequence, teams tended to focus only on critical incidents. Thus, video analysis tended to be largely qualitative with reconstructions of specific plays, often those in which a team had scored or had conceded a score. However, teams identified patterns of play based on very few observations, indicating a sample size limitation. Count data for invasion-territorial sports remained very limited in scope.

Stage 3: digital technology

The advent of digital technology and low-cost computing power in the 1990s accelerated the process of data collection in high-performance sport. The digitalisation of video images allowed the development of computer software to code and edit game videos so that the data collection process became much quicker. In particular, the use of image-recognition software indicated that the coding of games could be largely automated, with human intervention required only to resolve problems such as blind spots and conflicts when two or more players converged. Because of digital technology, count data for all of the different player actions in invasion-territorial sports became readily available.

The digital revolution in performance analysis led a number of commercial companies to offer data collection and analysis to elite sports. For example, in association football in the United Kingdom, three alternative commercial data systems have been available since the late 1990s: Opta, Prozone, and Amisco. All these data systems provide detailed count data on all aspects of games. Opta also supplies the detailed coding of games in spreadsheets involving around 1,600 rows of data for the typical games. Further, Prozone and Amisco combine the provision of the count data with graphic representations and the game video. Both of these systems also allow some degree of interactivity such that the analyst is able to control some of the parameters for reporting the data. Typically, teams rely on these systems to provide detailed statistical reports after the game, for being a source of video and count data on future opponents and possible scouting targets for player recruitment. Teams tend to produce their own in-game data using systems, such as SportsCode, to code and edit the live video stream of their games. Given the obvious time pressures, analysts can code relatively few features of a game in real time and, therefore, focus only on data of particular relevance to coaches and mostly likely to influence tactical changes. Sam Allardyce was an early adopter of in-game data collection and video analysis in association football in England when he was manager of Bolton Wanderers between 1999 and 2007. At home games in the Reebok Stadium, Bolton's performance analysts collected performance data and edited the video during games. A Smartboard was installed in the home dressing room so that players could be shown video clips during the halftime interval with a particular emphasis on set-piece play, a key aspect of Bolton's game plan. Allardyce would watch most of the game from a seat in the stands rather than from the dugout at pitchside in order to get a better view of the game and would relay instructions to the analysts and coaches through an intercom system.

The development of digital performance systems not only led to a massive expansion in the provision of count data in invasion-territorial sports, but also to the availability of tracking data. Tracking data involves continuous data on the position of players on the pitch. Initially, this type of data was collected from video-based image-recognition systems using triangulation of multiple cameras to continually locate the exact position of all players. This allowed distances covered and, when combined with time data, speeds to be calculated. For the first time, teams had reliable data on one aspect of the physical performance of players during games.

An alternative approach to video-based tracking systems is to use global positioning systems (GPS). Australian Rules Football was a first mover in this respect, allowing four players on either team to wear GPS devices during games in the 2005 games. Other sports, such as rugby union, have adopted GPS devices to provide in-game tracking data. However, possibly the most innovative use of GPS devices is to track distances covered and speeds in training sessions.

Expert data systems

The advances in data collection methods in high-performance sport, particularly the availability of software such as SportsCode, allows teams themselves to code and edit game videos quickly and has created the possibility of expert data systems. *Expert data systems* refer to systems in which data are defined and interpreted by coaches rather than relying on third-party commercial providers. The following example from association football can illustrate the difference between count data and expert data: Suppose a player (A1) has possession of the ball and plays it long beyond one of his team mates (A2) positioned out wide who is marked by a defending player (D1). D1 turns to chase the ball but is closed down quickly by A2 and forced to put the ball into touch. The attacking team now has a throw-in deep in the opposition half near the penalty area. How would this be coded? Typically, count data produced by third-party commercial providers would code the long ball by A1 as an incomplete pass, to be regarded as a negative since it led to a loss of possession. Further, D1 would most likely be credited with a clearance. A2's contribution would often not be coded at all unless it involved an attempted tackle and, again, since A2 did not win possession directly, the tackle would be designated as a missed tackle and treated as a negative. Therefore, the play could be quite easily coded as two negatives for the attacking team (i.e., an incomplete pass and a missed tackle) and a positive for the defending team (i.e., a clearance). However, the attacking team has gained 'second-ball' possession (i.e., a throw-in) in a dangerous area of the pitch close to the opposition penalty area. Indeed, this was a tactic frequently employed by Bolton Wanderers in the English Premiership under Sam Allardyce. If this incident was coded internally by the Bolton analysts based on expert knowledge of the coaches' tactical plan, then both A1 and A2 would have been credited with positive contributions – A1 for the well-placed long ball and A2 for closing down D1 – forcing a thrown-in to be conceded. This example highlights that count data is far from being an objective reporting of frequencies of different actions. The definitions of actions involve interpretation and experts with more detailed tactical and technical knowledge may have a very different interpretation of an observed event than an external analyst applying a standardised set of generic definitions.

The example of second-ball possession also raises another key aspect of expert data systems: Expert data can go beyond the observed event to analyse and interpret the more fundamental dimensions of performance. In particular, both the long ball played by A1 and the chase by A2 involve tactical decisions and their technical execution. A1's decision to play the long ball needs to be evaluated relative to the other available options. Further, the technical execution of the long ball in terms of distance and speed needs to be assessed relative to the positioning of both A2 and D1. If the ball is hit too long and/or too fast, there would be no opportunity for an effective chase by A2. Similarly, A2's decision to chase and the technical effectiveness of that chase in forcing D1 to put the ball into touch can also be expertly evaluated. Coaches can assess both the selection of actions (i.e., the decision) and their execution (i.e., the technique). Ultimately, it is all about 'doing the right things' (i.e., selection) and 'doing things right' (i.e., execution). Only the team's experts – the coaches and the analysts – can evaluate the tactical and technical aspects of their own players' performances.

An important component of tactical decision-making in invasion-territorial sports is the spatial positioning of players. Sports players must continuously make decisions on where to position themselves both when their team is attacking and defending. Attacking players need to provide options for the player in possession either by moving into positions to receive the ball or by making decoy runs to create space. Defenders must make positioning decisions in order to cover either a specific attacker or a specific area of the pitch. Tracking technology has greatly aided the ability of coaches to assess the positioning decisions of players. For example, Prozone provides an animated reconstruction of a game with a bird's eye view of the positions of players on the pitch, using a video-based tracking system. Connecting lines between players can be added to the animation to facilitate a better understanding of how players are coordinating their movements. This feature is particularly useful in association football to check the alignment of the back line of defenders. This feature also helped a leading English Premiership team to recognise that one of their defenders, an established international player, often lagged behind the rest of the back line when they moved out quickly and, therefore, undermined any attempt to catch opponents offside. Once the player was made aware of the problem using video clips and game animations, he rectified this aspect of his game and started to take greater responsibility for calling this defensive play.

One of the teams that embraced expert data systems was Saracens – one of the leading rugby union teams in England. Under the leadership of their Director of Rugby, Brendan Venter, a former South African international and a qualified medical practitioner well-versed in evidence-based approaches to decision-making, Saracens adopted a coach-led system of evidence-based performance management in 2009. Each coach has specific areas of responsibility and, after every game, collates the data on these aspects of player performance using internal definitions based on the team's own tactical approach. The data include assessments of key decisions by individual players, as well as the technical execution of particular actions. From this internal data, a set of key-performance indicators (KPIs) for the team as a whole as well as for individual players has been identified and these are monitored across the season using a traffic-lights system classifying the KPIs as excellent (green), satisfactory (amber), or poor (red). The KPIs are used to evaluate team and player performances and feed into coaching decisions on training priorities, game tactics, and team selection. In contrast, when it comes to opposition analysis, Saracens relies on count data supplied by Opta for the quantitative data analysis of future opponents. Time and cost constraints make it infeasible to collate expert data on opponents beyond the detailed qualitative analysis of the videos of their most recent games.

The development of sports analytics

Sports analytics is the use of quantitative data analysis of performance data to support coaching decisions. Sports analytics is not only the analysis of performance data, but also analysis with an explicit practical purpose. Specifically, sports analytics is analysis directed towards informing coaches' decisions on the optimal choice of intervention regarding, for example, training programmes, game preparation, and player recruitment.

There has been a long history of the statistical analysis of performance data in sport – particularly in baseball where paper-and-pencil methods have captured most of the key data from the very early days of the professional game in the 1860s. Important landmarks in the analysis of baseball include the contributions of Evers and Fullerton (1910), Rickey (1954), Cook (1964), and Mills and Mills (1970). Further, Scully (1974) used baseball data to show how the economic value of player performance could be calculated. For example, Scully developed a two-stage procedure in which he first estimated the win contribution of players by applying regression analysis to quantify the relationship between player performance and the team win percentage using the slugging average to measure hitter performance and the strikeout-to-walk ratio to measure pitcher performance. Using regression analysis, Scully then estimated the relationship between team win percentage and team revenues to calculate the financial value of an incremental change in team performance and, by implication, the financial value of a player's contribution to the team win percentage.

Probably the most influential contributor to the development of the statistical analysis of baseball – or 'sabermetrics' based on the acronym for the Society for American Baseball Research – is Bill James, who first started publishing articles on baseball in the mid-1970s and launched his *Baseball Abstract* in 1977. James questioned the usefulness of conventional performance metrics for hitting, pitching, and fielding and provided a number of important advances. One of his most important contributions has been including walks in the evaluation of hitting performance. James showed that on-base percentage, the percentage of at-bats in which a hitter gets to base, is a much better predictor of team success than either batting or slugging averages which only considered hits. Traditionally, walks had been perceived as a pitcher error but the ability of hitters to select which pitches to leave is a skill in itself, yet one ignored by the conventional hitting metrics and, as a consequence, largely ignored by teams.

None of these contributions to sabermetrics constituted analytics at the time since they were not motivated by any intention to influence decision makers in the game. The following classified advertisement in *The Sporting News* for the first *Baseball Abstract* by Bill James in 1977 gives a clear sense of the somewhat whimsical nature of the enterprise: 'The 1977 *Baseball Abstract*: Contains 18 Statistical Categories That You Just Can't Find Anywhere Else, And a New Table Baseball Game'. However, the *Baseball Abstract* led to the development of sports analytics when MLB teams started to take account of the insights of James and other sabermetricians. The team that led the way in using sabermetrics was the Oakland Athletics, who had pioneered the provision of statistics to fans in the early 1980s with STATS Inc. (Schwartz, 2004). The Oakland A's – a small-market MLB team with a very restricted player budget – then took the lead in the application of sabermetrics to player recruitment in the mid-1990s, initially under the General Manager, Sandy Alderson, and then most famously, by his assistant General Manager and successor, Billy Beane. The story of how the A's used analytics as a 'David' strategy to compete with resource-richer rivals, such as the New York Yankees, is recounted in Michael Lewis's (2003) book *Moneyball: The Art of Winning an Unfair Game*, which was subsequently turned into a Hollywood movie with Brad Pitt starring as Billy Beane.

Moneyball was a game-changer in high-performance sport, with an influence stretching well beyond baseball. The timing was incredibly fortuitous since the publication of *Moneyball* coincided with the beginning of the widespread use of digital technology for data collection and the establishment of commercial companies providing performance data in the invasion-territorial sports particularly association football and the other North American major leagues, including

American football, ice hockey, and basketball. Nothing persuades more in sport than winning, so inevitability the success of the As led coaches and analysts in other team sports to ask whether or not the *Moneyball* approach was transferable particularly to the invasion-territorial sports (Gerrard, 2007). Proponents of a statistical approach to performance analysis viewed the complexity of invasion-territorial sports as an opportunity rather than a barrier. From a statistical perspective, the high degree of interdependency coupled with a multitude of different types of player actions is ideally suited to multivariate analysis, such as multiple regression, to separate out the effects of individual actions.

One of the main functions of statistics is the reporting function – the purely descriptive task of summarising data using measures of central tendency (e.g., mean and median), dispersion (e.g., standard deviation and interquartile range) and distributional shape (e.g., skewness and kurtosis). The reporting function should also include the provision of comparisons between different metrics as well as comparisons of the same metrics for different entities and/or different time periods. The other principal function of statistics is the analytical function, which involves the analysis of the observed variation in the data to determine if it is systematic or random, followed by an investigation of the factors associated with the systematic variation. These two functions are interlinked. Statistical analysis of the data, particularly the identification of the most significant factors associated with the systematic variation in match outcomes, is necessary in order to determine which KPIs should be reported and tracked. Statistical reporting of summary statistics and comparisons for selected performance metrics does not constitute analytics. What to report becomes the critical issue, especially in an era where technology allows the capture of data on all aspects of performance and databases can be programmed to automatically generate statistical reports. Coaches increasingly face the problem of information overload with so much data available and thus, the primary role of the statistical analyst or data scientist is to determine the most appropriate data for the specific purpose. Statistical reports on performance must always include reliable statistical analysis that combines rigour and relevance.

The provision of tracking data has opened up new challenges for sports analytics. One line of enquiry is the link between player and team performance as measured by count data on player contributions and the physical data on speed and distance covered. In much the same way as in association football and many other invasion-territorial sports, there is often a weak relationship between the share of possession and match outcomes, and there is no unambiguous link between distances covered – and speed of movement – and match outcomes. Many teams track high-intensity distance (i.e., distances covered at sprint speeds) as a KPI, but there is no necessary link between high-intensity distance and effective performance. For example, players with excellent tactical awareness may be quicker and more effective in their positional decision-making and thereby reduce the need to sprint to get into the optimal position. In the case of distance covered and speed of movement, it is often the same principle as with the share of possession. It is not the quantity that counts as much as the quality of the physical work rate and player contributions. Additionally, quality can only really be captured by expert data, not count data.

A second challenge in tracking data is determining how best to summarise and report the available data on spatial positioning of players. As already noted, this data can allow coaches to assess the effectiveness of the positioning decisions of players; therefore, it is important to find the best ways to present this data to provide a reliable representation of the spatial distribution of players. One of the sports in which this work has progressed most is basketball. Shea (2014) suggested two key metrics for summarising the spatial distribution of basketball players: (a) the *convex hull area*, which measures the perimeter of the five-sided polygon created by the players in an a team; and (b) the *distance from average*, which measures the average distance of the players from the central point of the polygon. Shea defined these measures for both the attacking team and the defending team and then analyses the interaction. One particularly innovative application is to analyse how individual attacking players affect the spatial distribution of the defensive team – which Shea calls 'defensive stretch'. Shea also provided an example in which two attacking players, Allen and Wade, are compared. Although Wade averaged 6 inches further away than Allen from the attacking team's central point, it was in fact Allen who had the bigger impact on the defensive stretch of the opponents since Allen's defender averaged 14 inches more from the centre of the defending team than Wade's defender.

Managerial implications

The overall message of this chapter is that the technology now exists to collect comprehensive and very detailed data on all aspects of athlete performance even in the most complex sports such as the invasion-territorial sports. 'Knowing the numbers' is now a critical component in an effective competitive strategy for organisations operating in any sector, not just high-performance sport (Davenport and Harris, 2007). It is the growing recognition of the strategic importance of developing a leading-edge capability in analytics that accounts for the universal appeal of the *Moneyball* story of how a small resource-constrained organisation managed to compete effectively by knowing the numbers and using them better than their competitors. The Oakland As provide an example for any organisation that wants to compete effectively in an ever-changing environment, particularly when confronting resource-rich rivals.

For analytics to become an effective competitive tool, an organisation must develop a culture that values an evidence-based approach to decision-making and is, therefore, supportive of the use of data analysis. This culture requires leadership and senior management that is fully committed to building an analytical capability and able to clearly articulate the critical role of data analysis in improving future performance. Without a convincing vision of how analytics will contribute to improving performance, there will be little buy-in from the coaches, and without the buy-in of the coaches, the project will never succeed. Analytics must be coach-led, with the coaches setting the agenda for the analyst whose responsibility is to provide rigorous and relevant evidence in a timely fashion to inform coaching decisions. Coaches must also be fully involved in designing the data collection system, given that the most significant data are expert data involving the interpretation of performance relative to the coaches' tactical and technical expectations.

The effective use of analytics in high-performance sport also requires greater integration of both data storage and data usage. In the early stages of an organisation's development of an analytical capability, however, it is common for data collection and analysis to be fragmented across individuals and functions. This leads to the creation of data silos with specific individuals collating and analysing data in their own spreadsheets quite independently of others with limited interactivity. Yet some of the most important questions involve the relationship between different types of data, for example, the relationship between count data on player contributions and tracking data on physical performance. This requires an integrated database that houses all the different types of data being collected and analysed within the sporting operation. But effective integration requires not only the physical integration of data, but also greater cross-functional coordination of the analysts, with closer working relationships between performance analysts – both qualitative video analysts and quantitative data analysts – and sports scientists.

Conclusions and outlook

We have reached the stage in many high-performance sports where the capability to collect data far exceeds the capability to use data. This 'capability gap' is partly due to the explosive acceleration of data collection capabilities as a consequence of the digital revolution; however, it is also clear that cultural barriers have contributed by restricting the adoption of analytics by coaches. It follows, therefore, that coach education plays a key role in closing the capability gap. For example, modules on sports analytics need to become a core component in coach education programmes in all sports. Just as importantly, there also need to be better sport-specific training opportunities for data scientists who want to work in high-performance sport. Universities and colleges also need to offer sport-specific courses for data scientists akin to those now offered to performance analysts and sports scientists.

Looking forward, high-performance sport faces three analytical challenges. First, as already discussed, the greater availability of tracking data on player positioning is opening up a mass of questions on the spatial aspects of invasion–territorial sports which will create a demand for analysts with a strong background in geometry and trigonometry. Second, as more '24/7' data is collected on individual athletes' competitive performances, training, and general lifestyle, then there will be greater demand to use this data to design personalised training and lifestyle programmes to optimise competitive performances. These challenges will put a real premium on analysts with a multidisciplinary background, able to work with tactical, technical, physical, and psychological data. The final challenge, related to the increasing diversity of the data available on individual athletes, is the increasing need for integrated real-time control systems to analyse and synthesise the totality of the data being collected so that significant changes in the likelihood of under-performance or injury can be flagged up and acted on immediately.

In summary, technology has transformed the data collection process in high-performance sport. As a consequence, it is increasingly likely that the most successful athletes and teams will be those who are supported by a strong analytical capability that exploits data analysis to help create a winning margin.

References

Cook, E. (1964). *Percentage baseball*. Cambridge, MA: MIT Press.

Davenport, T. H. and Harris, J. G. (2007). *Competing on analytics: The new science of winning.* Boston, MA: Harvard Business School Publishing.

Evers, J. J. and Fullerton, H. S. (1910). *Touching second: The science of baseball*. Chicago, IL: Reilly and Britton.

Gerrard, B. (2007). Is the Moneyball approach transferable to complex invasion team sports? *International Journal of Sport Finance, 2*, 214–230. Retrieved from www.fitinfotech.com/IJSF/IJSF.tpl

Hughes, M. and Franks, I. M. (eds). (2008). *The essentials of performance analysis*. London: Routledge.

Lewis, M. (2003). *Moneyball: The art of winning and unfair game*. New York: Norton.

Mills, E. G. and Mills, H. D. (1970). *Player win averages: A computer guide to winning baseball players*. New York: Barnes.

Rickey, B. (1954, August 2). Goodbye to some old baseball ideas. *Life*, 79–89.

Scully, G. W. (1974). Pay and performance in Major League Baseball. *American Economic Review, 64*, 915–930. Retrieved from www.aeaweb.org/aer/index.php

Schwartz, A. (2004). *The numbers game: Baseball's lifelong fascination with statistics*. New York: St. Martin's Press.

Shea, S. (2014). *Basketball analytics: Spatial tracking*. Marston Gate, UK: Author.

Further reading

Anderson, C. and Sally, D. (2013). *The numbers game: Why everything you know about football is wrong*. London, UK: Viking.

> A very readable account of the state of play of analytics in association football. It contains a considerable amount of data analysis interspersed with insights from analysts working in the professional game. The authors cover a variety of topics including the increasing rarity of goals, the undervaluation of defensive play, the importance of possession, the optimal timing of substitutions, and the performance effects of sacking the manager.

Carroll, B., Palmer, P. and Thorn, T. (1988). *The hidden game of football*. New York: Warner Books.

> One of the earliest attempts to provide a detailed statistical analysis of an invasion-territorial sport, in this case American football. They argued for the importance of the situational context – score, field position, and time remaining. At the core of their analysis is the valuation of different plays based on the impact on win probabilities. The authors were one of the first to question the conventional wisdom of kicking on fourth down.

Hughes, M. and Franks, I. M. (eds). (2008). *The essentials of performance analysis*. London: Routledge.

A very comprehensive introduction to the many aspects of performance analysis. The chapter by Liebermann and Franks is a very useful survey of technological developments in data collection in high-performance sport.

Lewis, M. (2003). *Moneyball: The art of winning and unfair game*. New York: Norton.

This book was a real game-changer in high-performance sport, providing a success story to inspire other teams to emulate the As in the use of analytics. The author, Michael Lewis, was a financial trader before becoming a writer and has a real empathy with how Billy Beane used analytics to exploit misperceptions of market value. Read the paperback edition published in 2004 for an afterword on the hostile reaction of the baseball industry to the book.

Schwartz, A. (2004). *The numbers game: Baseball's lifelong fascination with statistics*. New York: St. Martin's Press.

This book tracks the history of statistical analysis in baseball and, as the subtitle suggests, shows that the interest in analysing baseball data is almost as old as the sport itself. Read this before reading *Moneyball* to properly appreciate the antecedents of sabermetrics use by the Oakland As.

16

A GENERAL THEORY OF THE USE OF TECHNOLOGY IN SPORT AND SOME CONSEQUENCES

Harry Collins and Robert Evans

Sporting events depend on referees and umpires getting decisions right. Prestige and prize money depend on the ability of officials to award points or goals correctly and detect unfair play. In this chapter, we examine the role of technologies in supporting match officials and argue that getting the 'right' outcome should be seen as a problem of increasing 'justice' rather than increasing 'accuracy'.

The chapter has four components:

1   a general, philosophical framework for understanding the role of officials and their relationship with players and, especially, spectators and TV watchers;
2   a five-way classification of the different kinds of technologies available to assist match officials based on their degree of intermediation or 'directness';
3   an analysis of why less 'indirect' technologies are to be preferred, with a particular focus on the problems created by the use of simulations and computerised reconstructions of events to take decisions; and
4   an example of how these concepts and principles can be combined to support the use of TV replays by match officials in soccer and argue against the need for ball-tracking technologies.

A theory of umpiring

The role of an umpire or referee is to apply the rules and determine how to classify and record certain events. Amongst other things, they are responsible for determining when the game has started, when it has ended, whether or not a particular passage of play has infringed the rules and whether or not a point has been scored or a player dismissed. In short, umpires and referees have ontological authority. Ontology is about what exists and, in a sporting context, having *ontological authority* (Collins, 2010) means having the power to determine whether a particular passage of play constitutes a new thing – a goal, the completion of injury time – or event. Crucially, whatever happened is neither a thing nor an event unless and until the referee or umpire says it is – a situation reflected in the match officials' oft-quoted remark to a player who disputes a decision: 'Look in tomorrow's newspaper'.[1]

Giving ontological authority to match officials has two justifications. First, match officials have received special training and have a detailed knowledge of the rules and their application. Second, and more important to the discussion of technologies, match officials are typically closer to the action than spectators and so have a better view of the game. Epistemology is about how we know things, and we can say that match officials' ontological authority is usually accepted because they typically have *epistemological privilege*. Typically, spectators just assume that match officials are using their epistemological privilege to ensure justice is done even if they, from their less privileged position, cannot see it happening; this assumption is analogous to the one we make in respect of legal judges when we did not attend the trial. It is important to preserve this 'presumptive justice' as far as possible if the relationship between sport and the public is to remain secure.

Sports technologies classified by level of intermediation

Sport measurement technology is a matter of capturing events. Match officials have to deal with fleeting moments and must 'grab the event' and hold it back for further examination so as to further enhance their epistemological privilege. We can call sports measurement technologies *capture devices*. The moment of capture can also be timestamped for comparison with the time of other captured events, such as in the case of the start and end of a race. We now examine the technologies used in different sports and classify them in terms of five degrees of intermediation, or indirectness, as shown in Table 16.1. Level 1 technologies are the most direct, with the least amount of intermediation between the event itself and its frozen counterpart. We work up to increasingly indirect technologies in which the captured event is more and more distant from the original; more things have to happen in order for the event to be captured.

Level 1: minimal intermediation

The cup on the golf green is a good example of a Level 1 capture device; there is almost no technology between the ball reaching the target and its fall into the cup where its position is held for all to see. Other Level 1 devices include the high

TABLE 16.1 Classification of capture devices

Level of indirectness	1	2	3	4	5
Examples	Bails, golf-cup, high jump bar	Photo-finish	TV replay	Manipulated TV-replay, Hot Spot, Snicko	Reconstructed Track Devices

jump bar, the sand in the long-jump pit, the embedded javelin, the mark in the turf caused by discus or shot, the surrounding wall in baseball, the chain between two verticals in American football and the pockets on snooker and pool tables. In other sports, the signal created does not last as long, but the principle is the same. Thus, even though a basketball net does not trap the ball, it does slow it down enough to capture the action for all practical purposes; something similar applies to the goal net in soccer and the winner's tape in athletics. In these cases, the technology enhances match officials' epistemological privilege and ontological authority.

Some capture devices actually *redefine* the event so as to make it easier to trap. Consider cricket. The basic transaction involves the bowler trying to strike the wicket (which comprises three vertical 'stumps') with the ball while the batsman tries to defend it. There are occasions when it is difficult to tell whether the ball struck the wicket with a grazing or gentle blow or missed by an imperceptible margin. To settle this kind of issue, two small sticks called 'bails' are balanced on top of the three stumps and the notion of striking the wicket is redefined as 'breaking the wicket', which means one or both of the bails must fall to the ground. The falling of the bails traps the event – the bails are either both still balanced or at least one of them is on the ground – while redefining the event as a matter of dislodging the bails.[2]

Needless to say, things get complicated from the outset as no technology is infallible and, even at Level 1, events cannot always be captured. The golf ball sometimes teeters on the edge of the cup and the player is not allowed to wait too long for it to fall but must walk up to it and tap it in without delaying overlong; it is the job of match officials to interpret what is to count as an 'acceptable' delay. In soccer, the net does not always bulge when a goal is scored as the ball can cross the line and bounce back out without touching the net.[3] It is also true that a high-jump bar can be dislodged by the wind, not the athlete, and there have to be rules about how these things are to be judged. In other words – and this is an important point to which we will return repeatedly in this chapter – there are cases where even the most simple technologies have to give way to, or be supplemented by, human judgement.[4] In these cases, it is the ontological authority of the match official that determines the outcome.

Level 2: minor intermediation

Now we come to capture devices that involve a little more intermediation. The photo finish in horseracing is an example of a Level 2 technology in which the positions of the horses at different times are presented in a single image captured by a high-speed camera looking down onto the finish line. The photograph is indirect because the horses are separated from the film on which their image is captured by the passage of light. Nevertheless, the technology is well understood and widely trusted. For example, no one worries that light takes a little longer to travel from the far horse than from the near horse so the far horse might be around

1/10,000th mm, give or take a zero, further ahead than the photo finish shows. On the other hand, the delay in transmission of the sound of the sprint-race starting pistol could disadvantage the far runner by hundredths of a second – and sprints are nowadays timed to 100ths or even 1,000ths – so in important races, each lane has its own loudspeaker with the signal transmitted across the track at the speed of electricity (light).[5]

Crucially, however, the image produced for the photo finish still must be examined and interpreted by a match official in order to determine who has won. In many cases, this is relatively straightforward, but there are cases where match officials' judgement and interpretation is crucial in explaining and justifying the decision. For example, in the 2014 Winter Olympics at Sochi, a close photo finish in which three skiers appeared to cross the line simultaneously was eventually awarded to Russia's Egor Korotkov because he threw his arms in front of him and crossed the line head first rather than feet first (Gripper, 2014).

Turning to the spectators, from their point of view, capture devices help them share the decision. They can see the golf ball topple, the bails fall, and the net bulge. The photo finish image is a public document that explains why the match officials classified the result one way rather than another. These devices improve the transparency of sporting justice.

Level 3: moderate intermediation

Matters become complicated when several different pieces of information have to be integrated. Returning to cricket, consider the 'run-out' or 'stumping' decision. This is like the decision in baseball as to whether a runner has made his or her ground before being tagged. In both the run-out and the stumping decision, the batters (we will use the American term to avoid having to continually write 'batsman or woman') strive to gain or regain their ground before an opposition player – often the 'wicketkeeper' – breaks the wicket. To avoid being given out, some part of the batter-plus-bat must touch the turf between the 'crease' – a line painted on the turf about a yard in front of the wicket – prior to, or simultaneous with, the wicket being broken. The wicket can be broken by the ball or by a player's hands, so long as the ball is held. In this case, it is not only a question of the exact moment when the wicket is broken – a much more difficult thing to judge than whether it has been broken at all – but also whether it was fairly broken (e.g., it would not be fairly broken if the player broke the wicket while the ball was spilling out of their hands) and the exact moment a third event took place a yard or so away – the grounded-crossing of the crease. In most cricket matches, there is no way to capture the exact moment the wicket was broken, the fairness of the wicket-breaking, or the split second at which the grounded-crossing of the line occurred. Instead, the match officials' ontological authority rests solely on their epistemological privilege: Using their own perceptual abilities and viewpoint on the pitch, they must decide and categorise in real-time and without the benefit of any technological support.

In televised games, however, technology can be used to assist the umpire: TV replays can provide a Level 3 capture device. It is a little more indirect than a photo finish because of the electronics in a TV camera, and little more fallible than the photo finish because the technology is not designed for the sole purpose of assisting the umpires. As a result, the position of the cameras is less than optimal; the frame rate is slower than would be preferred for a purpose-built device and more manipulation of the images – such as zooming in and out and replaying in slow motion – is needed in order to provide the necessary information. In a typical stumping or run-out decision, a dedicated match official, known as the *third umpire*, has access to the various broadcast camera feeds and, by zooming in or selecting different views, can reach a judgement about whether or not the batter should be given out. This decision is then relayed to the on-field umpire and to the spectators. This system works well in cricket and a number of other sports, including rugby union, American football and Formula One motor racing. As with the photo finish, the TV footage used to reach the decision can be made available to spectators and, again like the photo finish, the technologies involved are pretty well understood and widely trusted.

Needless to say, there will be some occasions where the TV replays do not provide a clear image; however, when this happens, spectators can see the ambiguity too. For example, a difficult judgement that cricket umpires often have to make is whether or not the ball just brushed the edge of the bat before being caught by the wicketkeeper – a 'catch' – or if it just missed. The visible effects of such slight contact are very hard to see in real-time and are often below the resolution and frame rate of the TV cameras. As a result, television replays provide little extra information and rarely provide a sound basis for overturning the on-field umpire's decision. Level 4 devices (see below) have been introduced to try to resolve this kind of problem but, in their absence, spectators can at least see that whatever the umpire's decision, no glaring error has been made. In other words, given the resources available, they could not have done any better and there was no obvious injustice.[6]

More seriously, there are circumstances in which TV replays are known to be misleading. One is the decision over whether a ball has been fairly caught. As in baseball, a player is 'out' in cricket if the ball is struck and caught by an opposition player before bouncing. With a low fast catch it is sometimes not clear if the ball flew straight into the hands or hit the turf just in front of the hands before being held. All commentators agree that the foreshortening effect of TV replays means they often appear to show that the ball did bounce and many commentators point out that this kind of TV replay almost always gives the benefit of the doubt to the batter, who then is determined 'not out'.[7]

Level 4: significant intermediation

Level 4 devices differ from Level 3 devices, as the intermediating technologies do more than re-present events that were, in principle, available to an on-field match official with perfect vision and discrimination. Instead, Level 4 technologies generate new data that would enhance even the most perfect human the perceptual abilities by allowing them to see things from new angles and via non-visible wavelengths and transpose sound into a visible waveform.

In cricket 'Hotspot', a Level 4 device uses infrared cameras to detect the heat produced by contact between bat and ball to indicate whether the ball has touched the bat in case of a disputed catch. Here, the intervening medium is infrared light, which is more complicated and less well-understood than standard photography. Because they are complicated and involve novel applications of new technologies, higher level capture devices tend to have unexpected failure modes. Thus, only after some years was it realised that Hotspot may not work well in very hot weather, and that it may not detect a slight contact if the edge of the bat is greasy. In modern cricket, Hotspot is often complemented by another Level 4 technology, 'Snicko', which generates an oscilloscope-type image of the sounds made at the crucial moment. This chart is synchronised with and superimposed over TV film to show whether the sounds heard were caused by contact between ball and bat or some other object. Because the shape of the trace is different for different kinds of contact, Snicko enables umpires to distinguish between the ball hitting the bat and some other kind of contact such as the ball striking the batter's pad, the bat striking the ground and so on. When used together, and alongside TV replays, Hotspot and Snicko seem to provide an acceptably reliable combination of Level 3 and Level 4 capture devices and to perform a useful function in correcting errors and reinforcing match officials' epistemological privilege and ontological authority with the process viewed and understood by the TV audience (see, for example, Hoult, 2013).

A combination of capture devices is also used by pundits and commentators to reveal the accuracy of offside decisions in soccer. Here the simultaneity of two events has to be judged, but they are not co-located and may even be as far apart as the length of the pitch. The two events are the moment the ball leaves the boot of the player passing it forward, and position of the receiving player in relationship to other players *at that moment*. At that moment, no part of the receiving player's body must be further forward than the last opposition player (goalkeeper aside). The optimum position from which to judge the relative position of the receiving player is level with that player, while the optimum position from which to judge the moment the ball was kicked is level with the kicker. The duty of making this judgement is given to a specialist 'assistant referee' (once called 'linesman'), who is advised to patrol the sideline keeping up with the front players. TV replays, which capture the whole field, can usually reveal the moment when the ball was kicked, but are less good at indicating the relative position of the front player because the view of the TV camera will almost always be at an angle rather than along the line of the front players.

Introducing more intermediation moves us nearer to a solution to the offside problem. Computer graphics techniques can be used to capture the crucial TV frame as a virtual image, rotate the scene, and draw a virtual line across the pitch which is level with the front players at the moment the ball was kicked; the TV viewer seems to be able to look along this line. Such transpositions are used in the BBC's *Match of the Day* programme but do not, as yet, influence match officials' decisions. There are no published statistics about the accuracy of such methods and one might argue that this does not matter, as they are not used by the referee. This is not strictly true, however, as the availability of these images does contribute to a wider trend – discussed in more detail below – in which match officials' episte-mological privilege is being eroded as more information becomes accessible to the TV audience. Spectators, who now have more epistemological privilege than match officials, can see that bad decisions have been made and that the ontological authority of the match official is groundless.

Level 5: maximum intermediation reconstructed track devices

Now we move to the highest level of intermediation in which technologies, known as reconstructed track devices (RTDs), are used not just to record or re-present data, but also to generate simulations of the on-field events. The Hawk-Eye system is perhaps the most well-known of these technologies.[8] Using specialist cameras, RTDs gather data that indicate the position of the ball in play and try to reconstruct its track in computer-generated graphical form within a virtual version of the playing area complete with boundary and other play-defining lines. The resulting animated computer graphic is taken to show the path of the real ball and, crucially, exactly where it bounced or struck some other feature of importance, such as a batter's leg. With the appropriate use of computer-generated images, the reconstruction offered by an RTD can appear to be the equivalent of a television replay, but a much greater amount of inference, calculation, and computation stands between the events and reconstruction. Also, the position of the reconstructed ball within the simulation is always judged in relation to the virtual model of the playing area and not against the actual playing surface.[9]

The problems RTDs create for spectators and officials are twofold. For spec-tators, the problem is that Hawk-Eye cannot be as accurate as the reconstructions – which typically claim single-millimetre accuracy – make it appear. In fact, for tennis, Hawk-Eye's website is currently reporting an average error of 3.6 mm based on tests carried out in 2006, whilst for cricket the accuracy is reported as within 5 mm, with a figure of 2.6 mm quoted for a particular set of tests.[10] There is error because RTDs must base their reconstructions on estimates of the position of the centre of the ball taken from the smeared set of pixels in each image, and must reconstruct the track from a series of such estimated points between which the ball travels considerable distances. This is often while decelerating along a path with changing curvature, with additional calculations needed to represent the way in which the ball may skid and/or be deformed as it hits the ground, and all set within a virtual rather than real playing area. Worse the quoted errors are averages – implying that larger as well as smaller errors will sometimes be made – yet no one explains or even admits to the existence of this *error distribution* in the reconstruct-ions made available to the public.[11] The result is that spectators are misinformed about what kind of information is being provided and, to the extent that they believe the technology is as accurate as its media-friendly outputs imply, they will prefer such technological decision-making to that of the on-field officials.[12]

The problem for match officials flows from the erroneous impression of extreme accuracy attributed to RTD technology. When the match official has actually made a large mistake and the RTD suggests that the original decision was incorrect, then there is no problem as the discrepancy is well outside the average error of the device. This is true even when the RTD errors are potentially very large, such as when a leg before wicket (LBW) appeal has to be judged after the ball has bounced very close to the batter's leg, because the umpire's error is even larger. The difficulty arises in those circumstances where the outcome of the RTD reconstruction must be more accurate than its average error. For example, what should an umpire or referee do when an RTD with a mean error of 3.6 mm shows that the ball was in (or out) by 1 mm? To know how to deal with this requires greater knowledge of the error distribution than is currently available in the public domain, but if the decision is taken that the technology is always right – as it has been assumed in tennis – then the outcome of very close calls, literally (and ironically, given the way RTD technology is often justified in terms of eliminating 'chance' outcomes) becomes a near random process. This is now reflected in the behaviour of tennis players who will often 'use up' any remaining opportunities to challenge the decisions of line judges as the set draws to a close on the chance that the system may decide in their favour.

Principles and practice in the use of sports decision aids

We now use concepts and typology to make recommendations for the use of sports decision aids and then apply them to a concrete example.

Why lower levels of intermediation are better

If a Level 1 capture device is available, it is likely to be better than any higher level device for a number of obvious reasons. First, it is likely to be cheap. Golf cups, bails, high-jump bars and goal nets are cost effective. Furthermore, they require little expertise to operate and they have been familiar for decades, if not centuries. Everyone knows how they work, everyone accepts that they work, and everyone can see them work. Moreover, on the odd occasion when they do not quite work – the golf ball teeters, the wind blows the high-jump bar – everyone knows what they should do nearly all of the time. Something similar applies at Level 2, where the photo finish has long been an integral part of horseracing and athletics.

Things are a little less clear at Level 3 because TV replays are most useful in continuous sports (e.g., cricket and soccer) as opposed to single events (e.g., races), and TV replays take time to review and may not be readily available for viewing on the pitch by the principal match referee. Furthermore, the reviewing process may not always provide a clear answer, which is why Level 4 technologies (e.g.,

Hotspot and Snicko) are also used, while rotation of virtual frames as used on TV programmes currently happens long after the match is over. These problems, among others, have been used to argue for the introduction of Level 5 devices, as they can process the material relatively quickly and appear to be able to provide clear answers where lower level capture devices cannot. We argue, however, that Level 5 devices should mostly be avoided in decision-making, if not in performance summarising, for reasons in addition to their cost.

In some sports, cost may not be crucial because Level 5 devices offer a great deal of interesting information to the TV viewer that has nothing to do with decision-making, and sports broadcasting companies might be willing to pay for them for these reasons alone. The aggregation of data about every individual ball bowled in a cricket match and the ability to compare a bowler's performance in one match with that in another, or note the point at which the batter strikes the ball at different times or places, is fascinating. None of this is problematic since it does not depend on millimetre accuracy; in fact, it seems to be a really good use of technology with integrity. The issue that concerns us, and which should concern all those involved in the management and development of sports, is the use of RTDs to usurp the on-field officials' position and act as decision-makers where very close decisions are concerned. The major objections, discussed in more detail below, are:

1   The output of RTDs is presented in a misleading way that does not acknowledge the existence of measurement error; this is dangerous for more than sport, as it risks creating an unwarranted faith in the power and accuracy of various other technologies.
2   The aim of sports technologies is miscast as achieving accuracy rather than justice: The inevitability of measurement error means that RTDs can never recreate 'exactly what happened', but they can, if used appropriately, contribute to avoiding major errors and so help to maintain a sense of justice and fairness in sport.
3   TV replays do a better job in respect of most decisions and a good enough job in respect of those decisions where they are challenged by RTDs.

RTDs can be misleading

The use of RTD technologies in tennis and cricket nicely exemplifies the different choices available, as well as the costs and benefits of each. In cricket, RTD technologies are used in a sophisticated way that reflects their limitations and preserves the traditions and spirit of the game. Priority is given to the on-field umpire's initial decision, with an overrule only when the evidence of a mistake is outside the bounds of error. In practice, this means that in LBW decisions, the flight of the ball as projected by the RTD must be shown to be leading to an impact by at least half the ball if an umpire's 'not out' decision is to be reversed.[13] A reconstructed brushing impact or even quarter-ball impact is not taken to indicate a definite umpiring mistake. Although there are ways in which this use of RTD technology could be improved still further (e.g., the potential error could be shown in graphic form by using a fuzzy outline twice the diameter of the ball itself to indicate where the ball might be), in terms of how the technology is used to support decision-making, the procedure helps the match official without usurping authority and is transparent to TV viewers. This is as it should be.

In contrast, tennis uses RTDs in a misleading way that provides no public acknowledgement of the inevitable measurement error. Instead, crowds become enthusiastically involved with RTD projections in which computer graphics create a perfectly defined court with a perfectly defined trajectory and clearly defined bounce footprint which, seemingly, allows definitive in–out decisions to be made. The display gives no indication of any uncertainty, even when the hair's breadth distances reported are less than the *average* error produced in official tests. Indeed, there is no acknowledgement anywhere that errors will sometimes be larger than the average, that the ball footprint is the result of a calculation rather than observation, that the lines are virtual and – unlike those in real life – are straight and sharp edged, and that a real-life tennis ball is also fuzzy and furry with no clear sharp edge.[14]

RTDs used in this way are misleading because they imply that technology of this kind is much more accurate than it is and may lead ordinary people to fail to question the potential efficacy of all kinds of new 'intelligence-based' technologies both within and beyond sport. There is already evidence from the ways in which commentators and others describe these technologies that they do not really understand how they work. For example, the ex-England cricket captain and now regular broadcast commentator, Ian Botham, is often heard complaining that cricket's use of RTDs is unfair and inconsistent because the same reconstructed ball flight will lead to either 'out' or 'not out' depending on the umpire's initial decision. Botham thinks the same reconstruction should always lead to the same outcome – what he thinks of as consistency. But what Botham does not appear to understand is that the reconstructed ball flight is consistent with the actual ball ending up in a number of different places; this is why it would be useful to present the display in these terms, with a fuzzy ball, removing the impression of inconsistency when there is none.

Tennis demonstrates further evidence of the potential for confusion, where the misleading presentation appears to confuse commentators even more fundament-ally. In the case of LBW in cricket, the path of the ball is projected after it hits the batsman such that its path beyond the last point of contact is an obvious estimate. In contrast, tennis appears to involve no such extrapolation leading to the belief, as voiced by another ex-England cricket test captain-turned-commentator, David Gower, that the use of RTDs in tennis shows 'fact in graphic form' (Gower, 2009, para. 3). In fact, this is wrong. There is usually a forward projection from the last frame before the bounce. If the ball is travelling quickly, then the distance over which the flight has to be projected can be large – depending, as always, on frame speed. That intelligent people who are not used to thinking in terms of measure-ment error make these kinds of mistakes is not surprising, but it is disappointing that such misunderstanding is not discouraged by the promoters of RTDs. Once more, if the reconstructed tennis ball were shown as fuzzy edged and, perhaps the series of points representing the individual TV frames were represented, Gower, along with the rest of us, would more easily see what is going on (for more detail, see Collins and Evans, 2008, 2012).

It could be argued that none of this matters and that what is actually happening is similar to what happens in the case of the bails in cricket. The in–out decision in cricket is being redefined as whatever the RTD decides it is and everyone ought simply to accept its decision. But if we really want to redefine the in–out decision, it would be less misleading in the case of close calls that are within the RTDs' error band to settle the matter with a toss of a coin – even an electronic, graphically represented, coin toss that the public could cheer. This would be no more inaccurate for the players and the spectators would understand what was going on. Doing this would make it clear that RTDs institutionalise rather than eliminate (statistical) chance in sporting decisions and, for this reason, we think a better process is that used by cricket in which, in the absence of any obvious error of judgement, the original umpire's decision simply stands. Alternatively, the point could simply be replayed.

Accuracy versus justice

The introduction of technologies into sport often assumes that ever-increasing accuracy and precision are needed. In some sports this may make sense. For example, touch sensors in the swimming pool may detect a winner even when cameras cannot discern who got there first and it makes some sense to try to time motor racing laps to a 1,000th of a second. Even in sports like cricket there will always be a role for technologies that can help disambiguate borderline cases and lead to fewer mistakes. For a while it seemed as if Hotspot had solved the problem of judging whether a batter has touched the ball before it is caught, though this, too, turned out to less than completely accurate. The crucial point is that there is no such thing as absolute accuracy in sport any more than there is in science and engineering, where every measurement is understood to be associated with an error. Error in science and engineering is not treated as a bad thing; rather, stating it is an integral part of the measurement. That there is often no exact measurement has been illustrated throughout this piece with the teetering golf ball, the wind-blown high-jump bar, the fuzzy tennis line, the squashed tennis ball, and so on. Moreover, even where pretty exact measurements are available, there is room for debating their value. It might be possible to time a swimming race to a 1,000th of a second, but would more dead heats be a fairer outcome given the tiny margins by which such a race would be 'won?'

More important, however, is the idea that, in pursuing ever-increasing accuracy in measurement, sports governing bodies are doing nothing to address the real harm being created by the widespread and blatant advertisement of injustice that has been around ever since TV replays become commonplace. In the case of soccer, for example, every week, TV viewers can see referees making mistakes over offsides, penalties, and sending-offs that affect the outcome of individual games and, by implication, the final positions of teams in their leagues – something worth huge sums of money to the clubs and huge amounts of emotional investment to the fans.

In the terminology introduced above, before TV replays came on the scene, the epistemological privilege of on-field officials was enough to preserve their onto-logical authority. Though referees and umpires have always made mistakes, it was a reasonable assumption that their judgements were as good as any judgements could be; they were close to the action and they were experienced in judging. It might well be that one or two of the players had a better idea of what was going on – in soccer whether it was a foul or a 'dive' – but only a handful of the public were in a position to claim they had a better view than the official – just those few at the game who might be very close to a particular piece of action. Nearly everyone else had to leave it to the official.

Things have changed. Epistemological privilege increasingly resides with the television-viewing public who usually have a better view of a disputed decision than the officials judging in real-time, as viewers can see slow-motion replays of incidents from a variety of angles. Sticking with soccer, it is worth remembering that many of the most important decisions in soccer do not turn on measuring the position of the ball, but on judging the intentions of players. Given this, what is the best way to award a penalty or send a player off? Is it a real-time judgement based on information fleetingly glimpsed from a less than favourable angle or after a few moments reviewing the incident using replays from several angles? Anyone watching a match on TV can tell you that the answer is obvious.

What this shows is that the big problem is *not* to get the judgement exactly right because there often is no 'exactly right' in these cases. Rather, the problem to be solved is how to rebuild match officials' ontological authority by restoring their epistemological privilege and enabling the match officials' judgements and the viewing public to be coordinated. It seems crazy to show the public, week after week, that referees are getting it wrong. It upsets the fans and destabilises the sport. The answer is to follow the precedent set by the use of Level 1 and 2 technologies and to make TV replays available to the match officials. This already happens in sports such as rugby, basketball, and ice hockey.

The principle of minimum intermediation

We now show how these ideas can be used. The case examined is the use of RTD *goal-line technology* in soccer with the intention of ensuring that goals are correctly awarded. Given the argument so far, it should be clear that this should be resisted because it violates the general principle of 'minimum intermediation'.[15]

Here is the logic. Consider the cup on the golf green. This could be replaced by a circle to guide the player's aim while multiple cameras set up around the green track and reconstruct the ball's path so that a computer model can determine whether the ball would have fallen into a cup had there been one. Likewise, the bails in cricket could be removed and RTDs could be used to reconstruct the path of a ball that brushed or came near to brushing the stumps and reach a conclusion as to whether it had touched or missed. And so on. But why would anyone want to do this? It is obviously much less expensive and much less trouble to work with lower levels of intermediation and it is also more transparent because there are no unknown error distributions and everyone can see what is going on.

Similar arguments can be made for most attempts to replace a successful low-level technology with one that introduces higher levels of intermediation and, in the case of soccer, the crucial choice is between the Level 3 technology of the TV replay and the Level 5 technology of the RTD. Large amounts are being spent on goal-line technology following some much publicised incidents where television replays demonstrate that a goal should have been awarded when it was not or vice versa. Bizarrely, the obvious lesson does not seem to have been learnt. The television replay revealed the problem, so the television replay could rectify it. What frame speeds are needed to correct the problem? Not the high frame speeds of modern RTDs, but the same frame speed as the technology that first revealed the problem: broadcast-TV frame speed. It is argued that play must not be interrupted for even the short time it would take to view a replay, but this is fallacious since in the case of a disputed decision, play could continue and be pulled back a few moments later if TV showed that a no-goal decision was incorrect.

Worse still, there are very few incidents of incorrect decisions in respect to goal or no-goal compared to the many other controversial decisions about which the RTD has nothing to say. Table 16.2 shows the results from a rough survey of about a quarter of the matches discussed by pundits on the BBC's *Match of the Day* programme over three seasons. As can be seen, goal-line disputes caused 16 discussions, with referees wrong only twice according to the pundits. In the third season, goal-line technology was introduced, but was only required on four occasions. In contrast, there were 238 other discussions about non-goal decisions that could have altered the course of the match, with referees being wrong 151 times according to the pundits.

TABLE 16.2 Analysis of 535 English Premiership matches out of the 2,280 played over three seasons

Pundits' discussions during 535 matches shown on MoTD: 2011–2014
Preliminary Unverified data

Officials are	Right	Wrong	GT	Total
Goal line dispute	14	2	4	20
Penalty dispute	44	70		
Goal related offside dispute	2	21		
Goal related corner or foul dispute	8	18		
Red Card dispute	35	40		238
TOTAL	103	151	4	258

Why not use TV replays?

The argument for not using TV replays hinges on the delay that would be caused while match officials review footage. This argument seems misguided. Even if we allow that soccer matches must not be unduly interrupted, there are ways to circumvent the problem.[16] Table 16.3 suggests ways in which TV replays could be used for almost all decisions without disturbing the normal flow of the game. It includes the suggestion that something equivalent to the flag thrown onto the pitch in American football be used to show that a decision is being examined by a TV judge. In the meantime play would continue as normal. A system of lights might be better than flags, but we will stick with 'flag' as generic for 'indication that play is being reviewed'.

Table 16.3 shows what would happen in the case of various passages of play. Starting at the top, if a penalty was awarded, the TV judge would review the decision while the players prepared for the shot at goal. If the decision was reversed, the game would be restarted with a drop-ball, a free kick, or a goal kick, depending on circumstances. As the rightmost column indicates, no extra delay would be

TABLE 16.3 How TV-replays could be used in football

Incident	Decision	Use of TVR	Extra Delay
Penalty	Awarded	If no penalty then restart with drop ball or free kick or goal kick	NONE
	Not awarded	Play on (with flag?) If penalty then pull back	NONE
Marginal Goal	Awarded	If no goal then goal kick	NONE
	Not awarded	Play on (with flag?) If goal, pull back, restart	NONE
Marginal Offside	Flag and play on; do not stop play	If offside pull back and free kick	NONE
	Not awarded	If no offside play on	NONE
Clear Offside	As now	None	NONE
Foul play no card	As now	None	NONE
Yellow or red card	Flag and halt play	TVR advice to ref	NONE
Ref misses off ball incident		(Flag?) TVR apprises ref Pull back and free kick, etc.	NONE
Corner throw in		TVR may tell ref to award goal kick or throw to other side	NONE

involved. If, on the other hand, one of the other officials thought the circumstances called for a review even though the match referee had not awarded a penalty, the appropriate 'flag' signal would be given and play would continue as normal unless the on-field decision was reversed. If reversed, fouls aside, the whole passage of play since the review signal would be cancelled out and play would be pulled back so the penalty could be taken. Again, there would be no extra delay.

Moving to the second row, and the kind of case that would now be settled by Level 5 goal-line technology, play would have already stopped if the referee awarded a goal but would continue during the review if the referee had not awarded the goal. Once more, play would be pulled back if the on-field decision not to award a goal was reversed. TV replays would be seen by the public, just as they are now, and if the replays were not quick, clear, and decisive there would be no change as there would be no evidence that a mistake had been made. This is the principle used in cricket. Whatever happened, there would be no extra delay and, crucially, no difference between the perspective of the viewing public and the match officials.

For marginal offsides, the game would normally not be stopped, but flagged for review by the referee or one of the other officials, perhaps using the Level 4 technology of computer-manipulated reorientation of the officials' perspective (so long as it is shown to be reasonably accurate). Play would only be pulled back if the TV judge concluded that an offside decision was in order. With clear offside or clear foul play things would continue as they do now, with the review taking place during the stoppage created by the on-field decision. Likewise, for red or yellow cards, play is already stopped and the only change would be an automatic TV review before the card was issued and the game restarted. Off-the-ball incidents missed by the referee would be reviewed by the TV judge and a card awarded and game restarted if the TV judge considered it merited. In the case of corners or throw-ins, again, the game is stopped anyway and the TV judge would advise if the decision should be changed.

The overarching rule would be that nothing is changed unless there is clear evidence for changing it and clear evidence means quick evidence, so the review period would always be short. As can be seen from the final column of Table 16.3, these procedures do not impose extra delays and the game should flow just as it does now. Teams whose players relaxed their efforts while reviews were taking place would be punished by teams playing at full pelt unless the game was stopped. Slowing down during reviews would be a very high-risk strategy.

Conclusion

We have set out a basic theory of umpiring in which the role of match officials is understood in terms of ontological authority exercised on the basis of an epistemological privilege relative to spectators. We have also classified the sports technologies used to assist umpires and referees according to their degree of inter-mediation and argued that such intermediation should be minimised. The key to this argument is recognising that technology should be used to bring about justice and fairness and not to chase some mythical notion of exactness. Life is not exact however much technology promises to make it so. In this context, low-level capture devices are cheap and transparent and serve the purposes of officials and spectators alike.

We have also argued that the notion that TV replays inevitably slow games like soccer down is misguided. Indeed, we would go further: the TV replay is a readily understood and readily available capture device that not only should be used, but must be used by match officials wherever it is already available to TV viewers. Only in this way can the epistemological privilege of match officials be restored, justice be seen to be done, and large public sports stabilised.

Notes

1   Ontological authority and the related concept of epistemological privilege were introduced in Collins (2010). The performative aspect of an umpire's call is also discussed in Russell (1997).
2   The laws of cricket are available at www.lords.org/mcc/laws-of-cricket/
3   The rules of golf are available at www.randa.org/en/Rules-and-Amateur-Status.aspx; the rules of soccer are available at www.fifa.com/development/education-and-technical/referees/laws-of-the-game.html.
4   This is an example of a much more general problem, namely that rules always need further rules to specify how they should be used; these meta-rules then require still further rules to regulate their application and so on, ad infinitum. The application and interpretation of rules is, therefore, a complex social phenomenon, the difficulty of which is masked by its ubiquity. It is only when expectations are breached that the fact there was a rule, and the need to determine how it should be applied, is foregrounded. For more on these ideas, see Collins (1992) and Winch (1953).
5   The important point here is that the technology is trusted to gather the necessary data in a sufficiently accurate and reliable manner. Where there is distrust and/or disagreement about the correct way to measure and interpret events, the result is both a technological dispute and a social controversy, with the resolution of one being co-produced with the resolution of the other. For examples of socio-technical controversies see Collins and Pinch (2010).
6   This is not to say that, in some cases, spectators and commentators will disagree about whether or not the available images provided 'clear evidence', but this is another instance of the 'rules regress' identified in Note 4. In such cases, it is the ontological authority of the match officials that breaks the regress.
7   These debates are also part of the public debate about the use of TV replays, with some players calling for self-regulation in respect to catches as a way of avoiding what they would see as bad umpiring decisions in which the benefit of the doubt is inappropriately given to the batter. See Lalor (2010) for an example.
8   We have discussed the Hawk-Eye system in detail in Collins and Evans (2008, 2012), identifying a number of concerns about the way in which the system is used by some sports governing bodies. Though the system is also described by Bal and Dureja (2012), this needs to be treated with caution. Not only is the discussion extremely superficial, but there are also several places where technical details reported (e.g., the type of cameras used) differ from those published by the system's manufacturers.

9   An extremely brief summary of how Hawk-Eye estimates the position of the ball in tennis is provided on the Hawk-Eye website: www.hawkeyeinnovations.co.uk/page/sports-officiating/tennis. In the 'Press' section, the website also contains links to downloadable pdf files in which Paul Hawkins, the creator of the Hawk-Eye system, responds to public criticism and debate (see Hawkins, 2015).

10   The 3.6 mm is published on www.hawkeyeinnovations.co.uk/page/sports-officiating/tennis; though in his response to Cricinfo (Hawkins, 2015), Paul Hawkins stated that the 'tennis error is 2.2 mm'. The average error for cricket is not published on the website, but is confirmed as 5 mm in the response to Cricinfo; further details of average errors relating to cricket, together with a summary of how the system is used in practice, are available in the 2010 article 'Hawk-Eye Accuracy and Believability' (Hawkins, 2010).

11   We found it impossible to obtain information related to error distributions, even though we asked both Hawk-Eye and the tennis authorities. At one point, Hawk-Eye threatened us with lawyers.

12   This is similar to the so-called 'CSI effect' in which it is claimed that fictionalised accounts of extremely precise forensic science create false expectations amongst citizens when it comes to the real-life application of forensic science in the court room (Ley, Jankowski and Brewer, 2012). Whilst there is some debate about the significance of this effect – the CSI dramas are a work of fiction after all – the routine use of unchallenged claims to hyper-accuracy in real-life settings seems more likely to have a deleterious effect on ordinary citizens' ability to critically engage with the increasingly complex technical systems in which they are embedded. In this sense, sports technologies are more like news reporting than works of fiction and so do raise legitimate concerns around public understanding (cf. Hargreaves, Lewis and Speers 2003).

13   The 'LBW rule' says that a batter is out in certain restricted circumstances if the pads alone stop a ball that would otherwise hit the wicket – this counts as out 'leg before wicket'. More detail, and an explanation of how Hawk-Eye is used to determine whether or not the on-field umpire's judgement that all elements of the rule had been satisfied, is available in the *Decision Review System* guide published by the International Cricket Council in 2009.

14   For this reason, the detailed analysis of umpire's performance (Mather, 2008) makes an orthogonal point to the one being made here, especially if the 'benchmark' data is taken to be the reconstructed estimate of an RTD.

15   We pick this topic because it is a current debate, with 'goal line' technology being used in some leagues and trials of TV replays being proposed in others (see 'Dutch FA Hopes', 2014; Khaled, 2015; World Football Insider, 2015).

16   The Dutch proposal was for TV replays to be used for goals, penalties, and red cards only, so our analysis goes further than is currently proposed. What is perhaps more significant is that, according to press reports, 'It is unlikely [TV replays] would eat up any more time than what is wasted by players inundating the referee and arguing every disputed decision. The Dutch claim as little as 15 seconds would be needed to make most decisions' (Khaled, 2015, para. 17).

References

Bal, B. and Dureja, G. (2012). Hawk Eye: A logical innovative technology use in sports for effective decision making. *Sport Science Review, 21,* 107–119. doi:10.2478/v10237-012-0006-6

Collins, H. M. (1992). *Changing order: Replication and induction in scientific practice*. Chicago, IL: University of Chicago Press.

Collins, H. M. (2010). The philosophy of umpiring and the introduction of decision-aid technology. *Journal of the Philosophy of Sport, 37*, 135–146. doi:10.1080/00948705.2010. 9714772

Collins, H. M. and Evans, R. (2008). You cannot be serious! Public understanding of technology with special reference to 'Hawk-Eye'. *Public Understanding of Science, 17*, 283–308. doi:10.1177/0963662508093370

Collins, H. M. and Evans, R. (2012). Sport-decision aids and the 'CSI-effect': Why cricket uses Hawk-Eye well and tennis uses it badly. *Public Understanding of Science, 21*, 904–921. doi:10.1177/0963662511407991

Collins, H. M. and Pinch, T. (2010). *The Golem at large: What you should know about technology*. Cambridge: Cambridge University Press.

Dutch FA hopes to introduce video referees this season. (2014, August 4). *The Amsterdam Herald*. Retrieved http://amsterdamherald.com/index.php/rss/1231-20140804-dutch-fa-plans-introduce-video-referees-this-season-netherlands-dutch-sport

Gower, D. (2009, December 20). Third umpire strikes back as review system improves. *The Sunday Times*. Retrieved from www.thetimes.co.uk/tto/news/

Gripper, A. (2014, February 20). So-chi close!! 10 fantastic photo finishes from sporting history. Retrieved from www.mirror.co.uk/sport/other-sports/sochi-2014-incredible-ski-cross-796763

Hargreaves, I., Lewis, J. and Speers, T. (2003). *Towards a better map: Science, the public and the media*. Retrieved from Cardiff University, Economic and Social Research Council website: www.cardiff.ac.uk/jomec/resources/Mapdocfinal_tcm6-5505.pdf

Hawkins, P. (2010). *Hawk-Eye accuracy and believability*. Retrieved from www.kitplus.com/articles/Hawk-Eye_Accuracy_and_Believability_in_Cricket/247.html

Hawkins, P. (2015, April 6). Paul Hawkins responds to CricInfo blog [Blog post]. Retrieved from www.hawkeyeinnovations.co.uk/news/39559

Hoult, N. (2013, July 29). Ashes 2013: Hot spot can miss fine edges, admits inventor ahead of third England v. Australia Test. *The Telegraph*. Retrieved from www.telegraph.co.uk/

International Cricket Council. (2009). *Umpire Decision Review System – a guide*. Retrieved from www.world-a-team.com/DRS_guide.pdf

Khaled, A. (2015, March 1). Fifa's refusal to introduce video technology will harm referees, not protect them. *The National*. Retrieved from www.thenational.ae/

Lalor, P. (2010, November 30). Catching referrals 'blight on cricket'. *The Australian*. Retrieved from www.theaustralian.com.au/

Ley, B. L., Jankowski, N., Brewer, P. R. (2012). Investigating CSI: Portrayals of DNA testing on a forensic crime show and their potential effects. *Public Understanding of Science, 21*, 51–67. doi:10.1177/0963662510367571

Mather, G. (2008). Perceptual uncertainty and line-call challenges in professional tennis. *Proceedings of the Royal Society B: Biological Sciences, 275*, 1645–1651. doi:10.1098/rspb.2008.0211

Russell, J. S. (1997). The concept of a call in baseball. *Journal of the Philosophy of Sport, 24*, 21–37. doi:10.1080/00948705.1997.9714537

So-chi close!! 10 fantastic photo finishes from sporting history. (2014, February 20). Retrieved from www.mirror.co.uk/sport/other-sports/sochi-2014-incredible-ski-cross-796763

Winch, P. (1953). *The idea of a social science and its relation to philosophy*. London: Routledge.

World Football Insider. (2015, May 22). *Football technology – Rummenigge wants goal-line tech: Dutch FA assess video refs*. Retrieved from http://worldfootballinsider.com/Story.aspx? id=36965

Further reading

Collins, H. M. (1990). *Artificial experts: Social knowledge and intelligent machines*. Cambridge, MA: MIT Press. [Provides a sociological analysis of what intelligent machines can and cannot do and why.]

Collins, H. M. and Evans, R. (2008). You cannot be serious! Public understanding of technology with special reference to 'Hawk-Eye'. *Public Understanding of Science, 17*, 283–308. doi:10.1177/0963662508093370 [Provides an in-depth analysis of Hawk-Eye but also raises more general issues relating to public understanding of science and technology.]

Collins, H. M. and Pinch, T. (2010). *The Golem at large: What you should know about technology*. Cambridge: Cambridge University Press. [A good introduction to the sociological analysis of technology that contains a number of case studies ranging from economic forecasting to the Challenger space shuttle disaster.]

17

THE TYRANNY OF PERPETUAL INNOVATION

Global mobile media, digital communications and television

Brett Hutchins and David Rowe

Many established professional sport leagues and teams possess ingrained conservative cultures that have poorly anticipated and capitalised on the emergence of new mobile technology services and digital marketplace developments – contrary to their media and marketing messages. Organisational rigidity makes sport professionals typically ill-prepared to respond to a relentless cycle of innovation in the mobile, digital, and telecommunications sectors. For instance, a digital business consultant and advertising executive who worked for major football clubs on two continents commented that the outcome is 'very lame and very boring' content and products that are 'not disruptive [innovative] enough' (Project Participant 3).[1] These provocative statements were collected as part of a wide-ranging program of in-depth interviews with industry informants. Generated by means of an international research project investigating the relationship between mobile media and sport, data from this project inform much of the analysis presented throughout this chapter.

Some readers may take issue with the opinion just described or at least the strength of its expression. Yet, recent controversy over the new live video streaming app, Periscope (launched in late March 2015 and now owned by Twitter), indicates how sport organisations can be caught off guard by the unforeseen popularity of new mobile consumer technologies. An American journalist, Stephanie Wei, had her PGA credentials revoked after live streaming a practice round of the Phoenix Open via her smartphone. She was accused of stealing content, even though the practice round was not shown on broadcast television (Abbruzzese, 2015; Rugg and Burroughs, 2016). The NHL also banned fans from using the app inside playing arenas in order to protect the interests of broadcast rights holders. In contrast, the MLB claims to have no problem with fans using Periscope to stream live footage from games with their mobile devices. The organisers of the 2015 Rugby World Cup in England used Periscope to show a public event featuring British royal family member, Prince Harry, on 10 June of that year, which marked

100 days until the tournament kick-off. Inconsistent reactions to the diffusion of mobile live streaming speak to the challenge of running leagues and events that have existing broadcast television coverage and digital media rights deals in place. There is considerable uncertainty over whether to react defensively, offensively, or not at all to nascent technologies that change the 'conditions of possibility' (Lobato and Thomas, 2015, p. 42) for the production, presentation, and circulation of media content.

In this chapter, we explain why those managing professional sport often find themselves reacting to and following, rather than leading, developments in mobile and digital media. It is essential to understand the reasons for this situation given that it affects executives, managers and administrators at all levels of sport (Fujak and Frawley, 2014; Halbwirth and Toohey, 2013; Karg and Lock, 2014). The objectives of the chapter are to:

- outline the growing relationship between a 'perpetual innovation economy' and the allied global media sport industries (Morris-Suzuki, 2011; Rowe, 2011);
- explain that developments in mobile media and digital communications are having a growing impact on contemporary 'mediasport' (Wenner, 1998) but that, at the same time, many sport organisations are still heavily reliant on broadcast television revenue and audiences;
- explore an example of a media sport company – Red Bull Media House (RBMH) – that is well-suited to the prevailing conditions of global mobile media and its 'messy' communications ecology (Goggin, 2011); and
- discuss the managerial implications of media and commercial developments which, in our view, centre on defending the cultural, public and community values of sport in the face of the technology-driven commodification of sporting practices and competitions.

The tyranny of perpetual innovation

New media is a redundant term under the conditions of digital capitalism – a ceaseless cycle of innovation, or 'novelty in technology' (Banks, 2012, p. 159), in which new media forms become familiar and then unremarkable at an accelerated rate. Media change, therefore, occurs through shifting configurations of digitisation, networking, and mobility. Varying combinations of sensor, data, wearable, and haptic features are threaded throughout these configurations. Such characteristics fuel a global digital and mobile economy built on the constant development, release, and upgrading of services, platforms, interfaces, devices, software, hardware, and network infrastructures. The structure underpinning this cycle can be summarised as follows:

- Turbocharged market competition is stimulated by digital technology behemoths such as Google, Apple, Amazon, Facebook, Samsung, Microsoft, IBM, Electronic Arts and Cisco. These companies sit above a complex ecosystem of smaller competitors, developers, publishers, investors, start-up tech firms, and venture capitalists that compete across the world.

- Located within this digital market ecosystem is a layer of specialist sport industry operators, including Perform, MLB Advanced Media, STATS, Sporting Innovations, DraftKings, Fancred, Catapult and GoPro.
- All of the names listed above play direct and indirect roles in the provision of myriad products and services to major sport organisations and events, such as website creation and management, mobile video, live streaming, social media, fantasy sport, tablet computer and smartphone supply and sponsorship, statistics and performance data analytics, wearable media, mobile app development, consumer database and customer relationship management software, locative media services, cloud computing, licensed interactive computer games, stadium Wi-Fi and distributed antenna system networks. These technologies and services have been created to target fans and consumers and are also increasingly distributed throughout the internal structures of sport organisations, adding to their operational and communications complexity (Frandsen, 2015).

The interlocking markets, sectors, and services detailed here have grown over the last two decades and, as a result, exposed sport to the dynamics of a perpetual innovation economy (Morris-Suzuki, 2011). While there may be physical and material limits to the amount of sport that can be staged, there are fewer limitations on how sport-related media content, digital data, and networked fan communication can be produced, aggregated, repurposed, augmented, and packaged. The continual reimagining and production of digital and mobile media innovation – or novel ways of consuming and commodifying sport-related content and experiences – is the generator of value in this economy. The effects of this mode of innovation include uncertainty, high levels of risk, and boom and bust cycles, underpinned by the unpredictable character of technology uptake and profitability (Kline, Dyer-Witheford and de Peuter, 2003; Lobato and Thomas, 2015; Morris-Suzuki, 2011). According to an entrepreneurship and business development expert, these dynamics are not immediately familiar to many professionals working in the national, transnational, and global sport industries:

> If you look at sport as being an industry and you compare it against the financial services or the retail sector, sport is still quite a long way behind in using digital and mobile to monetise. That's where the real pressure is… . Sports need to innovate, they need to be better at corporate governance, and they need to start monetising better.
>
> *(Project Participant 20)*

Adjusting to the tempo of a perpetual innovation economy presents considerable challenges for sport on a number of fronts, including the development of flexible media and communications strategies, negotiating the length and terms of media and technology contracts, staffing expertise and hiring decisions, and the purchase and allocation of digital and mobile technology resources and services. For instance, the international sport business and technology trade press is currently paying particular attention to the commercial opportunities presented by Snapchat Stories, the Apple iWatch, and virtual reality headsets for coaching and consumer applications. Only 12 months earlier, attention was lavished on Instagram, iBeacons, and Google Glass.[2] The names change but the emphasis on innovation and hype continues unabated, making investment decisions and strategic planning difficult and uncertain.

Many professional clubs, leagues, and mega-events have developed historically and commercially in relation to broadcast television systems. As we have written elsewhere, there are distinctions between the industrial conditions presented by 'broadcast scarcity' and 'digital plenitude', such as with regard to alternative institutional settings, economies of scale, user practices, and speeds of technological innovation (Hutchins and Rowe, 2009, 2012). Importantly, sport remains overwhelmingly reliant on commercial free-to-air and subscription broadcast television for the majority of its media revenue and audiences around the globe (Rowe, 2011). This reliance triggers an awkward balancing act between satisfying a rising demand for content-hungry mobile platforms and digital media services, and the protection of exclusive coverage and content rights for broadcast partners. In Australia, for example, watching live broadcast television is still a popular pastime, with viewers devoting an average of 88 hours and 50 minutes per month to live TV sport (Regional TAM, OzTAM and Nielsen, 2014). This popularity outstrips the time spent viewing video content on mobile devices by a considerable margin. However, television viewers frequently use a tablet or smartphone while watching, giving rise to the phenomenon of 'social television' and audience measurement indicators such as Nielsen Twitter TV Ratings. For example, an estimated 86 per cent of tablet users and 77 per cent of smartphone users in Australia, aged 14 years and over, reported accessing the Internet or apps while watching television in the previous 12 months (Regional TAM *et al.*, 2014). However, 'second and third screen' practices do not necessarily displace broadcast television viewing, and may even be positively related to the amount of time spent on television–viewing activity (Greer and Ferguson, 2015). The outcome of this multiple-screen use is that television, mobile media, and digital communications are redefining each other's conditions for the production and consumption of content:

> Broadcast and television, rather than being replaced by online viewing systems, are quickly becoming part of social media's logic; the growing interdependence between television and video-sharing platforms, and the frictionless exchangeability of YouTube, Facebook, and Twitter's features, simultaneously reflect and construct the emergent culture of connectivity.
>
> *(van Dijck, 2013, p. 111)*

This culture of connectivity enacts a complicated interchange between a historically dominant broadcast media system and an emergent set of mobile and digital media practices and technologies, as indicated by the controversies over Periscope. Therefore, often uneasy commercial relationships transpire that pivot on the generation of premium content, the sharing and/or exclusive control of this content, and the subsequent distribution of advertising revenue and audience data.

There is notable resultant tension due to the involvement of digital technology and telecommunications industries in sport. For example, sport industries are demonstrating concerted efforts to influence the rhythms of perpetual innovation, rather than being consigned to following and reacting to the latest technological developments. Initiatives are occurring internationally and take multiple forms; for example, in the United States, the L.A. Dodgers baseball team and the R/GA digital advertising agency have teamed up in introducing a new 'Dodgers Accelerator' programme. The ten start-up tech companies selected for this programme receive funding, development, and branding services and strategic support in an effort to achieve market scale. Claiming to be the 'first ever sports technology and entertainment accelerator' (L.A. Dodgers and R/GA, 2015, p. 1), this investment programme seeks to 'create more powerful consumer experiences, heighten fan engagement, and improve efficiencies' (p. 1) in areas such as fan relationship management, e-sport, sponsor integration, and data and analytics. A parallel initiative in the United Kingdom involves Scottish tennis star, Andy Murray, partnering with an equity crowd-funding platform, Seedrs, which is based in London (Fuller, 2015). Together, they are supporting British start-ups and entrepreneurs by fostering 'a community of support' for innovation in health, sport, and wearable technology. Another organisation with related objectives is the Australian Sports Technologies Network (http://astn.com.au/). Founded in 2012, this not-for-profit industry-led network has members including sport technology firms, national sporting organisations, governments, and investors. According to a business professional involved in the Australian Sports Technologies Network since its inception,

> There's a strong focus on innovation. So sports were being told to innovate, but how do you innovate? What do you do to innovate across high perform-ance game development, game participation and commercial operations? So there was a real opportunity to engage with sport and see what their problems or opportunities were, and around how technology could play a role....There is an investment pitching competition that really tries to be the avenue or the test-bed for new innovations in sports technologies. The really high-potential ones [pitches] can go into an accelerator program where they get direct mentoring advice from organisations, to help them pull them through to investment potentially.... So it's about trying to teach sport how to innovate.
>
> *(Project Participant 26)*

Terms such as *accelerator, start-up, opportunity,* and *potential* suggest that these early stage developments will take time to produce lasting impacts, and their results are also likely to be uneven given the risk-averse cultures of many sporting organisations that matured during the era of analogue media (Hutchins and Rowe, 2012).

RBMH: born digital and mobile *Red Bull Media House (RBMH)*

In contrast, this section offers a brief overview of RBMH, a company that epitomises the logic of perpetual innovation. The media and content strategies *7* developed by RBMH resemble, in some ways, those now being developed by the likes of MLB Advanced Media, NFL Media, and AFL Media.

RBMH has evolved within the complex structures and flows of global digital and mobile media culture, and, according to sociologist Holly Thorpe (2014), blurs 'previously conceived divisions between media, events, corporations and celebrity' (p. 62) in action and lifestyle sporting pursuits. Launched in 2007, RBMH has over 135 employees working in offices in Austria and California. It explicitly addresses a global audience and is a central driver of advertising and marketing efforts for Red Bull energy drinks. Red Bull's promotional activities encompass a wide range of cultural events, programs, and sponsorships around the world and extend to a telecommunications and mobile media service arm (i.e., Red Bull Mobile), a record label (i.e., Red Bull Records), a magazine (i.e., *The Red Bulletin*), and the development and publication of console and mobile games (e.g., Red Bull Air Race – The Game). Exemplifying the emergence of a transnational action sport culture, RBMH also sponsors more than 500 athletes (Thorpe, 2014), including Austrian skydiver and BASE jumper Felix Baumgartner, American BMX rider Tyler Fernengel and Australian wave windsurfer Jason Polakow. Furthermore, RBMH helps to create and organise international events such as the Red Bull Air Race World Championship, the 'X Fighters' Freestyle Motocross World Tour, the 'Crashed Ice' Ice Cross Downhill World Championship and the Global Rallycross series.

RBMH presents itself as a global 'umbrella brand' that produces original content for television, mobile, digital, audio, and print media (www.redbullmedia house.com). The key to its success is the prodigious production of content from assets owned and controlled by Red Bull. The RBMH library has more than 5,000 videos and 50,000 photographs (Thorpe, 2014). In addition, Fry (2014) indicated that RBMH reportedly adds around 1,000 hours of long-form programming annually, the content of which is generated and distributed in four main ways:

1 Digital and mobile platforms, including the online video service, Red Bull TV (e.g., Crashed Ice and X Fighters).
2 Broadcast television networks such as NBC in the United States (e.g., Red Bull Signature Series and the Global Rallycross series).
3 Red Bull's third-party sponsorships, which enable access to behind-the-scenes stories and content. An example of this arrangement is the Red Bull Formula One motor-racing team.
4 Endorsement of individual action sport athletes, who produce photographs, short-videos, and blogs that are distributed via Red Bull's digital channels and

other platforms such as Facebook, Twitter, and Instagram. These endorsements do not, however, afford athletes ownership over the content produced by their exertions, which are profitably deployed by the RBMH promotional media machine (Thorpe, 2014).

RBMH's ascendancy is linked to the Google-owned video-sharing site, YouTube. Reflecting the creeping professionalisation and commercialisation of user-generated content uploaded to this site (Kim, 2012), the first Red Bull video appeared on YouTube in 2006. RBMH has since grown into one of the most popular sport channels on this platform, boasting over 4 million subscribers and videos that achieve measured views that range from the tens of thousands to millions. The Red Bull channel and YouTube have also developed alongside each other. Action sport cultures such as surfing, snowboarding, and skateboarding have been at the forefront of 'do-it-yourself' portable and mobile media content creation for several decades, using devices to collaborate, record and share footage among participant communities (Gilchrist and Wheaton, 2013). YouTube's (2015) invocation to 'broadcast yourself' dovetails with these impulses, with half of all views now sourced from mobile devices. RBMH represents a highly adaptable model of media production and consumption in which sporting activity, mobile media, digital platforms and corporate brands are indivisible.

Managerial implications

The expanding interaction between sport and a perpetual innovation economy has implications for the ways in which sport is collectively understood. A conspicuous effect of this interplay is to embed the value of sport ever deeper within digital and mobile media consumption, branding of content, commodification of data, and the operation of technology-suffused market forces (Hutchins, 2015a; Wenner, 2014b). The momentum of commodification stimulated by this process is even greater than that perpetuated by the broadcast television industries, which at least have a history of public service telecasts that emphasise the ideals of universal accessibility and the notion of a common culture (Scherer and Rowe, 2014). It is a pattern that under-mines the cultural, public, and community meanings of sport that, in many ways, have long underwritten its popular appeal and economic value. The challenge for the managers of sport is, then, to articulate and protect these qualities while also recognising the realities of a contemporary media landscape that has not witnessed such thoroughgoing change since television supplanted radio and print as the main sport medium in the mid-twentieth century.

Professional sport has long placed itself in the service – usually willingly – of the state and commerce (Horne, Tomlinson, Whannel and Woodward, 2012). The main managerial dilemma has been how far their demands can be accommodated before control is lost over sport governance and practice, and even over the extent to which it remains recognisable as sport. The most enduring and troubling question for the sport–media nexus has been the extent to which sport's principal paymaster

– the media – may call the tune (Rowe, 2004). With the bewildering and rapid-fire innovation that has been discussed in this chapter insinuating media technologies ever further into the fabric of sport and, indeed, into the bodies of professional and amateur athletes, the earlier preoccupation with the media's influence over the timing of sport events and their rules of play now appears almost quaint.

Cultural citizenship

All interested parties, including governments and citizens, must carefully consider the implications of contemporary developments regarding sport's relationship to *cultural citizenship*. This concept goes beyond familiar questions of the rights of citizens to protection under the law, to vote or to receive fair remuneration for labour (Miller, 2007); it involves the important – though necessarily less tangible – domain of facilitating symbolic inclusion, preventing exclusion from national cultures and signifying the relationships between nations and other collectivities. Because sport has been so central to collective life in many societies, digital media and technology innovation cannot be permitted to erode cultural citizenship rights in the name of enhancing the opportunities for a limited range of privileged sport consumers. The concept of the 'citizen-consumer' is a vexed one, but it is important for those engaged in sport management to assure that they do not allow the latter part of this dual concept to overwhelm the former.

As has been well documented, the commercial stakes in sport and media are higher than ever before, involving very large sport organisations and major corporations seeking to monetise both sport content and relationships (Szymanski, 2014). Although it is common to declare that the media world has now moved well 'beyond television' and that screen video content can be accessed in many ways, broadcast television (the content of which is now deliverable by various techno-logical means) remains persistently popular (Wolff, 2015) – not least because of its attachment to sport. But there are persistent concerns that freely available sport television may be corralled in ways that lock out many citizens who have traditionally been able to partake in the great festivals of sport, such as the Olympic Games and the FIFA World Cup.

The International Olympic Committee (IOC) has historically favoured television audience 'reach over revenue' by insisting on the wide availability of Olympic broadcasts at the expense of subscription-only deals. In fact, with public broadcasters, such as the BBC, increasingly using online platforms alongside television, tournaments (e.g., the 2012 Summer Olympics and the 2015 FIFA Women's World Cup) can now be shown without change in their entirety. However, changes to the media environment are bringing in new corporate media players who are less committed to open access to major sport events. In 2015, the IOC notably awarded the European television and other media rights for future Olympic Games to a private pan-European sport network and its U.S.-based controller:

Discovery Communications and Eurosport have snapped up most European multiplatform broadcast and distribution rights for the four Olympic Games between 2018–2024 in a landmark deal inked in Lausanne, Switzerland, with the International Olympic Committee that ups Discovery's game in the sports-rights field and boosts the status of Discovery-controlled Eurosport as Europe's top sports platform.

Discovery acquired the exclusive rights, valued at EUR 1.3 billion (US $1.44 billion), across all platforms – including free-to-air and pay TV, online and mobile phone in all languages across 50 countries and most territories on the European continent... . Discovery said the deal marks the first time the IOC has sold the bulk of these European rights to a single media company.

(Vivarelli, 2015, paras. 1–3)

This centralisation of intellectual property rights in one commercial corporation, and the extension of its control over media sport platforms, has the potential to infringe upon cultural citizenship rights traditionally reserved for most of Europe's population. Although countries such as the United Kingdom and France retain Olympic broadcast rights until 2020 and receive some free-to-air protection from the listing of events by their media regulators, there is no doubt that this new arrangement shifts the balance of media sport power from public to private organisations ('Eurosport Wins', 2015). The justification for the change, presented by IOC President Thomas Bach, is that it maximises media platform choice for sport fans and provides additional revenue to support the development of sport across the world. It also involves a partnership that will develop a new Olympic Channel dedicated exclusively to Olympic sport, especially those pursuits that receive reduced media coverage – including those involving women – in the four-year intervals between both the Summer and Winter Games ('IOC Awards', 2015).

The implications for media sport management are significant in all of the following three respects: (a) the possibility that free-to-air viewing availability will be reduced at the expense of subscription platforms; (b) intensified competition between elite and grassroots sport organisations for the expanded media sport rights revenue; (c) and the advancement of the ambition of peak sport bodies like the IOC and FIFA to own, produce, sell, and distribute their own media sport content, rather than sell the rights to media companies, such as NBCUniversal and Discovery Communications. To date, sport-initiated media production has been largely limited to the operation of subscription television channels and websites by peak organisations (e.g., NFL and AFL) and clubs (e.g., Manchester United and Real Madrid) which are careful not to impinge on their expensively sold broadcast content to major television networks. However, digital technologies and new market entrants are providing unprecedented opportunities to display sport and to connect with audiences. For example, in June 2015, the NFL and Yahoo! announced the first ever free live-stream of a regular season game to viewers around the globe (Hutchins, 2015b). Played in London on 25 October of the same year, Yahoo! paid a reported U.S. $20 million for the digital rights to the match-up between the Buffalo Bills and Jackson Jaguars. Another example is the surprise securing of exclusive Australian broadcast rights to the English Premier League by telecommunications company Optus at the expense of the previous rights holder Fox Sports (Siracusa, 2015).

Enhanced use of the Internet and mobile media in carrying diverse sport texts to audiences – and, as we have seen, between audience members and the media – adds considerable complexity to the media sport environment. Managing relationships amongst sport organisations, media companies, telecommunications carriers, sponsors, advertisers, governments, athletes, fans and the general citizenry is an increasingly difficult task. Constant cycles of disruptive innovation open and close the possibilities for monetisation, surveillance, control, access, communication and, of course, leisure and pleasure. In the media sport sphere, in particular, conflicts between the maximisation of intellectual property rights and the protection and extension of cultural citizenship rights continue unabated. Exacerbated by 'the rise of networked media sport' (Hutchins and Rowe, 2012), the material and symbolic rewards that can be derived from media sport are uncomfortably matched by the consequent dilemmas involving their management and governance.

Conclusion: managing media sport innovation – a paradox

There is something of a paradox in discussing the management of innovation in media sport and in other domains. As has been discussed above, perpetual, rapid change demands a series of responses that, in many cases, are done 'on the run', with little knowledge of effects or anticipation of unintended consequences. Regarding media sport, it has been suggested that the profound shift from analogue to digital and mobile media, and from a largely one-way communication to high levels of interactivity, is unprecedented in its disruptiveness to the production and consumption of content (Miller, 2011). The history of sport media offers several earlier instances of profound, rapid change. For example, the major expansion of newspapers in the early twentieth century led to improved literacy; domestic television became rapidly popular in many countries after the Second World War and forever changed the presentation and format of popular media forms. Furthermore, new media technologies do not simply obliterate and supersede earlier ones, but coexist and are combined in a range of ways (e.g., multiple-screen use during major sport events allows fans to upload content that is then captured and carried by major institutional media, such as newspapers and broadcast television). It is more plausible to describe relatively ordered and limited periods, such as the transition from black-and-white to colour sport television, or from wave-based to digital audio radio sport broadcasting, which are punctuated by periods when the necessarily temporary *status quo* is challenged. At such times, sport and media industry players – and those who regulate and analyse their operations – are required to interpret and predict the outcomes of these developments, with demonstratively mixed results.

It is, therefore, obvious that the large, dynamic 'media sports cultural complex' cannot somehow be stabilised to accommodate those who are seeking to divine its trends (Rowe, 2004). For example, the academic journal *Communication and Sport*, edited by Wenner (2014a), devoted a research forum to Twitter in seeking to understand the impact of micro-blogging on sport media and communication and on its research and scholarship. Given that Twitter has only existed since 2007 and has become a publicly listed company as recently as 2013, any authoritative conclusions could only be provisional. The same can be said of wearable sport technologies or virtual reality, the latter having been heralded as the 'future present' of immersive media at the end of the last century (Rheingold, 1991). However, as we have noted through our own media sport industry research (Hutchins and Rowe, 2012), analogous analytical exercises are being conducted in both sport and media organisations and with similar degrees of speculation and inconclusiveness.

As Stuart Cunningham (2013) has argued with regard to the creative industries in an analysis influenced by Joseph Schumpeter's concept of *creative destruction*, there are,

> emergent modes that have seized opportunities thrown up by the crisis of business models in media production, the embedding of social media in everyday consumption and communication patterns, and the response of major platforms like YouTube to challenges to their own sustainability. What we seem to be witnessing is the 'co-evolution' of the market and non-market domains under the pressure that new forms of participative culture have opened up.
>
> *(p. 25)*

Media sport is implicated in these difficult questions of co-evolving – and, it should be said, frequently intersecting – market and non-market domains. Those engaged in media sport management have no choice but to negotiate these contending pressures. It is important that they recognise that their fiduciary duty to the sport industry does not overshadow their corresponding responsibility to respect sport's pivotal role in contemporary cultural citizenship.

Notes

1   Interview data presented in this chapter are de-identified in accordance with the conditions of clearance provided by the relevant University Human Research Ethics Committee. These data were collected through 48 semi-structured, in-depth interviews completed during 2014, featuring sport and media industry informants based in the United States, United Kingdom, Europe, Australasia and Southeast Asia.

2   This claim is supported by a trade press database produced from the content of major sport business and technology media outlets in the United States, United Kingdom,

other regions in Europe and Australia. Organised by date, theme, sport, headline, key words, nation and key quotations, this database is built from daily online subscriptions, weekly e-mail updates and magazine subscriptions for publications such as *Sport Business International, Mobile Sports Report* (United States), *Sport Techie* (United States), *Sports Geek HQ* (Australia), *Sports ProMedia* (United Kingdom and Europe) and *The UK Sports Network*. At the time of writing (i.e., late 2015), 1,075 stories had been collected and organised since 2 January 2014.

References

Abbruzzese, J. (2015, May 7). Periscope could change sports broadcasting, but leagues are still scared. *Mashable*. Retrieved from http://mashable.com/

Banks, J. (2012). The iPhone as innovation platform: Reimaging the videogames developer. In L. Hjorth, J. Burgess and I. Richardson (eds) *Studying mobile media: Cultural technologies, mobile communication, and the iPhone* (pp. 155–172). New York: Routledge.

Cunningham, S. (2013). *Hidden innovation: Policy, industry and the creative sector*. St. Lucia, Australia: University of Queensland Press.

Eurosport wins Olympic TV rights for Europe. (2015, June 29). *BBC News*. Retrieved from www.bbc.com/news/entertainment-arts-33311902

Frandsen, K. (2015). Sports organizations in a new wave of mediatization. *Communication and Sport*. Advance online publication. doi:10.1177/2167479515588185.

Fry, A. (2014, July 1). Content is king. *Sport Business International*. Retrieved from www.sportbusiness.com/sportbusiness-international

Fujak, H. and Frawley, S. (2014). Broadcast inequality in Australian football. *Communication and Sport*. Advance online publication. doi:10.1177/2167479514552672

Fuller, M. (2015, June 9). Tennis star Andy Murray investing in UK technology startups. *Sport Techie*. Retrieved from www.sporttechie.com

Gilchrist, P. and Wheaton, B. (2013). New media technologies in lifestyle sport. In B. Hutchins and D. Rowe (eds) *Digital media sport: Technology, power and culture in the network society* (pp. 169–185). New York: Routledge.

Goggin, G. (2011). *Global mobile media*. London: Routledge.

Greer, C. F. and Ferguson, D. A. (2015). Tablet computers and traditional television (TV) viewing: Is the iPad replacing TV? *Convergence, 21*, 244–256. doi:10.1177/13548565 14541928

Halbwirth, S. and Toohey, K. (2013). Information, knowledge and the organization of the Olympic Games. In S. Frawley and D. Adair (eds) *Managing the Olympics* (pp. 33–49). Basingstoke, UK: Palgrave Macmillan.

Horne, J., Tomlinson, A., Whannel, G. and Woodward, K. (2012). *Understanding sport: A socio-cultural analysis* (2nd ed.). New York: Routledge.

Hutchins, B. (2015a). Tales of the digital sublime: Tracing the relationship between big data and professional sport. *Convergence*. Advance online publication. doi:10.1177/13548 56515587163

Hutchins, B. (2015b, June 23). For football, the future has already arrived. *Inside Story*. Retrieved from http://insidestory.org.au

Hutchins, B. and Rowe, D. (2009). From broadcast scarcity to digital plenitude: The changing dynamics of the media sport content economy. *Television and New Media, 10*, 354–370. doi:10.1177/1527476409334016

Hutchins, B. and Rowe, D. (2012). *Sport beyond television: The internet, digital media and the rise of networked media sport*. London, UK: Routledge.

IOC awards all TV and multiplatform broadcast rights in Europe to Discovery and Eurosport for 2018–2024 Olympic Games. (2015, June 29). *IOC News*. Retrieved from www.olympic.org/news/ioc-awards-all-tv-and-multiplatform-broadcast-rights-in-europe-to-discovery-and-eurosport-for-2018-2024-olympic-games/246462

Karg, A. and Lock, D. (2014). Using new media to engage consumers at the football world cup. In S. Frawley and D. Adair (eds) *Managing the football world cup* (pp. 25–46). Basingstoke, UK: Palgrave Macmillan.

Kim, J. (2012). The institutionalization of YouTube: From user generated content to professionally generated content. *Media, Culture and Society, 34*, 53–67. doi:10.1177/0163 443711427199

Kline, S., Dyer-Witheford, N. and de Peuter, G. (2003). *Digital play: The interaction of technology, culture, and marketing*. Kingston, Canada: McGill-Queen's University Press.

L.A. Dodgers and R/GA. (2015, April 14). *The LA Dodgers and R/GA announce first-ever sports technology and entertainment accelerator* [Press release]. Retrieved from www.dodgersaccelerator.com/wp-content/uploads/2015/04/LA_Dodgers_Accelerator_Release_final.pdf

Lobato, R. and Thomas, J. (2015). *The informal media economy*. Cambridge: Polity Press.

Miller, T. (2007). *Cultural citizenship: Cosmopolitanism, consumerism, and television in a neoliberal age*. Philadelphia, PA: Temple University Press.

Miller, V. (2011). *Understanding digital culture*. London: Sage.

Morris-Suzuki, T. (2011). *Beyond computopia: Information, automation and democracy in Japan*. Abingdon, UK: Routledge.

Regional TAM, OzTAM and Nielsen. (2014). *Australian multi-screen report: Quarter 3*. Retrieved from www.nielsen.com/content/dam/nielsenglobal/au/docs/reports/australian-multi-screen-report-q32014.pdf

Rheingold, H. (1991). *Virtual reality*. New York: Touchstone.

Rowe, D. (2004). *Sport, culture and the media: The unruly trinity* (2nd ed.). Maidenhead, UK: Open University Press.

Rowe, D. (2011). *Global media sport: Flows, forms and futures*. London, UK: Bloomsbury Academic.

Rugg, A. and Burroughs, B. (2016). Periscope, live streaming and mobile video culture. In R. Lobato and J. Meese (eds) *Geoblocking and Global Video Culture* (pp. 64–73). Amsterdam: Institute of Network Cultures.

Scherer, J. and Rowe, D. (2014). *Sport, public broadcasting, and cultural citizenship: Signal lost?* New York: Routledge.

Siracusa, C. (2015). Optus snatches English Premier League rights from Fox Sports in Australia. *The Sydney Morning Herald*. Retrieved from www.smh.com.au/business/media-and-marketing/optus-snatches-english-premier-league-rights-from-fox-sports-in-australia-20151101-gkoedn.html

Szymanski, S. (2014). Economics in sport. In J. Maguire (ed.) *Social sciences in sport* (pp. 165–189). Champaign, IL: Human Kinetics.

Thorpe, H. (2014). *Transnational mobilities in action sport cultures*. Basingstoke, UK: Palgrave Macmillan.

van Dijck, J. (2013). *The culture of connectivity: A critical history of social media*. Oxford: Oxford University Press.

Vivarelli, N. (2015, June 29). Discovery, Eurosport snap up exclusive 2018–2024 Olympic rights for Europe. *Variety*. Retrieved from http://variety.com

Wenner, L. A. (ed.). (1998). *Mediasport*. London: Routledge.

Wenner, L. A. (2014a). Much ado (or not) about Twitter? Assessing an emergent communication and sport research agenda. *Communication and Sport, 2*, 103–142. doi:10.1177/2167479514527426

Wenner, L. A. (2014b). On the limits of the new and the lasting power of the mediasport interpellation. *Television and New Media, 15*, 732–740. doi:10.1177/1527476414532957

Wolff, M. (2015, June 29). How television won the internet. *The New York Times*. Retrieved from www.nytimes.com

YouTube. (2015). *Statistics*. Retrieved from www.youtube.com/yt/press/statistics.html

Further reading

Boyle, R. and Whannel, G. (2010). Editorial: Sport and the new media. *Convergence, 16*, 259–268. doi:10.1177/1354856510367549

Evens, T., Iosifidis, P. and Smith, P. (2013). *The political economy of television sports rights*. Basingstoke, UK: Palgrave Macmillan.

Hutchins, B. (2014). Sport on the move: The unfolding impact of mobile communications on the media sport content economy. *Journal of Sport and Social Issues, 38*, 509–527. doi:10.1177/0193723512458933

Lefever, K. (2012). *New media and sport: International legal aspects*. Berlin: Springer.

Rowe, D. (2014). New screen action and its memories: The 'live' performance of mediated sport fandom. *Television and New Media, 15*, 752–759. doi:10.1177/1527476414527835

18

SOCIAL MEDIA ANALYTICS FOR SPORT MANAGEMENT

Pitfalls, tools and best practices

Larena Hoeber and Orland Hoeber

Because a significant number of stakeholders within many sport organisations make extensive use of social media, the analysis of this data can provide valuable insights into a broad range of sport management concerns, including fan behaviour, sponsorship activation, risk management and sociocultural issues in sport. This chapter will discuss social media in the sport context, outline analytics from a research perspective, and provide an overview of some common commercial and free social media analytics software. Analytics pitfalls and best practices will be discussed, and a case study will be presented to illustrate the exploratory analysis of emerging themes within a large collection of tweets. Finally, there will be a discussion on the managerial implications of social media analytics and an overview of future directions.

The primary objectives of this chapter are (a) to advocate for the inclusion of analysis within a social media strategy, (b) to build awareness of the commercial and research-oriented tools available to assist with social media analytics, and (c) to highlight the broad reach of social media within sport management issues.

Social media and the sport context

In recent years, there has been a significant influx of social media platforms. While the most popular of these within the English-speaking world include Twitter, Facebook, Google+, Pinterest, and Instagram, the ever-changing landscape of web- and mobile-enabled services may result in new platforms taking over in the near future. Therefore, the discussion on social media analytics in this chapter will start with a general explanation of the key features of social media, and then will focus on Twitter, which has become a very popular media platform within the sport community.

Social media can be characterised by three fundamental features: (a) user-generated content, (b) immediacy, and (c) mechanisms for supporting social connections. In traditional media, content is generated by a small number of individuals (e.g., reporters, bloggers) and distributed via controlled and independent channels (Hutchins, 2011). Social media has democratised both the creation and distribution of news, allowing anyone with access to a computer or smartphone to produce content (Murthy, 2012). In contrast to the timeframes that are normally involved in traditional media, the time from creation to distribution is almost negligible with social media platforms. Similarly, consumers of social media can view posts instantaneously. Beyond these features, what truly sets social media apart from traditional media is the ability for media consumers to personalise their news feeds by choosing to follow or not follow specific media creators (e.g., 'friends' on Facebook, 'following' in Twitter).

An important feature that has contributed to the rise in popularity of social media in recent years has been the transition from web-based access to mobile access; this has been particularly important in the context of sport. With a smartphone, individuals can not only engage in the creation and distribution of content while watching a sporting event, but this can also be done quickly and easily, with minimal distraction from the actual event. In addition, a character limit that discourages long descriptions but supports photo uploads has made Twitter a very popular platform in this domain. As a result, we focus from this point forward on social media analytics in the context of Twitter, but also caution sport management practitioners and researchers to be mindful of other platforms that might eventually supplant Twitter within sport communities.

Twitter's popularity stems from its ability to allow individuals and organisations to post and share short messages in an open and unfiltered medium. It is an attractive and distinctive source of information because it is 'free to use, public (or perhaps semi-public), multicast (i.e. many to many), interactive, and networked' (Murthy, 2012, p. 1061). The widespread adoption and the willingness of users to comment on a broad range of topics have resulted in Twitter becoming a valuable source of information regarding public opinion, citizen reporting, and social interaction. For example, O'Connor, Balasubramanyan, Routledge, and Smith (2010) found that the sentiment expressed on Twitter can be used as a surrogate for public opinion polls.

Within the sport context, Twitter has been embraced and promoted as a mechanism to enhance communication among sport organisations, athletes, fans, and the media (Hambrick, Simmons, Greenhalgh and Greenwell, 2010; Pegoraro, 2010). Sport organisations are well aware of the popularity of social networks among their stakeholders and are investing in social media engagement from strategic, operational and user-focused perspectives (Filo, Lock and Karg, 2015). Fans and other stakeholders highly identify with their sport, their team, or particular sport personalities, often resulting in a willingness to share, build, and maintain reputations on behalf of their team (Brown, Brown and Billings, 2015). Athletes, teams, leagues, sponsors and other key players in the sport landscape are all actively participating to build followers; success in this endeavour is critical in the process of converting followers into fans.

From a managerial perspective, it is not sufficient to simply use social media for these purposes; it is also important to monitor and analyse the outcomes. Knowledge of both macro-level (e.g., descriptive statistics, timeline visualisations of sentiment) and micro-level (e.g., who is saying what in relation to events) content can provide valuable insight into the effectiveness of the communication, the networks involved, long-term and short-term trends, and a host of other information that can guide and inform managerial decisions and actions. While cursory analysis is possible via random or pseudo-random inspection (e.g., simply looking at the tweets of one's followers), there is too much information that is being posted too quickly for this approach to be effective. The textual and visual nature of social media data makes it difficult to analyse in the best of situations; this is even more acute within the larger network of social media. These issues have been identified within both the research community and commercial software world. In order to perform effective social media analytics, software tools must be employed to tease out the information that is relevant to a particular managerial need.

Analytics and sport management research

Although Twitter is an insightful and readily accessible source of data, analysis of such data beyond simple descriptive statistics and managerial reports presents significant challenges for both sport management practitioners and researchers. Currently, there is a polarisation between two approaches for analysing Twitter and other social media data (Tinati, Halford, Carr and Pope, 2014). Micro-approaches, which have been commonly used in sport studies, involve identifying and analysing small-scale or random samples (Boyd and Crawford, 2012). For example, Hambrick *et al.* (2010) used stratified random sampling to choose athletes to study and then selected the 20 most recent tweets from each athlete. In their study of the Giro d'Italia, Kassing and Sanderson (2010) used stratified sampling to select athlete Twitter accounts and then analysed all tweets posted during a specific period of time. For their study of how sport fans respond to a crisis – in this case, the Penn State sexual abuse scandal – Brown *et al.* (2015) chose every sixth tweet for a final sample of 2,000 tweets. Such a micro-approach is favoured because the sizes of the datasets are more manageable, particularly when conducting traditional manual content analysis. However, they have been critiqued for 'imposing an external structure by sampling users or tweets according to *a priori* criteria' (Tinati *et al.*, 2014, p. 3), discounting the dynamic, interactive, and temporal relationships of the data (Hutchins, 2014) and providing only descriptive findings (Hardin, 2014).

Others have argued for macro-approaches using descriptive statistics, data mining, and automated scanning and analysis, thus enabling an exploration of large datasets. While there is little evidence of sport management research incorporating these approaches, in other domains they have been critiqued for their inability to provide meaning to findings or for missing the social context of the data (Boyd and Crawford, 2012; Mahrt and Scharkow, 2013). Further, Mahrt and Scharkow (2013) argued that 'Big Data analyses tend only to show *what* users do, but not *why* they do it' (p. 23).

There is a similar problem with the managerial focus of many of the existing social media analytics approaches. However, we argue that any information about one's social media presence is better than no information. We, therefore, advocate for the measured use of both approaches, combining 'technical capabilities with in-depth qualitative search methods' (Tinati *et al.*, 2014, p. 6; see also Lewis, Zamith and Hermida, 2013; Murthy and Bowman, 2014); these approaches, such as our work on Vista – which will also be discussed in the following section – allow for the dynamic generation of purposeful rather than random samples, while main-taining large-scale views of the data. With careful analysis and purpose-guided exploration, such approaches can support the investigation of outliers and minorities (Foucault Welles, 2014). Further, we argue that sport managers should look for and use 'small-scale solutions that can leverage the power and potential of Big Data technologies [and] can be replicated, implemented, and maintained with low cost and minimal expertise' (Murthy and Bowman, 2014, p. 2).

Analytics software

There is a broad range of software available to support the tracking and analysis of social media data such as that posted on Twitter; these include free services, com-mercial packages, and experimental/research software. As with social media platforms themselves, the software available to support the analytics of social media are constantly changing and improving. Thus, we limit this discussion to the general functionality provided by a sample of such software, with a focus on the types of analyses each can support. Our intent is not to cover every possible feature of each system, but to provide a flavour for the range of analyses that are possible.

Twitter analytics

Twitter Analytics (http://analytics.twitter.com) is a free service provided by Twitter to support the analysis of a specific account. It provides simple statistics and visual summaries of tweet impressions, profile visits, and followers, grouped by month. More detailed analyses of tweets are possible, showing both an overall view as well as detailed analysis of the engagement with specific tweets, such as the impressions over time, whether or not links have been followed, how many times posts have been retweeted or favourited and whether or not it has led to a view of the user profile. Such analyses provide a glimpse into the level of engagement with one's followers and with some effort, can allow a social media manager to learn what kinds of tweets are well received.

Hootsuite uberVU

uberVU (https://hootsuite.com/products/ubervu-via-hootsuite) provides a real-time visual dashboard for the analysis of social media data, including all the major social media platforms. Users can specify an arbitrary topic to follow (e.g., one's team name), which will generate graphical reports based on simple metrics (e.g., gender distribution, language), complex metrics (e.g., sentiment trends over time) and the terms and phrases most commonly used in the context of the topic. uberVU is primarily geared to the creation of managerial reports and can be used to not only follow one's own social media interests, but also those of one's competitors.

Topsy

Topsy (http://topsy.com) provides both a free service and a pro version, both of which allow arbitrary querying of Twitter data. The list of corresponding tweets can be filtered by time, content, and language. The system provides a basic overview of the general sentiment – positive or negative – among the tweets and provides a timeline that can be used to compare the number of tweets for different topics. While the analytics that can be performed here are simple, they do provide a more detailed view of the data than the search feature provided by Twitter itself. The pro version allows for more detailed analysis, such as the extraction of topics, geospatial representations, and sentiment analysis.

Hashtracking

Hashtracking (www.hashtracking.com) supports querying Twitter and Instagram data based on specific hashtags. The free version provides the list of search results, along with analytics tools that summarise the type of interaction (e.g., original tweets, re-tweets, messages) and rank the users that are contributing to the topic based on followers and the number of tweets. Advanced features in the pay-for-use version provide analytic tools including timelines, geospatial representations, word clouds, and comparisons of topics.

These advanced approaches are generally focused on account tracking, managerial reporting, or following a specific hashtag or arbitrary query and provide a high-level analysis of the social media data. However, there is often a need to dig deeper into what people are saying on Twitter. These tasks can be supported by commercial qualitative data analysis software, or cutting-edge research prototypes.

NVivo NCapture

NVivo (www.qsrinternational.com) is a popular qualitative analysis toolkit which includes a feature to support the import of web-based resources for further analysis. NCapture can be used to query Twitter, relying on the built-in search features of this platform itself. The tweets and additional metadata are stored in a tabular format and can be analysed using the full range of features provided by NVivo.

Leximancer

Leximancer (http://info.leximancer.com) is a popular text analytics software package that supports the lexical analysis of text, including concept clustering and sentiment analysis. When provided with Twitter data – extracted either manually or using software such as NCapture or the Twitter application programming interface – Leximancer can be used to analyse and visualise the connected nature of the themes within the data.

Vista   12

Vista is a research prototype developed by the authors of this chapter, for the purpose of exploring the temporally changing sentiment and emergent themes within Twitter data (Hoeber, Hoeber, El Meseery, Odoh and Gopi, in press). Much of the existing social media analytics software focuses on the production of dashboards and managerial reports or provides simple overviews of a user account or arbitrary query. The research-centric approaches either place a significant effort on the researcher to analyse the data, or include automatic analyses for the researcher. Vista was designed to balance the value of automatic analysis with the power and insight of human-guided exploration and analysis. In particular, Vista supports the interactive exploration of the sentiment, temporal, geospatial and topical elements of Twitter data. A social media analytics case study of discovering emergent themes within sport-based Twitter data is provided later in this chapter.

Analytics pitfalls and best practices

In deciding which tools or approaches to adopt for social media analytics, sport managers should be mindful of some pitfalls and strive to follow best practices.

Pitfalls   13

Analysis without purpose. It is easy to get caught up in running analyses of social media data, because there is so much data; however, this results in analysis without purpose. While managers can explore the data, they need to have some ideas of what to look for.

Overreliance on automated approaches. Another pitfall is reliance on the computer to do the analytical work. Sentiment analysis often incorporates a supervised learning approach, whereby existing collections of text, tagged with a specific sentiment or emotion, are used to classify new text (Feldman, 2013). While this approach can speed up the analysis process, automated classification is not always accurate or valid. For example, outside of the sport world, the word 'fight' is usually associated with a negative sentiment (e.g., conflict, physical assault). In contrast, in the sport context, fight may be associated with a positive sentiment; for example, a 'fight to the finish' implies a close battle. Managers should also be involved in the analytical process because of the contextual nature of human behaviour and language.

Lack of critical analysis. Some social media analysis – particularly in the academic field – has been critiqued for being too descriptive and formulaic (Hardin, 2014;

Hutchins, 2014). There is a tendency to assume that what is presented in social media is reflective of larger societal trends; however, as Billings (2014) pointed out, 'Twitter is worth studying because it is *not at all* representative of any generalized population' (p. 108). Managers, therefore, need to critique who is using Twitter (and other social media platforms) and how it is having an impact both within and outside the sport world.

Best practices

Mindful sampling. Twitter provides an exciting opportunity to explore data from temporal, social, and interactive dimensions. Yet, random samples compromise an understanding of these dimensions. Tools that allow the collection of large Twitter datasets also allow for the purposeful selection of smaller subsamples, such as a set of tweets related to a specific topic or from a specific group of users (Foucault Welles, 2014; Hoeber *et al.*, in press).

Adherence to ethical principles. Many social media platforms are viewed as public information. While this information may be easily available to the general public, we need to carefully consider the ethical implications of using this data. People are not expecting that their comments or photos will be used for other purposes, such as research or marketing (Boyd and Crawford, 2012). Boyd and Crawford (2012) stated that 'data may be public (or semi-public) but this does not simplistically equate with full permission being given for all uses' (p. 673).

Computational support, but human control. While there is a broad range of auto-mated text mining approaches that can be applied to social media data, tools that permit human control or direction are more appropriate and meaningful than ones that rely exclusively on automated analysis.

Informative and varied visualisation. Sport managers should look for tools that provide informative visualisations of the data, at both the overview and detail levels. They should also look for ones that allow for different ways to see the data, such as the geospatial, temporal, and relational aspects of it. For example, beyond our own work in Vista, the social network aspect of Twitter can be examined by visualising re-tweets (Lotan, 2011), clustering the user and message contents of the tweets (Cheong and Lee, 2010) and visualising summaries of tweets using hierar-chical tag clouds (Archambault, Greene, Cunningham and Hurley, 2011).

Case study

To illustrate the value and benefits of combining automated analyses with human control in analysing Twitter data, we present a case study using Vista to explore the tweets posted during the 2013 Tour de France. This mega-sport event was held from 29 June to 21 July 2013, with cyclists racing every day except for two rest days. The event is broadcast globally, with a large and dedicated following. The event organisers actively promoted the use of Twitter, publicising their own Twitter account (@letour) as well as a specific hashtag to use when discussing the event (#tdf).

Using this official hashtag for the event, a dataset of over 409,000 tweets was collected during the three-week period of the event. In this case study, we show how Vista can provide a visual overview of this large collection of tweets, assess how high-level patterns within these tweets can be identified with respect to the positive, neutral, or negative sentiments, and how analysts can zoom into a smaller temporal range in order to study the patterns in greater detail. We explain how the data can be filtered with sub-queries, either selected from the top hashtags, terms, user mentions, and authors or entered by the analyst based on specific interest, supporting interactive discovery, and exploration of the topics embedded within the data. This filtering and exploration process provides a mechanism for selecting a meaningful subset of the data, which can be inspected and exported for further analysis using other qualitative research tools such as NVivo.

An initial visual inspection of the data (see Figure 18.1) shows that there are many more neutral tweets than positive or negative ones; this is an indication of the large number of informational tweets that are posted during a live sporting event (e.g., score or position updates, overall event status updates, and links to images and videos of the live action). This visual overview also shows daily spikes of tweets that are occurring at regular points in the race, highlighting the bursty nature of the data. Some of the spikes are higher than others indicating more tweet activities related to specific micro events during the race. The top hashtag per sentiment is #tdf – the official event hashtag. After that we can see hashtags related to particular athletes (e.g., #vavafroome for Chris Froome), the sport (e.g., #cycling), and the significance of the event (e.g., #tdf100 for the hundredth anniversary of the event in 2013).

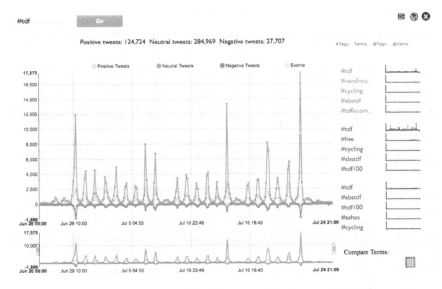

Figure 18.1 Temporal distributions of all of the tweets for the event (including two days before and two days after)

In Figure 18.1, one can readily identify that the two highest bursts occurred on the first (29 June) and last days (21 July) of the event. It is reasonable to expect a significant amount of Twitter activity on the final stage of the event, as the overall winner is decided. Additionally, there was likely significant discussion of the conclusion of the hundredth running of Le Tour de France. The heightened activity at Stage 1 (29 June), however, warranted further examination, since the Twitter activity exceeded what one would expect for the start of the race. Using the zoom feature allowed us to examine the Twitter activity in more detail during the first day of the race (see Figure 18.2). Here we can see a considerable amount of tweeting happening around 3:00 p.m. – near the end of the stage. There were over 2,000 neutral posts and 422 negative posts at that time.

Zooming further into this data, we isolated a two-hour window for more detailed inspection (see Figure 18.3). This was particularly interesting in that there were a relatively high number of negative posts, suggesting that a negative incident had occurred during the event. From here we could inspect the tweets to determine the nature or context of what people were discussing. By clicking on one of the points in the timeline, we could see that people were tweeting about a bus – also referred to as a coach – crashing into the finish line. Team buses travel along the route of the race, and park near each stage's finish line. On this day, one team's bus hit a banner above the finish line and got stuck with just minutes left before the first cyclist was due to finish.

A subquery of the data allowed us to explore how the official organisers (@letour) handled this situation (see Figure 18.4). This feature highlights the value of searching the data to understand how organisations use Twitter for crisis

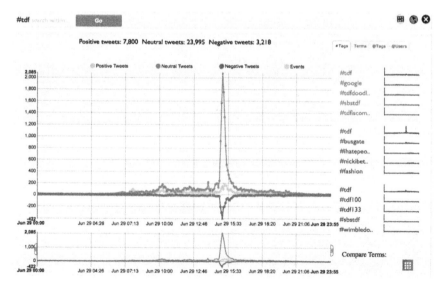

Figure 18.2 Zooming into the first day of the race at five-minute intervals shows a sudden peak in neutral and negative posts near 3:00 p.m

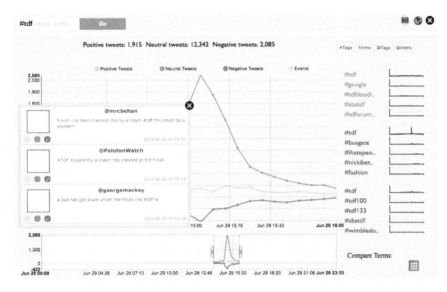

Figure 18.3 Looking at a two-hour span more clearly shows the abnormal spike in Twitter traffic; examination of the tweets revealed that people were tweeting about a bus crash

communication (Brown *et al.*, 2015; Procter, Vis and Voss, 2013). A manual inspection of the individual tweets posted by the official organisers showed that they provided basic, descriptive information about the bus crash (e.g., 'Bus crash changes finish', 'Finish: 3 km shorter than planned'). There were few details related to any

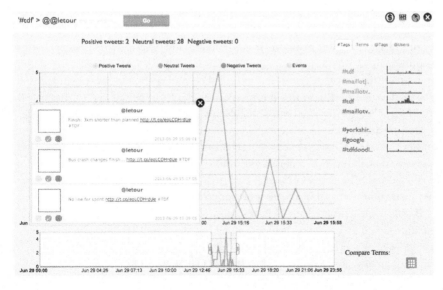

Figure 18.4 Viewing the official @letour tweets at this same time period shows the organisation's response to the crash

injuries to spectators or team staff, or how the crash may have impacted the cyclists' strategies. Further qualitative analysis could be done to determine if other stakeholders (e.g., cycling teams, fans) provided different details in their description of the incident or how they responded to the posts from the event organisers.

Managerial implications

Visual analytics approaches, such as Vista, provide powerful mechanisms for observing and understanding numerous sport management activities, processes, and issues that occur within the realm of social media. These include those related to sport communication, sport marketing, sponsorship, and consumer behaviour, but also in the areas of human resource management, leadership, sport tourism, risk management, and sociocultural issues. Even with the user-centric and managerial-focused social media analytics software that have become commonplace, there is value in monitoring and analysing – at a deeper level – the content and activity associated with social media posts. While we provide a few examples of managerial implications, sport managers must be aware of the multiple ways in which social media influences sport.

As noted earlier, sport managers need to stay abreast of the latest social media technology and platforms. Although managers are likely to be most aware of the platforms used by their own social cohort, they also need to be familiar with the social media that other stakeholders, target markets, or user groups are using. For example, Snapchat is currently popular with those under 20 who have long since abandoned or completely avoided Facebook, and Pinterest is more popular with women than men. But it is not enough to know about different platforms and create content for them; sport managers need to also know how to monitor social media.

Fundamentally, sport managers need to understand why analytics of social media is important. From a marketing perspective, analytics can be used to better understand the behaviours and interests of their audiences and users (Murthy and Bowman, 2014), and with this information, content can be tailored to these users (Corrigan, 2014). Advanced tools can also be used to monitor and analyse stakeholders' opinions and sentiments about relevant issues. These may include issues specifically related to sport teams (e.g., changes in team colours, player trades), sport events, and facilities (e.g., security, location) or sponsors (e.g., appropriateness), but they could also be larger societal issues, such as environmentalism, race relations, and social unrest, that impact the sport industry (Murthy and Bowman, 2014).

People expect immediate responses and communication, particularly in crisis situations, such as weather warnings, unstable community relations, or viral comments. When a crisis strikes, a sport organisation should immediately employ carefully orchestrated crisis response strategies in order to minimise the impact on the organisational reputation. Brown, Brown, and Dickhaus (2014) argued that 'in the new era of social media, sports organizations have … lost some of the control they once possessed over the crisis narrative' (p. 177).

Social media analytics tools provide a means for monitoring situations based on citizen reporting, allowing the organisation to intervene in a timely manner (Brown *et al.*, 2015). Further, identities and discourses are constructed, framed, and shaped via social media (Bruce and Hardin, 2014; Meân, 2014; Vincent and Kian, 2014). Sport managers need to be aware of the discourses associated with athletes, coaches, officials, management, and so forth. Such discourses are created and shaped within social media – although not exclusively – in the context of critical issues such as ability, social class, gender and race and ethnicity. Social media is a powerful place for this construction because the general public is part of the process – not just the elites – and the construction happens in real time.

We recognise that the most significant management challenge with monitoring and analysing social media is finding tools to enable these activities. Many sport organisations do not have the capacity to develop their own tools for visual analytics. One option is to keep track of analytical tools that permit exploration and monitoring of social media content and trends – we have provided a few options in this chapter. Another option is for sport organisations to partner with technology, information technology, or software development companies to design and develop software or tools to assist them with this task (Hoeber and Hoeber, 2012).

Conclusion and outlook

Knowledge is a critical resource in today's society and social media is a source of knowledge. As stated earlier, it is not enough that sport managers be aware of and provide content for social media platforms. Rather, sport managers must be able to find relevant information and understand that information within social media. Doing so allows sport managers to make informed decisions, address risks, recognise and respond to trends and shape sport discourse, in addition to communicating with key players in the sport world.

Social media is an ever-changing landscape. While we can expect it to transform and reshape itself in the coming years, what is certain is that it is not going away. Because of the abundance of information being generated, there is a need to develop robust and scalable ways for making sense of what people have to say on social media as well as the context in which they say it. The constant difficulty is the textual and visual nature of this data, both of which pose significant analysis challenges even in well-controlled circumstances. What is needed out of social media analytics software is not just confirmation of what we know, but actionable insight into what is unknown. We must, therefore, strive to harness the information that is being made available, and not let the information harness us.

References

Archambault, D., Greene, D., Cunningham, P. and Hurley, N. (2011). ThemeCrowds: multiresolution summaries of Twitter usage. In I. Cantador, F. M. Carrero, J. C. Cortizo,

P. Rosso, M. Schedl and J. A. Troyano (eds) *Proceedings of the International Workshop on Search and Mining User-Generated Contents* (pp. 77–84). doi:10.1145/2065023.2065041

Billings, A. (2014). Power in the reverberation: Why Twitter matters, but not the way most believe. *Communication and Sport, 2*, 107–112. doi:10.1177/2167479514527427

Boyd, D. and Crawford, K. (2012). Critical questions for Big Data. *Information, Communication and Society, 15*, 662–679. doi:10.1080/1369118X.2012.678878

Brown, N. A., Brown, K. A. and Billings, A. C. (2015). 'May no act of ours bring shame': Fan-enacted crisis communication surrounding the Penn State sex abuse scandal. *Communication and Sport*. Advance online publication. doi:10.1177/2167479513514387

Brown, N. A., Brown, K. A. and Dickhaus, J. (2014). When crisis strikes: The evolution of sports crisis communication research in an era of new media. In A. C. Billings and M. Hardin (eds) *Routledge handbook of sport and new media* (pp. 177–188). London, United Kingdom: Routledge.

Bruce, T. and Hardin, M. (2014). Reclaiming our voices: Sportswomen and social media. In A. C. Billings and M. Hardin (eds) *Routledge handbook of sport and new media* (pp. 311–319). New York: Routledge.

Cheong, M. and Lee, V. (2010). A study on detecting patterns in Twitter intra-topic user and message clustering. In *Proceedings of the International Conference on Pattern Recognition* (pp. 3125–3128). doi:10.1109/ICPR.2010.765

Corrigan, T. F. (2014). The political economy of sports and new media. In A. C. Billings and M. Hardin (eds) *Routledge handbook of sport and new media* (pp. 43–54). London: Routledge.

Feldman, R. (2013). Techniques and applications for sentiment analysis. *Communications of the ACM, 56*, 82–89. doi:10.1145/2436256.2436274

Filo, K., Lock, D. and Karg, A. (2015). Sport and social media research: A review. *Sport Management Review, 18*, 166–181. doi:10.1016/j.smr.2014.11.001

Foucault Welles, B. (2014). On minorities and outliers: The case for making Big Data small. *Big Data and Society, 1*, 1–2. doi:10.1177/2053951714540613

Hambrick, M. E., Simmons, J. M., Greenhalgh, G. P. and Greenwell, T. C. (2010). Understanding professional athletes' use of Twitter: A content analysis of athlete tweets. *International Journal of Sport Communication, 3*, 454–471. Retrieved from http://journals.humankinetics.com/ijsc

Hardin, M. (2014). Moving beyond description: Putting Twitter in (theoretical) context. *Communication and Sport, 2*, 113–116. doi:10.1177/2167479514527425

Hoeber, L. and Hoeber, O. (2012). Determinants of an innovation process : A case study of technological innovation in a community sport organization. *Journal of Sport Management, 26*, 213–223. Retrieved from http://journals.humankinetics.com/jsm

Hoeber, O., Hoeber, L., El Meseery, M., Odoh, K. and Gopi, R. (in press). Visual Twitter analytics (Vista): Temporally changing sentiment and the discovery of emergent themes within sport event tweets. *Online Information Review*.

Hutchins, B. (2011). The acceleration of media sport culture. *Information, Communication and Society, 14*, 237–257. doi:10.1080/1369118X.2010.508534

Hutchins, B. (2014). Twitter: Follow the money and look beyond sports. *Communication and Sport, 2*, 122–126. doi:10.1177/2167479514527430

Kassing, J. W. and Sanderson, J. (2010). Tweeting through the Giro: A case study of fan-athlete interaction on Twitter. *International Journal of Sport Communication, 3*, 113–128. Retrieved from http://journals.humankinetics.com/ijsc

Lewis, S. C., Zamith, R. and Hermida, A. (2013). Content analysis in an era of big data: A hybrid approach to computational and manual methods. *Journal of Broadcasting and Electronic Media, 57*, 34–52. doi:10.1080/08838151.2012.761702

Lotan, G. (2011). Mapping information flows on Twitter. In *Proceedings of the ICWSM Workshop on the Future of the Social Web* (pp. 23–27). Retrieved from www.aaai.org

Mahrt, M. and Scharkow, M. (2013). The value of Big Data in digital media research. *Journal of Broadcasting and Electronic Media, 57*, 20–33. doi:10.1080/08838151.2012.761700

Meân, L. J. (2014). Sport websites, embedded discursive action, and the gendered reproduction of sport. In A. C. Billings and M. Hardin (eds) *Routledge handbook of sport and new media* (pp. 331–341). New York: Routledge.

Murthy, D. (2012). Towards a sociological understanding of social media: Theorizing Twitter. *Sociology, 46*, 1059–1073. doi:10.1177/0038038511422553

Murthy, D. and Bowman, S. A. (2014). Big Data solutions on a small scale: Evaluating accessible high-performance computing for social research. *Big Data and Society, 1*, 1–12. doi:10.1177/2053951714559105

O'Connor, B., Balasubramanyan, R., Routledge, B. R. and Smith, N. A. (2010). From tweets to polls: Linking text sentiment to public opinion time series. In M. Hearst (ed.) *Proceedings of the International AAAI Conference on Weblogs and Social Media* (pp. 122–129). Retrieved from www.aaai.org/Library/ICWSM/icwsm10contents.php

Pegoraro, A. (2010). Look who's talking – athletes on Twitter: A case study. *International Journal of Sport Communication, 3*, 501–514. Retrieved from http://journals.human kinetics.com/ijsc

Procter, R., Vis, F. and Voss, A. (2013). Reading the riots on Twitter: Methodological innovation for the analysis of big data. *International Journal of Social Research Methodology, 16*, 197–214. doi:10.1080/13645579.2013.774172

Tinati, R., Halford, S., Carr, L. and Pope, C. (2014). Big data: Methodological challenges and approaches for sociological analysis. *Sociology, 48*, 663–681. doi:10.1177/0038038 513511561

Vincent, J. and Kian, E. M. (2014). Sport, new media, and national identity. In A. C. Billings and M. Hardin (eds) *Routledge handbook of sport and new media* (pp. 299–310). New York: Routledge.

Further reading

For further reading, see the books and journal article below. Also see the *International Journal on Sport Communication*; *Communication and Sport, Big Data and Society*; and the Proceedings of the MIT Sloan Sports Analytics Conference.

Billings, A. C. and Hardin, M. (eds). (2014). *Routledge handbook of sport and new media*. London: Routledge.

Filo, K., Lock, D. and Karg, A. (2015). Sport and social media research: A review. *Sport Management Review, 18*, 166–181. doi:10.1016/j.smr.2014.11.001

Fu, Y. (ed.). (2014). *Human-centered social media analytics*. Cham, Switzerland: Springer.

19

DIGITAL TECHNOLOGY AND SPORT SPONSORSHIP

Christopher Rumpf and Christoph Breuer

An increasing interest in sport as a branding platform is evident in the annual sponsorship growth rate of 5.2 per cent in the Asian-Pacific market. Worldwide sponsorship expenditures are projected to reach US $60.2 billion in 2016 still outperforming traditional forms of marketing in terms of growth (International Events Group, 2016). Many companies invest a significant share of their marketing budget in sport properties with the goal of building associations between their brand and a popular sport property. In order to exploit the commercial potential of such associations, companies actively communicate their involvement in the event – or any other property – to stakeholders. Sponsors, therefore, place signage around popular sport events, teams, or athletes, in almost any area of major sports.

Despite the steady growth of sponsorships, their marketing effectiveness compared with alternative communication instruments is unclear. Since sponsorship investments fall into a broad set of marketing communication options, it is likely that marketing managers will only invest in a sponsorship activity if it serves the overall marketing objectives more effectively and efficiently than alternative investment options (Breuer and Rumpf, 2012). Digital technologies facilitate the impact of most general marketing activities. The following chapter will discuss how far the adoption of digital technology can also enhance the effectiveness and efficiency of sport sponsorship.

The chapter consists of two sections. In the first section, new technology-based measurements, recently employed to better analyse the effectiveness of sport sponsorship platforms, are introduced. The section will provide a general understanding about the application and usefulness of automatic measurement techniques such as eye tracking, the Implicit Association Test (IAT), and electroencephalography (EEG) in sponsorship research.

In the second section, a media technology known as digital overlay is introduced. Digital overlays allow sponsors to communicate variable brand messages in different geographical markets. This technology has already been implemented in four major sport leagues and might have fundamentally changed the sponsorship market.

Finally, managerial implications of digital technologies in sponsorship research and practice are discussed, followed by a brief summary and future direction of sport sponsorship.

Digital technology in sponsorship research

Most sponsors invest in a sponsorship to connect their brand with emotional experiences in situations where the consumer is critically engaged; for example, in a football match or car race (Cornwall, 2014). Brand messages in these events are directly communicated to the on-site spectator or indirectly to the wider media audience via traditional media (e.g., TV, newspaper) and new media (e.g., social media).

Considering the key marketing objective of connecting the brand to the emotional character of sports, the measurement of sponsorship effectiveness should be suitable to capture (a) the visual processing of brand stimuli in cluttered environments and (b) the emotional perception of brands as an outcome of visual processing. It is claimed that self-reported data (e.g., gained through questionnaires) barely capture these constructs since consumers can hardly recall their viewing behaviour and emotional perception (Pessoa, 2005); therefore, there is an urgent need to seek new research techniques to assess sponsorship effectiveness. In this section, three technology-based measurements – eye tracking, IAT, and EEG – are critically discussed in terms of their application and usefulness relative to self-reported measures.

Eye tracking

The function of eye tracking is to measure the reflection of infrared light to record the position of the pupils and a reflection point on the eye (corneal reflex) as horizontal and vertical coordinate values. Based on the ratio between the pupils' position and the position of the corneal reflex, the system calculates the direction of the gaze, independent from head movements. While the gaze direction is tracked, a scene camera captures the test person's field of vision. To measure brand gaze hits and brand glance, the gaze coordinates are matched with the individual scene film on a frame-by-frame basis with a frequency of at least 60Hz (Holmqvist et al., 2011). Figure 19.1 shows an eye-tracking heat map taken from a study on viewer attention in Formula One.

Sponsorship as a visual communication tool can only be successful if sport viewers pay a sufficient amount of attention to the sponsor's message (Breuer and Rumpf, 2012). Therefore, the analysis of brand gaze hits and brand glance duration means a significant first step in the evaluation of sponsorship effectiveness. Eye tracking is a useful technique to study these parameters both on-site and in a sport media environment (Duchowski, 2007).

Figure 19.1 An image of an eye-tracking heat map in Formula 1

Eye tracking provides valuable insights into the effectiveness of sponsorship communication strategies, particularly within a controlled experimental research design. Further, cause–effect relationships can be assessed through the systematic manipulation of visual properties of brand stimuli (e.g., colour, form, motion). For example, Breuer and Rumpf (2015) recently assessed the impact of colour variables and different types of animation in a lab setting. Sport broadcasts were manipulated in terms of brand colour and animation and then presented to a sport-interested sample. Breuer and Rumpf found that light- and high-contrast colours as well as certain types of animation (e.g., blinking) facilitate the visual perception of brands during TV sport consumption.

Such evidence-based findings enable researchers and managers to better understand the drivers of successful brand communications in emotionally loaded environments. Such environments are characterised by their potential to arouse strong emotional reactions among the audience such as sport events or concerts. For example, in another eye-tracking study, Rumpf, Noël, Breuer, and Memmert (2015) found that brand placements during highly arousing scenes are less likely to be visually processed and, therefore, branding objectives might not be met in high-arousal environments. They suggested that an individual's perception of brand stimuli in more exciting environments might have to compete with perception of a larger frequency of more intense stimuli. Therefore, Rumpf *et al.* also argued that a moderate level of surrounding intensity for brand placements is preferable.

Despite its evident strengths, eye tracking does not reveal if brands are significantly associated with the emotional sport experience. The challenge of measuring brand-related emotions is that they occur, to a large extent, unconsciously (Bal, Quester and Plewa, 2010). Thus, brand emotions cannot be validly retrieved through traditional questionnaires; a promising psychophysiological approach is EEG, which measures electrical activity along the scalp. If a participant has an emotional association to a brand, certain brain areas will be activated approximately 300 milliseconds after viewing this brand stimulus. Building on the 'oddball paradigm' (i.e., an experimental design in which the presentation of neutral stimuli is interrupted by target stimuli), event-related potentials are measured for the brand stimulus in comparison with neutral stimuli. Due to plenty of noise in EEG data, the target stimulus (i.e., brand) is randomly presented 15 to 20 times within a set of 150 to 200 neutral images (Luck, 2014).

Electroencephalography

It makes good sense to use eye tracking in combination with EEG. In a first attempt, the authors presented virtually embedded brand stimuli to participants in a manipulated video treatment in an experimental study assessing the emotional impact of sponsorship-linked communication on brand perceptions. Subsequently, the test brand was displayed in a neutral context on a computer screen. Whereas eye tracking was used to measure the frequency and duration of gaze contacts 4 during the video treatment, EEG data indicated the cortical reaction to repeated brand exposure. Based on both data sources, the relationship between visual processing and emotional reaction was analysed. Figure 19.2 shows a participant during EEG data recording.

The Implicit Association Test

Even though EEG is a powerful method of measuring cortical reactions as an indicator of emotions, it does not provide an understanding about the valence of such emotions. The IAT can, therefore, be used as a supplement to EEG. The IAT

Figure 19.2 Image of EEG data recording

is based on the assumption that respondents can react faster to objects if they fit into a particular category. Applied to sponsorship research, the IAT can be used to assess implicit (i.e., unconscious) associations with the brand.

With the help of a computer-based procedure, the participant is asked to classify pleasant and unpleasant pictures taken from the International Affective Picture System (Lang, Bradley and Cuthbert, 2008) by pressing either a left or right key. This task is done as quickly as possible to elicit an automatic (i.e., affective) reaction rather than a conscious reflection of the decision. In the next block, the test brand appears in between a similar set of pleasant and unpleasant pictures. The participant is then asked to classify the pictures (i.e., select *pleasant* or *unpleasant*). Following the logic of the original IAT (Greenwald, McGhee and Schwartz 1998; Greenwald, Nosek and Banaji, 2003), the reaction time is assumed to be shorter if the key is compatible to the perceived valence of the brand.

Compared with traditional approaches such as data collection via questionnaires, the advanced methods described above have the potential to provide less biased data. This is due to the fact that they measure outcomes to sponsorship activities without the conscious introspection required for self-reporting. Thus, deeper and more valid insights into the inner working of sponsorship communication can be achieved through the application of technology-based methods.

Digital technology for advanced sponsorship communication

Most companies nowadays operate in various countries around the world. To touch upon a worldwide customer base, marketing communication is often adapted to country-specific needs and preferences. For example, a car manufacturing company heavily promoting its sport utility vehicle in the U.S. market possibly sells most premium cars in China and might be most successful in the French market with its compact car. Accordingly, the car manufacturer would run separate marketing campaigns in all these geographical markets.

Even though most major sport events are broadcast worldwide, international companies cannot make full use of the global audience reach due to inflexible sponsor signage. That is, the brand messages on the perimeter boards exposed to the U.S., Chinese and French sport TV viewers is literally the same. However, global companies which use sports as a branding platform demand greater interactivity, territorial specificity, and flexibility from sport properties which have to keep up the pace with the changing media landscape (Tom, Tyre and Waln, 2008). The lack of adaptability of sponsorship communication can be regarded as a major disadvantage compared to alternative marketing approaches, and thus, a threat to the further growth of corporate spending.

Traditionally, sport properties, such as leagues or teams, have a sponsorship portfolio including one main sponsor, several premium sponsors, and co-sponsors. The categorisation of sponsors is often denoted as a pyramid, placing the main sponsor at the top and the co-sponsors at the bottom of the pyramid. By becoming part of the sponsorship pyramid, a company obtains the right to use the league or team as a marketing communication platform. However, the number of sponsors in the pyramid is usually limited to about ten to 15 brands. Consequently, sport properties can only increase their sponsorship revenues by marking up the fee per sponsor.

A technological approach which could help to overcome the aforementioned shortcomings is called *digital overlay*, a media technique which allows inserting a virtual brand message – static or animated – during the ongoing live broadcasting of a sport event. Such virtual brand messages can be placed onto, for example, the perimeter board around a pitch and are visible only to the TV broadcasting audience in a certain territory. Given the ability of digital overlay to simultaneously cater to multiple markets with different sponsor messages, it has the potential to fundamentally change the sponsorship business of the future.

By applying digital overlay technology, sport properties could affix different brand messages on visible locations (e.g., perimeter boards, interview backdrop) for different territories in which the corporate sponsor is operating. In this way, digital overlay is also termed *virtual overlay*, or *virtual advertisement*, and enables sport properties to reposition sponsorship – one of their most important financing instruments – as a more targeted form of marketing communication. It allows sport properties to trade sponsorship rights in a country-specific manner, and thus, maximise revenue. The time and space on a perimeter board would be offered to different sponsors in different countries and could engage local and global sponsors. As a result, sponsorship communication rights would be traded as more customised solutions to companies.

Further, digital overlays give existing sponsors the opportunity to change their brand message according to game and country. For example, Sponsor X would present a German brand message to the TV audience in Germany, whereas the same sponsor would present a Chinese brand message located in the same spot to the Chinese TV audience. Further, cognitive psychologists Masuda and Nisbett (2006) suggested that visual perception and cognitive information processing differs between cultures. Sponsor X could, therefore, adapt the design of the brand message to different cultural backgrounds. For example, the use of colours and animations should be ideally adjusted to the cultural background of a customer segment. The increased flexibility in terms of presenting territorial specific brand messages could be of high value to corporate sponsors, in particular when it comes to international events which are typically followed by huge TV audiences in different countries.

Moreover, digital overlays can be used as a means to overcome the prohibition on promotion of alcohol and/or tobacco in many countries. Such legal prohibitions can be avoided by simply replacing the alcohol and/or tobacco brand with another brand message. For example, Saudi Arabia has no legal restriction on the advertisement of tobacco; therefore, the application of digital overlays can extend potential marketing attraction to the multinational tobacco brands to sponsor the event if being broadcast in Saudi Arabia. Likewise, all other territorial specific prohibitions could be resolved through digital overlay.

Figure 19.3 Image of digital overlays in the Dutch Football League Eredivisie

An early adopter of this technology, the Dutch Football League Eredivisie has made use of digitals overlays since 2011 to place virtual sponsor signage next to the goals without compromising the screen flexibility and high-quality production. Figure 19.3 depicts a scene from a football broadcast in the Eredivisie where two sponsor messages have been virtually embedded into the live footage using the digital overlay technology. Recently, the Spanish La Liga, the American NFL, and the Italian Seria have implemented the technology, while other leagues, such as the German Football Bundesliga, are still testing the latest technological advancements.

Internationalisation strategies as a driver of digital overlays

A growing number of professional sport properties expend internationally to create a larger media audience and fan bases for their events around the world (Dolles and Söderman, 2005). For example, leading European football clubs, such as Liverpool FC, AS Rome, and Bayern Munich, have opened sales offices in the United States. English football club Manchester City has even gone a step further by building a joint venture with the American baseball team the New York Yankees to reach strategic goals in the U.S. market (Sandomir, 2014).

Another recent example is the German football club Borussia Dortmund, which signed a regional sponsorship contract with the Japanese travel agency, Highest International Standards (H.I.S.; Connolly, 2015). In exchange for their spending, H.I.S. is able to exploit Borussia Dortmund's growing fan base in Japan. With the help of digital overlay, it would be possible to show the association between the brand and club by embedding the H.I.S. message on the perimeter board during the live broadcast of Borussia Dortmund home games. Given the popularity of the club among Japanese football fans, digital overlays would attract other companies to join as one of Borussia Dortmund's official sponsors in Japan and benefit from in-game visibility.

Further, the international cooperation between FC Bayern Munich and Tmall Global – a Chinese online shopping platform – could presumably benefit from the digital overlay technology. Tmall Global will soon launch an official FC Bayern Munich online shop for consumers in China; with the new online shop, over 90 million Chinese football fans will be able to purchase official FC Bayern Munich fan merchandise products. Considering that Tmall Global is only operating in the Chinese market, the online shop's brand visibility in countries other than China would be irrelevant. Thus, consumer awareness of Tmall Global as a provider of FC Bayern Munich official fan merchandise could be addressed efficiently by the use of digital overlay during the home games broadcast in China (DHL International, 2015).

As a pioneer in the internationalisation of sport teams, English football club Manchester United has been successful in building a global fan base over the last few decades. To exploit its high popularity, particularly in the Asian market, Manchester United has created country-specific sponsorships. For example, the official telecommunication sponsor of Manchester United differs around the globe: 'TM' in Malaysia, 'STC' in Saudi Arabia, 'Viva' in West Africa, 'TrueMove' in Thailand, and 'PCCW Global' in Hong Kong (Turner, 2014). Though not implemented yet, digital overlay would provide sponsors the opportunity to generate brand visibility during Manchester United's home games in their respective territories.

Two of the U.S. major leagues, the NBA and the MLB, are also developing international markets. In 2013, the NBA played ten games in six countries and opened its first Indian office in Mumbai. To ensure high media coverage, the NBA commissioner has signed a deal with an Indian TV station, providing the channel with exclusive broadcasting rights in India and to host several basketball events across the country (Riches, 2013). NBA broadcasts in emerging countries, such as India, offer sponsors additional value provided that these companies are targeting a customer base in this market. Thus, the added value for the existing sponsors would justify an increase in sponsorship fees.

However, the NBA's sponsorship portfolio also includes companies which only focus on the U.S. market and thus, do not gain any benefits from their sponsor logo exposure in foreign markets. In this case, the use of digital overlay means a straightforward solution to replace such sponsor brands with a local sponsor from the foreign market. Thus, the digital overlay technology has the potential to maximise NBA sponsorship revenues by making country-specific sponsorship contracts.

Similarly, one of the most popular football leagues in the world – the UEFA Champions League – generates larger audiences outside Europe than within the continent itself. Thus, digital overlay technology offers an enormous potential for existing sponsors to communicate more pinpointed sponsor messages in non-European markets. Further, the technology would enable the UEFA to increase its sponsorship revenues through additional sponsorship deals – for example, selling specific sponsorship communication rights in the Asian-Pacific market.

Sport marketing agencies as facilitators of digital overlays

There is an ongoing trend in the international sports business that sport properties sell their media and/or marketing rights to intermediate players which have the competencies to handle these rights more efficiently (Cornwall, 2008). Such sport marketing agencies buy national and international media and marketing rights and sell these rights to the broadcasting stations and corporate sponsors in various countries across the globe. For example, one of the leading sports marketing agencies, Sportfive, has recently traded the media rights for the Rio 2016 Olympics in 40 territories of Europe. Building on a well-coordinated trading process, Sportfive is able to generate higher income than costs; that is, the revenue gained through country-specific selling of broadcasting rights exceeds the fixed amount paid to the sport property and the operating costs.

Through digital overlays, sport marketing agencies can expand their ambit and sell sponsorship rights not only to a limited number of international brands which are interested in worldwide brand exposure during a sport event. Also, regional sponsors from a certain territory would be interested in buying a regional sponsorship right. Digital overlay has the potential to create a mutually beneficial situation for both the sport properties that can charge a higher surplus in exchange for their marketing rights and the sponsors which are naturally interested in more efficient brand communication solutions. As it clearly serves the generic business model, sports marketing agencies have an obvious interest in the application of digital overlays. In addition, international sports marketing agencies, such as Sportfive or IMG, have the market power to push the technology further, as they control large portions of the sponsorship market.

Potential downsides of digital overlays

After discussing the marketing potential of digital overlay technology, it is equally important to critically evaluate the potential downsides. Critics claim that the integrity of sports will be at risk because broadcast media will manipulate sport events by inserting virtual signage during the game. The decision-makers in the German Football Bundesliga are, therefore, still sceptical about using digital overlays. They argue that the current technology cannot perfectly detect players and the ball appearing in front of perimeter boards. Further, heavy rain or snow still means a technical challenge for digital overlays. As a consequence, virtually embedded brand messages could stand out against the environment, and thus, reduce sport TV viewers' overall viewing experience.

Issues may also arise with regard to premium brands, such as Mercedes-Benz. For example, Carrillat, Harris, and Lafferty (2010) found that premium brands prefer visibility in a clean and exclusive environment because image attributes spill over not only between sport properties and sponsor brands, but also among concurrent sponsors. With the advent of digital overlays, it will become difficult for sponsors to control for the quality of exposure with regard to clutter and dubious co-sponsors. The uncertainty about the concurrent sponsors in certain territories might induce premium brands to withdraw their sponsorship investments.

Managerial implications

As a basis for rational decision-making, marketing managers require solid data on the effectiveness and efficiency of sponsorship activities in the planning, implementation, and evaluation stage. Traditionally, decisions are based on media exposure figures and sponsor-awareness ratings. However, such data can neither explain the sport-viewer attention devoted to brand messages nor the consumers' emotional reactions to sponsor brands. To gain a deeper understanding about the effectiveness of sponsorship activities, this chapter suggests taking into account a more sophisticated set of research methods.

With the help of eye-tracking studies, marketing managers can learn about the optimal positioning and design of sponsor messages. To maximise viewer attention, marketing managers should place brand messages in positions where the intensity of sport action is at a moderate level. Further, the use of light colours compared with dark colours might increase the saliency of brand messages. A higher level of colour contrast is also able to facilitate viewer attention (Breuer and Rumpf, 2015).

Further, the IAT and EEG can be employed to better understand the preconscious and affective processing of sponsor messages. Marketing managers should use these technology-based approaches in a pre–post design to identify relative improvements in brand perception. Moreover, the effectiveness and efficiency of collateral marketing activities (e.g., social media campaigns) could be also be assessed.

Marketing managers use sponsorships to touch upon customers in various geographical markets. When it comes to internationally broadcast events, digital overlays should be used to communicate country-specific brand messages to customers in each territory. Digital overlays can also be used to enhance sponsorship efficiency as brand visibility would be limited to territories of relevance to the brand.

For professional sport properties, digital overlays mean a cost-effective way to increase their income in terms of sponsorship money. Therefore, they should further develop the technology to make it ready for regular use. At the same time, sport properties should avoid confusing sport viewers with intrusive sponsorship communication, as it may jeopardise the audience's interest in watching the sport activity (Breuer and Rumpf, 2015).

Conclusion

With the rapid evolution of digital technology, the sports industry in general and sports sponsorship in particular are going through fundamental changes. In this chapter, the impact of digital technology on both the research and the practice of sponsorship have been discussed; evidence indicates that digital technology will change the way sponsorships are managed in the future.

On the research front, technology-based methods, such as eye tracking, IAT and EEG, are now employed to provide decision-makers with deeper insights about how sponsor messages are perceived in the consumer's mind. Whereas traditional approaches of sponsorship evaluation rely on survey data, advanced methodology adapted from psychometrics and neuroscience is able to explain affective and even preconscious outcomes of sponsorship activities. Based on evidence-based insights, the return of sponsorship activities in terms of brand growth can be assessed more holistically and with greater validity.

Despite their given advantage, psychometric and neurobiological methods have thus far received limited attention in sponsorship research. This might be due to the fact that the application of these technologies is relatively costly and time-consuming. Whereas online or telephone surveys can reach large sample sizes within a few days, lab research employing eye tracking, IAT, and/or EEG techniques often takes several weeks and is typically based on rather small samples. Nevertheless, it can be assumed that advanced research techniques will be increasingly used in the future as they are able to better reflect the effectiveness of sponsorship activities.

Sponsorship communication has come a long way over the last few decades; whereas simple perimeter boards were used until the early 2000s, nowadays LED boards are predominantly employed to display sponsor messages in sport arenas. With the digital overlay technology, the next era of sponsorship communication is fast approaching. Given the global audience reach of major sport events, digital overlay means a straightforward technology to achieve a higher efficiency in sponsorship communication. Compared with the costly adoption of LED board systems, the digital overlay technology demands no investment into physical infrastructure, and thus, can be regarded as highly cost-effective.

References

Bal, C., Quester, P. and Plewa, C. (2010). Emotions and sponsorship: A key to global effectiveness? A comparative study of Australia and France. *Asia Pacific Journal of Marketing and Logistics, 22*, 40–54. doi:10.1108/13555851011013146

Breuer, C. and Rumpf, C. (2012). The viewer's reception and processing of sponsorship information in sport telecasts. *Journal of Sport Management, 26*, 521–531. Retrieved from http://journals.humankinetics.com/jsm

Breuer, C. and Rumpf, C. (2015). The impact of color and animation on the sports viewers' attention for televised sponsorship signage. *Journal of Sport Management, 29*, 170–183. doi:10.1123/jsm.2013-0280

Carrillat, F. A., Harris, E. G. and Lafferty, B. A. (2010). Fortuitous brand image transfer: Investigating the side effect of concurrent sponsorships. *Journal of Advertising, 39*, 109–123. doi:10.2753/JOA0091-3367390208

Cornwall, T. B. (2008). State of the art and science in sponsorship-linked marketing. *Journal of Advertising, 37*, 41–55. doi:10.2753/JOA0091-3367370304

Cornwall, T. B. (2014). *Sponsorship in marketing: Effective communication through sports, arts and events.* London: Routledge.

Connolly, E. (2015, January 13). Dortmund sign Japanese regional deal with HIS. *Sports Pro.* Retrieved from www.sportspromedia.com

DHL International (2015, May 27). *FC Bayern Munich launches exclusive flagship store on Tmall Global to offer official merchandise to Chinese fans* [Press release]. Retrieved from www.dhl. com/en/press/releases/releases_2015

Dolles, H. and Söderman, S. (2005). *Implementing a professional football league in Japan – challenges to research in international business.* Tokyo, Japan: German Institute for Japanese Studies.

Duchowski, A. (2007). *Eye tracking methodology: Theory and practice* (2nd ed.). London, United Kingdom: Springer.

Greenwald, A. G., McGhee, D. E. and Schwartz, J. K. L. (1998). Measuring individual differences in implicit cognition: The implicit association test. *Journal of Personality and Social Psychology, 74,* 1464–1480. doi:10.1037/0022-3514.74.6.1464

Greenwald, A. G., Nosek, B. A. and Banaji, M. R. (2003). Understanding and using the implicit association test: An improved scoring algorithm. *Journal of Personality and Social Psychology, 85,* 197–216. doi:10.1037/0022-3514.85.2.197

Holmqvist, K., Nyström, M., Andersson, R., Dewhurst, R., Jarodzka, H. and van de Weijer, J. (2011). *Eye tracking: A comprehensive guide to methods and measures.* Oxford: Oxford University Press.

International Events Group. (2016). *IEG projects global sponsorship spending to increase 4.7 percent in 2016.* Retrieved from www.sponsorship.com/About-IEG/Press-Room/IEG-Projects-Global-Sponsorship-Spending-To-Increa.aspx

Lang, P. J., Bradley, M. M. and Cuthbert, B. N. (2008). *International affective picture system (IAPS): Affective ratings of pictures and instruction manual* (Technical Report A-8). Gainesville, FL: University of Florida.

Luck, S. J. (2014). *An introduction to the event-related potential technique* (2nd ed.). Cambridge, MA: MIT Press.

Masuda, T. and Nisbett, R. E. (2006). Culture and change blindness. *Cognitive Science, 30,* 381–399. doi:10.1207/s15516709cog0000_63

Pessoa, L. (2005). To what extent are emotional visual stimuli processed without attention and awareness? *Current Opinion in Neurobiology, 15,* 188–196. doi:10.1016/j.conb.2005. 03.002

Riches, S. (2013). Basketball and globalization. *The New Yorker.* Retrieved from www.new yorker.com

Rumpf, C., Noël, B., Breuer, C. and Memmert, D. (2015). The role of context intensity and working memory capacity in the consumer's processing of brand information in entertainment media. *Psychology and Marketing, 32,* 764–770. doi:10.1002/mar.20816

Sandomir, R. (2014, July 31). Deep-pocketed Bayern Munich is open for business in US. *The New York Times.* Retrieved from www.nytimes.com

Tom, A. S., Tyre, J. and Waln, B. (2008). *Stepping beyond the 30 second spot ad with digital overlays* [White paper]. Retrieved from https://rgbnetworks.com/resources/

Turner, R. (2014, October 17). *Sports sponsorship* [White paper]. Retrieved from www.two birds.com/~/media/Sports%20sponsorship.pdf

Further reading

Breuer, C. and Rumpf, C. (2015). The impact of color and animation on the sports viewers' attention for televised sponsorship signage. *Journal of Sport Management, 29,* 170–183. doi:10.1123/jsm.2013-0280

Cornwall, T. B. (2014). *Sponsorship in marketing: Effective communication through sports, arts and events.* London, UK: Routledge.

20

CURRENT TRENDS AND FUTURE RESEARCH CHALLENGES IN GLOBAL SPORT MANAGEMENT

Stephen Frawley and Nico Schulenkorf

As outlined in Chapter 1, this book was developed with the clear intention to engage with current, critical, and applied global sport management issues. In order to achieve this aim, leading international sport management scholars have contributed 18 cutting-edge chapters dealing with the big issues that are shaping the management of sport around the globe today. In this final chapter, we as editors reflect on a number of the key debates highlighted in the book. Moreover, with the use of practical examples, we critically discuss how current issues, challenges, and emerging trends in global sport are likely to develop in the future.

Governance, integrity and welfare

The first section of the book highlights the critical importance of maintaining high levels of integrity and governance in global sport. As outlined by Ordway and Opie in Chapter 4, the challenges faced by senior sport administrators and executives in attempting to uphold the integrity of sport in the face of massive financial incentives to cheat cannot be underestimated. In particular, with the flow of vast sums of capital into professional and elite sport over the past three decades – through sources including broadcast rights, sponsorship, ticket sales and merchandise – the potential gains for athletes from cheating have escalated dramatically. Examples for systematic bribery and corruption can easily be found across different sports and leagues, including international cricket and tennis matches, professional boxing, and European top-tier football competitions. In addition to athlete involvement, the expansion of sports betting through the rise of the Internet and associated digital technologies has also provided numerous opportunities for other parties to gain from corrupt sport practices.

As suggested by Breuer and Kaiser (Chapter 5), has been a popular topic for the sport and non-sport media for a while now; however, very little work has been undertaken by journalists and/or academic researchers to examine more complex sport integrity problems, such as those that emerge when investors have a stake in more than one club competing in the same competition (e.g., the European Champions League). While we agree with the sentiments of the chapter authors in this section – that there is no one single solution to these complex problems – we argue that global and local sport organisations need to increase their levels of transparency and accountability, with the overall aim of improving the way international sport is governed. Against the background of ongoing crises at FIFA and national football bodies (e.g., the German Football Association), this space should provide exciting opportunities for further investigatory research and the development of new approaches to sport management practice, theory, and policy making.

Another common form of cheating discussed in the book is that of doping. Whilst there has been a significant amount of material written on doping in sport both from an academic and popular press perspective, we agree with Woolf (Chapter 6) that this area of study is often reduced to very simple and underdeveloped arguments. In truth, the management of doping issues remains complicated, as it involves diverse legal, medical, and scientific themes that deserve careful consideration. For example, designing and then enforcing doping policy on a global scale is a highly complex task, as can been seen through the recent problems encountered by the IAAF. In order to deal with this level of complexity, the international agency responsible for sports doping control, World Anti-Doping Agency (2015), recently stated that they need to be even more targeted and sport-specific in designing their doping control strategies. We agree that a more targeted approach will be needed in order to be more effective and sustainable; moreover, with the emergence of micro-dosing and gene doping techniques, it will be an important and necessary step for the global doping agency to stay ahead of the 'game'.

Moving on from doping control, Greenhow and Gowthorp (Chapter 7), discuss one of the biggest issues faced by sport over the past couple of decades. The issue of concussion management, though widely examined and debated in the media, has surprisingly seen very little collaboration across the impacted football codes. Many of the impacted sports, for instance, have responded in different ways, even though key medical bodies such as the Australian National Health and Medical Research Council stated in 1994 that a coordinated approach across all sport was required.

For the above issues to be successfully addressed, the global sport system needs to embrace good governance principles. From this perspective, Adriaanse and colleagues (Chapter 2) explored the critical intersection between corporate social responsibility, governance, and diversity. While many sport organisations across the globe have embraced corporate social responsibility strategies in order to position their brand and organisation as 'good corporate citizens', in practice, not a great deal has changed with regard to diversity, inclusion, and good governance. This is best witnessed by the lack of women accessing positions of power within the world's two major sporting organisations: the International Olympic Committee (IOC) and FIFA. However, not only FIFA and the IOC can be blamed. As Adriaanse (Chapter 3) points out in forensic detail, the slow rate of progress in these matters can also be witnessed across most international sporting federations. For instance, in 2014 only 13 per cent of board members of international sport federations were women while just 21 per cent maintained the position of CEO. Given this poor representation of women at the senior levels of international sport, it is easy to see why so many international sport organisations have failed miserably to maintain a high level of good governance. In short, by not having all stake-holders equally represented (or represented at all), sport organisations are failing to maximise their potential through balanced decision making.

Globalisation

Against the background of the issues presented above, Dickson and Malaia (Chapter 8) investigated further challenges and opportunities faced by sport through globalisation. They argue that a global workforce engaged in sport needs to be diverse and possess a strong understanding of cross-cultural sensitivities. Having an understanding of these sensitivities is not only beneficial for sport staff and managers, but also for the consumers of sport. Drawing on Choi and Kim (2007), Dickson and Malaia state that underrepresented groups will continue to lack a psychological ownership to sport if they are continually treated as 'second class citizens' and are not involved in the highest levels of decision making.

Another central feature of sport globalisation has been the rise of the new media. While specific aspects related to technology and social media are discussed under the final theme in this book, Chapter 10 by Scott and colleagues relates specifically to globalisation as it examines the impact social media has had on international sport and relations. Not only has social media become an important tool for sport organisations to communicate with fans and related consumers, but it has also provided fans from around the world with the power to highlight negative issues and comment on unacceptable practices (e.g., the lack of diversity in some sports). Thus, social media is not only a tool that can engage and promote goods and services, but it can also be used to assess and highlight all that is wrong with global sport. The relentless treatment FIFA has received from football fans on outlets such as Twitter over the past couple of years serves as an excellent example for fans who are discussing corrupt practices and poor governance around the world.

Another area that deserves critical attention and well-designed management responses is the handling of football hooligans. In Chapter 11, Rookwood argues that football hooliganism is not a static global phenomenon, but rather one that is constantly changing and evolving. He suggests that the culture of hooliganism is made up of many sub-cultures that develop within the context of contemporary conditions and local, as well as global, environments. As a response to hooliganism, policing and legislation have been implemented to both deter and punish offenders. In Chapter 12, Pearson and Stott explore this perspective in further detail, arguing that recent developments in alternative liaison-based strategies have had a positive impact on reducing violence at football matches, especially in the former hooliganism hotspot, Great Britain. In other words, the authors also suggest that managing hooligans is not just a matter of monitoring, controlling, and/or banning, nor is it just about limiting the sale of alcohol or improving security measures. Instead, a more nuanced approach is required to manage football crowds effectively, which may mean reducing the level of riot police tactics used and increasing facilitation and communication. In particular, Pearson and Stott's research demonstrates that the introduction of dialogue officers at football matches has led to a more favourable perception of police by fans. In short, higher tolerance levels could be established, which may in turn prevent small incidents from turning into major problems. Further research along these lines would be welcomed in other international settings; for example, studies could be conducted in Australia where recent incidents at football matches have left the sport suffering from negative media coverage and public outrage.

At the other end of the spectrum, small-scale sport-for-development (SFD) initiatives are increasingly used as a strategic vehicle to achieve different development outcomes. In Chapter 13, Schulenkorf and colleagues built on their previously published review of SFD literature (Schulenkorf, Sherry and Rowe, 2016) and discuss some of the current challenges and future opportunities for both practice and research. For example, association football has received by far the most attention by SFD practitioners and academics and while this dominance may well be justified by the global reach, cost-effectiveness, and easy-to-follow rules of the game (Martinez, 2008), other team sports such as basketball, volleyball, and ultimate frisbee – or general physical activities such as walking or gardening – may be equally relevant to specific development efforts. In particular, the authors argue that in the future, SFD practitioners and scholars may investigate non-traditional alternative sports in more detail, herewith opening up SFD to new markets. An 'out-of-the-box' approach to sport delivery and research may also be interesting in the context of disability programmes, which have been proven to benefit significantly from innovative forms of leisure and play. However, to date, SFD-specific disability studies remain hard to find and it is argued that more can and should be done to build (research) capacity in this space.

Under the previously introduced banner of global SFD, the increasingly important topic of international sport diplomacy is addressed in Chapter 14 by Baker and Baker. The authors argue that one of the main challenges faced in the realm of sport diplomacy is the decline of available funding for diplomatic-based sport programmes, especially given that most of these programmes are not financially self-sufficient but reliant on government funding or philanthropic support. Given this resourcing reality, the challenge for organisations involved in this space is to demonstrate their programmes' efficacy. Exaggerating the claims that diplomacy programmes are remarkably impactful without providing thorough and independent evaluation results will therefore be a thing of the past. Instead, development bodies and non-governmental organisations (NGOs) will need to demonstrate that their investments are worthwhile and supported by strong evidence based on rigorous evaluation and associated research. For this, more use of innovative methods and techniques – including data analytics and new media technologies (see also Chapters 15 and 18) – may assist organisations in demonstrating the impact of their programmes in communities around the world.

At the other end of the scale, Manzenreiter and Horne (Chapter 9) examined the social and economic impacts of sport mega-events. In their chapter, they argue that much more research focus is required to distinguish the intended from the unintended impacts that can develop from the staging of such events. Too often in the past, the organisers and promoters of sport mega-events have over-promised and under-delivered when it comes to social, economic, and environmental legacies (Frawley and Adair, 2013, 2014). Thus, much more consideration by host governments and event organisers is required to balance the event requirements with the longer term outcomes for the host communities. So far, the legacy left by sport mega-events has often been underwhelming, especially from an infrastructure perspective, as can be seen by poor post-venue usage related to the Olympic Games (e.g., Athens 2004 and Sochi 2014) and recent Football World Cups (e.g., South Africa 2010 and Brazil 2014). However, the past decade has seen greater awareness of this issue and the inclusion of sustainability aspects as a requirement in the event-bidding processes of the IOC and Commonwealth Games. Despite these well-intended changes, much more still must be done to ensure sport mega-event planning moves well beyond the event start and finish dates.

Technology and social media

The third and final theme addressed in this book explored critical issues that emerge from the development and advancement of technology and digital media platforms. Gerard (Chapter 15) started this section by examining the rise and usefulness of sport data analytics. He argued that one of the major issues for this particular area is the 'capability gap' that has resulted from the quick explosion of data collection techniques due to digital innovation. While the ability to collect all different types of data has increased at rapid speed, the resistance to embrace change by sport stakeholders such as coaches and club owners has dampened and restricted analytics adoption. In an attempt to break down these cultural and knowledge barriers, coach education will play an important role moving into the future. This also suggests that sport management education in universities in particular should see this gap as an opportunity and consider providing specialised sport data analytics courses for undergraduate and postgraduate students to start the learning process and to fill the knowledge gap.

The advancement of technological knowhow is further discussed in Chapter 16, where Collins and Evans explore issues and challenges with adopting technology to assist referee decision making. The authors argue that sport technologies should be adopted to assist umpires and referees to bring about result fairness, and not to achieve a 'mythical exactness'. They also suggest that low-level capture devices are providing cheap support that will serve not only the officials, but also benefit the fans. One such capture device is television replay, a technology that according to Collins and Evans should be used wherever it is available to television viewers. Importantly, the authors dismiss claims that the use of television replays would slow games down (e.g., in football). Given the rapid pace of professional sports and the inconsistent support mechanisms provided by different governing bodies (e.g., goal-line technology vs. goal-line referees), this topic will continue to provide opportunities for critical investigation and discussion among sport stakeholders.

Chapter 17 by Hutchins and Rowe looks at technology from a different perspective. The authors investigated the rise of global digital media and innovation and argue that in some ways, there is a paradox when discussing the *management* of the new media. In other words, the authors question the ability to truly manage this space, when in so many cases decisions are made 'on the run' due to the relentless speed of digital media innovation. While in the past the media was considered a one-way street – in the sense that sport was covered by media outlets and distributed to the public – today, fans co-create sport content through various social media (i.e., Twitter and Facebook) and in some circumstances can actually re-broadcast events through innovations such as Periscope. Surprisingly, given the vast amount of disruption in the sport media field, dominant sports, such as football codes, and sport mega-events, such as the Olympic Games or World Cups, have still managed to significantly increase their broadcast rights deals year upon year. From this perspective, the 'rich' have actually got 'richer', while mid- to lower ranking sports have, in some instances, struggled to achieve reasonable broadcast deals. It is, therefore, suggested that those sports that in the past have failed to access traditional television space should aim to maximise and leverage their sport through online technologies including live-streams. A good example is provided by the professional surfing community, who have been able to showcase online many World Surf League competitions.

Following the new media theme, Chapter 18 by Hoeber and Hoeber explores the opportunities provided by the digital revolution to capture and analyse the vast amount of data that is now available to sport managers. In line with arguments provided by Gerard (see Chapter 15), data analytics is the next frontier for those involved in the management and administration of sport. Rather focusing on the coach and the sport performance side, Hoeber and Hoeber examine how sport managers can extract and analyse data generated by fans through social media platforms such as Twitter. They argue that more robust and scalable approaches are required when analysing social media data. Particularly given the large array of textual and visual aspects of social media data, the analysis of this material on a mass scale results in significant complexity and deserves to be supported by sophisticated applications that provide actionable insights.

Finally in Chapter 19, Rumpf and Breuer continue investigations into the digital technology theme and they do so in the context of sport sponsorship. The authors explore how changes in digital technology have impacted sponsorship evaluation and practice. In particular, the chapter discusses how eye-tracking technology, such as the Implicit Association Test, has been deployed to provide detailed analytics on how consumers perceive sponsor messages. This approach is a significant change to the usual methods of survey and interview data collection in that it utilises the latest advances from both neuroscience and psychology to understand consumer perceptions. Through such approaches, it is argued that sport sponsorship research validity will increase significantly, and better marketing decisions can be made by sponsors that are based on objectively identified evidence.

Looking back and looking forward

This book had a clearly defined goal: to critically examine the key issues shaping global sport management today. Based on the content presented and discussed by the contributing authors – and our reflections of all chapters provided here – global sport has a number of significant problems and challenges to tackle. First and foremost, the global sport system is lacking strong, ethical, diverse, and responsible leadership. In particular, global sport institutions have failed to take decisive collective action with problematic issues that have been around for many years, including gender equity, the physical impact of athlete concussion, the detrimental consequences of sports betting, and the rather slow uptake of new technologies and analytical tools that could significantly enhance sport both on and off the field. While some of these issues have started to be addressed, it remains to be seen how sport managers around the world find innovative solutions to implement and achieve much needed social, cultural, technological, economic, and managerial change.

Given the magnitude and diversity of managerial challenges presented, we are convinced that this edited volume will be useful for a wide range of sport management scholars including academics, students, and the wider sport community. It has been conceived as an alternative to 'plain' textbooks with the intent of making reading, learning, and classroom discussions relevant, meaningful, and enjoyable. While we believe that our book has achieved this goal, a future edition of this book may expand into other critical areas that were beyond the scope of this first volume. For example, much more attention is required on the rise of sport management and commercialisation in Asia; the importance of sport governance and responsible leadership in low- and middle-income countries; the impact of austerity measures on the funding of community sport programmes and sport infrastructure; the analysis of 'local voices' in sport, including the impact on fan protests regarding continuous increases of ticket prices and the (potential) power of fans to collectively resist the over-commercialisation of sport; and finally, the impact of financial fair-play measures and related control mechanisms to improve competitive balance and the sustainability of global sport.

References

Choi, C. J. and Kim, S. W. (2007). Women and globalization: Ethical dimensions of knowledge transfer in global organizations. *Journal of Business Ethics, 81*, 53–61. doi:10.1007/s10551-007-9480-7

Frawley, S. and Adair, D. (2013). *Managing the Olympics.* London: Palgrave Macmillan.

Frawley, S. and Adair, D. (2014). *Managing the Football World Cup.* London: Palgrave Macmillan.

Martinez, D. P. (2008). Epilogue: Global football. *Soccer and Society, 9*, 300–302. doi:10.1080/14660970701811214

Schulenkorf, N., Sherry, E. and Rowe, K. (2016). Sport-for-development: An integrated literature review. *Journal of Sport Management, 30*, 22–39. doi:10.1123/jsm.2014-0263

World Anti-Doping Agency [wadamovies]. (2015, June 25). *WADA talks with Sir Craig Reedie* [Video file]. Retrieved from www.youtube.com/watch?v=9j1eEfX-mxQ

INDEX

Made in the USA
Coppell, TX
21 January 2021